Comparing Public Policies

*Issues and Choices in
Six Industrialized Countries*

Jessica R. Adolino
Charles H. Blake

Comparing Public Policies

Issues and Choices in
Six Industrialized Countries

CQ PRESS

A Division of Congressional Quarterly Inc.
Washington, D.C.

CQ Press
A Division of Congressional Quarterly Inc.
1414 22nd Street, N.W.
Washington, D.C. 20037

(202) 822-1475; (800) 638-1710

www.cqpress.com

Printed and bound in the United States of America
04 03 02 01 00 5 4 3 2 1

Typeset by G & S Typesetters, Inc.
Interior designed by Dennis Anderson
Cover by Rich Pottern

⊚ The paper used in this publication meets the minimum requirements of the American National Standard for Information Sciences—Permanence of Paper for Printed Library Materials, ANSI Z39.48-1992.

Library of Congress Cataloging-in-Publication Data

Adolino, Jessica R. (Jessica Rose), 1962–
    Comparing public policies : issues and choices in six industrialized countries /
Jessica R. Adolino, Charles H. Blake.
        p. cm.
    Includes bibliographical references and index.
    ISBN 1-56802-449-5 (pbk.)
    1. Industrial policy—Case studies. I. Blake, Charles H., 1962– . II. Title.
HD3611.A34   2000
338.9—dc21   00-045527

Contents

List of Tables and Figures

Preface

At the dawn of the twenty-first century, we see countless news stories reminding us of the growing interconnectedness of the world. Countries have never operated in complete isolation, but today we increasingly define ourselves and our national priorities in a global context. Although learning about politics and governance by comparing different national experiences dates back to ancient civilizations, both Eastern and Western, we are perhaps more keenly aware than ever before of the relevance of other countries' actions.

This book is about comparative public policy in industrialized countries. It includes a conceptual discussion of policy making as well as treatment of specific areas from a cross-national perspective. The conceptual discussion provides a foundation for conducting political analysis of policy-making practices in the six largest industrialized economies with the six largest populations in the industrialized world—France, Germany, Italy, Japan, the United Kingdom, and the United States. We focus on large, industrialized countries so that the lessons drawn will have the greatest relevance for the United States—the largest industrialized country in terms of both economic output and population. The book is devoted to seven policy areas: immigration, fiscal policy, taxation, health care, social policy, education, and environmental policy. We chose these policy areas to expose readers to a variety of major issues on the policy agenda in the industrialized world. Although other policy concerns also form relevant elements of national agendas, each of these seven policy areas has maintained a visible profile for decades. Furthermore, by organizing this book across such diverse policy concerns, we encourage readers to ponder which policy-making dynamics are particular to a given issue and which travel across many issues.

We wrote this book as a primary text for courses on comparative public policy. Most books on this topic tend to be written for professional analysts and graduate students and assume too much contextual and conceptual knowledge on the part of the reader. Conversely, books that provide such contextual and conceptual knowledge tend to provide minimal treatment of existing policy choices and even less analysis of the dynamics of those choices.

This book meets these dual challenges in a single text designed for undergraduates and general readers. Chapters 1 and 2 use real-world examples to summarize the field of comparative public policy and the literature on policy-making dynamics. Chapters 3 and 4 are intended for readers with little or no knowledge of political science or of the six countries studied in this book. Some readers, therefore, could skim this material or skip it entirely. The policy-oriented Chapters 5 through 11 form the core of the book. The first half of each chapter provides background material on policy issues, on the study of policy making regarding those issues, and on international factors framing domestic policy making. Then, in national case studies, readers are informed about contemporary policy efforts and about the dynamics of those policy decisions. In working through the case studies, readers are encouraged to apply the examined theories of policy making. These policy chapters are intended to be read in their entirety, but instructors and readers with an interest in only some of these six countries can focus on the case studies of interest to them without entirely losing the thread of the book. Similarly, each policy chapter can be read on its own. Chapter 12 reexamines the internationalization of public policy in industrialized countries and returns to the opening theme: cross-national learning and the political constraints on learning, as observed in the case studies.

Throughout the book, terms defined in the glossary appear in bold print the first time they are used. We have included two types of feature boxes. "In Depth" boxes provide examples of issues examined in the book, while "Country-at-a-Glance" boxes offer readers a quick review of the political institutions of each country. A series of tables summarize theoretical frameworks and provide data regarding national policy decisions and policy outcomes. The data focus on the 1980s and 1990s, thereby presenting readers with current information.

This book can also be used as a text for courses that cover politics in industrialized countries (European governments or, more generally, industrialized societies). Many instructors devote increasing amounts of time to policy issues. However, the major textbooks designed for these courses usually include too-brief sections addressing contemporary public policy issues in the countries they examine. We provide policy-oriented instructors with the opportunity to compensate for this deficit by providing highly detailed discussions and analyses of policy concerns.

Acknowledgments

While writing this book, we have benefited directly and indirectly from many exchanges about the politics of policy making with students and instructors here at James Madison University. In the years to come, we look forward to hearing from students and faculty using this book. We encourage you to send your comments to CQ Press.

We have also benefited from the counsel and hard work of many people beyond our campus. Don Reisman was generous in the early stages of this project with advice about how to organize a textbook on comparative public policy. At CQ Press, we have had the help of many talented individuals— beginning with Brenda Carter, who supported the book as a useful enterprise.

Charisse Kiino provided a stimulating editorial climate in which to develop this project. All of the reviewers selected—Steve Mazurana at the University of Northern Colorado, John C. Morris at the University of Mississippi, and S. Tjip Walker at the University of North Carolina at Charlotte—contributed helpful suggestions that have improved the content and the structure of this book. In the final stages, we have been ably guided through the production process by Belinda Josey and have profited from the constructive copyediting of Amy Marks. Finally, we would like to thank our families for their ongoing love and support during this project and during all of life's many adventures.

An Introduction to Comparative Public Policy

In 1965 newly elected president Lyndon Johnson promised to extend health benefits to the elderly. Later that year, the U.S. government created the Medicare program to provide senior citizens with hospitalization insurance paid for out of general government revenues. Many of the legislative leaders who voted in favor of the Medicare program had participated in failed efforts to create some form of national health insurance over the prior two decades. Medicare marked a change in legislative strategy from the original goal of comprehensive health insurance for all residents to a guarantee of hospitalization care for the elderly. This strategic change was a response to political obstacles facing prior initiatives. Advocates felt that it would be easier to build legislative and public support for public health insurance for retirees alone (and not discuss the merits of extending it to people still in the labor force). In part, this strategic change was also an effort to build on the experiences in neighboring Canada where a national hospitalization insurance policy had just been created.

Three decades later, in 1993, newly elected president Bill Clinton renewed the call for some form of national health insurance program. It was the first time that sweeping health policy reform had reached a visible place on the presidential agenda since the Nixon administration in the early 1970s. President Clinton named a council on health reform that studied the current U.S. health care system as well as health policies in other industrialized countries. That council drafted a proposal based on the concept of managed competition and influenced by health policy reforms in the Netherlands and the United Kingdom. Meanwhile, legislative leaders proceeded to develop their own alternatives. Half of the subsequent major congressional bills proposed policies adapted from abroad. Sen. Paul Wellstone, D-Minn., sponsored a single-payer reform based on the Canadian system. Reps. Jim Cooper, D-Tenn., and Fred Grandy, R-Iowa, and Sen. John Chafee, R-R.I., sponsored bills advocating a form of employer-mandated health insurance—the most frequently observed health policy in the industrialized world.

These proposals sparked serious debate and controversy in the legislature, in the news media, and among a variety of interest groups during the 1993–1995 legislative session. By the end of that session, none of the various proposals had been passed by Congress. In fact, for reasons we explore later in this book, none of the proposals advanced to a general floor vote in the legislature.

This brief discussion of health policy making in the United States illustrates three important features of public policy making. First, public policy making is an ongoing process. Over the years the United States has frequently discussed major modifications in its health policy. This is not unique to health care as an issue. Governments are always implementing and evaluating existing policies while they consider reform proposals for the creation of new programs, the modification of existing programs, and the termination of some current policies. Throughout this book we attempt to provide you with a richer understanding of policy making as an ongoing endeavor.

Second, you can see from the history of health policy making in the United States that countries try to learn from one another. Perhaps this is truer today than ever before. Marshall Raffel discussed this issue at the conclusion of a recent analysis of health reform in industrialized countries:

> The countries in this book are especially inclined to look at one another's efforts at reform because of the economic and social similarities and ties that exist among them. The Nordic countries are a case in point: they are in regular consultation and use the Nordic Council to facilitate the process. New Zealand has historically looked to the United Kingdom for leadership and many of its health care reforms were, and still are, adaptations of what the United Kingdom was doing. Government agencies in the United States have increased their study of the leading industrialized societies as witnessed by dedicated issues of the *Health Care Financing Review* (a journal published by the Health Care Financing Administration of the U.S. Department of Health and Human Services), and by reports from the General Accounting Office (an agency of the U.S. Congress) on Canada, Sweden, the United Kingdom, France, Germany, and Japan. Private professional journals such as the *New England Journal of Medicine, Journal of the American Medical Association, Health Affairs,* the *Journal of Medical Practice Management,* and the *Journal of Health Politics, Policy and Law* have also printed accounts from time to time of the health systems in various industrialized countries (1997: 293).

When countries study one another to draw lessons about which policies work best to reach particular goals, they are engaged in policy analysis. Policy analysts ask questions aimed at learning lessons about different policy options' strengths and weaknesses. Policy analysis begins with a definition of the policy problem government wants to address. In turn, what are the policy objectives? How successful were the policies chosen in achieving those objectives? How should one account for these policy successes or failures? In this book we engage in policy analysis concerning seven major policy issues: immigration, fiscal (or budgetary) policy, taxation, health care, social (or welfare) policy, education, and the environment.

Third, in addition to viewing policy making as an ongoing process in which countries try to learn from one another about which options are desirable, you can also see in contemporary U.S. health policy that political dynamics can limit countries' willingness and ability to borrow from other countries.

Although much of the health policy legislation proposed in 1994 was inspired in good measure by foreign experiences, none of the proposed legislation was enacted. Even if policy analysts can document that some form of universal health insurance is the norm across all other industrialized countries, that does not mean that U.S. policymakers are going to focus wholeheartedly on the foreign evidence in their public and private deliberations. Writing at the conclusion of another recent volume on health policy reform in the industrialized world, Theodore Marmor examined how political dynamics influence lesson learning:

> Policy-makers are busy with day-to-day pressures. Practical concerns incline them, if they take the time for comparative inquiry, to pay more attention to what appears to work, not academic reasons for what is and is not transferable and why. Policy debaters—whether politicians, policy analysts or interest group figures—are in struggles, not seminars. Like lawyers, they seek victory, not illumination. For that purpose, compelling stories, whether well-substantiated or not, are more useful than careful conclusions. Interest groups, as their label suggests, have material and symbolic stakes in policy outcomes, not reputations for intellectual precision to protect. None of these considerations are new—or surprising. But the increased flow of cross-national claims in health policy generates new reasons to reconsider the meaning of cross-national policy learning (1997: 361).

Marmor's comments about the limits to learning make it clear that policy analysis should be complemented with political analysis. Public policies use government personnel and resources in response to challenges deemed worthy of government effort. Because the sum total of individual and collective complaints at any point in time is enormous, governments must choose which problems to address and how to address them. These choices are shaped by a variety of factors often common across countries. Political analysts study the dynamics of policy making in an effort to understand what sorts of policy choices are likely to be made in different scenarios. What policies have this and other countries enacted in the past? What factors influenced their decision-making processes? Do the cultural, economic, political, or institutional conditions that exist in one country differ from those in other countries? If so, how will these differences affect policy decisions or the probability of long-term success for borrowing a given policy option?

In summary, research in comparative public policy tries to improve our understanding of all three of these major facets of policy making: its ongoing nature, the efforts in and out of government to build a better mousetrap via policy analysis, and the intensely political nature of policy choices made by government officials. Because we concur with Marmor's view that politics shape how the lessons of policy analysis will be applied, the primary emphasis in this book is on political analysis. By examining policy making in six industrialized countries and in relation to seven major issues, we hope to enrich your understanding of other countries' policy making and increase your capacity to conduct political analysis. You will then be better positioned to consider strategies for adopting the policy option that seems preferable in light of a policy analysis of a given situation. Intervention in policy making—as a private citizen, as an interest group leader, or as a government official—also requires an understanding of the many stages of the policy-making process. If you do not get your way initially, you might later on in the process.

The Increasing Internationalization of Public Policy

Usually when we hear the term *public policy*, we think of national issues dealt with by national governing institutions. In turn, when we hear the phrase *foreign policy*, our attention shifts to policies toward other countries' governments and societies. Since the 1970s, however, many issues formerly considered purely domestic concerns are becoming increasingly internationalized. Before we begin thinking about how governments make national policy decisions, let us take time to consider how international obligations and pressures can frame public policy choices related to matters inside a country's own borders.

Perhaps the most overt examples of the internationalization of public policy stem from economic integration agreements adhered to by these countries. By ratifying the World Trade Organization agreement, all industrialized countries' governments have committed themselves to a series of decisions that go beyond the scope of a narrow definition of trade policy. Within the European Union, the Maastricht Treaty and other directives and accords are encroaching on national governments' traditional sovereignty in areas such as environmental regulation, monetary policy, product safety, and (more slowly) health and social policy. Furthermore, other changes such as the elimination of border controls among members and the drive for monetary unification have had tangible influences on immigration and fiscal policy, respectively. The North American Free Trade Agreement has not committed Canada, Mexico, and the United States to this degree of policy harmonization and supranational decision making. However, it has called for harmonization of certain areas (particularly investment laws and intellectual property rights) while focusing attention on differences in other areas such as education, the environment, fiscal and monetary policy, and social policy.

Beyond the realm of binding international agreements, market forces of various types are causing governments to internationalize their policy-making concerns and processes. If one conceives of human migration as a market choice, then the sustained high international demand to immigrate to wealthy countries has placed enormous pressure on these six countries. These pressures go beyond calls for a more restrictive immigration policy. Increased ethnic diversity also can make equal opportunity and equal protection more visible policy issues. Demands for services from new arrivals affect decisions in basic government services, such as education, health, and social policy, that influence fiscal policy. Illegal immigration can place special demands on taxation policy because of the existence of underground economies.

The internationalizing forces need not be physically present in the country to have an impact. Over the past generation, foreign economic pressures and dynamics have had a growing effect on a variety of domestic policy areas. Foreign exchange market transactions in the 1990s have had a significant impact on fiscal policy in Italy and the United Kingdom. The pressure to reduce deficits in order to stabilize one's currency influences just about every decision that governments make. Similarly, concerns about foreign economic competition affect a variety of policy realms that go beyond pressure for protectionist trade measures. Businesses in some countries lobby for educational reforms in the name of increasing economic competitiveness. In turn, business associations often complain that government environmental and social policies require too much taxation and impede economic growth and employment generation.

Given the growing sophistication and speed of communications and the importance of international trade in the global economy, this trend toward the internationalization of what were once considered domestic issues is unlikely to fade in the near future. Countries with poorer, less diversified economies than those in the industrialized world have long been seen as subject to international forces partially or wholly beyond their control. What is different as we enter the twenty-first century is the increased visibility of interdependence in large, industrialized economies like the six countries examined in this book.

The Organization of This Book

This book examines policy making in six major industrialized countries—the United States, Japan, Germany, France, the United Kingdom, and Italy. We chose to focus on industrialized countries so that the lessons learned will have the greatest relevance for the United States—the largest industrialized country in terms of both economic output and population. We selected the other countries to extend further the relevance of the comparisons involved by studying the six largest industrialized economies and the six largest populations in the industrialized world.

The first four chapters of this book provide a foundation for conducting political analysis of policy-making practices in our six countries across the ongoing policy process. In Chapter 1 we discuss conceptual tools for the study of policy making in industrialized countries and introduce a five-stage model of the policy-making process. In Chapter 2 we examine cultural, economic, political, and institutional theories that attempt to explain policy-making choices. In Chapter 3 we extend our consideration of influences on policy making by reviewing concepts central to those cultural, economic, political, and institutional influences on policymakers. In Chapter 4 we summarize the political systems of the six countries at the heart of this book—France, Germany, Italy,

Japan, the United Kingdom, and the United States—and we discuss the structure of the European Union as a key international influence on four of these six countries.

The main body of this book consists of Chapters 5–11. Considerable variation exists in the nature of policy making from country to country and across policy areas within a single country. For that reason, these chapters are organized by policy area rather than by country. In Chapters 5–7 we examine three broad sets of government decisions that frame individuals' prospects in their respective countries—immigration policy, fiscal policy, and taxation policy. In Chapters 8–11 we turn to four specific areas in which governments work to influence individuals' well-being more directly and often more overtly—health policy, social policy, education policy, and environmental policy. We chose these policy areas to provide exposure to varied, major issues in public policy. Although other policy concerns form important portions of the national debate, each of these seven policy areas has maintained a visible profile for decades.

In each policy chapter we begin by discussing the policy area's principal problems and the major policy options available to address those challenges. This discussion provides us with information based on policy analyses. We then review research in political analysis that tries to explain the dynamics of policy making. We then move on to case studies of policy making in our six countries—beginning with the United States.

In recognition of the increasing internationalization of national policy decisions, we frame the national case studies with a consideration of the international context for policy making in the issue area. Each case study starts with some background on the policy process and the history of policy making in the policy area. After that, we examine contemporary policy dynamics using the five-stage model of policy making presented in Chapter 1:

- Policy evaluation: How has the evaluation of past policy performance informed and shaped the current debate?
- Agenda setting: What policy problems are at the heart of the contemporary debate?
- Policy formulation: Who are the major participants in this policy area and what are their preferred alternatives for addressing the problem(s)?
- Decision making: What is the key arena to watch for a decision on this issue? What forces carried the day?
- Implementation: Are there any implementation concerns surrounding existing policies or the major alternatives under consideration?

Each case study concludes with an analysis of the choices made (or not made). This analysis is informed by the general political and policy dynamics discussed in Chapters 1 through 4 as well as by the nature of the specific policy issue(s) at hand.

At the end of each policy chapter we search for broader cross-national trends in policy choices, policy outcomes, and policy dynamics. The examination of policy choices and subsequent outcomes takes us to the task of policy analysis. Which governments have succeeded in reaching their major policy goals and why? Finally, we reflect on the central question of political analysis: What influences contemporary policy decisions in these countries?

In Chapter 12 we conclude by returning to our opening themes. First, we reflect on how international factors shape contemporary policy making across the policy process and across policy issues. We then review some of the limitations on learning discussed over the course of this book. Finally, despite several obstacles to borrowing from other countries, we consider how cross-national perspectives can and do provide lessons for policymakers about which policy choices to make and about how to pursue those goals in the political process.

Chapter 1 **The Policy Process**

In this chapter we introduce some conceptual tools designed for the study of policy making in industrialized countries. Specifically we use a five-stage model of the policy-making process. We start with the emergence of issues as policy problems on the political agenda and then move on to the formulation, adoption, implementation, and evaluation of public policies.

The Study of the Policy Process

The five-stage model is an analytical device used by researchers to study public policy; it is not a literal description of the policy-making process. Only on the rarest of occasions do governments march methodically from stage to stage in a given policy area. Most of the time, governments are working on all fronts simultaneously—continually shifting gears from the identification of problems to the creation of potential solutions and then back again. As an example, let's think this through in the area of health policy. At any given time, there are hundreds of health issues that different citizens want to see addressed (directly or indirectly) by public policy. Some people are concerned about the supply of certain health care options; others want government to help improve the quality of care for different health conditions; still others are concerned about the cost of health care; and so on. At the same time, many competing policy proposals are floating around that deal with each issue—several are being actively considered by the bureaucracy and the legislature (in a federal system of government, such as the U.S. system, this is going on at multiple levels of government). While the government is making decisions about which (if any) policy proposals to adopt for each issue, the bureaucracy is overseeing thousands of aspects of existing health policies. While existing policies are being implemented, people inside and outside of government are evaluating the effectiveness of each existing government program using multiple sets of standards. The array of policy-making activity in any country on any given day in any given year would be just as dizzying in other policy areas.

It would be decidedly difficult to use a single set of tools to analyze everything that is happening simultaneously. It would be like trying to explain the outcome of a battle by applying the same principles to components as varied as supply lines, geography, weather conditions, weaponry, combat experience, morale, and tactics. To gain a greater appreciation of the entire policy process, analysts have worked over the years to conceptualize components of policy making that share common dynamics and common challenges. In this chapter, we introduce these conceptual tools as lenses through which we can better understand public policy. We then apply these tools in analyzing public policy on seven different issues in industrialized countries.

Because the study of public policy involves the analysis of what governments do, it is central to the work of political scientists. However, this was not always the case. When political science emerged as an academic discipline at the beginning of the twentieth century, it focused largely on the analysis of formal government institutions and made normative judgments about what institutions were preferable. This **traditionalism** remained the prevailing focus of professional political science until the end of World War II—even as critics from the 1920s and later years called for the systematic study of the dynamics of political events and decisions (rather than comparisons of constitutional provisions often divorced from the performance of those systems in practice). In the postwar era, Harold Lasswell (1951) sounded a clarion call for the creation of a **policy science** that would focus explicitly on what governments do rather than on how they are organized. In his view, this policy science should be multidisciplinary (combining legal studies with insights from economics, political science, and sociology); problem solving (focusing on relevant real-life policy problems rather than on obscure, sometimes semantic, legal distinctions); and normative (admitting that the analysis of the policy process cannot be separated from the value judgments implicit in policy choices). Lasswell constructed a seven-stage model of the policy process: intelligence, promotion, prescription, invocation, application, termination, and appraisal. This model attempted to describe the steps taken by individual government decision makers: gathering information, promoting particular policy options, deciding on a particular policy, fleshing out that policy, carrying out the policy, deciding that the policy has outlived its usefulness, and evaluating the results of the entire enterprise.

This focus on people in government gave way during the 1960s and 1970s to efforts to conceptualize the policy process as one involving a variety of forces inside and outside of government itself. This broadening of Lasswell's initial formulation was driven largely by the other major development in political science during the 1950s: **behavioralism.** Whereas Lasswell reacted to traditionalist political science by focusing on government policies, other researchers such as Robert Dahl and David Truman led an effort to focus on the political behavior of individuals and groups throughout society. These two mid-century academic movements—policy science and behavioralism—combined to influence a new generation of public policy studies.

In the contemporary era, public policy analysts consider how and why governments enact and implement policies to address public needs and demands. **Public policies** are defined here as intentional courses of action designed by government bodies and officials to accomplish a specific goal or objective. These policies are usually enacted in response to a perceived need or demand and are thus problem oriented. In democracies, policy demands are made by a variety of actors, both within and outside government bodies, including private citizens, interest groups, bureaucrats, and legislators. Public policies may take the form of legislation (including budgets), government regulations, administrative and executive orders, or judicial decisions. They may also take the form of government actions that are not taken; in other words, the policy can be a decision *not* to use public authority to address a recognized problem. When we examine public policies, we are concerned not only with one specific decision to adopt a law or regulation but also with related subsequent decisions (such as amendments to the initial law or the regulations and procedures created to implement the law).

Studies of public policy and policy making examine not only government intentions but also specific government actions and the consequences of those actions. Thus such studies commonly examine **policy outputs,** or what governments actually do to implement and enforce their policies. Policy outputs can include the amount of money a government spends on education, the number of police officers it hires, the tax code provisions it passes to subsidize health care, and its penalties for violating environmental laws. Assessing the consequences of government activity involves the study of **policy outcomes,** or what the public policy has produced. This assessment entails evaluating a given policy's short-term effects and its long-term and unintended consequences. Analyses of policy outcomes examine whether public policies have, for example, improved literacy rates, reduced crime rates, made health care more accessible to the poor, or reduced air pollution.

Cross-national studies of the policy-making process in industrialized countries demonstrate that there is no single process through which public policies are made. Instead, different institutional frameworks, procedures, and traditions result in significant variation in the style and mechanisms of policy making. Despite such differences, however, it is possible to identify five stages of policy making that are common to all countries: **agenda setting, policy formulation, decision making, policy implementation,** and **policy evaluation.** The sections that follow are an introduction to what these commonly experienced stages entail in industrialized countries.

Agenda Setting

If we were to look at any given industrialized country today and attempt to catalog all of the needs and demands of its population, we would find the dimensions staggering. Most individual citizens and almost all organizations hold one or more pressing concerns that they believe merits government attention. These concerns, when combined with a country's domestic and international concerns more generally, create a seemingly endless list of potential items for the country's policy agenda. Many scholars refer to this potential list of policy issues as the country's **systemic agenda.** However, not all of these wants and demands occupy visible spots on the government's **institutional**

agenda. In fact, only a relatively small number of these demands attain such institutional agenda status and become the focus of public policy making.

How then do problems attract the attention of government officials and become the objects of public policies? Comparative research in the 1960s and early 1970s focused on the level of economic development as a possible determinant of agenda setting and of decision making on a wide variety of policy issues. Some scholars working in this vein developed the **convergence thesis,** which posits that as countries industrialize, they develop similar policy concerns. For example, focusing on social security policy, Harold Wilensky (1975) asserted that the level of economic development in a country (as measured by gross domestic product per person) was the most important factor driving the level of social security spending in sixty-four countries. Wilensky argued that as countries industrialized, governments (whether democratic or not) would face increasing demands for policies to improve individuals' standards of living. Over time, Wilensky reasoned, governments would respond by spending increasing amounts of money to address those concerns via programs such as social security pensions, unemployment insurance, welfare benefits, and national health insurance.

During the rest of the 1970s and into the 1980s, the convergence thesis was attacked from a variety of angles. Some critics charged that spending levels were not the most appropriate measure for agenda status. If research focused on the variety of ways that governments construct public policy to influence people's standards of living, then we would find much more divergence among industrialized countries than Wilensky's study revealed. Others focused on redefining the role of political factors to understand better their importance in the process. Still others highlighted the role of ideas in shaping the issues to which policymakers attend in a given situation. The consensus in the field of comparative public policy today is that no single factor is the smoking gun that drives agenda setting in all policy areas or in all countries. To understand agenda setting then, one must be open to exploring a variety of factors.

Instead of searching for universal determinants of agenda setting, many researchers have focused on understanding the process of agenda setting. Cobb, Ross, and Ross (1976) identified three different paths to agenda setting. In the **outside initiation** model, organized interest groups attempt to raise the profile of an issue on the systemic agenda. Interest groups form allegiances with other groups, raise citizen awareness, and lobby the government to get their concerns onto the institutional agenda. For example, during the 1960s a variety of grassroots organizations drew public attention to a series of environmental concerns in the United States. This dramatic change in public opinion and in the active expression of that concern through petitions and protests paved the way for the formation of the Environmental Protection Agency at the start of the 1970s—all for a set of issues that was nowhere to be found on the systemic and institutional agendas just a decade earlier.

In the **inside initiation** model, influential interest groups seek to pressure the government to address particular concerns without expanding the visibility of the debate on the systemic agenda. In this model, interest groups do not engage in advertising campaigns and public rallies but instead attempt to influence government policymakers almost entirely in private meetings. Here the principal tools of the trade are information and analysis of the issue(s) at hand along with, at times, the use of campaign donations. One of the most colorful examples of inside initiation in contemporary U.S. politics has been the quiet (and, to date, successful) effort of the honey industry to reinsert government subsidies into a series of budget proposals under successive presidencies that had initially removed the subsidies. The American Beekeeping Federation, the American Honey Producers Association, the National Honey Packers and Dealers Association, and other groups made campaign contributions to key legislators and provided a host of arguments about the importance of domestic honey—ranging from the jobs produced by the sector and its status as an environmentally friendly business to the purported need to maintain a substantial domestic bee population in the event of the arrival of so-called killer bees from abroad.

The **mobilization** model describes situations in which government constitutes the group interested in agenda setting. In these situations, government officials agree that an issue not currently visible in the systemic agenda needs to be addressed. The government works to get the issue onto the systemic agenda to increase public support for subsequent policy decisions and, often more crucially, for the implementation of those policies once created. The call for the privatization of several government enterprises during Prime Minister Margaret Thatcher's government in the United Kingdom provides one example of government officials expanding the visibility of an issue that had received much less attention prior to those efforts. The Clinton administration's attempt to increase support for sweeping health policy reform in the United States in the early 1990s provides another example of mobilization led largely by the government.

Cobb, Ross, and Ross originally posited that these three models were each associated with a particular sort of political system: outside initiation with pluralist democracies; inside initiation with corporatist democracies; and mobilization with authoritarian (and, especially, totalitarian) governments. Over time, however, many researchers have concluded that all three models are potentially applicable in a wide variety of political systems. The more important determinant of which model will apply is not the political system but rather the policy issue in question. As we demonstrated earlier, contemporary democracies have engaged in all three forms of agenda setting.

Peter May (1991) suggested a fourth model of agenda setting, **consolidation,** in which the government places an issue on the institutional agenda that already is visible on the systemic agenda. In this scenario the government does

Table 1-1 Four Models of Agenda Setting

		Public Support for Government Action	
		High	Low
Initiator of current debate	Societal actors	Outside initiation	Inside initiation
	Government	Consolidation	Mobilization

SOURCE: Modified from Howlett and Ramesh (1995): 116.

not need to mobilize support for maintaining the issue on the institutional agenda; it simply needs to work from the existing base of public interest in the issue. One could point to the increased activity of the Clinton administration in tobacco-related policy as an example of the consolidation model. Several of the proposed policy changes involving teenage smoking already had substantial support in public opinion polls.

The addition of the consolidation model leaves us with a basic typology of agenda setting that covers four different scenarios that vary from issue to issue in each country (Table 1–1). Low-profile issues tend to reach the institutional agenda via inside initiation or mobilization. More visible issues are more likely subject to the outside initiation and consolidation approaches.

As we move on in subsequent chapters to the study of specific policies in particular countries, we will observe a considerable degree of cross-national divergence in problem definition. A pressing problem in one setting will sometimes be viewed as insignificant in another. In addition, the process through which problems are brought to policymakers' attention varies from country to country, particularly as a reflection of different participatory structures. More specifically the structure and tactics of interest groups and the nature of political party systems (as well as the degree to which the political system is open to their influence) are key elements in defining the agenda-setting process in different countries. A new issue that is dominated by inside initiation in one country may be subject to the outside initiation model in another. In contrast, some long-standing policy issues (such as pension policy) may be so high on the systemic agenda that it would be difficult to take the inside initiation approach and unnecessary to conduct the mobilization gambit to place an item on the institutional agenda.

Policy Formulation

Once a problem has arrived on the institutional agenda, a course of action to solve, reduce, or dismiss the problem must be created. The formulation stage entails developing and evaluating proposed solutions and programs. At this stage, many conceivable policy alternatives are rejected because they are viewed as technically not feasible or politically unacceptable by major participants in the policy-making process. Given the subjective nature of the technical and political judgments at issue here, understanding policy formulation requires an assessment of who the important participants are and where policymakers look for policy alternatives.

There is rarely a rational march from careful problem definition to the meticulous consideration of options. Often the agenda-setting process gets an issue on the institutional agenda without generating an accepted or clear definition of the policy problem and its causes. As a result, the policy formulation process involves not only the evaluation of policy alternatives but also a vigorous debate about the nature of the problem itself. Consider for a moment the drug abuse problem in various countries. A wide variety of public and private organizations provide differing estimates of the percentage of the population that abuses narcotics and of the economic and human costs of that abuse. Opinions differ even more over the forces driving drug abuse that government efforts might try to tackle. People point their fingers at the personal background of drug abusers, the failure of law enforcement to stop trafficking in illegal narcotics, the dire economic circumstances of many abusers, the failure of mass media to condemn universally drug use, and so on. This disagreement over what constitutes the drug problem creates a dizzying universe of potential policy proposals. Even when there is considerable agreement about the essential elements of the problem, multiple solutions are often proposed.

The government plays a crucial role in policy formulation. Government research often serves to frame policy problems once they reach the institutional agenda. Our understanding of the dimensions of the problem are often shaped by government statistics. Different government agencies measure everything from the unemployment rate and the amount of air pollution to the infant mortality rate and the educational achievement of secondary school students—to name only a few examples. In addition, the bureaucracy provides formal and informal evaluations of different policy proposals in an effort to influence the debate over which options are more desirable. The historical stances of political parties in the legislature (as well as the partisan balance of forces) also tend to filter out some options while promoting others. For example, conservative legislators are likely to turn rather quickly to market-oriented policy instruments, but they can be slower to consider direct government intervention than are legislators from centrist or leftist parties.

In addition to the nature of relationships within government, the connection between society as a whole and government policymakers has an important effect on policy formulation. One of the oldest concepts in the analysis of U.S. policy making is the notion of an **iron triangle.** The iron triangle refers to a policy sub_ector controlled by the relevant bureaucratic agencies, the relevant legislative subcommittees, and the major interest groups dedicated to that policy area. For example, for many years national policy making on U.S. rivers and harbors was dominated by a small nucleus of actors: the Army Corps of Engineers (the key agency in charge of constructing and maintaining projects), the relevant congressional subcommittees with jurisdiction over public works in the House of Representatives and the Senate, and the

National Rivers and Harbors Congress (the major interest group on the issue). Without fanfare, these groups spearheaded policy activity on water projects for decades—often working cooperatively in pursuit of shared goals.

Subsequent research in the United States and other countries demonstrated that few policy subsectors were governed by such a limited number of actors for long periods of time. Drawing on a series of comparative research projects on policy subsectors, Hugh Heclo developed a competing term, the **issue network,** to refer to situations in which a mix of government and nongovernment actors actively involved in policy formulation is much more flexible over time. For example, in health care policy making, a wide variety of public and private groups can be interested in one or more aspects of health policy. The precise number of groups and individuals actively participating in the process depends on the issues involved and the perceived urgency of those issues. As Heclo explained,

> Iron triangles and subgovernments suggest a stable set of participants coalesced to control fairly narrow public programs which are in the direct economic interest of each party to the alliance. Issue networks are almost the reverse image in each respect. Participants move in and out of the networks constantly. Rather than groups united in dominance over a program, no one, as far as one can tell, is in control of the policies and issues. Any direct material interest is often secondary to intellectual or emotional commitment (1978: 102).

Over time, Heclo's notion of a continuum of policy formulation environments has formed the foundation of subsequent research that tries to describe the **policy network** at play for different policy issues. A policy network can be thought of as a map detailing the different actors who normally participate actively in a given policy area and, in particular, the nature of the relationship between government and nongovernment participants. Heclo's initial typology focused largely on whether a given policy area was captured by a small number of actors. In a recent summary of work on policy networks, Frans van Waarden (1992) presented a typology of various policy networks (Table 1–2).

Van Waarden's typology makes distinctions along two dimensions. First, is policy formulation dominated largely by government or by society? Second, how many major private groups are typically engaged in policy formulation in that issue area? In a bureaucratic network, government actors (especially in the executive bureaucracy) dominate with minimal effective participation from outside. The participatory statist network has the government bureaucracy playing the lead role in public but with key policy formulation conducted in private by major nongovernment actors (often in the business community). In a clientelistic network, the government uses its resources to ensure the loyalty of a major interest group active in the policy area. In a captured network, that power relationship is reversed: A major interest group forces the government to formulate policies to its liking. In a triadic network,

Table 1-2 Eight Types of Policy Networks

		Number and Nature of Network Participants			
		No Major Societal Groups	*One Major Societal Group*	*Two Major Societal Groups*	*Three or More Major Societal Groups*
Government-society relations within the network	*Government dominated*	Bureaucratic network	Clientelistic network	Triadic network	Pluralistic network
	Society dominated	Participatory statist network	Captured network	Corporatist network	Issue network

SOURCE: Modified from Howlett and Ramesh (1995): 130.

the government leads a policy network in which two major interest groups are key players. In a corporatist network, that power relationship is (again) turned on its head, and the two major interest groups tend to play the lead role in tripartite bargaining. In a pluralistic network, many interest groups are active, but more often than not government tends to retain the policy formulation initiative. In an issue network, as Heclo originally suggested, a large number of actors drop in and out of the policy formulation process, and government does not play a leading role over time (nor does any other single group).

This typology of policy networks will be a guide to thinking about policy formulation in the chapters that follow. In industrialized countries, most policy networks include one or more major interest group participants, and policy networks on major issues are often subject to multiple influences. In the policy-oriented chapters, we discuss who participates in several specific policy networks, and how they do so.

Decision Making

Once the political process inside and outside of government has weeded out many potential policy options, the moment arrives to make a decision to create a new policy, revise an existing policy, or, alternatively, take no new action. The decision-making stage is the component of the policy-making process that involves the smallest number of direct participants. With the infrequent exception of policy questions put to a vote via a referendum or an initiative, only the appropriate elected or appointed government officials can make decisions about the use of public authority. A wide variety of formal and informal rules determine the precise procedures by which the government can make decisions, and these rules vary considerably from country to country.

For instance, meaningful cross-national variation exists at the decision-making stage and hinges on the nature of executive-legislative relations. In presidential systems, decision making occurs in both the executive and the legislative branches of government—especially in the United States. In parliamentary systems, policy decisions are largely the responsibility of the executive branch with legislatures playing more limited, often symbolic, roles—

particularly when a single political party has majority control of the government, as has tended to be the case in the United Kingdom. When legislatures are important, one must pay attention to specific rules that govern how committees screen bills, how legislative proposals come to a full vote, what constitutes a quorum, and how new spending (if needed) gets authorized.

The distinction between a unitary and federal system also plays a key role in the decision-making stage. In a unitary system, formal decisions that shape policy must usually be made at the national level (although sometimes governments in unitary systems delegate authority to lower levels of government). In federal systems, many policy decisions can be made at the national, provincial, or local levels. This flexibility naturally expands the number of potential formal participants in the decision-making process. For example, educational standards in a federal system conceivably could be set by the national, provincial, or local legislature or by the relevant executive branch agency at the national, provincial, or local levels. Funding decisions also could be made by government at all three levels. Federalism also allows decisions at one level of government to be formed in reaction to decisions made at other levels. For instance, a national government might choose to modify its own educational standards to emulate a standards model first implemented at the provincial level. Alternatively a provincial government might choose to alter its own policy in response to an unwanted change in national policy.

Despite the formal exclusion of nongovernment actors from the policy process at this stage, government decision makers work in a context shaped by the policy preferences found in society as a whole. Individual citizens and organized interest groups voice their approval of some options (and, perhaps more crucially, their objections to other alternatives). The more important and visible the issue is to the public at large, the more decisions are constrained by public opinion. Not surprisingly, the less salient the issue is to the public, the more decisions are influenced primarily by the interest groups most directly affected by the policy under discussion.

Amid this variety of formal and informal constraints, how do decisions get made? In the early years of formal policy research in the postwar era, the **rational decision making** model emerged as the primary conceptualization of decision making. The rational model arose out of an effort to prescribe an ideal path to sound decisions rather than from an attempt to describe reality. After defining a policy problem, firm goals should be established; all possible paths to reaching those goals should be identified; each option's ability to achieve the stated goals should be evaluated, as should its cost; and, finally, decision makers should approve the option that has the greatest likelihood of reaching the goals at an acceptable cost. At its most formalized, the rational model calls for all items to be evaluated in monetary terms. The results of this **cost-benefit analysis** can be evaluated against different criteria. One such standard is **Pareto optimality,** according to which policy decisions must make at least one person better off while making no one worse off. However, because most public decisions involve transferring resources (directly or indirectly), few policy decisions can hope to be Pareto optimal. Instead, formal cost-benefit analyses tend to adopt the utilitarian principle of the **Kaldor criterion,** according to which a policy must provide more benefits than costs to society as a whole (even if some people suffer net losses), in order to be adopted. The preferred policy option then is the one that provides the greatest net benefits.

During the 1950s, future Nobel Prize winner Herbert Simon conducted a series of studies that detailed several serious limitations to the application of the rational decision making model under real-life conditions. First, all human beings have cognitive limitations that Simon termed bounded rationality—we cannot and do not consider all possible alternative courses of action. Instead, we consider a much more limited number of options. In the policy realm, these options are selected using the ideological or political filters that are part and parcel of the policy formulation process. Second, it is simply impossible for anyone to predict the positive and negative consequences of each examined alternative. To use the phrase favored by economists, people do not have perfect information—especially about the future. Finally, most policy decisions affect so many people in so many different ways that it is difficult to conduct formal cost-benefit analysis for society as a whole. Faced with these constraints, Simon argued that real-life decision makers could not hope to make Pareto-optimal or Kaldor-efficient decisions on most matters. Instead, they would engage in **satisficing decision making,** setting some basic guidelines for a decision and then trying to meet them. For further discussion of how formal cost-benefit analysis contrasts with Simon's satisficing model, see Box 1–1.

Over the next decade, the **incremental decision making** model emerged out of further criticism of the limited usefulness of the rational model. Political scientists embraced Simon's critique of cost-benefit analysis and they went further in detailing the real-life dynamics of public decisions. Charles Lindblom (1959, 1968) and others argued that in most circumstances the principal elements of bounded rationality are the existing policy and the institutions created to implement the policy. New policy problems emerge not from consideration of all conceivable alternatives but rather from specific problems associated with the existing state of affairs. In turn, the policy options under consideration need not be an exhaustive list but rather a short list varying only incrementally from the status quo. This incrementalism is driven by the cognitive limitations of human beings as well as a desire to minimize the political costs of the new decision. This model assumes that—under most circumstances—it is much easier politically to gain approval of minor changes in existing policies than to negotiate a decidedly different approach. Consider briefly the income tax code in any country. The tax code contains a wide variety of exemptions and deductions for various categories of personal and business expenses. Most proposed reforms in the tax code are generated by opposition to particular components of the existing tax structure. Even the

Box 1-1 **Decision-making Processes: Cost-benefit Analysis versus Satisficing**

Richard Layard and Stephen Glaister (1994) outline a specific framework for conducting cost-benefit analysis. This approach calls for the relative valuation of all costs and benefits at various points in time across the life of the project and an assessment of the costs and benefits accruing to residents at different income levels and with different relationships to the policy. From these valuations, analysts calculate the sum total of costs and benefits for each year of the proposed project. At that point, they then try to estimate the present value of the total project by discounting the costs and benefits in the future. This discount rate, like the cost and benefit totals, varies by category of resident and is an effort to make projections about the future more conservative because inflation and many other unpredictable factors can reduce people's enjoyment of the policy in the future. Finally, these individual calculations are compiled into the present value estimate, and policymakers can then determine whether benefits exceed the proposed costs of the project.

Herbert Simon argued that this detailed accounting of costs and benefits did not match up with reality. He wrote:

> While economic man maximizes—selects the best alternative from among all those available to him; his cousin, whom we shall call administrative man, satisfices—looks for a course of action that is satisfactory or "good enough." Examples of satisficing criteria that are familiar enough to businessmen, if unfamiliar to most economists, are "share of market," "adequate profit," "fair price."
>
> Economic man deals with the "real world" in all its complexity. Administrative man recognizes that the world he perceives is a drastically simplified model of the buzzing, blooming confusion that constitutes the real world. He is content with this gross simplification because he believes that the real world is mostly empty—that most of the facts of the real world have no great relevance to any particular situation he is facing, and that most significant chains of causes and consequences are short and simple. Hence, he is content to leave out of account those aspects of reality—and that means most aspects—that are substantially irrelevant at a given time. He makes his choices using a simple picture of the situation that takes into account just a few of the factors that he regards as most relevant and crucial (1957: xxv).

Simon's criticisms of the rational decision-making model have proven fairly persuasive. Few, if any, contemporary political analysts consider cost-benefit analysis as a model of how most decisions are conducted. Instead, cost-benefit analysis is seen as one of many ways that policy analysts attempt to inform (and to influence) the decision-making process. In the political process, if satisficing decision makers find a cost-benefit study that supports their position, it can be a useful tool in the debate. If they want to support a conclusion not supported by cost-benefit analysis, then they will try to find some reason to dismiss its importance.

calls for sweeping reform, however, are still potentially subject to the incrementalist tug highlighted by Lindblom: It is easier for politicians (and involved citizens) to hammer out minor deviations in the existing system than to embrace a wholesale change that might create new opponents of reform who see their favored elements of the current system under challenge.

The conservatism implied by the cognitive and political dynamics of incrementalism is bolstered by additional dynamics. First, people usually have greater confidence in their ability to predict the costs and benefits of minor changes than major ones; as a result, major reform proposals are vulnerable to the criticism that the proposed costs and benefits are miscalculated. Second, the existing policy already has a government bureaucracy conducting analyses of the current state of affairs and it tends to call for minor changes for a variety of reasons: an ideological commitment to the success of the existing policy, self-interest in the policy's continuation, and the bounded rationality constraints identified by Simon. Critiques of this incremental decision making model run the gamut from those who believe it encourages people to give up on systematic, rational decision making to those who believe the incremental model still describes a more orderly consideration of alternatives than exists in real life.

In the 1970s James March and Johan Olsen (1976) developed the **garbage can decision making** model, which rejected even the limited rationality of the incremental model. March and Olsen argued that policymakers do not engage in any systematic consideration of alternatives. Instead, a variety of circumstances thrust decision opportunities on the government. Unforeseen economic developments, political dynamics at home and abroad, the sum total of a variety of actions taken by elected and nonelected government officials, and the mood of decision makers can all shape the decision. March and Olsen called each decision opportunity a garbage can in an effort to dramatize the ad hoc, even chaotic nature of many policy decisions. A key notion in this garbage can metaphor is that spare policy problems and spare solutions are always sitting around in the can. This means that when the government is called into action, officials will sometimes choose a solution they find handy—for ideological or political reasons—rather than search for solutions specific to the problem at hand. For example, faced with public criticism of existing child care facilities, a governing party that favors government intervention on a variety of issues may be more prone to consider direct government provision of child care or greater public regulation. Conversely a more market-oriented party might consider issuing a call for personal responsibility or a public call for dedicated individuals to take advantage of market opportunities in child care. In the garbage can model, decision makers are often depicted as being addicted to a particular problem-solving approach—not unlike a child who enjoys drumming and looks at every household object as another opportunity to play the drums.

Although some decisions undeniably have a "garbage can" feel to them, many decisions are made more systematically. During the 1980s and 1990s, policy researchers moved from efforts to generate a one-size-fits-all characterization of decision making to the study of decisions as made in different policy areas. This contemporary approach departs from the premise that all the models described earlier occur in real life—depending on the context and on the will of the participants. To attempt to understand the likelihood of different decision-making styles, one must try to understand the specific policy area and the formal and informal rules governing decisions in that area. This subsystem decision-making model analyzes the context of decision making along two dimensions. First, how complex is the policy network for that issue? In other words, are the political constraints on decision makers high or low? Are there many groups and individuals actively lobbying with differing goals, or are there relatively few groups with goals that overlap in several respects? Second, how compelling are the logistical constraints? These constraints include the complexity of the policy problem, the pressure of time, and the availability of sound information. In short, are the logistical constraints high or low? The income tax reform dynamics we discussed earlier are an example of an area with high political and logistical constraints with many divided participants dealing with a laundry list of complex alternatives. Working from these two sets of constraints, Martin Smith (1994) generated a four-model typology of decision making at the subsystem level (Table 1–3).

In Smith's typology, the model of rational decision making is most applicable to situations in which the policy network is not complex and the logistical constraints are low. In turn, incrementalism is most likely at the other extreme—when the policy subsystem is highly complex and the logistical constraints are also high. Simon's satisficing behavior is most likely when logistical constraints are high but the policy network is not very large. Finally, Smith carves out a new model of decision making, **optimizing adjustment,** to refer to situations in which decision makers do not consider widely divergent options but are willing to consider fairly significant changes from the status quo. Such a model of decision making is deemed most likely when the political constraints are high and the logistical constraints are low.

If we pause briefly to reflect on the preceding discussion of decision making, we might assume that sweeping policy change is close to impossible in major policy areas. Only the rational decision making model holds out the possibility of tremendous change, and that model is not likely to occur in major policy areas. However, both common sense and the consideration of major reforms of the past in various countries tell us that change is possible—even in policy areas with major political and logistical constraints. What breaks the logjam in such situations? Since the late 1980s, a variety of analysts have argued that a perception of crisis is the driving characteristic common to most major policy changes. Studies of both industrialized countries (Hall 1990; Jenson 1989) and late-industrializing countries (Grindle and Thomas 1991) concur

Table 1-3 Four Scenarios of Subsystem Decision Making

		Complexity of the Policy Network	
		High	Low
Policy issue constraints	High	Incremental decision making	Satisficing decision making
	Low	Optimizing adjustment	Rational decision making

SOURCE: Modified from Howlett and Ramesh (1995): 148.

that an economic, political, or social crisis can drive sweeping policy change from the agenda-setting stage through to policy formulation—culminating in the adoption of decidedly different public policies. For example, the perception of an emerging ecological crisis in many industrialized countries in the 1970s helped to create a policy climate in which major departures from previous policies were considered and, in many cases, adopted by governments.

Be forewarned, however, that what constitutes a crisis is in the eye of the beholder. There is no ironclad, objective definition of crisis; it is entirely subjective. For that reason, in many policy settings we should anticipate that the advocates of sweeping change will be calling the current state of affairs a crisis. Conversely the advocates of lesser (or no) change will attempt to convince the general public and decision makers that there is no crisis that warrants major reform.

Policy Implementation

When speaking of the implementation stage, we are concerned with what is done to put a public policy into effect. In the early years of policy research, most analysts focused on the first three stages of policy making because they assumed that the real action centered on policy decision making (and the events leading up to the decision). However, by the early 1970s a variety of studies demonstrated that the implementation stage is crucial to the success or failure of a policy (Pressman and Wildavsky 1973).

Implementation is important because prior to this stage a great many public policy decisions are loosely defined. Those individuals and agencies responsible for policy implementation are often given a great deal of latitude in determining the specific terms and requirements of a new law or regulation. Because of this delegation of authority, in most countries the bureaucracy is the major location for policy implementation and enforcement and thus plays a large role in interpreting and elaborating the government's broad policy guidelines. How the bureaucracy approaches this task can vary widely from country to country and across policy areas within the same country. We consider both sides of the implementation coin: the specific provisions made to enforce the core elements of the policy and the behavior of the persons specifically responsible for policy implementation as they interpret and elaborate policies.

Many policy implementation studies examine issues such as the amount of money spent on a program, the types of fines or penalties to be imposed on those who violate the law, or the number of new employees hired to implement a program. In short, these studies consider the specific **policy instruments** used to put the policy into effect. Policy instruments can be grouped into four basic types. When most people think of public policies, they tend to think of the use of **direct government instruments**—whether through regulation, the direct provision of services, or the operation of state-owned enterprises. However, direct action is just one of several possible approaches to achieving policy goals. Sometimes governments attempt to reach policy goals by the operation of **market instruments**—ranging from deregulation to incentives intended to motivate certain behaviors within a largely free market. In other situations, governments mobilize their powers of persuasion to convince the public to address policy concerns via **voluntary instruments** at home or in their local communities. A fourth course of action remains: the combination of some or all of these options into a **mixed instruments** approach.

In the early years of scholarly research on implementation, theories focused on the nature of instrument choice at the upper levels of the bureaucracy via a focus on **top-down implementation.** In a top-down approach, the resources dedicated to an agency, its organizational structure, and the goals adopted by the agency are crucial to successful implementation. For instance, the analysis of implementation problems in secondary education focused on identifying the missing resources or organizational patterns that could improve schools' performance. As case studies of various programs in several countries showed, however, important decisions are often made at the lower levels of the executive branch. Civil servants can shape policies at the ground level not only by using the discretion left to them by the implementation decisions at higher levels but also by the speed and dedication with which they use their resources.

Critics of the top-down approach such as James Wilson (1989) have countered with a conceptualization of **bottom-up implementation.** The debate between top-down and bottom-up theories of implementation is not just about who shapes implementation but also about the core nature of implementation problems. In a top-down approach, the crucial issue in implementation is policy design: Good implementation is driven largely by sound, detailed decisions made at the highest levels of government. In a bottom-up world, the central concern is building a motivated, trained civil service that willingly carries out its duties in a professional manner and makes good instrument-choice decisions when reacting to situations that the policy designers did not anticipate. For example, can school principals motivate teachers and students while providing sanctions for those who do not meet certain expectations?

Since the early 1980s, researchers have shifted from trying to characterize entire countries to studying what drives instrument choice at the policy subsystem level within countries. Stephen Linder and B. Guy Peters (1989) argued

Table 1-4 Four Scenarios of Subsystem Instrument Choice

		Complexity of the Policy Network	
		High	Low
Government capacity	High	Market instruments	Direct government instruments
	Low	Voluntary instruments	Mixed instruments

SOURCE: Modified from Howlett and Ramesh (1995): 163.

that the two crucial factors determining decisions at this stage are the complexity of the policy network and the nature of government capacity in the policy area (Table 1–4). When the policy network is complicated (again, meaning that there are many participants in and out of government) and government capacity is low, government is most likely to resort to voluntary instruments—exhorting citizens to change their behavior to address the policy problem. Conversely, when government capacity is high and the policy network is less complicated, the government is most likely to use direct instruments. It may be surprising to see research indicate that the use of market instruments is associated with high government capacity. Linder and Peters (and others) argued that although the flexibility of market instruments lends itself to situations in which the policy networks are complex, only governments with high capacity are likely to use them. This is because governments need substantial administrative capacity to monitor market activity and to enforce market outcomes. They also need substantial political capacity to defend the use of markets in the face of opposition in complex, mobilized policy networks. For example, a responsive judicial system is needed to enforce contracts and an effective regulatory system is needed to monitor the provision of services such as education and utilities via the private sector. In both examples, the government that adopts market-oriented approaches to an issue must have sufficient support for tackling these concerns through the up-and-down world of the free market. Finally, Linder and Peters asserted that when the number of participants in the policy network is low and government capacity is low, an eclectic, mixed instruments approach is most likely.

In addition to analyzing instrument choice, many studies of implementation focus on the bureaucrats themselves. As noted in Table 1–4, the capacity of the bureaucracy plays a crucial role in public policy. Just as some instruments are not chosen because of a lack of capacity, other instruments can fail in practice because the bureaucracy lacks the motivation to carry out the program. Studies of implementation failure often focus on the human factor. For example, Wilson (1989) discussed how situational imperatives and the internal norms of police forces frame daily work activity in ways that differ from the stated goals and policies of the overall law enforcement policy.

When the focus turns to bureaucrats' motivations, many scholars turn to insights from the **principal-agent model** of delegation. The principal (here the supervisory government authority) may have one vision of policy implementation but cannot carry it out without the cooperation of many individual agents to whom specific responsibilities are delegated. The principal has certain potential sources of leverage over the agents' behavior including the power to hire and fire and the possibility of rewarding faithful implementation with raises and promotions. That said, there are constraints on the use of each of these strategies by elected officials because they usually have the power to hire and fire only the top-level appointed officials who, in turn, face legal and political constraints both on firing employees and on rewarding some employees disproportionately over others.

An even greater limitation on the power of the principal may be the problem of imperfect information. If the principal were all-knowing, perfect information could be used to identify implementation failure everywhere it happened and to propose specific remedies for each situation. However, legislators (and even executive agency heads) will never have anything approaching perfect information on the implementation process. Accordingly, it can be difficult to identify which bureaucrats are not carrying out the policy as designed. Clearly the larger the population to be served by a policy, the bigger this potential problem becomes. This information constraint on the principal is magnified further when you consider that the source of much of that information on implementation is the bureaucracy itself. As a result, managers and politicians have to try to motivate bureaucrats to carry out the work independently.

The implementation process can be critical in explaining cross-national differences in policy outcomes and effectiveness. In some instances, countries that have adopted similar policy goals and frameworks in response to a given problem have observed different policy outcomes. Often the resources for policy implementation and the specific instrument choices made by governments play major roles in determining policy effectiveness. In other situations, the willingness and ability of government officials to implement the specified program in a coherent manner can prove the deciding factors in policy success.

Policy Evaluation

The evaluation of policy effectiveness constitutes the fifth and final stage in the policy-making process. People in and out of government are often conducting formal and informal evaluations of government performance in different policy areas. The potential criteria for evaluation are diverse. Sometimes evaluations focus primarily on the nature of policy outputs—that is, the resources government uses to address a problem. An output-oriented study might focus on the amount of money spent on a policy area or on the number of government employees dedicated to work in that policy area. Other evaluations focus on policy outcomes, examining whether government action has produced desired objectives. For example, did education policies increase access to schooling or improve students' test scores? Still more ambitious evaluations might focus on policy efficiency, asking whether current policies constitute money well spent. In other words, are existing policy outputs the best path to the current outcomes, or would some alternative produce better outcomes using similar resources?

There are three major arenas for policy evaluation. **Administrative evaluation** is conducted by government itself. Most government programs are required to provide regular self-assessments that are reviewed by the upper levels of the executive branch or by the appropriate legislative committee(s). In addition, many programs periodically undergo external evaluations—by another government agency, by private consultants, or by some mixture of the two. Even external evaluations are shaped by information provided by the program itself.

Judicial evaluation is conducted by the courts in response to a particular legal complaint against the program. In most industrialized countries, the central issue of judicial evaluation is the legal authority of the government to make policy in that area. Many countries employ administrative courts to determine whether a particular government employee or agency had legal authority to take action in a certain sphere. Sometimes, however, especially in the United States, the courts examine not just the statutory authority to take action but also whether that action was in compliance with the policy intent of the law in question. In such a scenario, judicial evaluations may move from the determination of the scope of government authority to the determination of whether such authority was used appropriately in a given situation. For example, courts in the United States may determine that a local school board's plan for rezoning to generate a more racially integrated student body is insufficient. In most other countries, the courts would simply be ruling on whether the school board had the authority to engage in rezoning.

A third major arena is the realm of **political evaluation.** Sometimes governments attempt to gauge the public's evaluation of government policies via the interpretation of election results and by tracking public opinion polls on certain issues. However, it is difficult to interpret election results as turning on a single policy's evaluation, and public opinion polls are often better indicators of where governments should focus attention (rather than on how to approach a problem). Instead, most political evaluation takes place within the active policy network for each issue. Perhaps the major role of interest groups lies in their efforts to shape government (and, at times, public) opinion via formal and informal policy evaluation. For example, think briefly about the debate over welfare reform in the United States in the 1990s. Interest groups calling for major changes, such as work requirements and time limits for benefits, brought out analyses of the cycle of poverty associated with many welfare recipients, which they blamed on the dependency on those government benefits. In contrast, groups opposed to those changes presented analyses arguing that the major cause of that cycle of poverty resided in the insufficiency of benefit

Table 1-5 Four Scenarios of Policy Evaluation and Policy Learning

		Government-Society Links in the Policy Network	
		High	Low
Government capacity	High	Maximum learning in government and society	Substantial government learning with minimal societal learning
	Low	Formal evaluation with minimal learning	Informal evaluation with minimal learning

SOURCE: Modified from Howlett and Ramesh (1995): 177.

levels or in personal background factors that the proposed reforms would not resolve. A similarly diverse range of studies sponsored by interest groups dots the policy landscape of every major issue area.

Consultation within policy networks about the current state of affairs provides the feedback that closes the circle of the policy cycle by shaping the institutional agenda for the next round of policy formulation, decision making, and implementation. Such consultation among those dedicated to a policy area is shaped broadly by perceived trends in public opinion and voting. That said, decisions within the boundaries set by general public opinion at all five stages are in turn crucially influenced by the policy network for the specific issue.

Since the late 1980s, policy researchers have moved from the study of how to conduct different types of policy evaluation to a focus on how administrative, judicial, and political evaluations merge to influence subsequent choices in the earlier stages of the policy process. Again, contemporary research has focused on the policy subsystem level because of the wide variation within and across countries from one policy area to the next. Wesley Cohen and Daniel Levinthal (1990) argued that the crucial determinants of the effect of policy evaluation on future behavior are the level of government capacity and the nature of links between those in and out of government in the policy network (Table 1–5).

For Cohen and Levinthal, major changes in behavior are most likely when government capacity is high. When governments have expertise and good information, they are most able to learn from past experience. In turn, when policy networks have clear lines of communication between the public and private sectors, learning is likely to take place both in government and in society as a whole. When government has high capacity but has minimal links to those outside of government, past experience will have the largest impact on those within government itself. Conversely, when government has little expertise or minimal good information, policy evaluation continues but far less learning takes place. When nongovernment actors have multiple links to government in a policy network, the government is more likely to engage in formal policy evaluation than when the policy network is less vibrant. In both scenarios, however, the impact of those formal and informal evaluations will be smaller on future decisions in subsequent rounds of the policy cycle.

The Policy Process Revisited

The study of the five stages of the policy process indicates that it is difficult to make sound generalizations about any stage that apply to policy making throughout an entire country—much less to all countries. Perhaps the lone exception is in the number of participants in the policy-making process across the five stages. In most countries and in most policy areas, the number of active participants has an hourglass shape across the five-stage policy-making process (Figure 1–1).

The agenda-setting stage is filled with participants in and out of government at many levels. Once a policy problem reaches the active political agenda, the number of meaningful participants begins to decrease as the debate shifts from what is important to the analysis and promotion of competing policy solutions to the problem at hand. At the decision-making stage, given the rule-based nature of most public authority, we find the smallest number of active participants as government decision makers outline the new policy (or ratify the existing one). This decision, however, is not the end of the process. Instead, it leads to a wider struggle to implement the policy. The implementation process involves more participants as many more individuals in government (and often outside of government) have a direct role in bringing the policy to life. Implementation is complex not just because government policy decisions leave room for interpretation by the executive branch but also because the broader number of participants leaves multiple points for opponents of the prior decision to attempt to change the course of the policy.

Figure 1-1 The "Hourglass" Nature of Participation in the Policy Process

Stage of the Policy Process	Number and Diversity of Active Participants
Agenda setting	
Policy formulation	
Decision making	
Implementation	
Policy evaluation	

Finally, at the policy evaluation stage, the number of participants gets broader still as the executive, judicial, and legislative branches review policy performance—as do a wide variety of forces from outside of government. These evaluations form the context in which subsequent agenda setting takes place as the policy process continues.

Beyond this pattern of participation across the policy process, one finds substantial differences in the precise nature of policy making from country to country and across policy areas within a single country. For that reason, our examination of policy making focuses on the dynamics in different policy areas. In analyzing those policy areas, we consider what motivates government to create, reform, and terminate specific policies. Those decisions constitute choices made in an intensely political process shaped by many factors.

SUGGESTED READINGS

Ashford, Douglas E. 1992. *History and Context in Comparative Public Policy.* Pittsburgh: University of Pittsburgh Press.

Castles, Francis G., ed. 1992. *A Comparative History of Public Policy: Patterns of Post-war Transformation.* Oxford: Polity.

Castles, Francis G. 1998. *Comparative Public Policy: Patterns of Post-war Transformation.* Northampton, Mass.: Edward Elgar.

Howlett, Michael, and M. Ramesh. 1995. *Studying Public Policy: Policy Cycles and Policy Subsystems.* Toronto: Oxford University Press.

Kingdon, John W. 1995. *Agendas, Alternatives, and Public Policies.* 2d ed. New York: HarperCollins.

Marin, Bernd and Renate Mayntz, eds. 1991. *Policy Networks: Empirical Evidence and Theoretical Considerations.* Boulder: Westview Press.

Marsh, David. 1998. *Comparing Policy Networks.* Buckingham, England: Open University Press.

Miyakawa, Tadao, ed. 1999. *The Science of Public Policy.* Vols. 1–3. New York: Routledge.

Olson, David M., and Michael L. Mezey, eds. 1991. *Legislatures in the Policy Process: The Dilemmas of Economic Policy.* Cambridge: Cambridge University Press.

Palumbo, Dennis, and Donald Calista, eds. 1990. *Implementation and the Policy Process: Opening Up the Black Box.* New York: Greenwood Press.

Parsons, Wayne. 1995. *Public Policy: An Introduction to the Theory and Practice of Policy Analysis.* Northampton, Mass.: Edward Elgar.

Peters, B. Guy. 1995. *The Politics of Bureaucracy.* 4th ed. New York: Longman.

Rose, Richard. 1993. *Lesson-drawing in Public Policy: A Guide to Learning Across Time and Space.* Chatham, N.J.: Chatham House, 1993.

Sabatier, Paul. 1999. *Theories of the Policy Process.* Boulder: Westview Press.

Chapter 2 **Theories of Policy Making**

Across the policy process, what are the major factors that shape the policies adopted by governments? The attempt to explain why governments create, modify, or terminate policies has produced theories that focus on various potential influences. Cultural, economic, political, and institutional factors have received significant attention from scholars.

The Cultural School

The cultural school maintains that some societies are more skeptical about government than others. This skepticism reduces the probability of government policy creation and expansion. In other settings, cultural traditions, attitudes, and values are more supportive of government intervention and tend to support the expansion of government activity. In the sections that follow, we examine two major approaches to the study of cultural influences on policy making.

The Family of Nations Approach

Industrialized countries often differ in how they approach a given policy area; however, groups of countries may traditionally handle a given issue in a similar way. What explains those differences across groups of countries? Some researchers focus on deeply rooted cultural and historical traditions that lend themselves to different attitudes about society and distinct ways of organizing policy making. Francis Castles (1993) led a team of researchers to examine whether there are **families of nations,** that is, groups of countries whose cultural similarities help to produce similar policy-making dynamics and, in some cases, similar policy decisions. They identified four distinct cultural families in the postwar industrialized world: the Anglo-American family (Australia, Canada, Ireland, New Zealand, the United Kingdom, and the United States), the German family (Austria, Germany, and Switzerland), the Latin family (France, Greece, Italy, Portugal, and Spain), and the Scandinavian family (Denmark, Finland, the Netherlands, Norway, and Sweden).

What characterizes each family of nations is a particular set of historical and cultural traditions that have continued to shape policy making in the postwar era. For instance, the Anglo-American countries have had a greater tendency to emphasize the role of the individual than have societies from different cultural traditions. As a result, some scholars assert that Anglo-American traditions serve as a brake on government expansion (or as a force for contraction).

Conversely, the Scandinavian family of nations is seen as more collectivist in its cultural norms, which helped to fuel more support for government expansion in range and degree. The German and Latin families' traditions stand between those contrasting Anglo-American and Scandinavian traditions. The German family of nations has a deeply rooted federalist approach to political organization that serves as a check on government expansion. At the same time, societal groups have tended to organize nationwide in a more corporatist fashion that makes collectivist public policies more possible when those national groups work closely with government. The Latin family of nations, in turn, has a long historical tradition of support for a powerful central government, which many scholars attribute to its historical desire to catch up economically and militarily to northern European countries. This big government tradition, however, has been counterbalanced by a variety of cultural norms that center on the family and breed distrust of the national government.

The Public Opinion Approach

Some scholars prefer to focus not on broad, long-standing cultural and historical traditions but rather on the impact of contemporary, specific attitudes as reflected in public opinion polls. Working in this vein, scholars use responses to questionnaires to measure support for government intervention or, conversely, belief in the role of individual responsibility. Cross-national studies of public attitudes toward policy making began to flourish in the 1970s and expanded to include more countries by the 1990s.

Regarding the range of government activity, opinion surveys from the 1970s and later have found that considerable majorities in industrialized countries have supported government intervention in a broad range of policy areas. Table 2–1 shows that virtually all citizens in six European countries support government activity to provide health care and to care for the elderly. Large majorities support government responsibility for other issues as well. This pattern of broad support for some form of government intervention on a variety of issues characterizes the situation in the industrialized world since the 1970s: Government is expected to play a role. Support for some form of government action or responsibility places a dizzying array of policy concerns on every country's systemic agenda. This does not mean, however, that large majorities of citizens will consistently agree on the specific form of government activity in each policy area, nor do polls on attitudes about the range of government activity tell us very much about citizens' attitudes about spending priorities.

Indeed, public attitudes regarding the degree of government intervention (as measured by support for increased spending) have been less stable. In the 1960s and 1970s, there was overall support for the expansion of government spending in most countries—albeit with greater differences across countries than we observed on the range-of-activity dimension. During the 1980s and 1990s, this situation changed. On specific policy issues, majorities (albeit small

Table 2-1 Attitudes Toward the Range of Government Responsibility, 1990 (in percent)

Issue	Germany	Ireland	Italy	Norway	Sweden	United Kingdom[a]	Average
Provide health care	95%	99%	99%	99%	97%	100%	99%
Provide for the elderly	95	98	99	99	97	99	99
Provide for the unemployed	78	91	78	91	90	80	85
Provide jobs	74	71	85	84	75	63	75
Control prices	70	92	96	92	86	89	88
Assist industry	52	90	82	67	N.A.	94	77
Reduce income differences	64	82	78	72	74	74	74
Average	*75%*	*89%*	*88%*	*86%*	*87%*	*85%*	*85%*

SOURCE: Adapted from Huseby (1995): 96.

NOTE: Percentages of respondents who think the issue "definitely should be" or "probably should be" the government's responsibility.

[a]The respondents for the United Kingdom were all located in Great Britain.

N.A. = not available.

Table 2-2 Attitudes Toward the Contraction of Government Spending (in percent)

	Respondents		
Country (Year)	Support Reduced Spending	Neutral	Oppose Reduced Spending
Denmark (1987)	39%	24%	37%
The Netherlands (1988)	30	47	23
Norway (1985)	25	42	33
Sweden (1988)	39	18	43
United Kingdom (1987)[a]	46	13	41
United States (1980)	32	21	47
Average	*35.2%*	*27.5%*	*37.3%*

SOURCE: Data for the United States are from the 1980 General Social Survey. Data for all other countries are modified from Huseby (1995): 104.

[a]Data for the United Kingdom reflect only respondents in Great Britain.

ones) still favored higher spending. However, when one turns to the issue of total government spending, there is more division within societies as large minorities favored more spending and large minorities supported a contraction of overall spending by the 1980s (Table 2–2).

Despite President Clinton's State of the Union Address claim that "the era of big government is over," policymakers must face public opinion that is divided over the issue of spending. Elected officials attempt to satisfy calls for government program spending increases on certain issues (and from certain quarters) while avoiding visible increases in overall spending that are likely to alienate another sizable minority of voters. To avoid alienating one side or the other, governments must try to strike a balance. Continued overall government growth risks mobilizing one-third of the public; however, so, too, does a refusal to expand government on at least some fronts. To deal with this complex situation, policymakers would be well advised to examine the flow of opinion in each specific policy area.

The Economic School

The economic resources available to a country shape the expectations of citizens and policymakers alike. Efforts to study the influence of economic conditions on policy making have taken into account both short-term and long-term effects of economic change.

The Role of Short-term Economic Conditions

Economic perceptions can be based on short-term trends in the economy, such as the gross domestic product (GDP) growth rate of the economy as a whole. If the economy is growing, policymakers might be more prone to expand government activity for a couple of reasons. First, economic growth can also spawn policy reform by generating optimism about a society's ability to solve its problems through public action. Second, rising economic growth rates generate additional government revenues even if all tax rates remain the same. In short, more money is available to create new programs and to expand existing efforts. For a hypothetical example of how economic windfalls and crises can affect the public purse, see Box 2–1.

Some scholars have challenged the notion that economic growth will be associated with growth in the government's size relative to the economy as a whole. Among others, Aaron Wildavsky (1975) argued that governments blessed with growth rates that exceed the rate of inflation could expand government spending in real terms without taking a larger slice of the growing economic pie. For example, Wildavsky noted that Japanese public spending rose during the 1960s by 16 percent annually while inflation rose at an annual rate of 5.5 percent. As a result, spending rose in real terms (controlling for inflation) by over 10 percent annually. By the end of the decade, however, public spending comprised a slightly smaller share of the economy. How did this happen? Annual economic growth in Japan averaged nearly 12 percent during that time period (1975: 232–235).

Bad economic conditions can also influence fiscal policy making. A recession breeds a decline in government revenues that forces governments to borrow money if they want to maintain or increase spending. Amid a recession, the fiscal incentives to reexamine and curtail government activity can be substantial. Also, just as growth can breed optimism among decision makers and the general public, an economic downturn can generate pessimism about the prospects for successful government action.

A potential product of economic downturns—rising unemployment rates—deserves special attention in many policy areas. Unemployment presents complex challenges for policymakers. As just noted, economic problems can breed a pessimism that makes policy activity more difficult. At the same time, rising unemployment places new demands directly on existing policies such as unemployment insurance, poverty relief, and, at times, health insur-

Box 2-1 **The Relationship Between Economic Growth and Deficits**

Assume that last year your national government ran a balanced budget. In an economy that produced 100 dollars, the government collected 30 dollars in taxes and spent 30 dollars. For the current year, the government announces that it plans to increase spending to 31 dollars (an increase of 3.33 percent) but will leave the overall tax rate stable at 30 percent. Does this mean the government will be engaging in deficit spending this year?

Whether the government runs a deficit or surplus in this scenario is entirely contingent on economic growth. If the economy grows by exactly 3.33 percent, the budget will remain balanced. If it grows by more than 3.33 percent, the government will run a surplus. Conversely, the farther the economy falls short of that target, the larger the deficit will become as the table indicates:

Economic Growth Rate (%)	Gross Domestic Product (dollars)	Rate of Taxation (%)	Public Revenues (dollars)	Public Spending (dollars)	Budget Outcome (dollars)	Budget Outcome as a Percentage of GDP
−5%	$95	30%	$28.50	$31	−$2.50	−2.6%
−2	98	30	29.40	31	−1.60	−1.6
0	100	30	30.00	31	−1.00	−1.0
2	102	30	30.60	31	−0.40	−0.4
3.33	103.33	30	31.00	31	0.00	balanced
5	105	30	31.50	31	0.50	0.5
10	110	30	33.00	31	2.00	1.8

ance. These demands for increased government benefits raise issues for fiscal and taxation policy as governments must find ways to fund the increased services. These funding decisions are made more difficult than usual because rising unemployment is often associated with falling government revenues—due to a reduction in the workforce paying payroll taxes and to a fall in economic activity more generally. If that weren't enough, spikes in unemployment can spawn calls for immigration restrictions as a potential path toward alleviating unemployment problems among voting citizens.

The Role of Longer-term Economic Trends

Policy making can also be influenced by longer-term economic conditions such as the wealth of the country as a whole. For example, one could say that the greater a country's GDP per person, the wealthier the country is. This national wealth, along the lines of the convergence thesis of agenda setting we discussed in Chapter 1, can serve as a force pushing for the expansion of government. Overall national affluence helps to make the remaining pockets of poverty more noticeable while it also can generate confidence that poverty can and should be eliminated, that everyone can be provided a sound education, that health care can and should be made available to all, and that environmental preservation can be achieved—all without major sacrifices in the national standard of living. Harold Wilensky (1975) and others demonstrated in comparisons of countries from around the world that the affluence of industrialized countries was associated with greater welfare spending than was typically found in less wealthy countries. This is the essence of the convergence thesis: Wealth helps make national policy agendas and public spending levels in the industrialized world look different from those elsewhere.

The convergence thesis is not necessarily as useful in comparisons of policy dynamics within the industrialized world itself. Once we focus on the industrialized countries alone, we begin to see enduring differences in spending levels between countries. In the 1980s and 1990s, some countries tended to spend around one-fourth of the GDP whereas others tended to spend as much as half. In contrast to the logic of the convergence thesis, two of the wealthiest industrialized countries, Japan and the United States, have been among the lowest spenders. Another limitation of the convergence thesis is that spending is not the only way to characterize a country's policy outputs. Two countries might spend similar amounts of money to implement decidedly distinct policies. This is true even in policy areas that demonstrate the convergence detailed in Wilensky's worldwide study. Take health care, for example. Every industrialized country in the world except the United States has adopted some form of national health insurance, and each country spends between 6 and 10 percent of its GDP on those efforts. Even so, the precise nature of national health insurance provision varies considerably from country to country. Some countries have government-managed national health services. Others mandate that employers provide insurance. Still others use a mix of these strategies along with government-provided health insurance. Spending priorities are important policy decisions, but they are not the only concern facing policymakers in each issue area.

Another longer-term economic trend consists of demographic changes common to industrialized countries. In particular, these countries are experiencing a so-called graying factor: An increasing percentage of their residents are senior citizens. This shift, especially if it is not accompanied by an increase in the average age at which people retire, has implications for a variety of policy areas. Just as with unemployment, a rise in the percentage of retirees in a society tends to generate an increase in demands for certain government services—especially public pensions and health care. At the same time, the aging dynamic reduces the number of active workers per retiree. As Table 2–3 indicates, this trend will accelerate over the coming decades as the postwar baby-boom generation reaches retirement age. The potential influence of these demographic pressures will probably increase as this trend deepens in coming years.

Another long-term economic trend that became increasingly visible over the course of the 1990s is the increasing interconnectedness of the world

Table 2-3 Working-age Population per Elderly Person, 1960–2040

Country	1960	1980	1990	2000	2020	2040
Canada	7.7	7	5.9	4.9	3.1	2.3
France	N.A.	4.6	4.7	N.A.	N.A.	N.A.
Japan	11.2	7.4	5.8	4.0	2.4	2.1
Sweden	5.5	3.9	3.6	3.7	3.0	N.A.
United Kingdom	5.5	4.3	4.2	4.1	3.5	2.8
United States	6.5	5.9	5.3	5.4	3.6	2.7
Average	*7.3*	*5.5*	*4.9*	*4.4*	*3.1*	*2.5*

SOURCE: Organisation for Economic Co-operation and Development (1994c: 100).

N.A. = Not available.

economy. As trade increases, as production processes are less frequently national (but instead truly global), as communication speed increases, and as international economic agreements grow more complex, what were once considered domestic policy issues must now be decided with an eye toward a variety of international contextual influences. Sometimes those influences are ongoing phenomena with heightened visibility—such as a concern for the impact of government policies on the country's economic competitiveness. In other situations an increase in the number of intergovernmental organizations and international agreements can have direct implications for domestic policymakers. Sometimes international agreements redefine the existing problem in a policy area. On other occasions the agreements can place explicit and implicit limitations on national sovereignty in the exercise of government authority within national boundaries. The most ambitious example of this latter influence on industrialized countries is the European Union.

The Political School

In the 1970s a variety of policy analysts began to criticize what they saw as an overemphasis on the role of cultural and economic influences on policy making. Their chief contention was that policy dynamics were not necessarily primarily driven by those conditions. The political strategies and actions of political parties and interest groups could often play a central role as well.

The Role of Labor-oriented Political Parties

Many explanations of government activity (and, in particular, of the creation of the modern welfare state) have focused on the rise to popularity of political parties with ties to the organized labor movement. The contention that parties matter is the core of the **partisanship thesis** of policy making. Labor parties are likely to support an expansion in the scope of government in support of policy issues generally supported by labor unions, including education, the expansion of economic activity, health care programs, job creation and protection, old-age pensions, and unemployment insurance. Labor parties are considered likely to be faithful to this agenda for two main reasons. First, labor parties often have organizational or financial ties to organized labor that make the parties more likely to adopt policy positions in harmony with labor unions' priorities. Second, labor parties tend to focus their campaign efforts on citizens living at the lower end of the economic scale. In order to mobilize votes to gain and retain power, labor parties have an additional incentive to follow through on a welfare state agenda that has tended to be popular with working class voters in most industrialized countries during the postwar era. Scholarly research in the 1970s and 1980s provided empirical support for the contention that the range and degree of government activity was more likely to expand when labor parties had total or partial control of the executive and legislative branches (Castles 1982a).

Events in Europe during the 1990s caused modifications in the consideration of labor party influence on government spending. In the drive to reduce deficit spending, most European governments reduced spending levels. Some of those cuts were undertaken by labor party governments. Accordingly, it would be a misinterpretation of earlier research to conclude that labor parties will not engage in spending cuts. Instead one might hypothesize that labor parties are likely to make lower cuts than conservative parties (particularly in welfare spending) when spending reductions are adopted—just as they were likely to raise spending at a higher rate than conservative parties in past decades when spending was on the rise throughout the industrialized world.

The Influence of One-party Government

In addition to the ideologies and constituencies associated with major political parties, the partisan balance of forces in the legislative and executive branches also can play a role. When one party controls the executive branch and holds a majority in the legislative branch, the **party government** model argues that such one-party governments will find it easier to engage in quick reforms (Castles and Wildenmann 1986). In the industrialized world, the party government model has mainly referred in practice to three Anglo-American countries (the United Kingdom, Australia, and Canada) that employ the **Westminster model** of government, in which a parliamentary system is combined with a plurality electoral system. Other scholars (Pempel 1990) have also included Japan as an example of a parliamentary system in which a single party has controlled both branches of government for long periods of time. We explore the Westminster model and the party government model in greater detail in Chapter 3.

The party government dynamic has an influence on the ease of policy change and is not necessarily a force for government expansion or contraction. These majority governments could use this power in either direction—to expand or to contract the scope of government activity. Conversely, divided governments in presidential systems (that is, when the presidency is in the hands of a party that does not have a majority in the legislature) and multiparty coalition governments in parliamentary systems tend to be less likely to engage in sweeping reform because multiple parties must be consulted to generate a working majority.

The "Overloaded Government" Thesis

Other scholars working in the 1970s and 1980s focused on the implications of party competition itself on policy making (King 1975). In a democracy, political parties strive to win elections. The party or parties in control of the government often believe that spending increases can be useful to mobilize people to vote. Conversely, tax increases are dangerous because they mobilize votes against the governing party or coalition. As a result of these dynamics, the size of government will grow in good economic times but may also grow in bad economic times. However, because governments are reluctant to increase tax rates to pay for higher spending, they are prone to run budget deficits spending. Furthermore, over time, this pattern of government growth may generate demands for even more growth as voters and interest groups refine their strategies for increasing spending on behalf of their own policy priorities. In the end, this process generates an **overloaded government,** in which the sum total of demands grows faster than both public spending and public revenues.

The notion of overloaded government certainly captures an important portion of democratic policy making: Elected officials can and do attempt to retain office through the use of public authority. In fact, the gloomy implications of the thesis were lived out in many countries during the stagflationary economic crisis of the 1970s and early 1980s. Many democracies experienced increasing levels of deficit spending and a list of public demands that exceeded government efforts by increasingly larger margins. However, the last decade of the twentieth century did not witness an extension of the crisis of overloaded government. Many industrialized countries slowed the growth of spending and reduced their annual budget deficits. The overload dynamic can certainly have an impact on policymakers, but it is not always and everywhere going to be the dominant influence that it seemed to be in the late 1970s.

The Interest Group Politics Approach

Interest group activity is central to many discussions of agenda setting and policy formulation (Cigler and Loomis 1998; Norton 1999). The strategies of interest groups and their direct appeals to government officials also form part of the context of decision making and implementation. Indeed, interest groups are often directly involved in the implementation of public policies—especially regarding health care, education, and the environment. At the evaluation stage, many interest groups engage in political evaluation directly while others focus their activity on publicizing evaluations conducted by others in an effort to influence the agenda-setting process.

When are interest groups most likely to be influential? Generally speaking, increases in the size of a group's membership and in its financial resources improve its chances to be effective. However, organizational size and strength are only part of the story. As we noted in Chapter 1, the number of interest groups that are usually active in a policy network also affects the roles of those interest groups. In policy networks in which the issue is narrow and relatively low profile, the notion of an iron triangle emphasizes a particular interest group that has a predominant role above all others. Usually, however, the policy network is more complicated, and a variety of major interest groups have visible roles. This is perhaps especially true for the major policy areas covered in this book.

In policy networks in which many interest groups participate, the nature of interaction among groups and between those groups and the government become important influences on policy making. Two major conceptualizations of interest group activity exist for such complex policy networks: **pluralism** and **corporatism.** Under a pluralist scenario, many interest groups compete openly for the government's attention, and the government does not often make a clear effort to bring the different groups to the negotiating table to seek a consensus. In a corporatist scenario, fewer, larger groups participate actively, and the government tries more often to include the major groups in systematic discussions of policy-making issues relevant to the policy network. We discuss the pluralist and corporatist models of interest group activity in more depth in Chapter 3.

The Institutional School

Some scholarly analyses focus on how institutions frame policy-making decisions. Rules shape how decisions get made at many stages of the policy process. Within government, some rules make it easier for governments to take action, thereby making the expansion of government more feasible. A new institutionalist school of scholars has emerged that examines not only the impact of formal government rules but also the impact of informal norms in government and nongovernment institutions.

The Role of Formal Government Institutions

The study of government institutions' effect on policy making has tended to focus on two sets of rules: those structuring the relations between the national and subnational governments (**federal political systems** versus **unitary political systems**) and those framing the interaction between the executive and legislative branches (**presidential systems** versus **parliamentary**

systems). For many years, scholars have recognized that federal governments tend to have a harder time engaging in national policy reform. This notion begins from the premise that subnational governments are autonomous on some issues and share authority with the national government on other issues. This multi-tiered decision making makes federal systems prone to slower change because more people in and out of government have a chance to challenge policy proposals. This common-sense dynamic has been associated with long-term trends in the extension of the scope of government in the postwar era (Cameron 1978). Industrialized countries with federal governments tended to have smaller governments in both range and degree. In a unitary system, government claims ultimate authority throughout the national territory, which makes the national government the supreme policymaker unless it chooses to delegate authority to subnational government units. When unitary governments remain fairly centralized, there are fewer arenas in which decisions have to be ratified or carried out. This makes expansion of the government's range and degree easier to achieve because fewer decisions have to be made to ratify the expansion.

As in the party government model, the unitary system's relation to the expansion issue is ultimately indeterminate. The centralization of authority lends itself to faster change, but that change could occur in either direction. An expansionist central government could expand its activities more quickly, and a contraction-oriented central government could shrink government more quickly. The Conservative government led by British prime minister Margaret Thatcher provides a clear example of how centralized authority in a unitary state can be used to reverse the expansion of government.

Executive-legislative relations also can influence the government's ability to engage in policy reform. Some scholars have argued that a presidential system provides more decision points because the chief executive and the legislature need not be from the same party or governing coalition of parties. The presidential system, similar to the federal system, generates additional decision points that tend to slow potential changes in government activity. In contrast, a parliamentary system has rules that require the executive branch to retain the support of a majority of legislators. These rules may do a better job of ensuring that the executive and legislative branch will act together—thereby increasing the possibility of speedy reform. As with the centralization of power, this institutional factor has more of a potential role in shaping the pace of reform than its direction. When the executive and legislative branches work together, they can do so to expand government or to slow the growth of government. Thatcher's government was not simply working within a unitary system; it was working in the context of a parliamentary system in which Prime Minister Thatcher had a solid working majority in the legislature.

Formal institutions' effects on policy making can perhaps best be described as contingent on other policy-making influences. First, both federal systems

---

Box 2-2 **The Contingent Influence
of National Government Institutions**

In *Do Institutions Matter? Government Capabilities in the United States and
Abroad,* Kent Weaver and Bert Rockman reviewed comparative case studies
of issues such as energy policy, environmental policy, the management of ethnic and social cleavages, fiscal policy, industrial policy, pensions policy, national security policy, and trade policy. Their summary analysis captures the
complexity of policy making and reiterates the simple truth that national-level
government institutions are part of the larger whole (1993b: 446–453):

- Although institutions affect governmental capabilities, their effects are
  contingent.
- Specific institutional arrangements often create both opportunities and risks
  for individual governmental capabilities.
- Policy-making capabilities may also differ substantially across policy areas
  within a political system.
- Institutional effects on governmental capabilities are channeled through
  governmental decision-making characteristics.
- Differences in electoral rules and the norms which guide the formation of
  governments may have as much impact as institutions themselves.
- Parliamentary systems are not better than presidential systems, and vice
  versa.
- Divided party control of the executive or legislative branch exacerbates the
  problems of governance—especially that of setting policy priorities.
- Institutional arrangements involve a trade-off in capabilities.
- Governments may work around institutional constraints by generating coun-
  tervailing mechanisms.

---

and presidential systems can affect the speed of reform—provided that the
political party or parties in power desire reform at all. Other factors may create a climate so unfavorable to reform that the effects of institutional arrangements on those decisions are negligible. Second, if major actors in and out of
government desire change, reform can come despite the obstacles posed by
these institutional rules. In other words, federal systems and presidential systems often serve as obstacles to change, but they do not pose insurmountable
obstacles. If they were insurmountable, change would never occur in such
systems and that has clearly not been the case. Reviewing comparative research on the role of institutions in policy making, Kent Weaver and Bert Rockman (1993b) asserted that an institution's role is contingent on other policy
influences and that each set of governing institutions has its own strengths
and weaknesses (Box 2–2).

The Bureaucratic Politics Approach

The prior two sets of institutional influences focus on the nature of interaction among elected officials across levels and branches of government. A third set of institutional influences stems from the actions of nonelected officials—especially in the executive branch. Bureaucrats are particularly relevant in policy formulation and implementation. Peters (1995: 211–35) argued that a variety of characteristics shape a given agency's influence over policy making:

- the degree of consensus within the agency about its mission (and the path to achieving that mission)
- the degree to which the agency is seen as the prevailing expert authority regarding the feasible implementation of policies
- the personnel stability of the agency
- the managerial skill demonstrated by the agency over time
- the agency's ability to mobilize political support for its view
- the agency's ability to claim an apolitical distance from partisan and electoral disputes
- the degree of monopoly an agency holds over a policy sector (versus a situation in which two or more agencies compete for a role)

Generally speaking, the more each of these factors is present, the more effective the bureaucracy will tend to be in influencing policy making.

This list of characteristics makes clear the many reasons why the bureaucracy forms an important part of the politics of policy making. That said, it is important to remember two things. First, in many situations individual agencies lack several of these features in significant ways. Second, there are many more situations in which subunits within a single agency compete for leadership in a policy area. As a result, one should not think of the bureaucracy as a faceless, monolithic group working in unison toward a single vision of public policy. Instead, just as we are accustomed to hearing about disagreements within and among political parties and interest groups, we should be open to the possibility of divisions within and among bureaucratic agencies.

The New Institutionalism

Researchers in the 1980s and 1990s placed renewed interest in institutional influences on policy making. This **new institutionalism** has expanded the examination of institutions in a couple of senses (March and Olsen 1984). First, the concern for institutions has broadened from a focus primarily on formal rules to include consideration of how informal norms and patterns can frame policy making. For example, the seniority rule dominant in the U.S. House of Representatives in the middle half of the twentieth century was not a formal rule of the House. It was an informal tradition passed on from session to session within each political party. For decades, congressional committees elected as chair the senior member of the majority party within the committee. Only in the 1970s did both political parties explicitly embrace the possibility that nonsenior members could be nominated (and thereby elected) as committee chairs; however, the informal practice of seniority as a decision rule has continued to dominate committee chair elections to this day. During the age in which House committee chairs were not bound to many formal rules, this informal seniority system had a crucial impact on policy making. The policy impact of the seniority system was not lost on legislators often frustrated by the dominance of committee chairs. Indeed, that frustration led to a call for new formal and informal institutions that would constrain House committee chairs over the last quarter of the twentieth century.

Second, although government rules remain an important potential influence, scholars have begun to consider the role of institutional considerations that frame the participation of nongovernmental organizations in policy making (Hall 1986; Scharpf 1997). For example, in the debate over health care reform in the United States, the directors of the U.S. Chamber of Commerce initially voted to endorse the drive for some form of national health insurance. Most of the directors were representatives of large firms who generally felt that health reform would work to reduce their costs. In the membership rolls of the Chamber, however, small and medium-sized firms greatly outnumber the large firms. Since voting within the Chamber is based on the principle of one vote per firm, the members voted not to endorse national health insurance because the smaller firms feared that reform would raise their costs. If the Chamber had voting rules based on the size of the firm, the vote might have affirmed the directors' inclination to support health care reform. This reversal of course had a visible impact on the push for reform because it deflated the Clinton administration's claim that the Chamber's initial decision demonstrated that the business world supported the president's plan. This is but one of many examples of how institutional rules in nongovernmental organizations influence policy making.

An Eclectic Approach to Examining Policy Theories

Past efforts to explain public policy dynamics demonstrate the need to examine policy making from several theoretical perspectives. There is no single set of factors that emerges as the dominant influence on policy making in the second half of the twentieth century. Cultural, economic, political, and institutional influences all play a role.

As we saw in Chapter 1, many studies of the creation, reform, and termination of policies remind us that the context of policy making varies not just from country to country but also across policy areas within each country. Similarly, the specific nature of factors that influence policy decisions will vary from one policy area to another. Accordingly, our effort to explore the influence of cultural, economic, political, and institutional factors on policy choices and outcomes also focuses on the individual policies.

Although each policy area has its own particular context and dynamics, the national context for policy making forms an essential element of the backdrop that shapes policy making on each issue. Before we move on to specific policy issues, we consider national conditions more thoroughly. In Chapter 3 we review a variety of societal dynamics that frame policy making. Then, in Chapter 4, we explore the context for policy making in each of the six countries featured in the policy chapters that follow.

SUGGESTED READINGS

Borre, Ole, and Elinor Scarborough, eds. 1995. *The Scope of Government.* Oxford: Oxford University Press.

Campbell, Colin, and B. Guy Peters, eds. 1988. *Organizing Governance: Governing Organizations.* Pittsburgh: University of Pittsburgh Press.

Castles, Francis G., ed. 1982. *The Impact of Parties: Politics and Policies in Democratic Capitalist States.* London: Sage.

Castles, Francis G., ed. 1993. *Families of Nations: Patterns of Public Policy in Western Democracies.* Aldershot, England: Dartmouth Publishing.

Flora, Peter, and Arnold J. Heidenheimer, eds. 1981. *The Development of Welfare States in Europe and America.* New Brunswick, N.J.: Transaction.

Pempel, T. J., ed. 1990. *Uncommon Democracies: The One-party Dominant Regimes.* Ithaca: Cornell University Press.

Peters, B. Guy. 1995. *The Politics of Bureaucracy,* 4th ed. New York: Longman.

Scharpf, Fritz W. 1997. *Games Real Actors Play: Actor-centered Institutionalism in Policy Research.* Boulder: Westview.

Thompson, Grahame, et al., eds. 1991. *Markets, Hierarchies and Networks: The Coordination of Social Life.* London: Sage (for the Open University Press).

Weaver, R. Kent, and Bert A. Rockman, eds. 1993. *Do Institutions Matter? Government Capabilities in the United States and Abroad.* Washington, D.C.: Brookings Institution Press.

Wildavsky, Aaron. 1975. *Budgeting: A Comparative Theory of Budgeting Processes.* Boston: Little, Brown.

Wilensky, Harold. 1975. *The Welfare State and Equality.* Berkeley: University of California Press.

Chapter 3 **Political and Economic Dynamics in Industrialized Countries**

W e do not have to stretch our imaginations far to recognize that a country's policy-making process is affected by its political and economic institutions and traditions. For example, the policy-making process in an authoritarian political system looks different from the policy-making process in a democratic system. We also expect policies to look different in market economies and centrally planned economies. Among democracies, meaningful variations in policy-making processes are based on a country's institutions and its society. In this chapter we examine the basic distinctions in industrialized countries' political and economic dynamics and the relevance of these dynamics to the policy-making process. In so doing we lay the foundation for the specific policy analyses offered in the remainder of the book.

Social Cleavages

The pattern of **social cleavages,** or social divisions, is an important contextual factor for understanding any country's political system. Social cleavages are those social criteria by which people are grouped in a society. The politically relevant social cleavages found in industrialized countries have traditionally included socioeconomic status (or class), religion, ethnicity, region, and language. These cleavages find expression in various interest groups and political parties and are important for understanding a country's patterns of conflict, its distribution of political authority, its choice of an electoral system, and the formation of individuals' political attitudes and their political behavior.

The manner in which social cleavages are expressed through a country's interest group and political party systems is of particular significance for our understanding of the policy-making process. A country's social cleavages can be linked directly to certain patterns in this regard. For example, in industrialized countries from 1945 to the late 1980s, upper-middle-class voters were more likely to vote for right-wing parties, whereas working-class voters were more likely to vote for leftist parties. Thus class was a strong predictor of partisan identification and the vote. Similarly, until at least the late 1960s, religious cleavages were strong predictors of party choice and voting behavior. Social changes (for example, a growing middle class and increasing secularization) in industrialized countries since the 1970s, however, have reduced the degree to which these two cleavages are related to political behavior. Both class and religion have decreasing influence on party identification and voting choice in many industrialized countries.

Having observed this change, researchers have begun to look at new sources of social cleavage in industrialized countries, including divisive issues among the growing middle class (such as environmental protection and women's rights) that appear to influence individuals' political behavior. As we discuss later in this chapter, changes in social cleavage patterns have had an impact on contemporary patterns of partisan competition in industrialized countries, particularly through the emergence of new social movements and political parties. These changed patterns often have resulted in less predictable voting practices in these countries. For example, as noted earlier, through the 1980s in most industrialized countries the working class voted for left-wing social democratic or labor parties; these parties tended to favor increasing social welfare spending, bigger government, and higher taxation rates. Consequently, when these parties were elected to office, public policies largely reflected these preferences. Today we no longer observe such a clear connection between working class status and support of such parties. Thus our ability to establish a clear relationship between social cleavages and party identification or voting choice, as well as the policy choices of a political party once elected, is no longer as strong. As a result, understanding the policy-making process in these countries is less straightforward than it once was.

Interest Groups

Political parties and **interest groups** serve as democratic linkage mechanisms, connecting citizens to their political systems by communicating citizens' interests and demands. However, interest groups define for themselves goals clearly different than those associated with political parties. Interest groups do not seek the election of their representatives to political office. Instead they set out to influence public policy in specific areas of concern to their members. Interest groups do not aggregate interests; instead they directly communicate the specific and particularized interests of their members, and, typically, most of their members share similar interests and concerns. Interest group systems tend to reflect a country's social cleavage patterns: the more socially and economically diverse a society is, the more interest groups we expect to find. Today interest groups proliferate in industrialized countries, with multiple, independent groups pressuring governments externally in most countries (although these groups have varying degrees of influence on the content of public policies).

Interest groups' prevalence, behavior, and effect are partly a reflection of the characteristics of a country's wider political system. Countries with more centralized political systems are likely to have few key interest groups that have privileged access to policymakers and a greater likelihood of meaningfully influencing the policy-making process. For example, interest groups in the United

Kingdom typically have had less influence on the policy process because policy making is highly centralized and party discipline is strong (making members of Parliament less subject to the influence of lobbyists). British interest groups tend to be relatively weak, their access to the policy-making process is limited (with the exception of a few large and powerful interests that are given special access to policymakers), and they have been less able to regularly influence policy decisions.

In more decentralized political systems, where there are multiple points of access to key policymakers, interest groups are often more numerous, active, and effective. In such systems, the greater the size, internal coherence, and financial resources of an interest group, the more influential it is likely to be. In addition, in systems where political parties and party discipline are weak, interest groups may be more active for at least two reasons. First, weak political parties tend to rely on interest groups for fundraising and for sparking the public's interest. Second, if party discipline is weak, interest groups will have a much better chance of influencing the votes of members of the legislature because those members are less likely to be subject to reprisals from their party for voting against the party line in favor of an interest group's position.

The best example of interest group activity in a decentralized political system is found in the United States, where strong interest groups (such as AARP and the National Rifle Association) have large membership numbers and substantial financial resources with which to exert influence. Complementing this strength is the fact that the political system offers to these powerful groups multiple points of access to the policy-making process via members of Congress as well as the executive branch. When this ease of access is combined with the weak party discipline found in congressional parties and the legislature's decentralized and powerful committee system, we find all the ingredients for a pervasive pattern of interest group influence on the policy-making process.

The pattern of interest group activity in a country, particularly the relationship between interest groups and the government, is crucial to understanding the impact of these groups on the policy-making process. All industrialized countries have interest groups, but we find important differences from country to country when we examine the nature of the relationship between interest groups and government. Political scientists usually describe this relationship as either **pluralism** or **corporatism.** In pluralist systems, such as those found in the United Kingdom, France, and the United States, power is dispersed throughout society rather than concentrated in a few actors within and around the government. Interests organize independently, compete freely, and have no formal connections to government. In such systems, competition between interest groups is viewed as making a vital contribution to the political process, and public policies frequently reflect interest groups' demands. In a pluralist setting the government responds to outside pressures but does not intervene in interest groups' activities in any systematic fashion. The extent of an interest group's influence on the policy-making process in a pluralist sys-

---

Box 3-1 **The Swedish Corporatist Model**

One of the best examples of a corporatist interest group system among the industrialized countries is found in Sweden. Sweden has a highly centralized, unitary parliamentary political system. Policy making takes place in an environment that emphasizes cooperation and compromise and in which government and interest groups act to develop a high degree of policy consensus. Sweden has many powerful interest groups that are formally incorporated into the policy-making process, enabling them to exert a considerable degree of influence over policy making.

Swedish interest groups work together in powerful associations empowered to represent all their members. For example, trade unions in all economic sectors operate under the umbrella of the National Federation of Trade Unions, while employers throw their lot together in the Swedish Association of Employers. These and other interest organizations are consulted regularly in the policy-making process, primarily through their work on state commissions. These commissions serve in a number of specific issue areas and play an important advisory role in the policy-making process. They are appointed by the Swedish cabinet and include members of relevant interest associations as well as bureaucrats and politicians. These commissions' recommendations are incorporated into government policy proposals and also may be an important source of policy initiation.

In addition to forming these commissions, the government is constitutionally required to submit all legislative proposals to those interests involved with any given policy. In this process, known as *remiss*, groups and the bureaucracy are given the opportunity to comment on pending policy proposals. Their comments are included with the legislation submitted to the parliament. When combined, the state commissions and the remiss procedure make for a strong corporatist arrangement between government and organized interests, and as a result of these arrangements, organized interests in Sweden have a direct influence on policy making.

---

tem often depends on an interest group's individual characteristics such as expertise, financial resources, and organizational unity.

In corporatist systems, fewer interest groups participate in the political process and the ties between interest groups and the government are often institutionalized and quite explicit. Among the countries we examine in this book, Germany is the most strongly corporatist, although Italy and Japan also demonstrate corporatist tendencies (see Box 3–1 for an example of a corporatist model elsewhere in Europe). Where corporatism occurs, we typically find one large interest group in each of the major interest sectors in a country (for example, labor, farmers, government workers). This one group will coordinate the demands of active organizations in that sector and speak authoritatively for them. Such groups usually are directly incorporated into the official policy-making process as members of a council or committee that is systematically consulted when policy is made and implemented. In corporatist systems, governments do not simply respond to interest group pressures at their own discretion, rather they create an institutionalized pattern of active consultation and cooperation between groups and the policymakers. Policy decisions therefore are viewed as negotiated outcomes between the government and those most affected by the policy. Corporatist arrangements are intended to reduce conflict in the policy-making process, to develop policy consensus, and to increase the likelihood of policies being implemented effectively.

Some evidence indicates that corporatist relationships are of declining influence in those industrialized countries where they once flourished (such as in northern Europe). This decline appears to be a flexibility issue: Corporatist arrangements tend to be quite rigid in that they reduce the ability of both governments and organized interest groups to respond to a more complicated policy environment because of the complex relationship between the two. As a result, it can be difficult for actors in corporatist arrangements to adjust to changing conditions. Further, corporatist arrangements require unanimity in group interests; in the contemporary era, it has become increasingly difficult for interest associations to organize diverse interests around one clear policy position. Finally, societies that emphasize corporatist relationships make it more difficult for new interests to be heard, which results in demands for weakening corporatist linkages. Despite some decline, however, these arrangements remain important in some countries in key policy sectors, particularly in agriculture and in more technical policy areas.

Political Parties and Party Systems

Political parties are widely viewed as the most significant political institutions in a representative democracy because they play a key role in linking citizens to their political systems and the policy-making process. Parties are fundamental to the policy-making process because of their role in **interest aggregation:** Political parties are responsible for taking a wide range of citizen viewpoints and demands (for example, on education, health care, and the environment) and translating them into a more manageable and more specific number of policy alternatives. Parties then enter elections and voters choose between the various parties' competing partisan programs. Once elected to office, parties form the basis for the executive branch and the legislature (usually, but not necessarily, as a reflection of partisan majorities) and then exercise control over the policy-making process, thus translating these policy alternatives into actual public policies. Because these political parties try to fulfill many of their campaign promises once in office, they play a key role in the policy-making process in any country.

There are several dimensions along which we must evaluate the role of political parties and party systems in the policy-making process. The first dimension involves those partisan characteristics that affect the way parties aggregate citizens' interests, namely, the nature of their membership bases and their internal cohesion. Traditionally in industrialized countries, the primary form of partisan organization was known as a **mass party.** This term describes parties that (1) have a large number of active members drawn from a specific social cleavage (for example, the working class or a religious group), (2) are well-organized, and (3) are committed to pursuing a particular political ideology or a distinctive set of policy goals (that clearly reflect their members' interests). Traditionally, European Socialist and Communist parties, especially those found in Italy and France, were considered to be model mass parties, in that their memberships tended to be drawn from one particular group (the working class) and they pursued a clear ideological vision—namely, some version of Marxist philosophy. Mass parties have become less common in modern political systems as political, social, and economic changes (such as the growth of the middle class and the declining strength of labor unions) have eroded their traditional bases of support.

Today, traditional mass parties have for the most part given way to far looser coalitions of voters with weaker organizational structures, memberships drawn from disparate backgrounds, and programs based on less clearly defined goals or visions. These forms of partisan organization are often described as **catch-all parties,** and they are commonly seen more as electoral organizations (focused on achieving elected office) than as membership parties (focused on pursuing a set of policy goals that directly reflect their members' concerns and ideology). The German Christian Democratic Union and the Japanese Liberal Democratic Party are both catch-all parties. These partisan organizations have broadly based memberships drawn from across socioeconomic and occupational groups, they are programmatically vague, and they are concerned with issues rather than ideologies. Further, these parties have historically been highly effective electoral machines, with most of their activities directed toward ensuring that their parties secured and maintained positions of political power.

Mass parties are generally seen as a far more effective mechanism for performing the interest aggregation function, particularly because their members, based on a set of shared characteristics, can be more easily focused and mobilized around a set of common goals. Catch-all parties tend to have diverse membership bases and are much less focused and unified around a common policy vision. Thus we might expect governing catch-all parties to provide less policy coherence than more traditional mass parties. Further, when catch-all parties are in power, we might expect the policy-making process to be less focused on large-scale reform, particularly reform driven by some wider vision or plan for society. Catch-all parties are the predominant form of partisan organization operating in the six countries we examine.

The internal cohesion of each party's behavior in the legislature is another key element of the policy-making process. The term **party discipline** refers to the likelihood of legislators voting with their own party in the legislature. The more often party members vote the party line, the more disciplined the party. A higher degree of party discipline implies a greater degree of partisan control over the policy-making process. More specifically, disciplined parties are considered to be more likely to fulfill their campaign promises because they can be confident that their members will support their party's policy proposals. British political parties are among the most disciplined of those found in the six countries we examine, whereas parties in the United States provide a clear example of undisciplined partisan organizations. In Britain, parties are structured, centralized, and cohesive, and their members vote as a bloc in the legislature. In the United States, none of this is true of political parties. Parties in the other four countries vary with respect to discipline, but all lean toward greater discipline than is found in U.S. parties.

Another important feature of a country's political system is the nature of its **party system,** meaning the number of parties viewed as having a serious chance of winning elections in that country as well as the extent of competition among these parties. The number of parties operating in a country affects the way in which parties aggregate interests. Two principal types of party systems are found in industrialized countries: **two-party** and **multiparty systems.** In the two-party systems of the United States and the United Kingdom, the two major political parties (both of which are increasingly "catch-all") present broad and relatively undefined policy alternatives to the electorate. This approach reflects the parties' desire to appeal to the broadest segment of the electorate possible and to avoid alienating potential supporters. As such, these parties do a great deal of interest aggregation. In contrast, in France the multiparty system is characterized by multiple parties that represent a much more narrow range of interests and thereby do very little interest aggregation. These characteristics are key factors in understanding the role that these countries' legislatures play in the policy-making process.

The emergence of two major parties may have roots in a country's political culture, its social cleavage patterns, or its political institutions (see the discussion of electoral systems later in this chapter). In two-party systems, two major parties receive the vast majority of votes cast at any given election. These two parties are not necessarily the only parties that run in an election, rather they are the only two parties that have a serious chance of winning. In two-party systems, the victorious party usually wins with a large enough majority to govern independently—the Labour Party in Britain currently finds itself in this position, where it enjoys a 180-seat majority in the House of Commons. As a result, this type of party system usually is associated with more stable patterns of governance, and public policies generally reflect the preferences of the majority party in the legislature (assuming that the majority party is disciplined). In such instances, **party government** is said to prevail. Two-party systems also encourage parties to moderate their policy positions to attract a wider base of support; this tendency toward centrist parties and policies further contributes to government stability in these systems.

Multiparty systems are more common than two-party systems in industrialized countries. This is true for two main reasons: First, many of these countries traditionally were characterized by social cleavages that created the basis for several different parties. Second, the use of proportional representation electoral laws in most industrialized countries makes it easier for multiple parties, and especially smaller parties, to take seats in the legislature.

A fairly clear association exists between multipartism and coalition governments. Coalition governments in multiparty systems are currently found in four of the six countries we examine: France, Germany, Italy, and Japan. In coalition governments, the executive branch must negotiate with coalition members to obtain support for policies and get them passed, or sometimes even to remain in office. The executive branch's success in acquiring and maintaining support for its policies will be affected by the degree to which the parties in the coalition are disciplined—if party leaders cannot ensure their party members support the coalition's policy proposals, the policy-making process is further complicated. Thus policy making in multiparty systems is often less straightforward than in two-party systems because no single party in the legislature controls enough seats to govern alone. In multiparty systems, political parties often continue the interest aggregation process well after being elected to office, as their policy positions are refined in negotiations between the parties in the coalition. As a result, the link between voters and policy choice can be less direct in a multiparty system than in a two-party system.

Countries with multiparty systems have a greater tendency toward government instability because of the difficulties associated with either forming or maintaining a governing coalition. The assumed culprit is the existence of too many parties in the coalition; however, evidence suggests that this instability is related to the degree of **polarization** between the parties in the system, or the amount of emotional or political distance between parties. It is argued that the more ideologically distant the parties are (referring to the distance between them on the political spectrum), or the greater the degree of antagonism and conflict between parties drawn together in a governing coalition (in other words, where there is **polarized pluralism**), the more likely political instability is to occur. Polarized systems are more likely to have extremist or antisystem parties in their midst. Conversely, in political systems where the "pulls" are toward a moderate center (in other words, where there is a centripetal tendency or **moderate pluralism**), multiparty systems are not associated with unstable government. In short, the greater the ideological distance between the parties involved in a governing coalition, the more likely we are to observe government instability.

The situation in France during its Fourth and Fifth Republics illustrates the effects of polarized and more moderate pluralism. Prior to 1958, the French party system consisted of multiple parties clustered around the extreme right and left, with a wide distance between these extremes, leaving a political vacuum at the more moderate center. The result was a debilitating tendency toward parliamentary and governmental instability and resulting governmental ineffectiveness. Since the beginning of the Fifth Republic in 1958, we observe a pattern of much more moderate pluralism and consequently a much more stable government structure. Today, France still has a multiparty system that continues to lack a truly moderate centrist party (or parties), although the number of politically significant parties has shrunk, so that we now observe two broad political blocs on the left and right. However, the ideological distance between the ends of the political spectrum has narrowed considerably, and the possibility of workable coalitions between parties of the left and right has risen. As a result, persistent government and parliamentary instability has not been a problem during the Fifth Republic. Instead, frequent transitions between right- and left-wing governments have proceeded easily, and coalitional arrangements have remained fairly secure.

France is not the only example of changes in degrees of partisan polarization. As social cleavages have declined in significance since the mid-1970s, we have observed in most industrialized countries a tendency for political parties to move toward the moderate political center because voters tend to look so much more like one another. As a result, we have also seen a general pattern of more stable party and political systems. Although increased government stability has some positive effects for policy making, this movement toward the center (or **depolarization**) can make it more difficult to identify significant policy differences between parties, so that at election time voters' partisan choices seem to be less about policy and more about perceptions of competence. This often complicates the policy-making process once parties come to office because they lack a clearly defined program and must quickly develop coherent policy proposals.

Voting Behavior

Voting is the most common form of political participation in industrialized countries. Citizens enter the voting booth with the expectation that their actions affect not only who governs but the policies that governments adopt. Voting citizens select candidates who have adopted certain policy positions that they will then try to enact in the legislature, thereby communicating their policy preferences. Thus some knowledge of why citizens decide to vote for a particular party or candidate is important for understanding the policy-making process.

In some industrialized countries, such as France and Italy, voters are given the opportunity to make policy choices directly through the use of a **referendum**—elections in which voters choose among specific policy options, typically involving a yes-no vote on one issue. For example, should we ratify the Maastricht Treaty? Should we increase education spending? In some countries such elections are used fairly regularly; in others they are used only for decisions considered to be of such importance that the people should be involved directly. In policy-making terms, when referenda are used, they can have a direct and significant effect on the policy-making process.

Because the use of referenda is not widespread, typically we are less concerned with citizens' voting patterns in referenda and more with their behavior concerning the selection of elected representatives. As mentioned earlier, in industrialized countries electoral choice traditionally was most directly related to group membership and social cleavage patterns and not to specific policy positions. Through the late 1970s, an individual's association with a particular societal cleavage (for example, class, religion, or region) or his or her attachment to a particular ideology gave that individual a certain set of characteristics that clearly made him or her part of the natural constituency of one political party over another. Thus voters traditionally were seen as making voting choices based on partisan ties that almost exclusively reflected their class background, ethnic identification, religious affiliation, or a shared ideological perspective. For example, belonging to the British working class until very recently was directly related to voting for the Labour Party. Although we observe today some lessening of working class support for Labour in Britain (for example, with the emergence of "working class Tories"—members of the working class who vote for the other major British party, the Conservatives or Tories), the Labour Party continues to receive the greatest proportion of the working class vote. In this situation, we talk about a form of party loyalty that reflects an individual's social characteristics more than his or her assessment of parties' and candidates' policy positions.

In most industrialized countries, voting based primarily on social cleavages has yielded ground to more **issue voting.** Rather than voting for the same party at every election because of their strong sense of party identification, voters are increasingly likely to compare policies advocated by competing parties on issues that matter to them and to make their choice on the basis of which party's program seems to best suit their own interests and beliefs. This is a much more pragmatic style of voting than traditional partisan voting and can result in a great deal of **volatility** in election results—patterns of partisan support may shift dramatically from election to election as both the issues of the day and parties and the electorate's positions change. Increasingly volatile voting patterns across industrialized countries demonstrate voters' growing willingness to punish governments that fail to deliver, as well as more widespread feelings of disillusionment among electorates.

A consequence of this volatility has been a marked rise in support for marginal parties as support for mainstream parties declines. For example, in both France and Germany left-wing green parties have enjoyed greater success since the 1980s; the same is true for far-right extremist parties. In Italy, we observe increased support for regional leagues and movement away from mainstream traditional parties. Such movement has raised some concern that volatility will destabilize party systems in the long run. This possibility does exist when voters move to the margins; however, in systems where vote swapping is between mainstream parties, this seems a less likely prospect. More worrying in the latter instance is increasing evidence that volatility is being accompanied by decreasing electoral participation overall.

Elections in France in the 1980s and 1990s clearly reveal such electoral volatility. Since 1978, French electoral majorities have moved back and forth from left to right in nearly every national election. Voting data indicate that parties' traditional bases of support have eroded. For example, Catholics who in the past were strong right-wing voters increasingly vote for parties of the left, and working class voters have moved from the left wing to the right wing. Such results support the view that a substantial number of **swing voters** demonstrate no strong loyalty to any political party but rather cast their vote on the basis of considerations such as candidates' personalities, perceptions of their competence and leadership abilities, or more specific policy promises of one party or another. These patterns hold true in France and in other industrialized countries.

Economic conditions also appear to have a powerful effect on electoral choice. Where we observe what is known as **pocketbook voting,** election results reflect the state of the national economy and, at times, individual economic fortunes. If the economy is seen as reasonably strong, the incumbent party tends to do well with many voters—regardless of their traditional party ties or ideology. Many analysts argue that such voting patterns were observed in the United Kingdom in the 1980s and early 1990s, when voters who seemed otherwise dissatisfied with the ruling Conservative Party (because of their policy positions or their views of the party's leader) continued to vote for the party because of their belief that the Conservatives were responsible for improving economic conditions and that they were the party of economic competence. (This pattern applied to both Tory voters and traditional Labour voters who switched to the Conservatives in this period because of their belief in their own party's economic incompetence.) With the emergence of issue voting and pocketbook voting, predicting the vote is much less straightforward today than it was when being a member of the working class meant that you would almost invariably vote for a party of the left, irrespective of the issues or the economic climate of the day.

Political scientists describe this general pattern of weakening ties to existing political parties and shifting voting behavior as **dealignment.** This pattern emerged as old cleavage patterns in industrialized countries have become less significant, particularly as class lines blur and shift (especially as a result of the increasing size of the middle class in most of these countries). As a result, parties become less meaningful agents for channeling political conflict. In addition, the process of building effective electoral coalitions has become more challenging.

There is some speculation that these changes may be part of a trend toward eventual **realignment,** in which individuals form attachments to new political parties resting on new bases of social identification. This trend is suggested by the appearance of several new partisan movements in industrialized countries, such as green parties in Germany and France, that have sought to attract voters concerned about issues that tend to cut across class lines, such as environmental problems, human rights, regional nationalism, or xenophobia. Such a process of realignment is blocked in some countries by institutional barriers, namely, electoral laws that impede the success of smaller, emerging parties. The absence of a meaningful green party movement in the United Kingdom or the United States, for example, can be attributed at least in part to electoral laws that discourage small parties from running for office.

The extent to which such issue-based politics may be forming the basis for enduring, institutionalized partisan alignments remains unclear. These new movements may turn out to be the major parties of the future, or it may be that a more fluid and volatile pattern will be the continuing trend, as more stable bases of partisan identification continue to erode. Following on this, political leaders are faced with a more uncertain policy-making environment. In particular, in policy terms increased volatility and partisan dealignment make it more difficult for governments to engage in widespread reform, particularly when reform involves actual costs to the citizens. For example, in France in the early 1990s, the right-wing government of Jacques Chirac and Alain Juppe attempted to reduce significantly levels of public spending by cutting public sector employment and reducing public sector benefits. These reforms were rejected by French citizens (as indicated by massive public demonstrations), and in subsequent parliamentary elections there was a clear swing away from a large right-wing majority to left-wing control. Needless to say, the new left-controlled government has been much more cautious in its approach to reform, presumably in recognition of the electoral risks associated with both large-scale change and the enactment of policies that reduce benefits for large numbers of French citizens—no matter how necessary the policies may be.

Changing patterns of voter choice affect the way parties develop their policy positions and have changed the very nature of parties themselves. As parties' traditional bases of support have eroded, they have struggled to redefine themselves. As part of this effort, parties seek to tailor their policy positions to capture as many votes as possible; this results in an overall moderation of parties in industrialized countries. Increasingly, we observe political parties trying to develop policies that will appeal to the widest range of voters (following what is known as the **median voter model**), regardless of whether those policy positions contradict the party's traditional perspective on the issue at hand. The result is a clear trend toward the aforementioned catch-all parties with elections becoming nothing more than contests for the median voter.

Electoral Systems

Electoral laws determine the manner in which the votes cast in an election are translated into seats in the legislature. The nature of a country's electoral system can have an important impact on election outcomes—the same percentage of votes can yield very different shares of seats in the legislature. Electoral laws are important for understanding the policy-making process because they affect not only the distribution of seats in the legislature and its subsequent operation but also citizens' access to politics and the nature of political party systems. For example, electoral laws influence whether smaller parties form in a political system, what sort of say they will have in the policy-making process, and whether such parties continue to exist at all. In most industrialized countries, two main types of laws are used to allocate legislature seats. Countries may either adopt **single-member district plurality** or **proportional representation** electoral systems, although some choose a combination of the two. Table 3–1 summarizes the electoral systems used in the six industrialized countries we examine in this book.

Single-member district plurality (SMDP) electoral systems (also known variously as plurality, winner-take-all, or first-past-the-post systems) divide a given country into a relatively large number of legislative districts and assign one seat in the legislature to each district. Once an election is held in a given district and the results are tallied, the candidate who receives the most votes (a **plurality**) is the elected representative from that district. A candidate may win a seat under such a system without capturing a majority of the votes cast (particularly when more than two candidates are running for a seat) and no seats are awarded to any other candidate receiving votes in that district. Some countries, such as France, require a candidate to win a majority of votes to be elected. This usually entails a second runoff election between a group of top vote-getters in the first round of balloting. This **ballotage system** variation of SMDP encourages the participation of smaller parties in the first round—when they are more likely to receive enough votes to make it to the second ballot—while ensuring that the eventual winner of the election enjoys strong support among the electorate. Of the six countries we examine, only the United States and the United Kingdom employ SMDP systems.

SMDP systems are often valued for the strong legislative majorities they produce, resulting in a politically stable legislature, and for the clear and direct ties they create between elected representatives and their constituents (because there is only one representative from a district, everyone living in that district knows who is representing them). These systems often are criticized, however, for favoring larger parties, particularly if support for smaller parties is not geographically concentrated in certain electoral districts, so that the smaller parties have some chance of achieving a plurality in at least a few districts. If a small party's support is spread across a country, the party is unlikely to win a plurality of the vote in a district. Because the prospects for such

Table 3-1 Electoral Systems in Six Industrialized Countries

Country	Type	Institution	System
France	Mixed	President	Two-ballot plurality
		National Assembly	Two-ballot SMDP (second ballot only if no absolute majority in first round)
Germany	Mixed	Bundestag	Half SMDP
			Half PR with party lists
Italy	Mixed	Chamber of Deputies	Three-fourths SMDP
			One-fourth PR with party lists
		Senate	Three-fourths SMDP
			One-fourth PR with party lists
Japan	Mixed	House of Representatives	300 seats SMDP
			200 seats PR with party lists
United Kingdom	SMDP	House of Commons	Plurality of popular vote
United States	SMDP	President	Plurality of popular vote
			Electoral college majority
		House of Representatives	Plurality of popular vote
		Senate	Plurality of popular vote

SMDP = single-member district plurality; PR = proportional representation.

parties are so poor, support for small parties generally declines over time or never emerges in countries using SMDP systems. Two-party systems are more likely to evolve and endure under SMDP systems, and those parties are more likely to be moderate in the interest of attracting the widest possible range of voters. As a result, it is often argued that SMDP systems sacrifice the wider representation of political interests (by creating two-party systems) for the sake of greater political stability (resulting from single party control of the legislature rather than coalition governments), which in turn produces greater policy coherency and follow-through but may exclude important interests from having a say in the policy-making process.

Proportional representation (PR) electoral systems involve a smaller number of large electoral districts, with multiple seats in the legislature allocated to each district. Instead of voting for individual candidates at election time, voters under PR systems usually cast one vote for a single party, or choose several candidates from a party list. When the votes are tallied after an election, the seats available in the district are allocated roughly according to the proportion of the vote that the party's slate received. For example, if ten seats are available in a district and party A received 40 percent of the vote, and parties B, C, and D received 20 percent each, then party A would win four seats in the legislature and parties B, C, and D would win two seats each. This is in contrast to a SMDP system in which only party A would win the only available seat. The precise formula used to translate the vote into seats varies from country to country. Strict proportionality often is qualified somewhat in PR systems through the introduction of a threshold of votes: a minimum percentage of the votes cast nationally (usually between 4 and 9 percent) that a party must receive to win any legislative seats. This threshold is intended to consolidate the representation of parties in the legislature by reducing the participation of electorally smaller parties, thereby increasing the likelihood of government stability.

This emphasis on proportionality in PR systems results in their being rated as more equitable and representative than SMDP systems. Box 3–2 illustrates how the SMDP system compares to the proportional representation system. Because PR systems increase the electoral chances of smaller parties, countries that adopt these laws tend to have multiparty systems with both small and large parties and a wider array of ideological positions represented in the legislature—thus the belief that they are more representative and fair. Rather than excluding smaller interests from political institutions, PR systems are designed to ensure their inclusion. For example, under a PR system, sixteen different parties took seats in Italy's Chamber of Deputies after the 1992 national elections (over fifty parties sought office). Since 1994, the Italian electoral system has been based less on PR, thereby reducing the significance of smaller parties and encouraging the formation of two party blocs (although the absolute number of parties operating in Italy remains large).

PR systems often are argued to produce a weaker linkage between representatives and their districts because citizens are less clear about who is really charged with representing them. Further, although they expand inclusiveness, PR systems also increase the likelihood of multiparty coalition governments by making it more difficult for a single party to achieve majority control of the legislature. In addition, depending on the degree to which a country's population is divided and prone to conflict, and the extent to which the electoral system has allowed the representation of more radical and extreme groups, a pattern of parliamentary instability can emerge. This consideration is important for the policy-making process because stable government means more straightforward and effective policy making. If a coalition has numerous, hostile parties, it is often impossible for that coalition to work together cooperatively and govern effectively. Italy again serves as the best example of such a pattern—here multiparty governing coalitions have been the norm because of PR. These coalitions often were formed by parties that had little in common and were unable to form effective working groups. This resulted in fifty-five different governments from 1946 to 1997 (each averaging less than one year in office)—more than in any other industrialized democracy. Some of this instability was clearly related to the presence of too many parties in the parliament, although this was not necessarily the sole cause; parties in Italy also lack internal cohesion, have ideological differences, and have leaders who are prone to personality-based conflicts with one another. Taken together, these factors account for the observed patterns of Italian governmental instability. The results of this instability for policy making were important: Citizens lost confidence in the political process, and policy making was defined by the lack of a consistent vision or coherence.

Box 3-2 **The Effects of Electoral System Choice**

1997 General Election Results in the United Kingdom

	Voter Support (percentage)	Seats in House of Commons	
		Percentage	Number
Conservatives	30.7%	25%	165
Labour	43.2	63.7	419
Liberal Democrats	16.8	9.7	46
Scottish Nationalists	2.6	1.5	10
Other	6.7	2.7	18

The results of the 1997 British general election illustrate the effects of a single-member district plurality (SMDP) electoral system on the distribution of the seats in a legislature. The Labour Party commands an overwhelming majority of seats in the House of Commons, despite having received less than a majority of the votes cast (only 43.2 percent). The Liberal Democratic Party, which garnered nearly 17 percent of the vote, received only 46 seats in the House, which is less than 10 percent of Parliament. As these results demonstrate, the SMDP system overrepresents the strength of the larger parties and underrepresents the smaller ones—in so doing, the distribution of seats in Parliament becomes a distortion of the electorate's political preferences.

1998 General Election Results in the Federal Republic of Germany

	Voter Support (percentage)	Seats in Bundestag	
		Percentage	Number
Social Democrats	40.9%	44.6%	298
CDU/CSU°	35.2	36.6	245
Greens	6.7	7.0	47
Free Democrats	6.2	6.4	43
PDS	5.1	5.4	36
Other	6.0	0	0

°CDU/CSU = Christian Democratic Union/Christian Social Union; PDS = Party of Democratic Socialism.

In the German system, where a variant of a proportional representation electoral system is used, the relationship between the votes cast in the election and the actual distribution of seats in the legislature is much less distorted. In comparison to the British system, German electoral laws deliver a far more equitable distribution of legislative power among political parties. The use of a form of proportional representation after the 1998 general election resulted in a far closer alignment between partisan strength in the legislature and the distribution of votes in the election, thereby creating a far more accurate expression of the public's preferences. The only parties who fail to gain representation are those who do not reach a 5 percent threshold, which ultimately creates a more stable pattern of governance because fringe parties do not gain representation.

Executive-Legislative Relations

Industrialized countries have two general models of executive institutions: presidential and parliamentary governments. Despite the heightened awareness of the presidential model in the United States, the presidency is clearly in the minority as a framework for executive-legislative relations. The vast majority of the world's enduring democracies have parliamentary arrangements. Of the six countries we examine in this book, only the United States has a presidential system of government; France has a mix of presidential and parliamentary institutions; and Italy, Japan, Germany, and the United Kingdom operate under parliamentary arrangements (Table 3–2).

Presidential democracies have one chief political executive—the president—who is directly elected for a fixed term of office. Perhaps the most distinctive feature of presidential democracies is their formal **separation of powers** between the executive and legislative branches of government. In presidential systems, central-level policy-making authority is constitutionally divided among the executive, legislative, and judicial branches of government. This formal separation of powers involves a system of checks and balances in which each branch is given certain constitutionally defined mechanisms through which it controls the actions of the other branches (through the use of vetoes, overrides, filibusters, and the like). This division of authority was intended primarily to prevent the abuse of power by any one government branch. In practice, it has three direct effects on the policy-making process: (1) It decentralizes power, (2) it requires negotiation and compromise among government branches, and (3) it creates inefficiency in the decision-making process.

In addition to recognizing the importance of a separation of powers, we must also consider the effects of a **separation of mandate** on presidential systems. The chief executive derives his or her strength from the fact that the president is elected independently from the legislature and therefore has a personal mandate to govern. At the same time, the legislature has its own independent electoral mandate. A president's personal mandate means that, in theory, he or she should be able to take charge of the policy-making process and provide clear policy leadership. In reality, however, the legislature often goes against a president's wishes, claiming that it is rightfully pursuing its own electoral mandate.

The emphasis of presidential systems on the structural independence of the government branches is argued to have several negative consequences for policy making. Because the legislature is independent of the president, it is not bound by law or tradition to support the president's policies. One of the central premises of the system, then, is the legislature's freedom to deny the president's wishes. In other words, its members must be convinced to offer their support. As such, presidents cannot ensure that they will be able to fulfill their campaign promises unless they secure the legislature's support. In the United

Table 3-2 Governmental Forms in Six Industrialized Countries

Country	State Form	Government Form	Executive		Bicameral Legislature	
			Symbolic	*Political*	*Upper*	*Lower*
France	Republic	Presidential and Parliamentary	None	President Prime minister	Senate	National Assembly
Germany	Federal republic	Parliamentary	President	Chancellor	Bundesrat	Bundestag
Italy	Republic	Parliamentary	President	Prime minister	Senate	Chamber of Deputies
Japan	Constitutional monarchy	Parliamentary	Emperor	Prime minister	House of Councillors	House of Representatives
United Kingdom	Constitutional monarchy	Parliamentary	Monarch	Prime minister	House of Lords	House of Commons
United States	Republic	Presidential	None	President	Senate	House of Representatives

States, the president cannot even introduce legislation independently to the Congress; he or she needs the support of a legislative sponsor who will introduce the bill. To receive such sponsorship, the president usually compromises over policy content or offers the sponsor incentives. Reflecting this relationship, the legislative agenda and calendar are not under the president's control but are set by the legislative leadership. Given these dynamics, most adopted policies reflect a series of compromises between the legislature and the executive branch rather than the clear intentions of the executive branch alone. The policy-making division of labor in presidential systems usually is described as one in which the legislature is responsible for decision making, and the executive branch is responsible for policy implementation, that is, making sure that policies are carried out.

In presidential systems, the smooth flow of the policy-making process may be interrupted by a clear tendency toward government immobilization. This often occurs when there is **divided government,** that is, when the legislature and the president are from different parties, as has been the case in the United States in the late 1990s. In such a situation, the president often finds it difficult to achieve much of anything. Instead, we often observe a process in which the executive branch and the legislature set out to frustrate each other rather than cooperate, mostly for political and electoral gain. This condition is often described as **gridlock**—when political, ideological, or other differences between the executive branch and the legislature make it more difficult for the government to develop policies to address important problems. Even when gridlock does not occur, the weak position of the president relative to the legislature also may reflect a tendency of presidential systems toward weak party discipline. Parties tend to be less disciplined because of the separation of mandate; legislators do not directly owe their election success to the president and vice versa. Often, a lack of party discipline in the legislature makes it difficult for presidents to secure support for their policies, even if their party controls a legislative majority.

Such obstacles make comprehensive policy making, in particular, large-scale reform, difficult to pursue in presidential systems. Instead, policies require extensive bargaining and negotiation and usually represent a compromise between the two branches. Voters find it difficult to assign responsibility for policies—because it is not immediately apparent which branch or institution created a particular policy (despite a clear focus on the president for policy leadership). As a result, voting in elections is not typically seen as an opportunity to pass judgment on a party's or an individual's ability to fulfill policy promises.

A presidential system does have some positive policy-making features. Because presidents serve a fixed term of office and are not subject to immediate removal by the legislature if their opinion poll ratings drop precipitously once a policy is implemented, they are freer to make politically less-popular policy choices (particularly when they have the support of the legislature). Further, policy making in presidential systems tends to be a slow, deliberative legislative process in which many actors have the opportunity to weigh in on the decision—thus increasing the possibility for citizen participation and input, and avoiding the problem of snap decision making by politicians for immediate political gain. Finally, separation of powers results in a fragmented decision-making process (which may reduce efficiency), but citizens have many more opportunities to influence the policy-making process.

Parliamentary systems usually have a dual executive that consists of a ceremonial head of state and a chief political executive known most often as the prime minister. Citizens vote for parties, not individual candidates, and members of the parliament are selected from the winning parties. The majority party in the parliament (or a coalition of parties that forms a majority of the legislature) then selects a prime minister. Typically this individual serves as the leader of the majority (or largest) party in the parliament and continues to act in this capacity while serving as prime minister. Thus the prime minister is not directly elected, and we observe a **fusion of powers**—meaning the executive derives from and is responsible to the legislature.

The prime minister and the cabinet (collectively known as the government) play both a policy-making and a policy implementation role in parliamentary systems. They control the overall process by formulating policies, overseeing their passage in the legislature, and controlling implementation. Whereas in presidential systems, chief executives must find sympathetic members of the legislature to sponsor their bills, in parliamentary systems the government introduces its legislation directly and independently into the parliament. (Few individual members' bills are introduced, and even fewer are passed.) The government controls the legislative calendar and agenda as well. Generally speaking, parliaments play a secondary role in the policy-making process in these systems—their role is essentially advisory, particularly when one party controls a strong majority.

There is almost a guarantee in parliamentary systems that the executive's policies will be adopted and implemented provided that party discipline is intact. When the governing party (or coalition) controls a strong and disciplined majority in the parliament, the executive is virtually assured of obtaining its policy wish list. Only a small percentage of bills introduced by the government will not be successful (unless party discipline has broken down, in which case the government will resign or be removed by the legislature). Under these conditions, legislative policy making tends to proceed quickly because there are no meaningful barriers to policy adoption in the legislature—an opposition party or parties will be present and participate in debate in the parliamentary chamber, but they typically will not be able to influence the policy-making process. Further, and unlike presidential systems, the lines of policy responsibility are clear in parliamentary systems—the electorate expects the government to fulfill its campaign promises, and at election time voters know who to blame or reward for policy decisions: the party or parties in power.

Several characteristics of parliamentary systems can have a negative effect on the policy-making process. First, prime ministers do not enjoy the same job security that presidents have: They may be removed from office at any time by a legislative majority. If the executive loses the support of the parliamentary majority, the prime minister will typically be forced to leave office. This may be accomplished by way of pressure to resign, a negative vote on a major piece of legislation, or a vote of no confidence. As a result, parliamentary executives are not likely to adopt policy positions that the legislature clearly does not support, for fear of being removed from office (although prime ministers are not typically so out of step with their parliaments that this occurs frequently). Second, prime ministers and their cabinets have the ability to dissolve the legislature at any time and call for new elections, or to call for a vote of confidence to confirm the executive's power. Thus the legislature is also unlikely to ignore consistently the executive's preferences because if legislative-executive interactions become too contentious, the legislature will be dissolved, risking the careers of its members. Third, although parliamentary systems are able to deliver policies quickly, some danger is associated with the pace of this policy-making process. More specifically, there is a risk of adopting inappropriate or poorly designed policies in the absence of a more deliberative process. Further, the faster pace at which policies are introduced, debated, and passed in parliamentary systems also decreases the opportunities for citizen input into the policy-making process.

Intergovernmental Relations

Any discussion of the policy-making process in industrialized countries must consider the degree to which a country's governmental authority is central-

Table 3-3 State Structures in Six Industrialized Countries

Country	Structure	Composition
France	Unitary	22 administrative regions with 96 metropolitan departments
Germany	Federal	16 *Länder* (states)
Italy	Unitary	20 regions and 94 provinces (several regions have some autonomy)
Japan	Unitary	47 prefectures
United Kingdom	Unitary	Municipalities and counties
United States	Federal	50 states

ized. Where are government policy decisions made? At the central level or by lower levels of government? Such discussions about the distribution of political authority usually focus on a single constitutional feature: Does a country have a unitary or federal political system? Among the six countries we examine in this book, only the United States and Germany have federal political systems (Table 3–3).

A **unitary political system** has only one meaningful level of government above the local level. In such systems, only the central government has constitutionally derived policy-making authority (for all stages of the policy-making process). For the most part, local governments in unitary systems are charged with simply administering decisions made at the central level. Under most unitary arrangements, central governments assign some decision-making authority in a few specific policy areas to local level governments as they see fit, with local governments having only limited independent policy-making discretion. In the United Kingdom, for example, acts of Parliament make local governments responsible for delivering many important government services (such as primary schooling, refuse collection, and policing); however, the central government strictly controls the ability of local authorities to raise revenue to pay for these services. In unitary systems government finances often are controlled by the center, thus limiting the scope of local efforts. Reflecting this distribution of authority, political power is centralized.

Unitary political arrangements are often praised for their simplicity, uniformity, and clear lines of accountability. Power is exercised at the central level, and the electorate will hold this level of government responsible for public policies. Policy implementation in most unitary systems is expected to be more uniform within the country because of the limited discretion given to local governments in administering policies. As such, we expect to observe a more equal pattern of government service delivery within a unitary system—that is, living in one locality or another should not affect substantially the type, quality, or quantity of service citizens receive, particularly because local governments operate with similar financial resources. A noted disadvantage of unitary arrangements, however, is their tendency to reduce citizen involvement in policy making because of the remote nature of the policy process. Policies are made in some distant, impersonal central government structure, rather than in citizens' own backyard by individuals with whom they have a more personal connection.

A **federal political system** involves one or two meaningful levels of government above the local level, and each level has its own institutionally defined policy-making responsibilities. Usually, lower government levels (including state, regional, or local governments) are assigned powers in specific policy areas (for example, education, policing, or transport) and these powers go beyond administration. Constitutionally, lower levels of government are given the power to determine policy in these areas at their own discretion. Typically they have their own revenue-raising capacity, thereby ensuring that their independent policy jurisdictions translate into a meaningful role in a country's policy-making process. Reflecting such distributions of authority, political power is fragmented.

Federal systems are most often adopted by larger countries (especially in terms of population size) because they provide for more flexibility in addressing the demands of their typically more diverse populations. This flexibility is viewed as federalism's strength: It enables governments to develop policies that are more responsive to the needs of smaller groups or more particularized interests. For example, in the United States a federal system of government is argued to make it easier to hold together such a large and culturally diverse political entity. The needs of different groups can be met at the state and local levels—wherever their populations may be more concentrated. For example, policies may be needed in California to address the needs of migrant farm workers from Latin America, whereas such policies have no widespread application in Minnesota, where such farm workers are not a significant presence. Federal political arrangements allow California to develop such policies, while Minnesota is free to address other concerns. If these problems could be solved only by a national government at the center, the likelihood of their being addressed would be far smaller. In this way, federalism is argued to make the political system more responsive to the needs of a diverse population. Federalism also encourages policy experimentation and innovation (whereby new solutions are tested at lower levels of government before being introduced nationwide). Because there are multiple points of policy decision making in federal systems, they also provide greater opportunities for citizen involvement.

Some disadvantages are associated with federal systems, however. Because significant variation exists in the type, quality, or quantity of government services delivered across a federal system, citizens may receive different treatment depending on where they live. This occurs for several reasons: differences in resources across levels of government (since lower levels of government typically have their own revenue-raising powers), with some localities or states more affluent than others; the effects of alternative policy choices across and within levels of government; and, more generally, variations in government performance. Difficulties can also arise owing to a lack of control by the central level over the pace and effectiveness of central-level policy implementation by lower levels of government. In addition, some duplication of government services is common in federal systems, when the central and the lower levels of government enact policies in similar policy areas. Such duplication often results in unnecessary government spending or government programs that pursue conflicting goals.

The Bureaucracy

Public bureaucracies play a powerful role in policy making in all industrialized countries. As the size of the welfare state and the role of government more generally (especially its economic activities) have expanded over the past several decades, public bureaucracies have increased in size as agents for both the formulation and the implementation of government programs. Even as governments seek to reduce their size, bureaucracies continue to flourish and to occupy a powerful role in the policy-making process.

Industrialized countries have well-established bureaucratic traditions. At one time, public bureaucracies were based on the distribution of the political spoils: People were appointed to the bureaucracy for their political loyalty and were expected to demonstrate this loyalty in their work. In European bureaucracies, these so-called spoils systems often involved wealthy citizens buying positions in the bureaucracy for their children. Such bureaucratic systems often were inefficient and of poor quality because of this lack of control over hiring—appointees were often unqualified and lacked any specific policy expertise. In addition, these systems generally lacked mechanisms for control over performance; employees would perform to get their jobs and then fail to perform once the position was secured, with no effective provisions for compelling them to actually do their jobs (their removal was unlikely given that they were protected by powerful political leaders). Today, however, industrialized countries pride themselves on having bureaucracies characterized by a modern civil service. By this we mean that bureaucratic institutions have become increasingly professionalized. They are viewed as impartial, permanent, and meritocratic; and bureaucrats are highly valued in the policy-making process for their knowledge, skills, and experience.

The question of political control of the bureaucracy, that is, the ability of the central government to control bureaucratic behavior and influence, has been raised now that the modern civil service has become the norm in industrialized countries. When bureaucracies consisted primarily of political appointees, political leaders exercised a significant amount of control over their actions. Leaders could simply remove the bureaucrats from office if they went against the leaders' wishes or political preferences. As a result, political appointees were not likely to contradict or challenge these leaders. Today, with professionalized and expert bureaucracies, there is some concern about bureaucracies' seeming immunity to the influence or control of politicians. Often this concern is expressed as a worry about a so-called democratic deficit, reflecting the fact that bureaucrats are not elected officials. When bureaucrats are seen as exercising too much influence on the policy-making process, citizens may question whether policy decision making is truly democratic.

Beyond the common denominator of a modern civil service, we observe a considerable degree of variation from country to country in the policy-making functions of bureaucracies. This variation reflects organizational factors, cultural traditions, and norms as well as the structure of party systems. Civil servants influence public policy in all political systems in some fashion, but the degree and manner of this influence vary. In particular, bureaucrats' ability to pursue and realize their own policy preferences, especially in the face of opposition from elected officials or the public, varies significantly both from country to country and across policy areas within countries. In some situations, the bureaucracy is seen as dominating the policy-making process, often going so far as to render parliaments and elected officials almost irrelevant. In other cases, the bureaucracy is seen as playing only a limited role beyond the implementation of policies made elsewhere. Bureaucratic policy making has traditionally been an important feature of the Japanese political system. In Japan, the majority of bills passed in the parliament are drafted by the bureaucracy. During the period of Liberal Democratic Party dominance in Japan (until 1993), bureaucrats worked closely with party politicians and representatives of special interests (especially big business) to develop and implement policies in what where known as iron triangles. Even after 1993, such patterns of policy making persisted. The bureaucracy's policy-making role was further enhanced in Japan because most adopted legislation is broad and vague, and the bureaucracy uses its power to draft rules and regulations to further control the nature of public policy.

The Judiciary

Industrialized countries also vary in the degree to which they have allowed judicial institutions to play a role in the policy-making process. In most of these countries, the judiciary traditionally was considered a branch of government that had no role to play in law making. This area was seen instead as the exclusive domain of the elected representatives of the people in the legislature and the executive. Despite this tradition, we now find constitutional courts in some industrialized countries, such as Germany, that have the power of **legislative judicial review,** meaning that they have the power to declare legislation unconstitutional and thereby nullify laws. From country to country, we observe significant differences in these courts with respect to their constitutionally derived powers, their interpretation of these powers, the kinds of decisions they make, and their levels of judicial activism (Table 3–4).

Generally speaking, constitutional courts do not seek out cases independently but instead consider issues that others (for example, a parliamentary

Table 3-4 Constitutional Courts in Six Industrialized Countries

Country	Court
France	Constitutional Council
Germany	Federal Constitutional Court
Italy	Constitutional Court
Japan	Supreme Court
United Kingdom	No court with powers of judicial review
United States	Supreme Court

party or the central government) send them. Because the policy-making process is not subject to the courts' independent influence or control, we do not consider the judiciary to play a consistent role in this process; however, they do have an important role to play. The courts' decisions cannot be overturned by any other institution; thus their ability to modify or nullify laws represents an important power in the policy-making process. In all countries we observe an increased willingness on the part of constitutional courts to engage in judicial interpretation and to make decisions about the substance of laws when cases are referred to them. A second and perhaps more apparent influence is that the courts' rulings set a standard or precedent by which future policies will be measured, not only by the courts but also by the legislatures and executives. Future policies must comply with the guidelines established by earlier court rulings; thus the courts become a participant in the policy-making process, albeit indirectly. Third, policy making begins to reflect some effort on the part of the legislature to anticipate the reaction of the court in developing policies—in this sense the legislature is not necessarily reacting to precedents but is attempting to avoid making policy decisions that might trigger the process of judicial review. Although the judiciary may not actively initiate policy-making activities, the fact that it may be asked to act, in conjunction with knowledge about how it acted in the past, can significantly influence policy decisions.

Economic Dynamics

Many of the policy decisions we examine later in this book undoubtedly affect countries' economies. At the same time, economic conditions and institutions clearly influence policymakers' decisions. An understanding of politics and policy making today requires some consideration of the role of economic factors in these processes for two reasons. First, many of the problems facing countries today are a byproduct of the economic choices they have made—for example, the commitment to the welfare state or a social market economy today presents real policy problems for many industrialized countries' governments as they are faced with skyrocketing costs and falling revenues. Second, a country's economic system often determines the manner in which the government responds to certain problems on its policy agendas. For example, an economic choice for trade liberalization may result in a loss of price protections for farmers, thus creating new policy demands in the agricultural sector.

Industrialized countries have in common one key characteristic: They are all capitalist **market economies.** They all adhere, with varying degrees of commitment, to certain core economic principles, although their economies do not all operate in the same fashion. Industrialized countries are considered to be capitalist because business remains predominantly in the hands of the private sector. In addition, the central coordinating mechanism for economic activities in these countries is the market, not the state. In a market economy, producers and consumers are key actors who enter the marketplace as individuals and behave in a rational manner. Their preferences and behaviors, through competition in the marketplace, set prices, control supply, and allocate resources, with producers responding to consumers' demands because of the profit motive. In this way the balancing effects of supply and demand are expected to provide maximum societal wealth and efficiency at minimum cost. A pure free-market economic system demands no strong role for government in the marketplace; the market is intended to regulate itself and requires minimal government interference. As such, market economies should be based on private sector rather than government decision making. In a pure market economy, therefore, the government's role is limited to maintaining order at home, enforcing laws to allow the market to function properly, and protecting the country from external threats.

Today, however, no industrialized country has reduced government to such an exclusively external role. Instead, the governments of industrialized countries play, to varying degrees, important economic roles—and these roles have expanded since the end of World War II. For example, all governments in industrialized countries provide for **public goods**—those services that are unlikely to be provided by the marketplace because it is not in any individual's self-interest to produce them but that are generally deemed necessary for a basic quality of life. Public goods include roads, schools, a clean environment, mass transportation, and public parks.

The governments of industrialized countries also determine to some extent how their economies operate overall: They regulate markets and industries to varying degrees, control inflation, oversee money supplies, and more generally enact policies designed to control or promote economic growth. In Japan, for example, where we clearly observe a capitalist market economy, government in the postwar era has played a major role in shaping the economy, especially through planning and assistance to specific industries. In some countries, the increase in the government's role since the end of World War II has been dramatic. This is particularly true in countries with **mixed economies,** such as France, Germany, Italy, and the United Kingdom. Mixed economies combine capitalist free-market principles, including private ownership, with some level of state ownership (usually of key industries and utilities), some central economic planning, and a higher level of regulation. As such, they mix public ownership with private control. Countries with mixed economies vary in the degree to which the state intervenes in the marketplace. In the United Kingdom, for example, the government does not engage in economic planning, it intervenes in the marketplace less directly, and it tends to regulate economic activities to a lesser degree than is observed in France or Germany. By the 1980s, some of these countries, especially the United Kingdom and France, began to reduce the economic role played by their governments in order to pursue policies of privatization, deregulation, and liberalization. These efforts were aimed at decreasing public spending and increasing government revenues (especially by selling off government assets). Despite these efforts, the economies of many industrialized countries are still characterized by a rather high level of government economic intervention.

In all of these mixed economic systems, **social insurance programs** provide for health care, old age and unemployment benefits, and the like and typically cover individuals from cradle to grave. Countries that provide such benefits are often referred to as **welfare states.** These programs generally involve a high level of public expenditure and high taxation rates, which, taken together, create some of the most vexing political policy issues faced by leaders in industrialized countries. Although the six countries we examine in this book provide some level of social welfare benefits to their populations (and all increased their levels of expenditure on these benefits after World War II), the French, German, and Italian governments do so far more comprehensively than do the governments of Japan, the United Kingdom, or the United States.

In Germany, we find a more specific type of mixed economy: the **social market economy.** Here the government combines support for the private sector and the free market (with nearly all enterprises under private control), with a high level of government intervention designed to create a framework for economic growth. The German government's economic activities are intended to achieve a clearly defined and widely accepted social goal—the well-being of all German citizens. Government thus is charged with providing a more extensive and generous array of social welfare benefits to its citizens than is found in most other industrialized countries. These generous social programs are viewed as essential to the workings of the marketplace. These economic arrangements are often described as "capitalism with a human face." The market is free and private, but government remains vigilant to ensure that citizens are protected from economic insecurity or other wants. Although public ownership is not an important dimension of the social market economy, close cooperation between public and private sector institutions is central to the development and implementation of economic policies. Both sectors work together in a consensual environment to create policies designed to provide maximum social gain.

Economic life in industrialized countries today also clearly reflects the effects of **globalization.** This term has many meanings but may be captured by the idea that national economic, social, and political life, in both industrialized and late-industrializing economies, is increasingly affected by what occurs beyond a country's borders. Those who consider the effects of globalization believe that the world has become more and more one market for goods and capital as a result of technological innovations and improved global communications. As a result, policy agendas and policy making in industrialized countries increasingly are influenced by events and conditions outside their territorial borders. Thus economic policies that once could be decided on in isolation are more subject to international constraints. Global financial and currency markets, multinational corporations, and the European Union are external forces that bring their influence to bear on national economic life in all industrialized countries, and their effects continue to grow. Further, events in the global environment, such as increasing industrial capacity in southeast Asia, increases in interest rates in the United States, and increasing civil war in Africa, may create policy problems for countries to address in an ever-more globalized context.

Economic systems in industrialized countries today are often referred to as **postindustrial.** If we look at where jobs are concentrated in most industrialized countries, we find that more people work in service industries (such as insurance, banking, and computing) than in manufacturing industries or agriculture. This represents a change in employment structures that began in the early 1980s and accelerated throughout the 1990s. This move to postindustrial status is argued to have several political implications. First, changing employment patterns can be associated with changes in the class structure of industrialized countries: The growing middle class discussed earlier is at least in part the result of the growing service sector and a higher standard of living associated with higher-paying jobs. Second, and following on the first implication, the relative decline of manufacturing jobs has produced a decrease in union membership that has reduced the political influence of these organizations in most countries. Today only public sector unions have seen their membership numbers increase. Third, the shift in employment away from traditional manufacturing occupations, which were often low-skill jobs, to high-skill service sector jobs has left many citizens in industrialized countries in a state of long-term unemployment, which has translated into higher levels of dissatisfaction with the performance of democratic institutions and political leaders in these countries and has created new political pressures and policy demands. It is often argued that this postindustrial development, when combined with rapid, unprecedented economic growth since World War II that vastly improved standards of living, also has produced attitudinal change in industrialized countries. Some political scientists believe that the new economic structure of these societies has produced long-term value change known as **postmaterialism.** This term was introduced by the political scientist Ronald Inglehart, who argued that by the early 1980s citizens in industrialized countries, who were increasingly members of the middle class, were less concerned about physical and economic security, or material well-being, than they were about less tangible concerns such as freedom of expression, quality of life, greater political participation, the environment, or gender and sexual equality. Inglehart claimed that because these new values were the result of generational, not short-term, changes, they would be of continuing political relevance.

The emergence of green parties in several industrialized countries, most importantly in Germany (where this party currently forms part of the governing coalition), as well as the strength of various new social movements, such as the women's and disarmament movements, support such arguments. Such groups often have a significant effect on public policies, even in countries where they do not have a share of governing power. Often they have been able to force the major parties in a country to adopt positions that reflect postmaterial concerns (as the parties attempt to reduce the effects of these movements on their own electoral support), and some of the partisan dealignment we discussed earlier is a result of the activities of new parties that espouse these postmaterial values. Supporters of the idea of postmaterial value change in industrialized countries argue that its effects on public policy are likely to increase in the future as a greater proportion of their populations consists of people born in the postindustrial era.

SUGGESTED READINGS

Aberbach, Joel, Robert Putnam, and Bert Rockman. 1981. *Bureaucrats and Politicians in Western Democracies.* Cambridge: Harvard University Press.

Baumgartner, Frank, and Beth Leech. 1998. *Basic Interests: The Importance of Groups in Politics and Political Science.* Princeton: Princeton University Press.

Beck, Paul Allen. 1997. *Party Politics in America.* New York: Addison-Wesley.

Bond, Jon, and Richard Fleisher. 1990. *The President in the Legislative Arena.* Chicago: University of Chicago Press.

Dalton, Russell. 1997. *Citizen Politics in Western Democracies.* Chatham, N.J.: Chatham House.

Dalton, Russell, et al., eds. 1984. *Electoral Change in Advanced Industrial Democracies: Realignment or Dealignment?* Princeton: Princeton University Press.

David, Rene, and John Brierly. 2000. *Major Legal Systems in the World Today,* 3d ed. Delran, N.J.: Legal Classics Library.

Doring, Herbert. 1995. *Parliaments and Majority Rule in Western Europe.* New York: St. Martin's.

Grofman, Bernard, and Arend Lijphart. 1986. *Electoral Laws and Their Political Consequences.* New York: Agathon Press.

Harrop, Martin, ed. 1992. *Power and Policy in Liberal Democracies.* Cambridge: Cambridge University Press.

Hayward, Jack, and Edward Page. 1995. *Governing the New Europe.* Durham: Duke University Press.

Inglehart, Ronald. 1997. *Modernization and Postmodernization: Cultural, Economic and Political Change in 43 Societies.* Princeton: Princeton University Press.

Jackson, Donald, and C. Neal Tate. 1992. *Comparative Judicial Review and Public Policy.* Westport, Conn.: Greenwood Press.

Laver, Michael, and Norman Schofield. 1990. *Multiparty Government: The Politics of Coalition in Europe.* Oxford: Oxford University Press.

Leduc, Lawrence, Richard Niemi, and Pippa Norris, eds. 1996. *Comparing Democracies: Elections and Voting in Comparative Perspective.* Beverly Hills, Calif.: Sage Publications.

Lehmbruch, Gerhard, and Phillipe Schmitter, eds. 1982. *Patterns of Corporatist Policy-making.* Beverly Hills, Calif.: Sage Publications.

Moe, Terry. 1980. *The Organization of Interests.* Chicago: University of Chicago Press.

Rose, Richard. 1974. *The Problem of Party Government.* New York: Free Press.

Rose, Richard, and Ezra Suleiman, eds. 1980. *Presidents and Prime Ministers.* Washington, D.C.: American Enterprise Institute.

Sartori, Giovanni. 1976. *Parties and Party Systems.* Cambridge: Cambridge University Press.

Strom, Kaare. 1990. *Minority Government and Majority Rule.* New York: Cambridge University Press.

Weaver, R. Kent, and Bert Rockman, eds. 1993. *Do Institutions Matter? Government Capabilities in the United States and Abroad.* Washington, D.C.: Brookings Institution Press.

Chapter 4 **The Policy-making Context**

The policy-making process in industrialized countries is often more dissimilar from country to country than we might expect in a set of countries that appear to have a great deal in common as fellow democracies and comparatively wealthy societies. As we touched on in Chapter 3, much of this variation is related to institutional arrangements that allocate power and resources in distinctly different patterns in each country. The choice, for example, between presidential and parliamentary systems of executive-legislative relations, or between federal or unitary patterns of organization, has a very real impact on the style and often the effectiveness of government policy making. In light of these and other important differences, we offer here a capsule discussion of the formal and informal political institutions in the United States, Japan, Germany, France, the United Kingdom, Italy, and the European Union (EU). Basic knowledge of these political systems provides useful background for the case studies offered in Chapters 5–11.

The United States

The United States has a presidential, federal system of government. This system is based on a separation of powers among the executive, legislative, and judicial branches of government, accompanied by a system of checks and balances that prevents each branch from overstepping its constitutional authority. The United States' policy process is often viewed as being less orderly and efficient than in parliamentary systems. In particular, the executive does not have the ability to control the legislative agenda in the United States. Instead, each house of Congress controls its own agenda and the president has a more limited capacity to generate legislative cooperation or compliance with the government's policy proposals or objectives.

The president may not introduce legislation directly to the legislature but must work with members of Congress to persuade them to adopt and propose the government's policy program. Presidential success in this regard usually depends on the pattern of party support in the legislature, the president's bargaining skills, and the state of public opinion. Thus policies are generally made by assembling issue-specific coalitions through a process of bargaining and deal making, typically involving all sorts of public officials, from bureaucrats to cabinet members to members of Congress, as well as interest group representatives. This approach results in less clear lines of policy accountability than are found in parliamentary systems. Unlike many of their prime ministerial counterparts, presidents must also constantly maneuver to avoid deadlock with the legislature, especially when the Congress is controlled by a party different from their own. This situation makes it especially difficult for the president to realize any broad policy goals.

The U.S. legislature exercises far more control over policy making than is the case in other industrialized (and in particular parliamentary) countries. This is partly a reflection of a strong congressional committee system that involves a large number of specialized, permanently staffed, and powerful committees. U.S. committees are independent and activist, and most of their decisions are supported by their relevant legislative branches.

The federal structure in the United States grants considerable powers of self-government to individual states. In addition, state and local governments in the United States have more independent sources of revenue than is the case in most industrialized countries. This structure has restricted the U.S. government's policy reach far more than is found in industrialized countries with unitary structures. In many policy areas, however, the division of policy making and administrative responsibilities between federal and state levels creates implementation and coordination difficulties.

Interest groups in the United States play a larger role in the policy process than in most other industrialized countries. This is partly a reflection of a much weaker party system. Parties in the United States generally lack the discipline, programs, and organization that characterize many European party systems. Party leaders in the United States do not have as much disciplinary authority as they do in other countries; as a result, party members often demonstrate low levels of party loyalty, especially when voting in Congress. Although party membership can be an important predictor of how members of Congress will vote, it is by no means the sole or even primary influence on their voting decisions. Hence, political parties in the United States are widely viewed as ineffective agents of interest articulation and aggregation—these functions are performed instead by interest groups.

With multiple points of access to the policy-making process in the United States, interest group activity is substantial and influential. Interest groups lobby bureaucrats and politicians at all levels of government—federal, state, and local. The large number and important role of congressional committees, when combined with weak party discipline, encourage widespread interest group activity because of the strong possibility of influencing legislators' decisions. These interest groups usually fall into one of two categories: political action committees that attempt to influence campaigns and elections at all levels of government, and groups that focus on lobbying members of Congress. Interest groups often make specific proposals for legislation to the bureaucracy and the legislature, and then work with executive and legislative officials in developing, enacting, and implementing policies.

Judicial review is an important aspect of the policy-making process in the United States. In comparison to other industrialized countries, the Supreme Court in the United States is a very activist institution. This is true not only

United States at a Glance

Political System
Federal republic
Presidential democracy

Administrative Structure
Federal state with fifty states and one district

Executive
Head of state and head of government: President
  Directly elected
  Bill Clinton, Democratic Party (since January 1993)
  1996 Presidential election results: Bill Clinton, 49.2 percent; Bob Dole,
  40.7 percent; Ross Perot, 8.4 percent; other, 1.7 percent

Legislature
Bicameral congress
• Lower house: House of Representatives (directly elected), 435 seats
  Majority party: Republican Party, 223 seats
  Other parties: Democratic Party, 211 seats
                 Independents, 1 seat
• Upper house: Senate (directly elected), 100 seats
  Majority party: Republican Party, 55 seats
  Other parties: Democratic Party, 45 seats

Party System
Two party
  Principal parties: Republican Party, Democratic Party
  Other parties: Democratic Socialists of America, Green Parties of North Amer-
  ica, Libertarian Party, Reform Party, Social Democrats

Judiciary
Supreme Court with powers of legislative review

Economic Indicators
Gross domestic product (GDP), 1999: $9,190.4 billion
GDP per capita, 1998, purchasing power parity: $32,328

Exports as a percentage of GDP, 1997: 11.5 percent

Economic growth, 1999: 4.2 percent
Average economic growth, 1990–1999: 3.01 percent

Unemployment, 1999: 4.2 percent
Average unemployment, 1990–1999: 5.75 percent

Inflation rate, 1999: 2.2 percent
Average inflation rate, 1990–1999: 3.0 percent

Budget surplus as a percentage of GDP, 1999: 1.0 percent
Average budget deficit as a percentage of GDP, 1990–1999: −2.86 percent

with respect to its position as the final arbiter of policies but also because of its tendency to initiate policy through its decisions. The Supreme Court is more powerful than the other constitutional courts because of its role as the highest court in the land for all matters—civil, criminal, and constitutional. This role gives the court more opportunities to make policy indirectly and also more status when it exercises the explicit power of judicial review.

The U.S. government has allowed the economy to operate according to the dictates of the market. Although there is government regulation of the marketplace in the United States, this takes place to a lesser degree than is observed in other industrialized countries. The U.S. economy is not based on a tradition of public ownership, and the public sector overall is smaller than in other countries. In general, the government does not engage in either long- or short-term economic planning nor does it coordinate economic policy. The government also does not provide guidance to various sectors of the economy (with the exception of agriculture and some defense-related industries). The United States is not a social welfare state, although the government maintains a variety of social insurance programs. The scale of this coverage is more limited than in most other industrialized countries.

Japan

The Japanese government is organized along parliamentary and unitary lines. Policy making in Japan is highly centralized, although it does not follow the traditional parliamentary policy-making pattern. Most notably, the Japanese prime minister does not have absolute control over the policy process, although the prime minister is still considered to be the country's most important policymaker. In contrast to the British or German executive, the Japanese prime minister lacks a disciplined majority party in the legislature and as such cannot enact major policy initiatives as easily. From 1945 to 1993 the majority party in Japan, the Liberal Democratic Party (LDP), was composed of a number of competing factions that resisted strong discipline. LDP members of the House of Representatives (the lower and more powerful branch of the Japanese Diet, or parliament), senior civil servants, and interest group leaders worked together in small groups referred to as subgovernments. These powerful groups exercised a large degree of influence over policy making in their areas of expertise, making it difficult for the prime minister and cabinet to intervene effectively in the policy-making process.

A related effect of this pattern of influence was the marked absence of comprehensive national policies. The strong influence of particularized interests allowed prime ministers to manage the policy process but made it difficult for them to control the policy agenda or institute overarching policy reform. Since 1993 and the end of continuous LDP control, the policy position of the executive has not changed dramatically in Japan. The first non-LDP prime ministers after 1993 were hampered by unstable multiparty coalitions. Since its return to power in 1998, the LDP still relies on an unstable coalition, resulting in a return to some old policy-making habits.

The majority of bills proposed to the legislature by the Japanese prime minister and cabinet are formulated by Japan's powerful bureaucracy. A highly professionalized bureaucracy that plays a large role in the process, its policies are formulated after consultation with relevant interest groups (especially business interests) and advisory councils (*shingikai*) comprised of experts in a given policy area. The bureaucracy's recommendations then go to parliamentary committees. The Japanese parliament has little influence over policy content but can be somewhat effective in blocking the passage of bills through the use of established parliamentary procedures. Because of bargaining between LDP factions, however, the Japanese parliament tends to play more of a policy-making role than other parliaments—although party discipline is still an important operating principle.

Through the national bureaucracy, the Japanese government also retains control over policy implementation. Laws passed in the Japanese parliament tend to be loose framework policies that leave ample room for interpretation at the implementation stage. Although local governments follow the lead of the national government under a system known as administrative guidance (reinforced by the local governments' high degree of dependence on the national government for funding), local adaptation of centrally defined policies is still possible. A notable feature of Japan's policy implementation process is the relative absence of policy coordination across bureaucratic jurisdictions. This lack of coordination can result in conflict, policy overlap, and inefficiency.

Japanese political parties as organizations play an insignificant role in the policy process. Unlike their counterparts in the European parliamentary democracies, Japanese political parties are elitist, with limited membership and weakly structured organizations. These parties do not seek to serve as agents of interest aggregation by representing local and grassroots-level interests, and they do not concern themselves with developing policy proposals to reflect those interests. Instead these parties (particularly the LDP) have close ties to interest groups and bureaucratic leaders who are concerned primarily with representing elite interests.

Japan's wide range of interest groups fall into two categories: those that are clients of government agencies and ministries, and those that are not. Groups in the first category have a close relationship with bureaucratic and relevant party officials and have a great deal of influence on public policy making through these personal contacts, and through their role on advisory councils and their influence on bureaucrats at the policy implementation stage. In this sense the Japanese interest group system is corporatist. Interest groups that participate in the system in a pluralist manner (that is, those in the other category) are not officially shut out of the policy-making process, but they do not have the privileged access that groups tied to the LDP traditionally have enjoyed and as a result have far less influence on policy making.

Box 4-2 **Japan at a Glance**

Political System
Constitutional monarchy
Parliamentary democracy

Administrative Structure: Unitary state with forty-seven prefectures

Executive: Dual executive
- Head of state: emperor (ceremonial)
    Hereditary
    Akihito (since January 1989)
- Head of government: prime minister
    Elected by National Assembly, leader of largest parliamentary party
    Keizo Obuchi, Liberal Democratic Party (since 1998)

Legislature: Bicameral parliament (Diet)
- Lower house: House of Representatives (directly elected), 500 seats
    Coalition government since 1998: Liberal Democratic Party, Liberal Party,
    New Komeito Party
    Largest party: Liberal Democratic Party, 265 seats
    Other parties: Democratic Party Japan, 93 seats
                    New Komeito, 52 seats
                    Liberal Party, 39 seats
                    Japan Communist Party, 26 seats
                    Social Democratic Party, 14 seats
                    Others, 11 seats
- Upper house: House of Councillors (directly elected), 252 seats

Party System: Multiparty (one party dominant until early 1990s)
- Principal parties: Liberal Democratic Party, Democratic Party of Japan, New
  Komeito, Liberal Party, Japan Communist Party, Social Democratic Party, Reform
  Club

Judiciary: Supreme Court with powers of legislative review

Economic Indicators
Gross domestic product (GDP), 1999: $4,380.1 billion
GDP per capita, 1998, purchasing power parity: $23,874

Exports as a percentage of GDP, 1997: 11.1 percent

Economic growth, 1999: 1.4 percent
Average economic growth, 1990–1999: 1.79 percent

Unemployment, 1999: 4.7 percent
Average unemployment, 1990–1999: 3.05 percent

Inflation rate, 1999: −0.3 percent
Average inflation rate, 1990–1999: 1.20 percent

Budget deficit as a percentage of GDP, 1999: −7.0 percent
Average budget deficit as a percentage of GDP, 1990–1999: −1.97 percent

Japan has an elected Supreme Court that has powers of judicial review. Unlike most of its counterparts in industrialized democracies, the Japanese court has not been activist. Reflecting a belief in parliamentary supremacy, the court has only rarely nullified parliamentary laws and does not appear likely to do so in the future.

The Japanese government plays a key role in the country's economy, while operating a free-market capitalist system. The government's immediate postwar industrial policies were central to Japan's rapid and remarkable economic growth. These policies provided financial assistance, tax breaks, foreign exchange, and imported technologies to targeted industries that were integral to economic development. The government intervenes in the market to guide investment decisions, and restrictive trade policies are implemented to protect key or developing industries. Most of the country's important domestic industries operate under the guidance and protection of bureaucratic agencies, especially the small but powerful Ministry of International Trade and Industry—this ministry and other economic ministries have a strong role in economic decision making. In the early postwar years these bureaucratic agencies, through administrative guidance, encouraged business mergers and cartelization to prevent counterproductive domestic competition. The government thus played a key role in directing the country's economic recovery through close collaboration with industry. Despite this strong guiding role for the government, the Japanese economy is not based on public ownership (the public sector is small relative to other industrialized countries). Free enterprise is the rule, although the government does not leave the market completely free to its own devices. The Japanese government continues to intervene in the market and restrict trade to protect its own industries and as such continues to play a major role in economic decisions.

Germany

The German government is a parliamentary system organized on a federal basis. Most legislation arrives in the German parliament through the executive—the chancellor's office is constitutionally responsible for setting the policy agenda, formulating policy, and overseeing policy implementation. As is typical of parliamentary systems, the legislature plays a more limited role in the policy process in Germany. Because policy initiation takes place at the executive level, the legislature is left with the task of evaluating and amending policies but only in a reactive manner. The German parliament typically plays a larger role in revising legislation than other parliamentary legislatures, through the efforts of both its committees and its legislative party groups. German parliamentary committees tend to be stronger than most of their counterparts, because they are more specialized, active, and powerful (although not to the degree observed in the United States). Nonetheless, the principle of party discipline reduces the likelihood of these committees making major changes to proposed legislation without government approval.

In most policy areas, responsibility for policy formulation is found at the federal level of government. The sixteen German states (*Länder*) are directly responsible for education, cultural, policing, and regional planning policies. Jurisdiction over some policy areas is shared between the federal and state levels (federal policy takes precedence over state policy in the event of conflicts). The states influence federal policy making and administration through the Bundesrat (the upper house of the German parliament), which is designed to represent state interests. A number of informal channels are used for policy consultation and coordination between the federal and state governments.

German states are integral to federal policy implementation. The states have primary responsibility for policy implementation and administration. In contrast to the situation in most other industrialized countries, German federal legislation and regulations tend to be very detailed to ensure that the government's objectives are met at the policy implementation stage. Because of wide-ranging responsibilities, state bureaucracies are larger than federal and local administrative agencies, and few federal ministries have sufficient resources to implement federal policies. The federal bureaucracy has the right to oversee state bureaucracies, but the German states typically have a good deal of autonomy and exercise some discretion in applying federal law. States typically are allowed to alter laws to fit local needs and circumstances when necessary, although this power is exercised within limits. In particular, states have limited policy latitude because their finances are centrally controlled—they have no independent revenue-raising powers. These characteristics of the federal-state relationship in Germany have created an environment conducive to effective policy implementation.

Germany has a competitive multiparty system, and parties play an important role in the policy process. German political parties are highly disciplined and have considerable influence on the government's policy agenda. In particular, parliamentary party groups in the Bundestag (the lower house) play an important policy-making role. They meet frequently to debate policy issues and are often successful in persuading the government to change the content of legislation, either before it is proposed or while the parliament is considering it.

The German interest group structure is considered to be corporatist because a clear pattern of cooperation exists between the government and interest groups—interest groups are systematically involved in making and implementing public policy. German law requires that the relevant interest groups be contacted when new policies are being formulated to ensure that the government benefits from the expertise of the groups and that the groups agree with and will cooperate with the new policies. The relationship between German administrative agencies and interest groups is strong. The leaders of major German interest groups are important actors in the policy process, and

Box 4-3 **Germany at a Glance**

Political System
Federal republic
Parliamentary democracy

Administrative Structure: Federal with sixteen states (*Länder*)

Executive: Dual executive
- Head of state: president (ceremonial)
  Elected by an electoral college consisting of federal and state parliament members
  Johannes Rau, Social Democratic Party (since July 1999)
- Head of government: chancellor
  Elected by Bundestag, leader of largest parliamentary party
  Gerhard Schroder, Social Democratic Party (since October 1998)

Legislature: Bicameral parliament
- Lower house: Bundestag (directly elected), 669 seats
  Coalition government since October 1998, Social Democrats and Greens
  Largest party: Social Democrats, 298 seats
  Other parties: Greens, 47 seats
  　　　　　　　Christian Democratic Union/Christian Social Union, 245 seats
  　　　　　　　Free Democrats, 43 seats
  　　　　　　　Party of Democratic Socialism, 36 seats
- Upper house: Bundesrat (elected and appointed from sixteen states), 69 seats

Party System: Multiparty
- Principal parties: Social Democratic Party, Christian Democratic Union, Christian Social Union
- Other parties: Alliance 90/Greens, Free Democratic Party, Party of Democratic Socialism, German People's Union

Judiciary: Constitutional court with powers of legislative review

Economic Indicators
Gross domestic product (GDP), 1999: $2,112 billion
GDP per capita, 1998, purchasing power parity: $22,998

Exports as a percentage of GDP, 1997: 26.5 percent

Economic growth, 1999: 1.5 percent
Average economic growth, 1990–1999: 2.18 percent

Unemployment, 1999: 8.7 percent
Average unemployment, 1990–1999: 7.49 percent

Inflation rate, 1999: 0.6 percent
Average inflation rate, 1990–1999: 2.51 percent

Budget deficit as a percentage of GDP, 1999: −1.1 percent
Average budget deficit as a percentage of GDP, 1990–1999: −2.51 percent

interest groups are seen as performing an important and necessary role at all stages of the policy-making process. A good deal of interest group lobbying occurs in the German legislature, particularly at the committee level, because German committees have some influence over the content of parliamentary legislation. Although this influence is not as extensive as is observed in the United States, it exceeds the legislative roles of many other industrialized countries.

The principle of judicial review is an important aspect of the German policy-making process. The German constitutional court has independent powers that enable it to nullify any law on constitutional grounds. The court hears appeals from private citizens; through referrals from lower courts; at the request of federal, state, or local governments; or in response to members of the parliament. In recent years, this court has played an increasingly activist role in the policy-making process, especially in the areas of human rights and federal-state relations.

Germany, like Japan, also experienced a remarkable postwar economic recovery, though in response to a different model of government intervention. In Germany, the government plays a leading but not directing economic role. The German economy is based on a social market model that emphasizes private ownership (although a small state sector exists), accompanied by an active role for the government in guiding the economy. In practice, the German government uses regulations to establish a broad framework for economic activity and within this framework encourages business organizations to coordinate their activities to achieve the government's objectives. The German government does not play a directing role like the Japanese government does; rather it allows market forces to operate within a framework of government supervision. The German economic system places a strong emphasis on social responsibility, and the government provides a generous social insurance system.

France

The French political system is commonly described as a hybrid because it mixes elements of presidential and parliamentary systems. The existence of both a directly elected president and a prime minister who represents the dominant party (or coalition) in the parliament creates a distinctive semi-presidential policy process. With the exception of periods of so-called cohabitation, when the president and prime minister represent different parties (as is the case as of this writing), nearly all government policy making since 1958 has been the responsibility of the French president and a small circle of advisers. The president, with bureaucratic assistance, dominates the policy process through the development of detailed legislative proposals and through control over policy implementation. During periods of cohabitation, control of domestic policy tends to move to the prime minister and the cabinet, whereas foreign policy remains in the president's domain. The few policies formulated by the prime minister and the cabinet outside periods of cohabitation generally require presidential approval.

The French parliament during the Fifth Republic has played a minor role in policy making, especially on important issues. This situation in part reflects an explicit constitutional decision to limit the parliament's policy-making role, especially its law-making powers. Nearly all legislation considered by the parliament is proposed by the executive, which has a wide range of specific powers to encourage (or even coerce) the parliament to adopt its policies. As tends to be the norm in parliamentary systems, the French legislature for the most part reviews and approves legislation formulated elsewhere. The parliament has begun to play a somewhat larger policy-making role in recent years as its committees have increased their influence (through their powers of amendment), but overall the policy-making activities of this institution remain limited.

France is a unitary state and has been one of the most centralized of the industrialized countries. The country is divided into 100 departments under the administrative control of a prefect. In addition, there are 22 French regions (consisting of the 100 departments and 36,551 communes or local governments). Each lower level of government is controlled by an elected body of some sort. Since the 1980s some movement has been made toward decentralizing policy responsibilities and power to these lower levels of government. However, compared to most countries, the French government remains highly centralized, with the bulk of policy development and implementation occurring at the central government level. The policy implementation process in France has been among the most effective of the industrialized countries because of strong linkages between the executive and the bureaucracy and the general public's tendency to support a strong government apparatus.

France has a weak multiparty system troubled by fragmentation and polarization. This, in combination with the strong role assumed by the executive, means that political parties do not have as much influence on agenda setting and policy formulation as is observed in parliamentary systems that have stronger partisan organizations. To some degree, parties exert greater influence on policy making in periods of cohabitation, especially when a partisan majority has strong control in the parliament.

The interest group system in France is generally considered to be pluralist, with multiple groups and actors vying for influence over policy making. French interest groups tend to be smaller, less organized, and less cohesive than those found in other countries. In particular, ideological divisions, both between and within groups (especially labor unions), have led to a marked pattern of interest group fragmentation that reduces their effectiveness. French interest groups generally do not have privileged access to policymakers. The possible exceptions to this pattern are agricultural and big business groups, which have some stronger connections to the government. Interest groups have a limited role in bureaucratic advisory committees in France, although not to

Box 4-4 **France at a Glance**

Political System
Republic
Semi-presidential democracy

Administrative Structure: Unitary state with twenty-two administrative regions containing ninety-six departments

Executive: Dual executive
- Chief of state: President
  Directly elected
  Jacques Chirac, Rally for the Republic (since June 1995)
  1995 Presidential election results (second round): Jacques Chirac, 52.6 percent; Lionel Jospin, 47.4 percent
- Head of government: Prime minister
  Appointed by president, leader of largest parliamentary party
  Lionel Jospin, Socialists (since May 1997)

Legislature: Bicameral parliament
- Lower house: National Assembly (directly elected), 577 seats
  Coalition government since June 1997, Socialists and Communists
  Largest party: Socialists, 250 seats
  Other parties: Communists, (36 seats), Rally for the Republic, (140 seats), Union for French Democracy, (113 seats), Greens, (7 seats), Others, (43 seats)
- Upper house: Senate (indirectly elected), 321 seats

Party System: Multiparty
- Principal parties: Rally for the Republic (center right), Union for French Democracy (center right), Socialists (left), Communists (left)
- Other parties: National Front, Greens, multiple smaller parties on right and left

Judiciary: Constitutional Council with powers of administrative review

Economic Indicators
Gross domestic product (GDP), 1999: $1,434 billion
GDP per capita, 1998, purchasing power parity: $21,150

Exports as a percentage of GDP, 1997: 26.4 percent

Economic growth, 1999: 2.9 percent
Average economic growth, 1990–1999: 1.64 percent

Unemployment, 1999: 11.3 percent
Average unemployment, 1990–1999: 11.24 percent

Inflation rate, 1999: 0.5 percent
Average inflation rate, 1990–1999: 1.94 percent

Budget deficit as a percentage of GDP, 1999: −1.8 percent
Average budget deficit as a percentage of GDP, 1990–1999: −3.73 percent

the degree observed in some other industrialized countries. Further, because of a generally strong pattern of party discipline in the French parliament and its committees, members of the parliament are not important channels of influence for lobbyists.

The French system does not fully subscribe to the principle of judicial review. Laws passed by the parliament are not subject to further scrutiny by a constitutional court; however, the Constitutional Council has the power to assess the constitutionality of a bill before it is adopted by the parliament. This council does not hear appeals from individual citizens but will examine legislation at the request of the president, the presiding officers of the parliament, or through a joint appeal from members of the parliament. Increasingly this council has been used by opposition party members seeking to block a law's adoption. Since the 1980s the council has been very partisan and controversial as it has increased both its scope and its willingness to reject bills.

The government plays an important role in directing and managing the French economy. Since the 1960s France has had one of the world's strongest economies, based on a high level of public ownership, regulated market competition, and government economic planning. This strong government role traditionally was advocated by both conservative and leftist governments in France, reflecting the country's strong statist tradition. Government economic intervention and state ownership increased markedly in the early years of Socialist rule in the 1980s but were then reduced because this approach was viewed as economically counterproductive. Despite recent widespread privatization and an emphasis on market forces, France still has a relatively high level of public ownership and a higher level of economic intervention than is found in the United Kingdom or the United States. Thus the general economic context is one of a free-market economy, with the government playing an important guiding role. France has a well-developed social welfare system that provides the most extensive cradle-to-grave coverage among the six countries examined in this book.

The United Kingdom

The United Kingdom is a parliamentary democracy organized around a unitary structure. Although parliamentary sovereignty is an important foundational principle for the United Kingdom, policy making is in reality the responsibility of the prime minister and the cabinet. Policy formulation takes place within both the cabinet and the bureaucracy: The cabinet is solely responsible for determining the parliamentary agenda, and civil servants play an important role in drafting the legislation sent to Parliament.

As a rule, the British executive is highly successful in seeing its policy agenda adopted in its entirety. A two-party system in the United Kingdom grants significant power to a prime minister who controls a strong majority in the House of Commons—and majority control by a single disciplined party is the norm. Parliament and its individual members play only a small role in the policy-making process. Opposition party members have no real ability to influence policy making and even the ability of majority party members to amend the government's policies is highly restricted. It is often argued that this pattern produces clearer lines of policy accountability between government and citizens than is the case in most other industrialized countries.

The unitary structure of the United Kingdom means that policy implementation is largely the responsibility of central government ministries. Adopted policies tend to be broad, with the bureaucracy left to work out the details. The British civil service has a strong reputation for efficient, professional, and effective policy implementation and administration. Policies that are made at the central government level are legally binding on local governments. Local government institutions serve as the mechanism for the delivery of services, but they exercise little discretion in the policy implementation process, largely because funding is controlled at the center.

The British interest group structure can best be described as pluralist, with many kinds of active interest groups attempting to influence politicians and bureaucrats. The bureaucracy maintains an important consultative relationship with interest groups, particularly in the development of administrative regulations included within the broad framework of parliamentary acts. Bureaucrats regularly submit draft regulations to interest groups for comment, in an effort to draw on the groups' expertise and improve the chances of successful policy implementation.

In recent years, interest group lobbying of both the government and members of Parliament (particularly the latter) has increased, in part reflecting the growth in the size and powers of parliamentary select committees. Generally speaking, however, parliamentary lobbying has not significantly reduced the importance of party discipline in predicting the vote in the House of Commons. Nonetheless, lobbying is argued to have made Parliament a more informed and critical participant in the policy-making process, as well as having given interest groups at least some voice in parliamentary debates. A notable feature of the interest group system in the United Kingdom has been the formal organizational linkage between labor unions and the Labour Party, which traditionally gave unions tremendous influence over Labour policies. The current Labour Party leadership under Prime Minister Tony Blair has endeavored to restructure and reduce this pattern of influence.

Courts do not have a policy-making role in the United Kingdom. The founding principle of parliamentary sovereignty denies the possibility of judicial review—only Parliament can overturn an act of Parliament. British courts may question the application of laws and the authority of government's actions, but their impact is on policy administration, not formulation.

The British government's economic approach traditionally involved a more limited role for the state than is found in France, Germany, or Japan, in that there has been no role for industrial guidance or economic planning.

Box 4-5 **United Kingdom at a Glance**

Political System
Constitutional monarchy
Parliamentary democracy

Administrative Structure: Unitary state with forty-seven counties and seven metropolitan counties

Executive: Dual executive
- Head of state: Monarch
    Hereditary
    Queen Elizabeth II (since 1952)
- Head of government: Prime minister
    Elected by House of Commons, leader of largest parliamentary party
    Tony Blair, Labour Party (since May 1997)

Legislature: Bicameral parliament
- Lower house: House of Commons (directly elected), 656 seats
    Majority party: Labour, 419 seats
    Other parties: Conservatives, (164 seats), Liberal Democrats, (46 seats),
                Others, (30 seats)
- Upper house: House of Lords (nonelected)
    Over 1,200 hereditary (four-fifths of all peers) and life peers
    Currently under reform, with plans to eliminate hereditary peers
- Other legislative bodies: Scottish Parliament (since July 1999), Welsh Assembly (since May 1999), Northern Ireland Assembly (to be determined)

Party System: Two party
- Principal parties: Labour, Conservative
- Other parties: Liberal Democrats, Referendum Party, Scottish Nationalist Party, Plaid Cymru, Ulster Unionist Party, Social Democratic and Labour Party, Democratic Unionist Party, Sinn Fein, Alliance Party

Judiciary: No constitutional court with powers of legislative review

Economic Indicators
Gross domestic product (GDP), 1999: $1,423 billion
GDP per capita, 1998, purchasing power parity: $21,675
Exports as a percentage of GDP, 1997: 28.0 percent
Economic growth, 1999: 2.1 percent
Average economic growth, 1990–1999: 1.91 percent
Unemployment, 1999: 6.1 percent
Average unemployment, 1990–1999: 8.24 percent
Inflation rate, 1999: 1.6 percent
Average inflation rate, 1990–1999: 3.71 percent
Budget surplus as a percentage of GDP, 1999: 1.1 percent
Average budget deficit as a percentage of GDP, 1990–1999: −3.65 percent

However, the British government in the postwar period played an active role in governing the economy through state ownership of key industries, the provision of a wide range of economic management policies, and the maintenance of a generous social welfare system. By the early 1980s, however, the country's economic decline persuaded the government to reduce its strong economic presence through privatization, deregulation, downsizing of public sector employment, and reduction of social welfare benefits. The government's current approach to the economy does not involve any overall planning or guidance but attempts to support fully market mechanisms and advocates pro-business and growth policies. The British government continues to support a wide array of social insurance programs, though not to the extent found in France and Germany.

Italy

Italy has a parliamentary, unitary system of government. The country has a strong tradition of parliamentary predominance. In comparison to other European parliaments, the Italian legislature is far more responsible for policy formulation and adoption, with party leaders developing and controlling the legislative agenda. Although most policy development takes place within government ministries, political parties and interest groups are also influential. Legislation is introduced by party leaders into parliamentary committees, and the president of each committee has a high degree of influence over the country's policy agenda. Unlike most other parliamentary committees, Italian committees are capable of completely rewriting legislative proposals. These standing committees have the right to pass bills on behalf of the Chamber of Deputies without sending them to the Chamber for consideration. About three-fourths of Italy's bills are passed in this manner.

The cabinet and prime minister have relatively limited control over the content of Italy's public policies. This unusual pattern is not only a reflection of a tradition of parliamentary dominance but also the result of a marked tendency toward cabinet instability that has resulted in a weak executive and the empowerment of the legislature and the political parties. Because of the multiparty nature of Italian cabinets, the cabinet and prime minister as a group are too weak to address divisive issues. They also have difficulty defining a clear government agenda and perspective—resulting in governmental immobility—a consistent characteristic of Italian government.

Although the Italian parliament plays a dominant role in policy making, much of its legislation takes the form of loose framework policies that are vaguely designed and difficult to implement effectively. The quality of these policies is yet another reflection of recurring and fragile multiparty coalition governments. It is also a reflection of the nature of Italy's political parties themselves. These parties lack clear and coherent policy visions and historically have been fragmented and polarized. The major political reforms of the early 1990s (including the adoption of a hybrid single-member district plurality/proportional representation electoral system) have not yet reduced the fragmentation of the political party system. Although members of the Italian parliament vote along party lines, their leaders find it difficult to adopt focused policy instruments. Most major policies tend to represent the least common denominator position on which the representatives of the many parties forming a majority coalition can agree.

Policy implementation is the responsibility of the Italian bureaucracy. Compared to most of its European counterparts, Italy lacks a strong bureaucratic tradition and its administrators have low status and command little respect. Overall, Italian citizens view the bureaucracy as corrupt, inefficient, and overly centralized—an institution renowned for its red tape. Such perceptions create significant problems for the implementation stage of the policy-making process.

Theoretically the Italian government has engaged in a process of decentralization. The country is divided into twenty regions whose powers have increased since the 1970s—today more than 30 percent of the national budget is formally under regional control. Even so, key policy areas, such as education, policing, and taxation, remain in the central government's hands, and financial control also remains at the center. Many policies that require regional implementation are ineffective, as a result of both poor policy design and a lack of sufficient central coordination or oversight of the implementation process.

Italian interest groups traditionally reflected divisions within the party system because they were linked directly to the political parties (in groups known as *parentela*, which resemble party factions, especially within the parliament). Today Italian interest groups increasingly act autonomously in both the parliament (especially in its committees) and the bureaucracy. Most bureaucratic agencies and departments have established sets of client groups (*clientela*) with which they regularly work to develop and implement policies. In this role, interest groups are an important source of political support for government agencies, and these agencies work to accommodate the demands of these groups.

Italy has a constitutional court that has powers of judicial review. The court may overturn any national law and has played a significant policy-making role, particularly with respect to civil liberties. It is far more activist than other such courts in industrialized countries. The court hears cases in response to appeals from private citizens, groups, or regional governments.

The Italian government has played a major economic role in the postwar period. In the early 1990s Italy had one of the largest state-owned sectors among the industrialized countries. The vast array of publicly owned enterprises in the country were controlled by public sector holding companies (such as the Institute for Industrial Reconstruction) that dominated all economic decisions and created close ties between government and industry. A

Box 4-6 **Italy at a Glance**

Political System
Republic
Parliamentary democracy

Administrative Structure: Unitary state with ninety-four provinces, twenty regions

Executive: Dual executive
- Head of state: President (ceremonial)
  Elected by parliament and regional delegates
  Carlo Azeglio Campi (since May 1999)
- Head of government: Prime minister
  Appointed by president, confirmed by parliament
  Massimo D'Alema, Democratic Party of Left (since October 1998)

Legislature: Bicameral parliament
- Lower house: Chamber of Deputies (directly elected), 630 seats
  Coalition government since October 1998: Democratic Party of Left, Popular
  Democratic Party, other small center-left parties
  Largest party: Democratic Party of Left (Olive Tree), 163 seats
  Other parties: Forza Italia, (109 seats), National Alliance, (91 seats), Popular
  Democratic Party (Olive Tree), (61 seats), Northern League, (48 seats),
  Communist Group, (21 seats), Democratic Party (Olive Tree), (21 seats),
  Others, (112 seats), (4 seats unfilled as of March 2000)
- Upper house: Senate (directly elected), 315 seats

Party System: Multiparty
- Principal parties: Olive Tree Coalition: Democratic Party of Left, Greens, Italian
  Popular Democratic Party; Freedom Pole: Forza Italia, National Alliance, Chris-
  tian Democratic Center, Democratic Union for Republic; Northern League; Ital-
  ian Communist Party; Italian People's Party
- Other parties: Numerous other small parties on right and left

Judiciary: Constitutional court with powers of legislative review

Economic Indicators
Gross domestic product (GDP), 1999: $1,162 billion
GDP per capita, 1998, purchasing power parity: $21,346
Exports as a percentage of GDP, 1997: 27.0 percent
Economic growth, 1999: 1.4 percent
Average economic growth, 1990–1999: 1.42 percent
Unemployment, 1999: 11.4 percent
Average unemployment, 1990–1999: 10.61 percent
Inflation rate, 1999: 1.7 percent
Average inflation rate, 1990–1999: 4.17 percent
Budget deficit as a percentage of GDP, 1999: −1.9 percent
Average budget deficit as a percentage of GDP, 1990–1999: −7.11 percent

large economic bureaucracy resulted that was prone to inefficiency and corruption. This close and corrupt relationship led to the scandals of the early 1990s that ultimately resulted in the collapse of the government system. The economy has traditionally been heavily regulated. Following the government crisis, a process of privatization and deregulation began, although the government still plays a significant role in economic decision making. The Italian government continues to provide a wide array of social benefits to its citizens, although these benefits are not as generous as those afforded to citizens in the other European countries examined in this book.

The European Union

The EU traces its roots to the European Economic Community that was created by the Treaty of Rome in 1957 with the intention of creating a common economic marketplace through the elimination of trade barriers between its member states (which then numbered six). The treaty also included common policies in areas such as agriculture and transport. The common market the treaty envisioned was established gradually through the 1960s. The 1987 Single European Act broadened the community's areas of responsibility, made changes to its decision-making processes, and established 1992 as the target year for the official completion of the single market—this latter provision was legally binding on member states. The 1991 Maastricht Treaty on European Union extensively revised the community's vision for the future. The treaty formally created the EU and introduced three pillars, or foundations, upon which this union would be built. The first pillar calls for cooperation on trade and economic affairs (including economic and monetary union), the second for the creation of a common foreign and security policy, and the third for cooperation on justice and domestic affairs. These three pillars create a substantial agenda for reform for the EU's member states. The 1997 Treaty of Amsterdam clarified, and in some cases extended, the union's vision under these three pillars and called for a strengthening of its governing institutions.

The EU currently consists of fifteen member states that are governed at both the supranational and intergovernmental levels.[1] The union's supranational elements have the authority to make decisions that are binding on all member states. The European Parliament, the European Court of Justice, and the European Commission are all supranational bodies—the members of these bodies act as representatives of the EU and its population rather than their own countries. The Council of Ministers and the European Council are both intergovernmental arrangements—representatives to these bodies act in

[1] The fifteen member states are Austria, Belgium, Denmark, Finland, France, Germany, Greece, Ireland, Italy, Luxembourg, the Netherlands, Portugal, Spain, Sweden, and the United Kingdom.

the interest of their own countries. Decisions made by the EU's intergovernmental bodies do not require the approval of the supranational bodies before they become binding—as a result, individual member states remain powerful actors in the EU's policy-making process. The EU is more than an international organization (primarily because it has legally binding authority over its sovereign member states), but at the same time its institutions do not replicate the legislative and executive bodies characteristic of political systems in industrialized countries. Policy making in the EU essentially takes place within three bodies, beginning with the European Commission.

As is the case in domestic political systems, responsibility for policy formulation in the EU is a bureaucratic function. The European Commission has twenty members (one from each member state, with two chosen from the five larger countries) selected by member state governments. These European commissioners are sworn to represent and act in the interest of the EU, and their activities are important in the push toward further integration. The commissioners oversee the EU's bureaucracy and civil service. The EU's bureaucracy resembles national bureaucratic institutions, although it is smaller.

The European Commission has the sole right to initiate legislation for the EU. In the policy formulation process, the commission interacts, as in other bureaucracies, with all those who have a stake in a given policy area. These actors include interest groups, individual national governments, national governments acting collectively in the Council of Ministers, and the European Parliament. The commission attempts to ensure that its proposals will be mutually acceptable to all relevant actors while at the same time developing policies that represent the interests of the EU overall. The commission is responsible for monitoring policy implementation in member states and for serving as the EU's administrative apparatus (although it depends on national bureaucracies to implement EU laws). The commission also issues technical and administrative laws.

The European Commission sends two types of legislation forward for adoption. Regulations tend to be general policies that upon adoption by the Council of Ministers automatically become national laws. Directives, in contrast, require member states to create policy instruments within a certain time period to put these directives into effect in the countries. Both types of proposals are sent to the Council of Ministers for approval. The commission has been an important institution for coordinating and promoting the process of European integration by developing policies that consistently focus on further integration as a primary policy goal. For example, the commission is widely seen as having maintained the EU's focus on specific objectives, such as economic and monetary union or the creation of the single market, even in the face of setbacks or waning enthusiasm.

The European Parliament plays the least important policy-making role of all the EU institutions. This is the EU's only directly elected body, and its

Box 4-7 **European Union at a Glance**

Political System

Intergovernmental organization with plans for full economic and political union
Intergovernmental and supranational institutions

Administrative Structure

European Commission
- Twenty commissioners appointed by member states (two each from France, Germany, Italy, Spain, and the United Kingdom, and one from each of the other member states)
- President Romano Prodi (since 1999), chosen by European Council
- Staff of 15,000
- Twenty-six directorates-general
- Supranational

Executive

Council of the European Union (also known as Council of Ministers)
- Various ministers of fifteen member states (depending on issue being discussed)
- European Council: fifteen heads of state and president of commission
- Rotating six-month presidency
- Intergovernmental and supranational
- Decisions based on both qualified majority voting and unanimity

Legislature

European Parliament (directly elected), 626 seats
- Close to 100 political parties represented, organized into eight political groups
- Twenty standing committees
- Supranational

Party System

Eight political groups in 1994–1999 European Parliament:
- Group of the Party of European Socialists
- Group of the European People's Party
- Union for Europe Group
- Group of the Liberal Democratic and Reformist Party
- Confederal Group of the European United Left/Nordic Green Left
- Green Group in the European Parliament
- Group of the European Radical Alliance
- Group of Independents for a Europe of Nations

Judiciary

European Court of Justice
- Fifteen judges appointed by member states for a six-year renewable term

members organize on a partisan rather than national basis. The 626 European members of the parliament adopt a European outlook, with their views varying as a reflection of the members' partisan preferences. Like the commission, the parliament tends to support policies designed to encourage further integration. The parliament itself cannot initiate or adopt legislation; it is intended to be a reactive institution. Policy proposals developed by the commission are sent to one of the parliament's eighteen policy-specific committees for review. These committees then make their recommendations to the full parliament; any amendments they call for will usually be adopted by the parliament and then referred back to the commission. The commission is free to accept or reject these amendments as it sees fit. Despite changes to its powers that were adopted under the Single European Act, the European parliament does not occupy a prominent policy-making position. At best, it provides the EU's only democratic forum for discussing EU affairs.

Policy proposals enter their third and most important round of consideration with their submission to the Council of Ministers. The council is simultaneously an executive and legislative body and is the EU's main decision-making institution. The council most often directly represents the interests of EU member states individually; national political concerns are a prime influence, despite its commitment to European goals (although the council sometimes acts on the basis of a unified European outlook, this is not the norm). The council is comprised of elected politicians, one from each member state, who are empowered to speak authoritatively for their countries. The council also has one nonvoting member from the European Commission. The exact membership of the council is not fixed; it changes depending on the issue being discussed. For instance, if environmental policy is being discussed, then the environment ministers attend. If agricultural policy is the topic, then each country's agriculture minister attends. If a more general topic is on the agenda, then the foreign ministers or the prime ministers attend. The council must approve all policies initiated by the commission before they can be implemented. The council is free to make policy decisions based on its own counsel alone; it may reject policies that have the support of either or both the parliament and the commission and may accept policies that both bodies oppose. Although the council cannot initiate policy proposals independently, it usually commands sufficient influence to pressure the commission to develop policies it considers necessary.

The European Court of Justice has binding jurisdiction over all EU member states, and its decisions overrule the decisions of national courts. The court does not have powers of judicial review—it does not overturn the policy decisions of the Council of Ministers. The court may, however, overturn national laws in member states that are judged to be in violation of EU laws. The decisions of the court pertain mostly to member states' application or interpretation of EU laws, not the content of the laws themselves.

SUGGESTED READINGS

Archer, Clive, and Fiona Butler. 1992. *The European Community: Structure and Process.* New York: St. Martin's Press.

Conradt, David. 1996. *The German Polity.* New York: Longman.

Edwards, George, Martin P. Wattenberg, and Robert L. Lineberry. 1999. *Government in America: People, Politics and Policy.* New York: Longman.

Furlong, Paul. 1994. *Modern Italy: Representation and Reform.* London: Routledge.

Norton, Philip. 1994. *The British Polity.* New York: Longman.

Richardson, Bradley. 1997. *Japanese Democracy: Power, Consultation, and Performance.* New Haven: Yale University Press.

Safran, William. 1998. *The French Polity.* New York: Longman.

Shafer, Byron. 1996. *Postwar Politics in the G-7: Orders and Eras in Comparative Perspective.* Madison: University of Wisconsin Press.

Chapter 5 **Immigration Policy**

The question of what to do about immigration and immigrants is on the systemic agendas of most industrialized countries today, as a reflection of changing patterns of population movement and settlement. In addition to addressing how much immigration to allow, governments also construct policies about asylum seekers and refugees, about residents without papers, and about foreign temporary workers—many of whom have resided in these countries for years. Increasing humanitarian immigrant flows and the permanent settlement of many temporary migrants have important ramifications for politics in industrialized countries. New political organizations and initiatives among immigrants have emerged that call for government responses to their concerns. At the same time, anti-immigration political parties have been formed that call for more restrictive policies. The electoral and political influence of these parties has increased significantly. The presence of racial, ethnic, and religious diversity has also created a new pattern of interaction among citizens that can be characterized by racism, hostility, and violence. In response to these developments, reformation of immigration control systems is a political priority. Most notably, governments are modifying policy instruments, or inventing new ones, to address the questions of who, how many, and why?

Common Policy Problems

Immigration in most industrialized countries takes one of three forms: **legal immigration** (usually as a result of family reunification or labor importation schemes), **humanitarian immigration** (involving asylum seekers or refugees), and **illegal immigration** (typically through clandestine entry or visa overstaying). Despite the introduction of substantial control mechanisms since the 1970s, legal immigration continues to constitute the bulk of immigration into most industrialized countries. The vast majority of legal immigrants arrive as a result of **family reunification** that is usually limited to the spouses and children of legal residents and citizens. A second major source of legal immigration is employment based, in which individuals are admitted on the basis of their specialized skills. Entry to a country through such legal means is often referred to as **front door immigration.**

Legal, employment-based immigration has been especially important in European countries. Following World War II, many of these countries instituted **guest-worker programs,** in which foreign workers were given temporary work and residence permits. These workers were expected to return to their home countries when their services were no longer needed; however, most of them remained in the countries to which they emigrated, and often their families were subsequently permitted to join them. The result is the presence of significant immigrant populations that lack a clearly defined status. Most European countries banned foreign workers in the mid-1970s but continue to allow limited employment-based immigration in sectors of the economy where labor is scarce. Entry to a country through a temporary labor program is often referred to as **side door immigration,** because these immigrants are not intended as permanent settlers.

The problem of humanitarian immigration encompasses the issue of what to do about asylum seekers and refugees. This has been especially important since the late 1980s, as a huge influx of immigrants from former communist countries and developing countries sought refuge. We must distinguish between asylum seekers and refugees. **Asylum seekers** are typically individuals who are already present in the country where refuge is sought or are at the border requesting entry. **Refugees** are usually found outside their home country (typically in refugee camps), where they are usually interviewed by a country's immigration officials before being given entry permits (see Box 5.1). Humanitarian immigration is often considered side door immigration.

Preventing illegal immigration is perhaps the most difficult problem for policymakers to address effectively. In this case, the term **back door immigration** is frequently used. A problem to most industrialized countries, illegal immigration is often the result of a variety of mechanisms. In the United States today, just over half of illegal immigrants entered the United States legally and then remained after their visas expired; others managed to cross clandestinely over relatively open borders, especially with Mexico. Illegal immigration has increasingly been a problem for European governments, as a result of their effective end to legal immigration by the mid-1970s and the more recent tightening of asylum policies, both of which forced would-be immigrants to find other means of entry. Until recently the bulk of European illegal immigrants were rejected asylum seekers who did not leave the country after their claims were refused.

A final area of concern is a government's ability to control so-called push and pull factors. In the immigration context, **pull factors** refer to a country's characteristics that make it attractive to immigrants. These factors include existing family ties, job opportunities, and the availability of public services and social welfare benefits. The nature of industrialized countries' labor markets—with abundant low-wage, low-skill jobs that these countries' populations are either unwilling or unavailable to fill—is another strong pull. National immigration policies usually attempt to modify or eliminate such pull factors, in the hope of reducing the incentive to immigrate. At the same time, **push factors** affect individuals' decisions to emigrate from their home countries. These factors include overpopulation, poverty, unemployment, natural disaster, and war. The ability of immigrant-receiving countries to control push factors is far more

---

Box 5-1 **In Depth: The International Refugee Problem**

The United Nations High Commission on Refugees (UNHCR) defines a refugee as a person who has fled his or her country because of a well-founded fear of persecution for reasons of race, religion, nationality, political opinion, or membership in a particular social group and who cannot or does not want to return. Some refugees flee from acts of terror perpetrated by their governments; others may be seeking refuge from violence resulting from ethnic conflict that does not involve the government or from other forms of oppression that the government can no longer control. Under existing international agreements, refugees have a right to safe asylum—defined as the right to seek and receive refuge from persecution or war. In this sense, refugees differ from other migrants in that they need protection because their own government has failed to protect their rights or physical security. Migrants applying for refugee status in a country are required to establish that their fear of persecution is well founded. Having done so, receiving countries are bound to afford refugees the same rights and assistance as any other foreigner who is a legal resident, including the extension of civil, social, and economic rights. Under these same agreements, receiving states may not forcibly return refugees to a country where they may face danger.

The problem of refugees has increased significantly in the postwar period, especially since the 1970s. At this time, a worldwide refugee crisis emerged as hundreds of thousands fled from such far-flung places as Vietnam, Cambodia, Laos, Lebanon, and Afghanistan—all of whom were seeking to escape repression, persecution, or civil war. By the 1990s refugees were moving across the globe, fleeing ethnic conflict in particular, with mass migrations from Rwanda, Sri Lanka, Somalia, Croatia, Sudan, Sierra Leone, and Kosovo, to name but a few.

The UNHCR estimates that the number of refugees worldwide rose from 17 million in 1991 to a record 27 million in 1995, dropping to just under 21.5 million at the end of 1998. This figure represents 1 out of every 280 people on earth. In Western Europe the number of asylum applications rose from under 170,000 in 1985 to more than 690,000 in 1992. Owing to stricter policies, the number of applications has declined steadily since 1992, to about 250,000 in 1996. Germany now receives about half of all asylum applications in Western Europe—after having received up to 80 percent before imposing more restrictive asylum practices in 1993. Asylum applications in the United States increased from about 20,000 in 1985 to nearly 148,000 in 1995. Of all the major industrialized countries, Japan receives the fewest asylum applications, only about 150 in 1996.

limited than is the case with pull factors. Industrialized countries attempt to control these push factors primarily through development assistance to the countries that provide them with substantial immigrant flows.

Major Policy Options

The most basic policy choice in the area of legal immigration involves the task of establishing who may legally enter a country for long-term or permanent residence. Beyond this, countries must also plan and manage the inflow of migrants to best serve national goals, whether economic, social, or demographic. The most common policy instrument is the **preference system,** which allocates a certain number of visas for categories of immigrants per year. Such systems may employ strict quotas, targets, or ceilings to regulate the flow of immigrants. Restrictions on the type of family reunification permitted have also been a common policy tool to control the flow of legal migrants. Family reunification policies have proven to be a rather ineffective control mechanism, largely because there is no accurate way to predict how many claims for entry on the basis of family ties will be made in any given year. Countries that permit employment-based immigration usually identify particular skills or economic sectors experiencing labor shortages for which immigration will be allowed. Some countries officially ban foreign workers entirely but continue to allow employment-based immigration on a smaller scale based on workers' skills and employment needs in particular economic sectors. These countries often have an immigrant labor quota, and governments reserve the right to deny work permits as they see fit, usually based on changing labor conditions.

In addressing asylum and refugee problems, governments generally are not completely free to develop policy unilaterally owing to international treaties and agreements that reduce their range of options. Most countries' asylum and refugee policies reflect the provisions of the United Nations Convention Relating to the Status of Refugees, which calls for the admission of refugees and asylum seekers "owing to well-founded fear of being persecuted for reasons of race, religion, nationality, membership of a particular social group or political opinion." The treatment of asylum seekers is a particularly difficult problem for democratic states to resolve because denying asylum is viewed by many citizens as compromising democratic values and a concern for human rights.

Despite these constraints, unprecedented flows of migrants since the early 1990s have produced increasingly restrictive asylum policies. Most countries have sought to regulate flows through policies making it more difficult for asylum seekers to enter countries and obtain resident status. These policies involve what are known as preentry (or external) and postentry (or internal) controls. Designed to prevent asylum seekers from making it across a country's borders, **preentry controls** may include sanctions against airlines for transporting individuals who lack legal documents, stricter visa requirements for citizens of countries known to be sources of asylum applicants, the invention of so-called international zones in airports to detain undocumented foreigners, or the streamlining of asylum procedures. Many countries have signed bilateral agreements with other countries that permit the return of asylum seekers at the border to the first so-called safe country they passed through before they arrived at the nation where they are seeking asylum. (Safe countries have asylum processes of their own, meet international standards, and are not themselves a source of asylum seekers.) Finally, many countries have increasingly used the standard of **manifestly unfounded claims** to assess requests for asylum. Claims may be rejected as such because of insufficient evidence of persecution or false evidence presented by the applicant.

Postentry controls attempt to control the rights and activities of asylum applicants who are already within a country's borders, including limiting access to social welfare benefits, denying work permits, and using computerized registration systems to prevent asylum seekers from disappearing into society before a decision is reached or after an application is rejected. Many European countries have also created government-run reception centers in which asylum applicants must reside until a decision is reached on their status. These policies are intended to reduce asylum claims by making life more difficult for applicants once they are in the country.

The task of controlling illegal immigration is clearly the most difficult problem in this policy area, because it involves controlling individuals who are deliberately attempting to avoid detection. Policy responses to illegal immigration generally take one of three forms: internal controls, external controls, and regularization programs. **Internal controls** allow for the legal supervision of immigrants to be sure they leave when their visas expire and that they do not work without authorization. Such policies include deportation programs for those with expired visas and sanctions against employers who hire illegal immigrants. **External controls** usually involve measures designed to prevent foreigners from entering the country without permission, such as more effective policing of borders and airports. **Regularization programs** provide legal amnesty (and usually naturalized citizenship) for illegal immigrants who satisfy certain conditions such as entry into the country before a certain date, good health, regular employment, or a valid passport. Regularization measures are usually adopted jointly with increased enforcement efforts to prevent additional inflows of illegal immigrants.

Explaining Policy Dynamics

The politics of the immigration policy-making process is an area of research that lacks any broadly comprehensive theorizing. In surveying the literature, we find relatively few attempts to clarify this process across the industrialized countries. The vast majority of empirical explanations are based on studies of a single country (or occasionally two or three countries). Based on this existing work, we can offer a set of potential explanations—cultural, economic, political, and institutional—for immigration policy reform.

Cultural Explanations

Cultural factors influence immigration policy reform. One cultural thesis focuses on a country's historical experiences with immigration. According to this view, immigration policy in countries that have longer histories of population inflows from abroad and larger immigrant populations overall (the so-called countries of immigration) differs from policy in countries that have experienced immigration for shorter periods of time and have smaller immigrant populations. In these latter countries, immigration is often unwelcome, particularly as immigrants become a permanent part of the population. More specifically, if immigration is incorporated into the country's "founding myth," that country is less inclined to favor more restrictive or exclusive immigration policies (Freeman 1998; Joppke 1998, 1999). Joppke (1999) argues that where immigration coincides with the nation-building process (in that immigration occurs as the nation is developing its self-identity), one finds a belief that immigration is a good thing and stronger support for continued immigration. National myths and self-images can be particularly important for understanding policy reform because they allow political leaders to portray their preferred policy outcomes as consonant with a nation's self-identity. In countries where immigration is not a crucial aspect of national identity, more exclusive immigration policy reforms are more easily adopted and implemented.

Other historical explanations for immigration policy reform consider the nature of the relationship between immigrant-receiving and immigrant-sending states. Immigrant-receiving states have less control over immigration policy relative to immigrant-sending states with whom they have strong historical ties. Often this argument points to the importance of past colonial relationships between countries that create special immigration obligations, although it may point to other aspects of a country's experiences as well, such as its record during World War II (Layton-Henry 1992; Rich 1990).

Pressures for immigration policy reform may also be explained by trends in public opinion. Today most governments face pressure to pass laws to slow or end immigration. Public opinion is often far more restrictionist than that held by political parties or government officials. Baldwin-Edwards and Schain (1994), for example, observe that most Europeans feel that there are too many immigrants in their countries. They note that the effects of these opinions on public policy are largely contingent on other factors. In particular, where political parties that specifically represent these negative views exist, reform tends to be more reflective of public opinion. In other contexts, these negative public sentiments do not dictate public policy. For example, Gimpel and Edwards (1998) argue that in the United States immigration is not usually an issue that motivates people to vote (unless the economy is weak), which they say explains an observed gap between public opinion and policy.

A final cultural explanation found in the literature on immigration policy reform concerns the effects of liberal political values on reform. These values are embedded in the fabric of industrialized countries, as well as in the international system in which they operate, and include nondiscrimination, political equality, and civil rights. Where rights-based liberalism figures prominently in policy making, it is difficult for states to treat immigrants in ways that violate these fundamental tenets (Heisler 1986; Hollifield 1992; Jacobson 1996; Soysal 1994). Because stricter immigration policies often require a rollback of civil and human rights for noncitizens, the prevalence of these norms can impede more restrictive reform.

Economic Explanations

Changes in a country's employment patterns also influence immigration policy reform. Schnapper (1994) notes that in recent years industrial restructuring has meant that there were fewer such jobs both for native populations and immigrants in industrialized countries. In response, immigrants (who, until the early 1970s had been accepted in most industrialized countries because of their economic contribution) are argued to cost more (in social welfare benefits) than they contribute to national economies. Support for more restrictive immigration policies is then mustered more easily among the general public, notably among the unemployed. Feelings of economic deprivation are frequently used to explain support for extreme right-wing parties and the more restrictive reforms they advocate (Money 1999). Economic depression, long-lasting unemployment, and budget deficits may all have an impact on the demand for immigration policy reform, especially where foreign workers are seen as unwanted competitors who take away jobs from native workers or who live on social benefits for which others have paid.

Short-term trends in economic growth can stimulate fluctuations in the focus of immigration policy, or its tendency to oscillate between restrictionism and liberalization. Some researchers claim that a close connection exists between business cycles and so-called admissionist or restrictionist reforms. Immigration is tolerated or even encouraged during periods of economic growth and prosperity. During bad times, immigrants are targeted as scapegoats for conditions they may have no part in causing, and immigration policies may become more restrictive (Brochman and Hammar 1999; Freeman 1998; Hollifield 1992; Kindleberger 1967).

A final economic explanation for policy reform concerns the effects of economic globalization and interdependence. Here, reform is viewed as a function of the connections between economic internationalization and labor market demands. In a world where economic change is in the direction of deregulation and liberalization, countries are pressured to keep their borders open. Sassen (1999) argues that it simply is not possible for countries to have an open policy for circulating capital and a very different regime for circulating people. The free movement of people is an integral part of the movement of trade and investment across borders. Transnational economic processes become key factors influencing immigration policy. Policy reform reflects the wishes of governments and private economic actors in immigrant-receiving countries, who are concerned with creating economic linkages with immigrant-sending countries—such linkages naturally serve as bridges for immigrants.

Political Explanations

Existing research points to two important political explanations for immigration policy reform. The first explanation emerges from studies of the growth and success of anti-immigration extreme right-wing parties in European countries. These parties, which base their appeals to the electorate on anti-immigration, racist, and xenophobic views, have disrupted traditional party systems by creating opportunities for the political expression of such sentiments. They increasingly influence public debates on immigration and immigrants. Perhaps more important for immigration policy reform, these right-wing movements also have forced the more moderate established political parties, on both the right and left, to place these issues high on their own agendas and to favor tougher reforms. Often these xenophobic, anti-immigration parties can force traditional parties to rearrange their policy platforms, their priorities for government, and, ultimately, the very nature of immigration policy reform (Brochman and Hammar 1999; Hollifield 1992; Messina 1995).

The second political explanation is based on research into the role of interest groups in immigration policy reform. Freeman (1995) advanced what he calls a client politics thesis in his examination of ethnic and economic interest group pressure on the immigration policy process. In his view, client politics involves a number of small and well-organized groups that have a strong influence on the policy-making process. He argues that such client politics is heavily oriented toward expansive immigration policies because of the more organized and effective efforts of interest groups (employers, ethnic advocacy groups, or human rights organizations) that favor more liberal policies. In Freeman's view, governments may pay more attention to these interests than public opinion because of the fear of promoting right-wing extremism if these issues are debated publicly. Thus they seek to reach an early and private consensus to avoid the emergence of these issues on the national systemic agenda, where they may quickly spiral out of control. This tendency for the major parties to try to defuse the immigration issue while responding to interest group pressure offers another explanation for situations in which policies do not reflect public opinion.

Institutional Explanations

Freeman's client politics perspective generated considerable debate among scholars in this area. Perlmutter (1996) responded that Freeman's model applies only when a strong political party controls the institutional agenda in a relatively unitary political system. In many other situations, the declining strength of mass parties creates the opportunity for other actors—dissident regional politicians, dissatisfied small parties in governing coalitions, or radical parties—to pose real challenges to immigration policy reform. Perlmutter argues that in multiparty or federalist polities, there are more chances to politicize immigration and only limited ability to keep these issues off the institutional agenda. In his view, the nature of immigration policy reform will be strongly influenced by the location of power in a political system. Perlmutter contends that because federalism allows for the regional expression of demands (which then often reach the national political agenda) and because immigrants tend to be concentrated in specific regions, the ability of advocates for change to influence policy reform could be increased in a federal system. Many other scholars make similar arguments about the effects of the long-term erosion of political parties and other traditional political institutions as policy-making bodies and as vehicles for political representation in industrialized countries. They note that as traditional actors lose influence, immigration policy falls increasingly within the jurisdiction of national courts or becomes the preoccupation of pro-immigrant welfare groups and activists or of anti-immigration extremists on the right. Hence, an area of public policy that was once controlled by executives and bureaucracies (and took place outside the domain of legislatures and electoral politics) becomes increasingly politicized and more difficult for governments and political parties to develop and implement (Betz 1991, 1994; Messina 1989, 1990; Schain 1987, 1988).

Other research describes an important role for the judiciary in immigration policy reform. In countries where the judiciary is inclined to (and empowered to) hold legislation to constitutional norms via judicial review, more restrictive immigration policy reforms are less likely to survive (Shapiro and Stone 1994). In many countries, courts also have limited the ability of governments to restrict or stop asylum seekers from crossing national borders (Cornelius, Hollifield, and Martin 1994; Hollifield 1992; Joppke 1998, 1999; Sassen 1998).

International Policy Making

Immigration policy is one of the least developed areas of international policy making because decision making in this area is most likely to take place at the national government level. Countries have demonstrated a marked reluctance to surrender their sovereignty and policy-making flexibility to a higher-level authority on this matter. This is true with respect not only to the European Union (EU) but also to broader international policies intended to govern population flows.

The most important international agreement affecting many countries' asylum and refugee policies is the 1951 Geneva Convention. Article One of the agreement calls on signatory nations to grant refugee status to any person who, owing to a well-founded fear of persecution on racial, religious, political, or other grounds, is unwilling or unable to return to his or her home country. This article, along with the 1951 United Nations Convention Relating to the Status of Refugees and the 1967 Protocol (which made the Convention more comprehensive), imposes both legal and moral obligations on countries not to reject foreign asylum applicants if such rejection entails their being returned to a place where they are in danger of being persecuted. This is known as the **non-refoulement principle.** Countries that have signed these agreements are to establish procedures for evaluating asylum and refugee claims and are obligated to admit those who qualify as refugees and have nowhere else to go. In practice, we observe considerable variation in how countries interpret their individual obligations under these commitments. Most industrialized countries have adopted more restrictive asylum and refugee policies than in the past; however, in keeping with their international commitments, they maintain that real refugees will not be turned away.

EU member countries have made progress on immigration and asylum policy coordination in only two areas: movement of EU nationals within the union and visa requirements. The elimination of borders between EU member countries was first proposed in a European Commission consultation in 1988, and by 1995 the removal of border controls had been largely implemented. Progress has been made on the adoption of EU-wide visa policies through the development of a common list of non-EU countries whose citizens require visas to enter any EU country. In most other areas of immigration policy, however, EU member states have not surrendered sovereignty.

Because immigration control policies involve questions of national sovereignty, most EU member states avoid coordinating policy in areas such as rights to asylum, the status of refugees, illegal immigration, and external border controls. Instead policies vary widely across member states. EU actions in these areas have involved resolutions, conclusions, and recommendations, which members adopt as they see fit. Thus the EU largely sets norms, and compliance is left to the discretion of each state. These actions are also beyond the jurisdiction of the European Court of Justice.

The 1991 Maastricht Treaty officially acknowledged for the first time an EU vision of immigration as an area of common interest for member states. Immigration policy falls primarily under the third pillar of the treaty, justice and home affairs, although these matters are also addressed in the first pillar on economic integration (in particular concerning visa policies). The most limited policy activity in the 1990s has occurred in areas that fall under the third pillar.

The 1997 Treaty of Amsterdam, which further defined some provisions of the Maastricht Treaty, commits the EU to creating a common "area of freedom, justice and security" by 2002. EU member states have agreed in principle to develop common immigration and asylum policies; however, it remains unclear how far European-wide policy integration will go in this policy area. To a greater degree than is observed in other policy areas, countries resist having more decision-making authority transferred to Brussels when it comes to immigration. This resistance arises from two concerns: first, that accepting supranational decision making on immigration policy involves the loss of yet another fundamental aspect of national sovereignty—border control; and second, that some member states cannot yet be trusted to effectively police their own borders, thus causing problems for other countries once inter-EU border controls are lessened. Because of this reluctance, many observers believe that a common immigration and asylum policy is still a long way off. Once the Treaty of Amsterdam is ratified, however, community decision-making procedures will apply to immigration policy, and any policy decisions made in Brussels will override national decisions.

In recent years European countries have been shaping their national immigration policies to reflect international agreements developed beyond EU institutions. The most important of these is the Schengen Agreement, which was implemented in 1995 among the Benelux countries, France, and Germany. The Treaty of Amsterdam fully incorporated the Schengen Agreement into the existing EU structure (with a five-year phase-in period). The Schengen Agreement abolished internal EU border controls and instituted common policies on visas and asylum applications. More specifically the agreement is intended to allow for the freedom of movement of EU nationals within the EU. The agreement is open only to EU member states. By 1999 all EU countries had signed on to the Schengen Agreement (the United Kingdom and Ireland were the last to join, in March 1999), although the United Kingdom reserved the right to maintain its border controls with other Schengen countries. Thus far the agreement's greatest contribution is a single computer system for maintaining immigration information that encourages customs policy cooperation.

Another agreement developed through intergovernmental negotiations but not within EU institutions themselves is the Dublin Convention on jurisdiction for asylum applications. Drafted in 1990, the convention has been signed by most EU members but has been ratified by only a few countries. The convention went into effect December 1, 1997. Under this agreement, individuals seeking asylum in Europe must apply for it in the first EU country they reach.

The 1993 North American Free Trade Agreement (NAFTA) signed between the United States, Canada, and Mexico does not directly mention immigration issues (beyond minor attention to the temporary movement of business persons). Unlike EU policies, NAFTA neither guarantees the right to free movement for workers between its signatory countries, nor does it impose strict requirements on member states' immigration policies or behaviors. In fact, NAFTA supporters argued before its signing that the agreement was likely to decrease immigration flows as increased trade flows would reduce immigration push factors. In North America, immigration policy is solely the province of national governments.

United States

Background: Policy Process and Policy History

Immigration policy making in the United States is controlled at the federal level of government. This control is relatively comprehensive, particularly because the Supreme Court has prohibited states from passing any laws that contradict federal policies in this area. At the federal level, policy making is led more by Congress than by the executive branch. There are two important congressional committees for immigration policy making: the House and Senate Judiciary Committees. The members of these committees typically have a strong interest in immigration policy and often initiate legislative proposals.

Immigration policy development, implementation, and enforcement is the responsibility of the cabinet-level Department of Justice and its Immigration and Naturalization Service (INS). Other federal agencies may also be involved in specialized areas of immigration, for example the Departments of Labor or Commerce may be involved in determining appropriate levels of foreign worker inflows. The judiciary also plays an important role in determining the constitutionality of many policy decisions in this area.

Because Congress plays a greater role in immigration policy making than do the executive or judicial branches, interest groups also figure prominently in the immigration policy-making process. Congress is very sensitive to immigration interests, and interest groups sometimes determine the political agenda or propose legislation that members of Congress will introduce and advocate. Prominent interest groups in this policy arena include ethnic, business, human rights, and community groups as well as trade unions.

Historically the United States has been considered by many to be a country of immigration, so much so that it is often referred to as a melting pot. Until 1875 the United States had no national restrictions on immigration. In the nineteenth and early twentieth centuries, policymakers viewed immigration as important to national economic growth and constructed policies to maximize the flow of immigrants. As a result, the vast majority of the U.S. population today are descendants of immigrants from the 1800s or early 1900s who came to the United States in search of economic opportunities. The total foreign population in the United States in 1990 was nearly twelve million, or 4.7 percent of the population overall.

The United States' legal immigration policy is largely independent of the dictates of the labor market, although labor needs are taken into account in determining immigration quotas. Most legal immigration today is based on family reunification, with only about 15 percent of population inflows consisting of skilled labor. Significant restrictions on legal immigration were last introduced in 1924. In marked contrast to the other countries examined in this book, in recent times almost all organized pressure related to immigration policy in the United States has been on raising immigration levels. The 1990 Immigration and Nationality Act substantially increased the United States' legal immigration quotas (by about 35 percent). Support for continued legal immigration clearly reflects a belief that restrictions on legal immigration are antithetical to the U.S. immigration tradition. Presently about 800,000 foreigners enter the United States legally each year.

Currently all immigrants are admitted under a preference system that allocates a certain number of visas for each category of immigrant. Employers seeking to recruit foreign labor must demonstrate that no similarly qualified citizen or resident worker is available for the job. Employers have devised numerous ways to circumvent this law, however, and permission for entry is generally not difficult to obtain. The 1990 act also protected the right to unrestricted visa provisions for immediate relatives of U.S. citizens and created a ceiling on overall immigration of distant relatives under a family preference system. Although some levels of family-based immigration (spouses and parents of U.S. citizens) declined in 1995, family-preference immigration (spouses and children of legal permanent residents) rose as a result of increases in the annual limits. Annual immigration levels in the United States are projected to rise further because of these less restrictive family reunification policies.

The 1980 Refugee Act sets targets for humanitarian immigration to the United States. Under the law, the number of applicants admitted per year is determined jointly by Congress and the president, with an annual recommended inflow of 50,000 refugees (although actual inflows far exceed this level). Refugees living in the United States receive immigrant status after one year of residence in the country. The number of refugees granted immigrant status has increased in recent years.

The asylum approval rate in the United States is very low when compared to the number of applications filed. In 1993–1994, nearly 300,000 asylum applications were filed, producing an enormous buckle in the processing system (just under 400,000 cases were pending in 1997). Of the nearly 100,000 cases closed in 1993 and 1ᴖ94, only 13,000 were approved. However, as a result of abuses and inefficiencies in the asylum application and review process, it is estimated that about 80 percent of all applicants will remain in the country illegally. This situation prompted new legislation to be introduced to shorten the application process.

Among the industrialized countries examined in this book, the United States faces the largest illegal immigration problem, mostly because of the country's vast geographic area. The country's long, unfenced border with Mexico as well as innumerable points of entry at airports and along an extensive coastline present a logistical nightmare for immigration officials. The INS estimates that about five million illegal immigrants are already in the United States, and an additional 275,000 enter the country each year. The illegal immigrant population is concentrated geographically, with 83 percent of illegal immigrants living in six large states—California has the largest share, followed by Texas, New York, Florida, Illinois, and New Jersey. Mexicans make up the largest proportion (roughly 50 percent) of illegal immigrants. The 1996 Illegal Immigration Reform and Immigrant Responsibility Act currently governs the country's approach to the problem of illegal immigration. Externally the act is designed to assist the INS by increasing the number of border patrols, strengthening enforcement abilities, improving detection technology, and improving barriers along the Mexican border. Internally the act restricts the rights of illegal immigrants already in the country and strengthens the ability of immigration officials to deny entry to the country or deport those who have already entered.

Contemporary Dynamics

U.S. policymakers face a continual challenge: to balance effectively the economic necessity of continued labor immigration expansion with rising anti-immigration pressures and popular calls for the end of immigration entirely. The conflict between expansionists (usually business leaders and immigrants' rights groups) and restrictionists (such as governors and citizens in states with large immigrant populations) flares up repeatedly, and the restrictionists figure more prominently among those pushing for reform.

The Clinton administration generally avoided the immigration issue until several developments pushed immigration reform onto the institutional agenda in 1996. Substantial inflows of Cuban and Haitian refugees in 1993–1994 made illegal immigration issues more visible in the public eye. This increased awareness, coupled with pressures after 1994 from the Republican-controlled Congress (which accused Clinton of losing control of the country's borders) and findings of the federal Commission on Immigration Reform (which recommended drastic changes in immigration policy, including cutting legal immigration by one-third and eliminating most family reunification opportunities), created a climate ripe for reform. In November 1994, California voters approved Proposition 187, which eliminated illegal immigrants' eligibility for state social welfare services and caused a chain-reaction backlash against illegal immigration across the country. These events led to the introduction of a sweeping immigration reform bill.

The bill as introduced in the House and Senate was intended to reform both the legal and the illegal immigration systems in the country. The decision to put two major reforms together in one bill proved to be a poor one. Because it was clear from the outset that Congress viewed illegal immigration as a problem that needed solving, this aspect of the reform was relatively uncontroversial. However, legal immigration is a sacred cow in the United States as many members of Congress cling to the image of the United States as a nation of immigrants. Thus this bill represented an attempt to attach a controversial policy proposal (reducing legal immigration) to one that was far more likely to succeed (addressing the problem of illegal immigration).

Decision making on this policy took place solely within Congress. Although the White House initially voiced its opposition to reforming the legal immigration system, it did not actively intervene in the decision-making process, reflecting a concern about the political fallout in those states with large immigration populations (which also happen to be some of the country's most important electoral states). The administration initially dragged its feet in opposing legal immigration provisions but then firmly supported the move to drop the provisions from the bill once it became clear that momentum was driving in this direction.

At the decision-making stage, congressional debate on the bill was highly politicized. Republicans initially were strong advocates for stricter control of both legal and illegal flows, although many Republican proponents of free trade and family values supported continued legal immigration. Democrats pushed hard to have the legal immigration restrictions dropped and proposed a more generous legal immigration policy. The debate between the two parties was intense, as was lobbying by various interest groups. Discussions of the bill in the House and the Senate resulted in alliances between groups that traditionally would not work together. Opposition to the bill came from both liberal and conservative interest groups, including business groups (especially high-technology companies that depend on foreign workers), the Christian Coalition, grassroots immigrant groups, immigration advocates, civil liberties organizations, and free-market conservative think tanks (that were strong free-trade advocates). These actors wanted to separate the legal and illegal immigration provisions in the hopes of killing the legal immigration restrictions entirely. They worked together in a determined, well-financed, and well-coordinated effort.

Congressional decision making on the bill was notably detached from public opinion. Although most Americans favored stronger immigration control, most people do not vote for candidates based on their stands on immigration. Consequently Congress tilted away from the electorate's preferences toward those of the interest groups, without any detrimental electoral effects. Further, the absence of any determined mass support for either immigration restriction or expansion made it fairly easy for Congress to be swayed by interest group pressure.

The lobby for legal immigration restrictions was not as organized or as well-developed as the lobby to kill the restrictions. First, none of the groups represented the views of Americans who favored increased restrictions. Second, because few of the anti-immigration forces (including population control advocates, pro-labor liberals, environmentalists, and those making economic arguments about the costs of further integration) were directly affected by immigration, they were not as highly mobilized. The pro-immigration forces had much more to lose, in the form of slower family reunification, fewer foreign workers and skilled workers, or more government regulation, which made them fight harder and with greater emotion.

Ultimately the power of immigration as a national symbol, when combined with intensive lobbying by pro-immigration forces, was sufficient to defeat the anti-immigration movement. The pro-immigration lobby made a powerful emotional appeal to Congress, focusing on America's tradition of welcoming immigrants. This lobby's first success was in having the bill separated into two pieces of legislation, effectively signaling the death knell of legal immigration reform, which was unlikely to pass alone. This lobby further succeeded in its efforts to block any changes to the legal immigration system with Congress's decision to postpone legislation on legal immigration. At the end of the day, the pro-immigration lobby achieved the concessions it demanded on legal immigration—significant parts of the original bill were weakened, and the key provisions regarding legal immigration were scrapped. However, the 1996 Illegal Immigration Reform and Immigrant Responsibility Act resulted in harsher provisions regarding the treatment of illegal immigrants already in the country than the Clinton administration, immigrant advocacy groups, and liberal Democrats in Congress had hoped.

Enforcing the act's illegal immigration provisions remains an implementation challenge because of the focus on immigration control. Thus major congressional activity today focuses on monitoring and improving the effectiveness of border controls. Beyond this, no major reforms of U.S. immigration policies are currently under way or anticipated. The United States will likely continue to engage in small-scale immigration reform, reflecting its annual reassessments of immigration quotas and targets.

The policy process just described reveals the importance of cultural, economic, and political explanations in overcoming anti-immigration policy reforms generally supported by public opinion. First, Congress's reluctance to support substantial legal immigration reforms reflected the power of immigration as a national symbol. Second, the business community's strong opposition to reducing legal immigration flows revealed the influence of economic considerations. This policy decision occurred at a time when the demand for highly skilled technology workers was rising; hence, high-technology employers (and others in the business community) were motivated to block any additional restrictions on legal immigration. Finally, the ability of interest groups to involve themselves directly in the decision-making process significantly weakened an initially sweeping anti-immigration proposal and blocked a policy option supported by public opinion. Congress's move away from the electorate's preferences reflected a high level of activism by those opposing restrictions and much lower levels of activity by individual citizens who favored controls.

Japan

Background: Policy Process and Policy History

Immigration policy making in Japan involves a number of cabinet-level ministries. There is no ministry specifically organized around immigration issues. Instead the following ministries play specific roles: Justice (through its Immigration Control Bureau, which is responsible for border controls), Labor, and Construction. All immigration policy decisions are discussed and debated among these ministries, with input from relevant governing officials and no meaningful opportunity for public input. Policy making in this area is often characterized as a tug-of-war, with the various departments and ministries involved struggling to represent the distinct interests of their constituencies. The prime minister and cabinet perform a coordinating rather than initiating role.

Historically Japan was not a country of immigration. It still has the smallest foreign population of any industrialized country, but immigration into Japan has increased substantially during the 1990s. Between 1950 and 1988, foreigners made up only 0.6 percent of the Japanese population, and by the end of the 1990s the foreign population had grown to just over 1.0 percent. The largest immigrant group in Japan is from Korea, and many others are from China or Southeast Asia.

Japan is known for its preference for cultural, racial, and ethnic stability that reflects a traditionally homogenous population. Japan in the postwar period was the only major industrialized country that was not forced to import foreign workers to fill low-level employment gaps. Guest workers were not needed because of a large rural labor supply and the massive use of labor-saving technologies by large industries. The situation had changed markedly, however, by the mid-1980s. Japan faced its first labor shortage as a result of a low fertility rate, a declining labor supply from rural areas, and government policies that encouraged employers and workers to reduce their working hours. A growing reluctance among younger Japanese to take so-called 3K jobs—*kitsui, kitanai, kiken* (dirty, dangerous, and demanding), as well as the greater availability of higher skilled jobs, also spurred the labor shortage. This shortage, in a time of economic boom in the late 1980s to early 1990s, created a strong pull for immigrants from other Asian countries.

Currently Japanese immigration policy is organized around three defining principles. First, the entry of foreign workers should be allowed only as a last resort in response to severe labor shortages. Second, under no circumstances will unskilled labor be admitted. Third, all foreigners will be admitted as temporary, not permanent settlers, regardless of their reasons for entry. Legislation adopted in 1990 limited legal foreign labor immigration to a supplementary role only when absolutely necessary and created a number of new categories, mostly professionals and those with specific expertise, who could enter and remain in the country legally. Japan discourages family reunification as a general policy.

Despite these restrictionist principles, side mechanisms exist through which unskilled foreign labor is imported, often on a permanent basis. One such mechanism permits descendants of Japanese emigrants to Latin America to immigrate and settle permanently in Japan. Since 1990 these individuals have had essentially unrestricted access to the Japanese labor market. This policy is widely accepted on the grounds that these individuals, being of Japanese descent, are not viewed as upsetting Japan's ethnic and cultural homogeneity.

The government also allows the entry of foreign workers through two other side door immigration policies: corporate trainee programs and student visas. These programs are basically legal labor importation programs the government has not formally recognized (and that it does not attempt to end) and through which a substantial number of foreigners flow into the country. The decision to use these side and back door mechanisms allows the Japanese government to import labor to meet an economic need without stirring up Japanese public opinion in opposition to the immigrant presence.

Despite its participation in the major international agreements concerning humanitarian immigration, there are essentially no asylum seeker or refugee problems in Japan because the government is generally hostile to applicants. From 1982 to 1998, Japan accepted 1,654 asylum applications and granted asylum to only 225 (14 percent) of them. The prime exception was the acceptance of about 8,000 Southeast Asian refugees who were accepted as political refugees from the Vietnam War in the 1970s and early 1980s. This situation clearly reflects a lack of support for accepting refugees, particularly economic refugees, as well as the principle that no foreigners should be admitted for permanent settlement. Any limited movement toward the acceptance of refugees has been in the interest of maintaining an image of international cooperation and humanitarianism rather than a wholehearted commitment to fulfilling Japan's international obligations.

A large part of the illegal immigration problem in Japan currently consists of foreigners who were allowed into the country on short-term visas (such as tourists, students, or those employed in the entertainment industry) but did not leave when their visas expired. The estimated number of foreigners who overstayed their visas increased threefold to nearly 299,000 between 1990 and 1993. By 1995, however, this figure declined to 285,000—through better enforcement of border controls and the use of more sophisticated detection systems. It is further estimated that over 90 percent of these illegal immigrants are participating in the workforce. This increase in illegal resident foreigners followed the implementation in 1990 of a more restrictive immigration law that involved severe employer and immigration broker sanctions and the extension of visa requirements to citizens of countries (primarily in Southeast Asia) known to be likely to remain in the country illegally.

Contemporary Dynamics

In recent years, immigration policies have not undergone significant reform in Japan. In the late 1980s the movement of foreign workers to Japan had begun to generate widespread national concern. The last notable immigration reform in Japan was the revision of the Immigration Control and Refugee Recognition Law in 1990, which simplified immigration procedures and strengthened existing restrictions on employment of foreign labor.

Since implementation of the 1990 revision, little immigration policy reform has occurred, in part because of a lack of governmental consensus about basic policy directions. The prime minister's office exercises little control over the immigration policy process, leaving agenda setting largely to the competing bureaucratic agencies. Similarly, although political parties have study groups or ad hoc committees to develop policy positions on immigration, they generally do not affect the immigration policy agenda. Rather the immigration debate is dominated by the Ministries of Justice and Labor. The Ministry of Labor is supportive of legal immigration in economic sectors facing labor shortages, but its support is for very restricted entry levels. These positions tend to be supported by those ministries involved with globalization (Foreign Affairs and International Trade and Industry) and by those involved with labor-scarce industries (Construction, Fisheries, and Transportation). In contrast, the Ministry of Justice has argued against expanding legal immigration on the grounds that it is harmful to Japanese workers and that immigrants are more likely to engage in criminal activities than are native Japanese. The ministry continues to push for additional employer sanctions against those who hire illegal immigrants. The level of debate between these ministerial forces was particularly heated after 1990, until the recession began in spring 1991.

As unemployment rates rose through the 1990s, the demand for foreign workers diminished. Most observers argue that immigration policy reform will happen only after a significant influx of immigrant workers has occurred and their settlement creates a resident foreign population. In this sense, Japan looks similar to many European countries. Rather than observing the dynamics of major policy reform in Japan, we find the absence of significant pressure for reform and a subsequent failure to develop a coherent or comprehensive national immigration policy framework.

There are few human rights or immigrant advocacy groups in Japan. The small groups that do exist exercise little influence. Public opinion weighs heavily on this process. Most policymakers view the strong anti-immigration sentiments of the public as a significant impediment to major reform. Eighty percent of Japanese do not want more foreign laborers allowed into the country, despite several conditions that would seem to suggest a need for an expansion of legal immigration, including slow population growth, rapid aging, and growth in the unskilled labor market. It is estimated that, given these conditions, Japan will need at least a half million new workers each year beginning in 2001. In the absence of public concerns about immigration or interest group activity, there is little to propel immigration issues onto the country's systemic agenda.

Despite slowing economic growth and rising unemployment, the demand for foreign workers in some economic sectors is not expected to disappear in the short term. The difficulty for Japan will continue to be the attempt to reconcile employers' demands for labor with the population's strong preference for social homogeneity. As such, a more realistic immigration policy (besides looking the other way) will be needed to forestall a significant rise in illegal immigration. There is an increasing sense among both outside observers and many in Japan that immigration policies must reflect a comprehensive vision of Japan's role as an economic power (and especially must acknowledge the existence of push and pull factors). In addition, these policies must address the country's changing demographics and the effects of technology and must foster the acceptance of what has started to become a multicultural society.

The absence of significant reforms to Japanese immigration policies in the 1990s reflects the country's rejection of immigration as an aspect of Japanese social or economic life. This is not a country with a historical pattern of immigration. Reflecting this legacy, a strong commitment to excluding foreigners continues today, despite evidence that such foreign labor will be needed in the future. Further, there continues to be little interest in policies that allow immigrants to settle in Japan and become citizens. This tradition, when combined with the country's economic slowdown in the 1990s (which reduced the demand for foreign labor), significantly reduced the salience of the immigration issue. Finally, the absence of any effective immigrant interest groups or political parties concerned about these issues also eliminated other sources of pressures for reform. Generally speaking, then, reform failed to occur in Japan in the 1990s because no one was particularly interested in pursuing policy change.

Germany

Background: Policy Process and Policy History

German immigration policy is developed at the central level but is implemented and enforced at the state level. Multiple institutions at the federal, state, and local levels are responsible for immigration policy making and implementation. The federal Ministry of the Interior is most involved with immigration policy making, although the Ministry of Foreign Affairs has several subdepartments that also address immigration issues. Each of the sixteen German states

(*Länder*) has an aliens authority charged with carrying out national immigration policies. Federal offices are responsible only for the initial reception of ethnic Germans (foreigners who share blood lines with Germans) and for deciding whether asylum seekers should be accepted as refugees. States decide, under federal guidelines, about family reunification, naturalization, and deportation. Little policy coordination occurs between individual states and the federal government, even though a working group that includes the federal interior minister and the interior ministers of each of the states has been created to coordinate policy enforcement. This distribution of authority means that immigration is governed by a variety of ad hoc rules and policies rather than a single overarching policy.

Germany receives more immigrants than any other European country. Immigration, however, is not a part of Germany's national self-definition, and preventing further immigration is the country's first principle of immigration policy making. What we observe in Germany is a discrepancy between the fact that immigration continues and a repeated denial of its existence by political leaders. Like citizens of many other immigrant-receiving countries, Germans are not pleased with a continuing and expanding immigrant flow into their country. As a result, recent reform trends echo the increased calls for immigration restrictions observed elsewhere. In 1996 the foreign population was 7.3 million, or 8.9 percent of the total population. This population consists primarily of immigrants from Turkey, Yugoslavia, Italy, and other European countries from which Germany used to recruit workers, as well as Central and Eastern Europe.

Germany was traditionally a country of emigration, although it had a small foreign worker population prior to World War II. Immediately following the war, until the early 1960s, the majority of immigrants to Germany were ethnic German refugees. However, reflecting postwar labor shortages, Germany's guest-worker population rose from 1 million to 2.6 million, or from 5 percent to 12 percent of the German workforce by 1972. In the early years of guest-worker importation, immigrants were largely of European origin, but by 1972 Turkish workers formed the majority of the immigrant worker group.

Amid the economic downturn of the early 1970s, the German government in 1973 put a stop to the recruitment of foreign workers. Policies tripled the employer-paid recruitment fee and banned all further foreign recruitment. This ban was highly ineffective in controlling immigration flows because of continued and increasing rates of family reunification. The most recent attempts to control immigration were enacted under the 1990 Aliens Law, which had three objectives: to promote the return of foreigners to their home countries, to restrict further immigration, and to facilitate the integration of those who remained. The law made it more difficult for foreigners to obtain permanent residence rights and made a clear distinction between EU nationals and non-European citizens (the former did not need work permits to enter the country and had complete freedom of movement within the country). The 1990 law did not, however, establish standards or categories, or numerical targets, to control population inflows.

Among the industrialized countries, Germany has one area of population inflow that is unique: the return of ethnic Germans. Throughout the 1980s and 1990s these individuals claimed full rights to German citizenship. German citizens tend to view these returning Germans as foreigners who speak different languages, who observe different customs and traditions, and who have no real right to German residence. In reaction, a 1993 law was implemented that restricts the number of entering ethnic Germans, limits the cash payments they can receive on arrival, restricts their access to language training programs, and provides funds for development and cultural assistance to discourage their emigration to Germany.

Germany has yet to adopt comprehensive policies that attempt to restrict the number of persons eligible to enter (except for ethnic Germans) or that disallow family reunification. Nor has it attempted to stem the tide of immigration by reducing push factors through development assistance. We find an unusual situation in Germany: The government announces that Germany is closed to immigrants, but few official policies ensure that this is the case.

Asylum seekers and refugees are admitted to Germany under Article 16 of the Basic Law, which, in an explicit commitment to human rights, states that "persons persecuted on political grounds shall enjoy the right of asylum." Before 1993 the number of asylum applications was not restricted, and applicants were entitled to social welfare benefits and housing until decisions were made about their applications. Such liberal policies made Germany the primary destination for asylum seekers among all the industrialized countries. Since 1945, Germany has attracted half of all applications for asylum in Europe. The number of asylum seekers entering Germany began to increase significantly in the mid-1980s. In response, and after lengthy political debate, Germany reformed its asylum process in 1993, through an amendment to the Basic Law. The constitutional right to asylum was protected in the reform process. However, asylum applicants who arrive in Germany through safe countries are required to return to these countries and make their asylum claims there.

Illegal immigration is not as significant a problem in Germany as it is in other industrialized countries (reflecting the effective policing of its borders), but it presents a growing policy challenge nonetheless. The size of the country's illegal immigrant population has increased since 1993, particularly as rejected asylum applicants manage to remain in the country. The number of illegal immigrants has also risen because of criminal trafficking operations that smuggle people in and because some foreign workers remain in the country after their work permits expire. Germany resists regularization programs for these illegal immigrants on the grounds that such programs would encourage further illegal immigration. Germany has yet to develop any comprehensive or systematic policies in response to the illegal immigration problem.

Contemporary Dynamics

Germany has offered a constitutional right to asylum since the creation of the Federal Republic in 1949. This policy was created and then maintained as an act of atonement for Germany's role in World War II. After the end of foreign worker recruitment in 1973, asylum became the principal means of entry available—resulting in an increased number of claims (many of which were unfounded) throughout the 1970s and 1980s. In response, no fewer than eight federal laws were introduced between 1978 and 1991 in an attempt to tighten the country's asylum policy. By the late 1980s the number of asylum seekers had risen dramatically—from around 20,000 in 1983 to 193,000 in 1991 to 438,000 in 1992. By 1992, 80 percent of all refugees to Western European countries went to Germany. It is estimated that Germany received at least three million new migrants between 1989 and 1992—all to a country that officially declares itself not to be a country of immigration. This massive inflow of asylum seekers, when combined with increasing inflows of ethnic Germans and population movement from east to west, triggered a serious domestic crisis, creating the perception that the government had lost its ability to control population flows.

As population flows increased, anti-immigrant violence and xenophobia spread throughout the country and extremist right-wing parties began to gain support. The rapid influx of people created financial and organizational problems for those localities receiving large numbers of immigrants. This was especially true because it was local level governments that were responsible for securing adequate housing for immigrants, which proved to be a costly endeavor. The media often exaggerated the nature of population inflows, and some politicians, particularly those associated with extremist parties, manipulated these issues to their own advantage. By 1992 the country was experiencing a public opinion backlash against further immigration. Eventually Article 16 itself came under attack. By late 1992 opinion polls revealed that three-fourths of Germans favored the government taking drastic action to contain asylum flows, including changing the Basic Law.

In the face of rising public discontent, as well as the need to control increasingly unmanageable population inflows, what had been a traditional consensus among the major parties to stick to Article 16 became strained. In response, the governing party, the Christian Democratic Union/Christian Social Union (CDU/CSU), introduced legislation to amend the constitution in 1993. The subsequent legislative debate was long and agonizing, focusing on the question of protecting, or abolishing, the constitutional right to asylum. Those who opposed amending the constitution—including the opposition Social Democratic Party (SPD), the Green Party, and the asylum rights organization Pro-Asylum—argued that the government was first obligated to its enduring human rights principles. Both the Free Democratic Party and the SPD faced heated internal debates between those who pleaded for asylum and immigration law changes so that inflows of migrants could be brought under control and those who feared that asylum law reforms would effectively eliminate the right to asylum in Germany. Pro-immigration groups voiced strong and, in some cases, strident opposition to any proposed reform.

The CDU/CSU argued that it had no choice but to act on its popular mandate, that it was accountable first to German citizens' preferences. Conservatives campaigned ardently and visibly, appealing to public opinion as much as possible. Assailed by public opinion and intense conservative campaigning, the SPD finally conceded the point. Against its deeply held beliefs and the vehement objections of its pro-immigration activists, the party's leaders ultimately argued that they had no choice but to come to the table or risk facing electoral ruin and the further politicization of immigration debates. The SPD's reversal resulted in Germany's most important immigration policy reform in the postwar period: the so-called asylum compromise of 1993. Both sides resisted giving in to hard-line demands that Article 16 be dropped completely; instead, when revision came it consisted only of a partial abandonment of previous obligations—as noted in the preceding section.

Implementation of the country's new asylum policy after 1993 proceeded smoothly regarding the legislation's primary goal. Immigrant flows decreased dramatically. By 1995 asylum applications dropped to around 130,000, less than half of 1993 levels. However, the new policy also had several unintended consequences. First, it resulted in substantially higher levels of illegal immigration. Second, it created a growing sense among some Germans that the country's immigration policy had become illegitimate because it directly violated constitutional norms. As a result, an active sanctuary movement has been created that focuses on protecting illegal immigrants. Finally, many critics argued that the new restrictions were fundamentally inhumane and had real human costs, especially to the extent that rejected asylum seekers were sent back to life-threatening situations.

Although many German political leaders (especially conservative leaders) continue to state that Germany is not, nor will it become, a country of immigration, the country has a substantial permanent immigrant population, and immigration inflows continue. A key challenge, therefore, is how to develop an immigration policy for the country that accurately reflects the problem at hand. Further reduction in immigration inflows appears unlikely, primarily because the country's large resident immigrant population makes family unification growth inevitable and because Germany remains an attractive destination for immigrants. The new Social Democratic government has no plans for a new immigration law and supports a zero-immigration policy, whereas its coalition partner, the Greens, wants a new immigration law based on quotas.

These reforms to Germany's long-standing liberal asylum policies can be explained in large part by cultural factors. The German population's response to a massive inflow of foreigners in the late 1980s and early 1990s was conditioned by a widespread and deep-seated belief that Germany is not a country of immigration. As the country experienced ever-increasing population inflows, public opinion strongly supported changes to the country's asylum policy. The climate of public opinion was so intense that even parties that were traditionally strong supporters of the constitutional right to asylum eventually agreed to the reforms—despite reservations—out of fear of an electoral backlash against them. These fears reflected the increasing, though relatively limited, mobilization of extreme right-wing parties in the country, especially in the eastern regions. The possibility that some of the electorate might turn away from the SPD if it failed to support these reforms, taking their support to the far right (or at least to the center-right conservatives), in part spurred the reform compromise.

France

Background: Policy Process and Policy History

As in Germany, immigration policies in France are developed at the central level of government. At the cabinet level, the Ministry of the Interior is charged with immigration control and oversees policing and border control. The Ministry of Foreign Affairs is responsible for refugee and asylum policy. Since 1994, illegal immigration issues have been monitored by the Central Agency for the Control of Immigration and the Struggle Against the Employment of Illegal Immigrants. Both the French Council of State and the Constitutional Council play important roles in immigration policy making, with the latter demonstrating a willingness to reject strict immigration and asylum policies on constitutional grounds. The Office of International Migration deals with the problems of immigrants who are already residing in the country. Immigration policies in France are implemented at lower levels within the government.

Among European countries, France has the longest history as a country of immigration; however, immigration is not part of the country's nation-building experience as it was in the United States. Rather, immigrants have entered France in large numbers since the mid-1800s in response to industrialization, lower French population growth, and a republican tradition that involves a respect for human rights and civil liberties and that prescribes a more open and inclusive idea of citizenship. By the early 1930s, 6.6 percent of the French population was foreign. Although this figure dropped during World War II and the early postwar years, by the 1950s immigration was again on the rise in response to labor shortages.

Despite its immigration legacy, the French population generally is reluctant to recognize immigration as either an economic or demographic necessity or benefit, with the result being an increasing emphasis on immigration control. In the 1990s weak economic growth, coupled with rising unemployment rates, strengthened anti-immigration sentiment. Although immigration into France slowed in the 1990s, the country's borders have remained relatively open, particularly when compared with its European neighbors. The 1990 census reported the foreign population at 3.6 million, or 6.3 percent of the country's total population. By 1997 the total foreign population was estimated at 7.4 percent, or five million people, including an estimated one million illegal immigrants. Over 40 percent of the foreign population in France is from Algeria, Morocco, or Tunisia, and a large Turkish population is present.

The French government maintained an open immigration policy from the early 1900s through the early 1970s. Labor shortages, as well as a falling birthrate, created continuing support for liberal immigration policies. Beginning in the 1950s and continuing to the early 1980s, the French set specific targets and imported foreign labor as guest workers who arrived in France on a temporary basis. These immigrants supplied France with the labor needed to keep its economy growing. In the early years of these programs, immigrants were mostly European in origin. By the 1960s immigration from North Africa (especially Algeria) became more widespread. The changing nature of the immigrant population, in combination with the economic recession that followed the 1973 oil crisis, made the open immigration policy more controversial. Immigrants quickly became scapegoats for rising unemployment. In response, the government declared an official end to worker recruitment abroad and announced a goal of zero immigration in 1974. However, France's agreements with its former colonies remained in place, and its borders remained porous to these immigrants.

The government's attempts to restrict immigration further in the 1980s and 1990s were largely unsuccessful. French law continues to allow legal immigration on a small scale for family reunification or based on labor needs for temporary, seasonal, or permanent skilled workers. Few permanent work permits are issued to foreigners who do not already have temporary residence or refugee status (the number of workers arriving from 1992 to 1996 dropped by 73 percent). Family reunification presently accounts for two-thirds of the total permanent immigration into the country.

After World War II, and through the 1970s, France had a liberal asylum and refugee policy, reflecting traditional support for civil and human rights and a desire to compensate for the discriminatory policies of the Vichy regime during the German occupation. Until 1960, an average of 15,000 asylum applications were received each year, and virtually all applications were accepted. The number of asylum seekers rose steadily from the mid-1970s to 1990, and their ethnic composition changed, with Europeans replaced by immigrants from developing countries. The government began to restrict significantly asylum claims in the late 1980s, resulting in reduced asylum seeker inflows in the 1990s. Asylum claims numbered 54,800 in 1990 and dropped to 21,400 by 1997. These numbers are now lower than those observed in Germany and the United Kingdom. The rate of acceptance for asylum seekers also decreased significantly in this period, falling from 77.7 percent in 1981 to 15.5 percent in 1990. French asylum policy now relies heavily on the principle of manifestly unfounded claims—asylum applicants are denied entry unless they provide absolute proof of political persecution. Relative to the other countries examined in this book, however, France has remained relatively open to asylum seekers.

Illegal immigration in France emerged in 1974 with the government's efforts to stop legal immigration. In addition, a considerable number of foreigners in temporary worker programs chose to remain in the country illegally when their work permits expired. Current estimates of the illegal immigrant population in France are around one million. In response to rising numbers of illegal immigrants in the 1970s, France enacted a generous amnesty policy for illegal immigrants in the early 1980s. Those who entered France prior to 1981 were eligible for temporary residence permits that allowed them to enter the application process for legal status. In 1995 the government introduced another regularization program that allowed some illegal foreigners to obtain temporary residence permits. This program was pursued again in 1997 and 1998, during which time over 200,000 immigrants were legalized. Those not legalized in the latter two programs were to be deported, but the government found this difficult to do, as we discuss in the next section. Legalizations, however, have not eliminated the problem of illegal immigration.

Contemporary Dynamics

French immigration policy in the 1990s has alternated between increasingly restrictive measures and public pressure to weaken those restrictions once their impact is recognized. Persistent unemployment problems, weak economic growth, increasing immigration pressures, and public opposition have compelled political leaders to enact more effective controls. At the same time, many on the left are committed to France's republican values, which makes stricter policies difficult to implement.

Agenda setting on immigration issues in France also is influenced by the success of Jean-Marie Le Pen, the leader of the anti-immigration, extreme right-wing party the Front National (FN). The electoral breakthrough of the FN in the 1980s and 1990s changed the face of French immigration politics. Le Pen's number one campaign issue is opposition to further immigration and a permanent foreign population, which compels competing parties across the political spectrum to exploit France's underlying xenophobia. The FN's success has created a sense that immigration is one of the country's most pressing issues, with public opinion polls indicating that most French citizens blame immigrants for France's economic and cultural decline and think immigration should stop. As the FN gained power and acceptance among the electorate,

French political leaders, particularly on the right, sought to redefine and re-assert themselves on immigration issues out of fear of losing their traditional bases of support to the FN.

Reflecting this increased politicization of immigration issues, policy for-mulation debates played themselves out in recent years both in the National Assembly and on the streets of the country. The new Socialist-led government that came to power in the National Assembly in 1997 was committed to elim-inating some of the harsh restrictions introduced by two previous conservative-led governments. This was in part a commitment to the Socialist Party's coali-tion partner, the liberal Greens, a strong advocate of continued immigration. Pressure from immigrant advocacy groups for an expanded and extended amnesty program for illegal immigrants also stimulated government interest in reform. In addressing these concerns, the Socialist Party is challenged by a desire to appear sympathetic to immigrants without seeming so lenient that it provides anti-immigration forces with a campaign issue that appeals to an electorate that generally favors stricter controls.

The decision-making stage for stricter controls began with the govern-ment's introduction of new immigration legislation, known as the Chevene-ment law, in the National Assembly in 1997. The government opted for amending, rather than repealing, the most restrictive provisions of existing laws, a decision that troubled many on the pro-immigrant left and created a divide within the governing coalition. In turn, the right-wing opposition saw this division as an opportunity to embarrass and weaken the government, and the FN saw an opportunity for free publicity. In response to the bill, immi-grant rights' organizations called for demonstrations against the government, and anti-racist groups called for vigilance against further outbursts of racism and xenophobia.

At the height of this controversy, the leader of the conservative Rally for the Republic (RPR) in the National Assembly accused Prime Minister Jospin's government of waving "a red cloth in front of the National Front voters" with this liberal legislation. Citing polls that showed a majority of French voters to be against increasing the rights of immigrants, the opposition RPR, along with the Union for French Democracy, called for a referendum on the reforms. Al-though the government had hoped to reawaken the republican consensus that characterized earlier periods of immigration policy making and appeal to a moral high ground to defuse the extreme right wing, the debate revealed how polarized the electorate and political parties had become on immigration issues.

The center-left coalition in the National Assembly responded by passing a new immigration law in May 1998 that established a stricter standard for is-suing residency permits to foreigners. The bill did not extend the amnesty or legalization provisions for illegal immigrants that had been introduced in 1997. It also eliminated a number of the more restrictive provisions of earlier legislation and created two new forms of asylum. After passage of the bill,

Prime Minister Jospin accused leftists of deliberately politicizing the immigration issue and of playing into the hands of right-wing extremists. He pointed out that 92 percent of the French population was in favor of the government further controlling immigration and that if the government was seen as failing to respond, then it ran the risk of sending voters to the far right.

Implementation problems plagued some aspects of the reform, and initial political evaluations were largely negative. Throughout 1998 the French government had trouble removing foreigners whose applications for legalization were rejected. Opposition was voiced by immigrant advocacy groups (such as groups for the so-called *sans papiers,* or immigrants without residency papers), trade unions (which did not oppose immigration in the 1980s and 1990s because their ranks include a significant number of immigrants), and religious groups and other pro-immigrant groups from other European countries. The French Roman Catholic Bishops' Committee on Immigration, as well as filmmakers and leftist deputies from the Green and Communist Parties in the National Assembly, urged the government to grant legal residence rights to more unauthorized foreigners. A series of protests in French churches, including occupation of a church by those to be deported along with their supporters, encouraged the Jospin government to modify its stance against extending its regularization programs and appearing too liberal on immigration issues.

Such backing down by a French government in the face of citizen outcry is an example of politics as usual in France. Policy implementation can be difficult in France because of the tendency of the French public to take their case to the streets. In July 1998 the government announced a plan to allow 70,000 immigrants without residence papers to remain in France as part of an amnesty program, thus allowing the government to avoid removing the foreigners who had applied for amnesty in 1997–1998 and were not granted resident status. As expected, this decision came under harsh criticism from the right, spurring yet another national discussion on the need for further immigration controls, as well as a heated debate among the parties of both the left and the right.

Immigration issues promise to remain prominent on the French political agenda in coming years, particularly as high unemployment rates and worldwide immigration pressures persist, as the public continues to associate unemployment with immigrants, and as the extreme right continues to agitate popular opinion. Although France will continue to admit immigrants, inflows are likely to fall, leaving the question of what to do about illegal immigration as the most likely reform issue for the future.

This contradictory reform pattern resulted from the interaction of various factors. Culturally, stricter controls reflected strong public sentiment favoring further restrictions on immigrants' ability to enter the country. When these sentiments were echoed and reinforced by the influential extreme right-wing party the Front National, the French government responded by placing stricter controls on the institutional agenda. The multiparty nature of French government at the time meant that decision making was affected by coalition politics, as the center-left coalition split on the issue of strict controls—illustrating the difficulties of enacting change when government has to satisfy its coalition partners. Divisions within the center-left coalition over the nature of the reform created an opening for those who opposed the reforms, since the government was viewed as operating from a weak position. At the implementation stage, the tendency of French citizens to voice their outrage in the streets was well illustrated on these reforms, as immigrant advocacy groups rejected key aspects of the new policies. Similarly the public's response to the Chevenement law points to the influence that rights-based liberalism may have on immigration policy making. Those who protested the reforms viewed them as violating fundamental human and civil rights principles. Ultimately these factors produced first stricter control policies and then more open, less restrictive ones as the government responded to interest groups' demands.

United Kingdom

Background: Policy Process and Policy History

The immigration policy-making process in the United Kingdom is centralized to a greater degree than in the other five countries examined in this book. Decisions in this policy area are made at the cabinet level, primarily through the prime minister's office, with little opportunity for influence from other interested parties. Although the House of Commons is often the site of heated debates over changes to immigration policies, it has not played an appreciable role in either policy formulation or amendment. Administratively the Ministry of the Interior is responsible for overseeing policy implementation. Local governments are charged with implementing some aspects of these laws, but they have no ability to interpret policies. To date, the judiciary has not played a role in immigration.

Among the six countries we examine, the United Kingdom is considered to be a model of successful immigration control. This reputation reflects a marked ability on the part of the British government to prevent unwanted immigration through effective policy instruments. Until the end of World War II, the British government dealt with emigration rather than immigration. Employment-based immigration in the postwar period, primarily from former British colonies, reversed this pattern, and questions of immigration control became politically significant. By 1996 the foreign population in the United Kingdom was nearly two million, or 3.4 percent of the total population.

Immediately after World War II, citizenship policy for residents of former British colonies was extremely liberal, reflecting a continuing sense among the British that they had a special relationship with their former satellites. Citizens of former colonies retained full British citizenship, including the right to enter the United Kingdom without restriction. Postwar economic conditions both in the colonies and in the United Kingdom served as powerful push and pull factors for these so-called New Commonwealth citizens. The flow of these citizens was substantial in the 1950s and 1960s (peaking at over 90,000 in 1962) and declined steadily during the 1970s and 1980s (to a low of 46,000 in 1987).

The British public did not, however, welcome the racially and ethnically distinct migrants from the New Commonwealth, believing they would not be easily assimilated. Thus strict controls have always been justified by political leaders as being essential for good race relations in the country. Traditionally, British policymakers of all political stripes championed policies of strict control and reaped political benefits in terms of the vote. Beginning in the 1960s a succession of increasingly stricter immigration control policies was adopted, resulting in the effective end to new immigration from former colonies in 1981 and to family reunification in 1988. Family reunification is now permitted only to persons who can prove that they have guaranteed housing and financial support in the country.

Continuing to reflect public opinion, Prime Minister Margaret Thatcher's government (in power from 1979 to 1990) emphasized strict controls on entry, employing visa requirements for New Commonwealth countries, genetic fingerprinting to establish family ties, and carrier sanctions for transporting undocumented foreigners. Immigrants who currently enter the United Kingdom (around 50,000 annually since the late 1980s) generally are spouses or dependents of legal residents. A small percentage of immigrants enter as highly skilled workers, professionals and managers, or refugees.

The United Kingdom has not faced the same sort of crisis in the 1990s as its European counterparts did with respect to asylum seekers and refugees. Although the United Kingdom also experienced a rise in asylum applications, the rise was tempered by the country's island geography, close scrutiny of asylum applications, and specific policies aimed at keeping the number of asylum seekers and refugees in check. In the 1980s the United Kingdom received fewer than 5,000 asylum applications per year. These numbers increased significantly beginning in 1989 to peak at around 45,000 in 1991 and ranged from 22,000 to 44,000 between 1992 and 1995 (applications fell to 27,900 in 1996). The increase in asylum applications reflected not an increase in the number of refugees but the fact that asylum applications were a means to evade the United Kingdom's strict immigration controls; criminal trafficking operations began to target the United Kingdom as well. A tremendous backlog of applications has resulted (51,000 applications were in the system in 1999).

The British government responded to these increases with a strategy of preentry and postentry controls. Because most asylum seekers enter the United Kingdom through another country (given the country's island status), the British government makes full use of the safe country concept, returning asylum seekers to the countries where they first landed. Further, the government levies stiff fines against airlines for carrying passengers who lack proper documentation and has also instituted a strict set of visa requirements as an important instrument of control.

Since 1993, postentry controls have also received significant emphasis. The 1993 Asylum and Immigration Appeals Act, while affirming the right to asylum in the United Kingdom, provides for a fast track procedure for manifestly unfounded claims. Although the act introduced the right of appeals for applicants who were refused asylum, the law imposed strict time limits on all stages of the application and appeals processes. In addition, the British government instituted a policy for detainment at ports of entry for those filing asylum claims deemed by immigration officers to be manifestly unfounded, in an attempt to deter individuals from seeking entry into the country in the first place. In 1996 a new Asylum and Immigration Act was passed that withheld asylum applicants' rights to benefits if they did not file an asylum application at their port of entry or if they were appealing an asylum decision. The law also imposed criminal penalties on employers hiring immigrants who did not have the right to work in the country and increased the use of the fast track application review process.

In 1999 the Labour government introduced another new Immigration and Asylum Bill into the House of Commons for consideration. The new act streamlines the government's approach to immigration and asylum with the intent of preventing abuse of the system. The 1999 act also introduces restrictions on marriages intended to help foreigners remain in the United Kingdom and stops the practice of giving applicants cash assistance while they await a decision—this assistance will be replaced with vouchers or in-kind benefits.

Because of a very effective and well-established policy of border control and strict monitoring of foreigners in the country, the United Kingdom traditionally has not had a significant problem with illegal immigration. By 1995, however, concern about the weakening of internal border controls in the EU prompted the government to introduce new proposals to ward off the problem of illegal immigration. Such measures included the government requiring employers to check the immigration status of prospective employees and denying social welfare benefits to suspected illegal immigrants. Having said that, illegal immigration is increasing steadily, especially as asylum restrictions increase.

Contemporary Dynamics

The British are far more successful than Germany or France at achieving zero immigration. This reflects a docile court system, a lack of constitutional protections for immigrants, and the dominance of parliamentary sovereignty. Further, it reflects a widespread national consensus about the desirability of strict immigration controls. The existence of an effective immigration policy since the 1970s means that immigration reform does not figure as prominently on the systemic agenda in the United Kingdom as it does in other countries. Consequently, contemporary reform dynamics have involved a series of relatively uncontroversial decisions designed to further tighten an already strict set of policies in the face of a consistently high number of asylum applications.

Traditionally the Conservative Party has been the party seen as responsible for strict immigration control policies, although the history of immigration control in the United Kingdom indicates that both parties have shaped this pattern of restrictionist policy. In the recent past, Margaret Thatcher was the first national leader to introduce the racial issue in the context of immigration policy; under her leadership in 1979 the Conservative Party campaigned on a platform promising strict controls for nonwhite immigrants. As a result, electoral support for the country's small National Front Party collapsed (and has never reemerged at the national level); its supporters were absorbed by the Conservative Party.

Public opinion in the United Kingdom continues to be pervasively restrictionist on immigration issues; in response, the Blair government has pursued stricter immigration policies. Because of numerous administrative problems associated with the country's asylum applications procedures, the Blair government moved in 1999 to further restrict entry into the country through asylum and refugee channels. In keeping with British traditions, this new policy did not meet with significant political or public opposition, and the legislation passed with ease. For their part, the Conservatives—still viewed as being tougher in immigration policy—noted that the Labour government's initiatives were not stringent enough. The immigration policy area has no powerful interest groups—those ethnic and human rights groups that do exist did not have a noticeable impact on the decision-making process surrounding this legislation. The British government has encountered little difficulty in implementing immigration policies: Once a policy is decided on, there is executive closure in implementation, with the Home Office firmly and uncontestedly in charge. The British preference for immigration restriction will likely be the country's policy standard in the foreseeable future.

The current state of immigration policy reform in the United Kingdom has two explanations. First, little in the way of significant reform is observed today because the British government has generally eliminated legal population inflows—thereby leaving little to control. Second, because the British population and its political parties remain strongly committed to restrictionist policies, reform is not likely to be an issue in the future. Immigration policy in the United Kingdom is not driven by those who benefit from continued immigration, such as employers or ethnic groups—rather it reflects the wishes of an overwhelmingly hostile public, with both political parties representing these views. The ability of the majority party to enact its policies as formulated—because of strong party government—means that this coincidence between public opinion and partisan views is fully represented in the country's immigration policies. The victory of the center-left Labour Party in 1997 resulted in little change in immigration policies; the Blair government continues the country's emphasis on limiting population inflows.

Italy

Background: Policy Process and Policy History

Italian immigration policy is developed by central government through the Ministry of the Interior. The successful implementation of immigration control policies in Italy is impeded by a fragmentation of authority on immigration matters and a lack of coordination between government agencies. Policies made at the central level tend to be loosely constructed, and when implemented at lower levels of government these policies are often misinterpreted. A pressing need exists for stronger monitoring from the center as well as for increases in resources allocated to authorities charged with maintaining border controls. The overarching political crisis of the early 1990s reduced the likelihood that a systematic and comprehensive immigration policy would be implemented.

Italy has traditionally been a country of emigration, not immigration. Between 1946 and 1975, over seven million Italians departed from their homeland, primarily in search of economic opportunities. Thus Italians constituted a large proportion of many of the guest-worker populations of other European countries. By the late 1970s immigrants began to outnumber emigrants in Italy for the first time. The delay in immigration to Italy partly reflected the belief that greater opportunities existed elsewhere. Also, the existence of a relatively large supply of low-skilled labor prevented the pull factor of labor shortages experienced elsewhere. Not surprisingly the increase in immigration to Italy occurred at the same time that Italy's European neighbors were closing their doors to economic immigration. These new population inflows included returning guest workers who had sought opportunities in other European countries as well as new immigrants from Africa, Latin America, and Asia.

The precise number of immigrants in Italy today is difficult to estimate because of poor accounting procedures. The 1997 reported estimate was one million legal foreigners (1.9 percent of the total population) present in the country. When an estimated 400,000 illegal immigrants are included in this figure, the foreign population is estimated at 2.6 percent of the total population.

Before 1986, Italian immigration policy was neither well defined nor adequately implemented. Immigration was controlled primarily through a series of ministerial directives that lacked a unifying vision of Italy's immigration future. In 1986 the Italian government introduced the country's first comprehensive immigration legislation, the Foreign Workers and the Control of Illegal Immigration Law, which constituted Italy's first attempt to regulate labor inflows (by tying immigration controls to the country's labor needs) and launched the country's first major regularization program. The law, however, was criticized as being too vague and excessively bureaucratic and for being so restrictive that it created an incentive for illegal immigration.

In response, the 1990 Martelli law established categories of foreign workers to be admitted on an annual basis and identified which countries' citizens would need visas to enter. This law was designed to bring Italy's immigration policies into line with those of other EU member states, particularly by focusing on more restrictive external controls. Legal immigration to Italy is currently restricted to those who have arranged employment or who are joining their families.

In response to criticism from other EU member states about Italy's lax immigration control approach, as well as to a more general sense that the 1986 and 1990 laws were ineffective and weak, a new comprehensive immigration control act regulating the entry and residence of foreigners was adopted in early 1998. The act focuses on immigration control and labor market regulation. Bureaucratically the law is designed for more effective implementation at both the national and regional levels of government, as well as for cooperation with employers and employees' organizations in regulating labor inflows. The 1998 law sets, for the first time, quotas for foreign workers, family reunification (while guaranteeing a right to such unification), and temporary asylum for humanitarian reasons.

The 1948 Italian constitution recognizes the right of asylum and the need for Italy to conduct itself within the requirements of international law. More specifically the constitution provides that "any foreigner who in his own country is denied democratic rights guaranteed by the Italian constitution has the right of asylum in Italy." In addition, Italy had ratified the Geneva Convention. The 1990 Martelli law eliminated geographic limits on asylum seekers and extended these rights to all nationalities.

Despite this relatively open policy, Italy has historically received few asylum claims (fewer than 2,000 asylum requests were received in 1993 and only 675 were received in 1996, although the number of requests rose in the late 1990s). Relative to other European countries, Italy does not treat asylum seekers well—they receive few benefits before the asylum decisions are made, and more than 83 percent of applications are rejected. The immigration environment in the 1990s has become one in which entering Italy and obtaining refugee status has become more, not less, difficult, despite the continuing open asylum and refugee policy.

The Italian economic system is distinguished from many other industrialized countries through the existence of a large and flourishing underground (informal or black market) economy. This underground economy accounts for 25–30 percent of Italian economic activity. For immigrants, this has meant disproportionate illegal employment opportunities in small- and medium-scale manufacturing and the service sector. For the government, this has meant that policies dealing with illegal immigrants differ from those of other countries not so much in their content (in that they involve attempts at regularization and the use of employer sanctions) but in their effectiveness.

Italy's first attempts at addressing illegal immigration, in 1986, involved employer sanctions and the introduction of a regularization program, both of which were largely unsuccessful. A second and more effective version of these programs was introduced with the 1990 Martelli law. This law was followed in 1992 by the Boniver Decree, which outlined new rules for the expulsion of undocumented immigrants, including asylum seekers and refugees. It permitted the police to transport foreigners who lacked visas or stay permits to the border for immediate expulsion without a court hearing. Finally, a decree issued in 1995 instituted a four-month regularization program for as many as 300,000 illegal immigrants who had been employed for at least four of the preceding twelve months, with a special provision for seasonal agricultural workers. The Italian government returned to the regularization approach again in 1998 and 1999 in a continuing effort to draw illegal immigrants out of the underground economy. In 1999 some 300,000 unauthorized foreigners applied for legalization, and 150,000 received legal immigrant status.

Contemporary Dynamics

As noted in the preceding section, Italy adopted its first major piece of immigration legislation in 1986, and for the most part between 1986 and 1990 immigration issues were not visible on the political agenda. Although the media continued to pay attention to immigration issues, public opinion was not terribly mobilized, and Italians were largely indifferent toward immigrants. Although trade unions tended to be mobilized around immigration issues, most of their efforts were ineffective in influencing the political agenda because of the fragmentation of these issues between various government ministries.

The murder of an immigrant in 1989 changed the political climate entirely. The public had once been indifferent and passive regarding immigration, but the murder (in combination with an increased tendency toward anti-immigrant violence overall) pushed immigration onto the systemic agenda and created an opening for government to initiate reforms. These events added urgency to what had been a mounting drive to scrap the 1986 law. In particular, as public opinion became increasingly mobilized following the murder (polls indicated a near consensus in support of action), the Socialist vice premier Martelli was able to force the issue onto the institutional agenda and formulate a policy response. The Socialists viewed this issue as providing a chance to show leadership and promote national solidarity. The 1990 Martelli law began as a decree law that would expire in sixty days if it did not receive parliamentary approval.

Italy in 1990 provided a classic example of a fragmented, multiparty system governed by an unstable coalition. This five-party coalition was dominated by the mass Catholic party, the Christian Democrats, which ruled with four other smaller parties: the Socialist Party, the Republican Party, the Liberal Party, and the Social Democratic Party. During the decision-making stage of the Martelli law, the mass parties, the Christian Democrats and the opposition Communists, sought to avoid taking visible public stands, out of fear of creating an opportunity for the extreme right. The small governing parties were, however, quite willing to take outspoken stands in favor (the Socialists) or in opposition (the Republicans). In fact, the Socialists—the largest of the minor parties—made liberal immigration legislation a key component of its political agenda.

The Martelli law as originally written emphasized a more open and liberal policy. The bureaucracy argued, however, that a more liberal policy would further annoy Italy's EU partners, who already viewed Italy's policies as too liberal. They argued that the new law should do no more than bring Italy's policies in line with those of the Schengen partners. Additionally, two parties—the Italian Social Movement (MSI) and the Republicans—decided to play the xenophobia card in the debates surrounding the law, in an attempt to test the waters with the Italian electorate. It turned out that although the Italian electorate is generally more restrictionist, it was not amenable to xenophobic appeals. The MSI had little influence over the legislation because of weak electoral support. Despite even lower levels of electoral support than the MSI, the Republican Party was more effective in its opposition because it was part of the governing coalition. The party stalled the legislation during parliamentary debates and threatened to create a government crisis by withdrawing from the governing coalition; it thus managed to extract some concessions before the House approved the law.

The decision to introduce a less liberal policy was initially opposed by labor unions, Catholic immigrant support groups, and the Christian Democratic party. However, the Socialist government managed to persuade these groups that adopting a too-liberal immigration policy created the possibility that an extreme right-wing party, like the Front National in France, would gain support in Italy. Immigrants themselves had no influence over the Martelli law, as they were not a coherent political force. Lacking leadership, resources, or a common vision or set of demands, immigrants are largely dependent on Catholic associations and unions to represent their interests. Italian policymakers chose the path of least public visibility on this issue, reflecting a reluctance to launch serious debate over restrictionist measures for fear of fueling the anti-immigration movement. Further, the need to keep the unstable parliamentary coalition together resulted in carefully mixed legislation. Some provisions of the Martelli law are fairly liberal (for example, a generalized right to asylum, an expansive regularization program), whereas others introduced a much more rigorous system of external controls.

The Martelli law proved difficult to implement effectively. Like the 1986 law, it was widely regarded as weak, overly bureaucratic, and often contradictory. Beyond regularization, it is not identified as having achieved much to reduce population inflows, largely because it failed to follow through on deportations and it had weak border controls. Between 1992 and 1995, immigration control issues were generally off the political agenda in Italy. They were still seen as a problem, but the political crisis and governmental uncertainty that emerged in 1992 meant these issues no longer had priority status. In recent years, however, immigration policy making has increased in response to growing problems with illegal immigration and in response to external pressures for better border controls. Since the mid-1990s, other EU member countries—especially Germany—have been highly critical of Italian immigration control efforts on two fronts: for failing to police effectively external borders and for allowing asylum seekers whose claims were rejected to remain in the country for two weeks—ample time for them to disappear and avoid expulsion.

In Italy, as in the other countries examined in this book, public opinion played a critical role in the policy reform process. Changes in public attitudes about immigration were critical in placing these issues on the country's institutional agenda and continued to influence the reforms as they moved through the policy process. The 1990 immigration policy reforms also reflect the difficulty of policy making by multiparty coalition governments. Differences within the governing coalition meant that the debate during the decision-making stage was heated and divisive, with the policy's supporters ultimately having to settle for a more restrictive bill because of pressure from their coalition partners. Further, the proportional representation electoral system enabled extreme right-wing parties to extend their influence to the immigration policy reform process, even though they were not part of the governing coalition. The potential appeal of these right-wing parties compelled some members of the governing coalition to play the xenophobia card in debates on the bill to improve their standing with the electorate. More important, fears of further mobilizing support for right-wing parties compelled the major parties to accept a final policy that was more restrictive than they originally intended, in order to prevent a right-wing backlash in the electorate.

Cross-national Trends

When considering the broader cross-national trends in these six countries, one must note the choices these countries make with respect to immigration policy and how effective they are in achieving their immigration objectives. Two clear patterns emerge. First, these countries all moved in the direction of increasingly stricter controls over immigration in the recent past. Second, despite their best efforts, they have not succeeded in reducing population inflows to their desired levels.

Policy Outputs

In comparing the immigration policies of these six industrialized countries, we see a marked convergence in their policies over the past several decades. The long-term trend is toward greater control over all types of population inflows. These countries all have adopted restrictive attitudes toward foreigners' right to enter and remain within their borders. In most of these countries, governments have tightened restrictions that apply to the flow of both legal immigrants for purposes of employment or family reunification and asylum seekers and refugees. Accompanying these stricter definitions of who has a right to enter legally, most industrialized governments also have fortified their border management systems to forestall further illegal immigration. The bottom line is that the industrialized countries have become less welcoming to foreigners. France, Italy, and the United States have adopted immigration control policies based on universal and nondiscriminatory principles. In contrast, policies in Germany, Japan, and the United Kingdom allow for selection on the basis of racial, ethnic, or national origin, with the explicit intention of maintaining a more homogenous population.

These six countries have restricted legal access so that entry is allowed for family reunification or to meet labor needs, although entry even on these bases has become more limited. The United States uses preference or quota systems to define the extent of legal immigration. The use of such preference systems is generally considered to be evidence of a strong planning instinct in the United States, in that an explicit effort is made to link immigration to labor or demographic needs. In most other countries, legal immigration is defined by categories (such as temporary workers, families, or seasonal migrants) but is not based on strict numerical targets or quotas for these categories. In countries without numerical targets, the goal is generally to admit as few new entrants as possible by eliminating whole categories of possible entrants.

Humanitarian immigration policies have also become more restrictive in these six countries, especially among the European countries. As popular opinion crystallized and mobilized against continued population inflows, governments in most industrialized countries responded with new policies that generally involved a stricter interpretation of the major international agreements protecting individuals' human rights and rights to asylum. Many countries introduced measures to control the entry of refugees, such as restrictions for those who are judged to have manifestly unfounded claims, the extension of visa requirements to include more countries, and the return of asylum seekers to safe third countries. These countries also increased the rates at which they process asylum applications and at which they dismiss applicants who make invalid or fraudulent requests. Most countries now attempt to evaluate asylum applications before individuals have the time to become settled in the country. Such moves are the norm in all but Italy and Japan, neither of which accepts a large number of asylum seekers or refugees.

In countries with large illegal immigrant populations, such as France and the United States, citizens place substantial pressure on government to stop all unauthorized entry. As a result, policymakers in these countries adopt much more stringent controls. Policies are designed that focus on the removal of undocumented foreigners (through deportation schemes and workplace inspections), increase barriers to illegal entry (such as visa requirements or stricter border controls), or penalize employers that hire illegal entrants (generally through employer sanctions and fines). Policy instruments of this sort are the norm in industrialized countries that are attempting to reduce the size of the illegal foreign population, especially in France and the United States. Other countries, such as Italy, have introduced policies intended to assist illegal immigrants already in the country (through regularization programs or the extension of legal and political rights). The United States and France have adopted similar programs (despite their stringent efforts to prevent illegal immigration), reflecting their commitments to individuals' human rights.

Policy Outcomes

In the previous section we observed a marked convergence among the types of immigration policy instruments used in these six countries. The effects of these policies have been nearly as uniform across these countries. Changes in immigration policy have enabled these countries to more effectively control their borders since the early 1990s. The overall trend among the industrialized countries is toward a leveling off of immigration since about 1993, after significant increases in the 1980s and early 1990s (Table 5.1). In many countries, immigration flows had either leveled off or declined by 1995, with a decrease in the absolute number of immigrants and in their percentage of the total population. Given the persistence of a wide range of push and pull factors that encourage immigration worldwide, these drops in population inflows were at least partially a consequence of each country's stricter immigration control policies. As Table 5.1 indicates, the United Kingdom did not experience a drop in population inflows, most likely because more restrictive policies were not imposed in this period.

Reflecting the intent of most immigration policies, family reunification was the principal form of legal immigration in all six countries in 1996. Between the early 1990s and 1996 in France, the United Kingdom, and the United States, family reunification grew to be the largest source of legal immigration. The second major form of legal immigration in the industrialized countries is employment-based immigration. This form of immigration in 1996 was relatively low in the United Kingdom but high in France. Worker flows rose in France, Germany, and the United Kingdom starting in the mid-1980s but began to drop by 1992. The type of employment-based legal immigration to these countries has changed in recent years, with lower rates of legal entry for less-skilled workers and increased emphasis on highly skilled and temporary workers.

Also reflecting recent policy changes, these six industrialized countries witnessed a decline in the number of asylum claims since the early 1990s. Policy measures designed to stem the flow of new arrivals, combined with efforts to lower rates of acceptance, led to a drop in the number of asylum applications

Table 5-1 Inflows of Foreign Population

Country	Foreign Population Inflow, by year (in thousands)		
	1986	*1991*	*1996*
France	38.3	109.9	74.0
Germany	478.3	920.5	708.0
Italy	N.A.	N.A.	N.A.
Japan	157.5	258.4	225.4
United Kingdom	N.A.	203.9ª	206.4
United States	601.7	1,827.2	915.9

SOURCE: From *Trends in International Migration: Annual Report* (Paris: Organisation for Economic Co-operation and Development, 1998).

ª1992 data

N.A. = not available.

Table 5-2 Inflows of Asylum Seekers

Country	Asylum Seeker Inflow, by year (in thousands)		
	1987	*1992*	*1997*
France	27.6	28.9	21.4
Germany	57.4	438.2	104.4
Italy	11.0	2.6	1.4
Japan	N.A.	N.A.	N.A.
United Kingdom	5.9	32.3	41.5
United States	26.1	104.0	79.8

SOURCE: From *Trends in International Migration: Annual Report* (Paris: Organisation for Economic Co-operation and Development, 1998).

N.A. = not available.

in France and Germany after 1992. The rate of refugee acceptance in most countries has also dropped dramatically since the early 1990s. For example, in France the percentage of accepted applications declined by two-thirds between the early 1980s and early 1990s, and in Germany the acceptance rate dropped from 29 percent in 1985 to just over 4 percent in 1992. In the United States, humanitarian immigration increased in 1996 after declining from 1993 to 1995. Asylum applications also increased in the United Kingdom, rising in 1994, 1995, and 1997. Requests declined in 1996 after legislation denying government benefits to applicants was introduced. The increases in asylum applications in the United States and the United Kingdom may reflect the imposition of stricter policies in the other industrialized countries, especially France and Germany (Table 5.2).

Success in controlling immigration through the front door (that is, legal immigration) and side doors (mainly asylum seekers and refugees) resulted in increased backdoor, or illegal, immigration to meet continuing labor demands in these six countries. A significant number of employers rely on foreign workers to fill labor gaps, which serves as a powerful pull factor for illegal immigrants. In this context, it is more difficult to control population inflows, especially because employers are willing to risk penalties. Further, as employment-based illegal immigration rises, so too does the likelihood of increased illegal family-based immigration. As the industrialized countries, particularly in Europe, adopted more restrictive controls on legal and humanitarian immigration, backdoor points of entry became increasingly significant, as witnessed by the rising numbers of illegal immigrants in most countries. Thus, although most countries have had some success in controlling important aspects of their foreign population inflows, they generally are not effective in ending immigration, especially when illegal population inflows are considered.

Understanding Policy Reform

The case studies in this chapter indicate that the interaction of cultural, economic, political, and institutional variables is key to understanding immigration policy reform. If we begin with cultural variables, we see that countries that have not traditionally been countries of immigration (such as the United Kingdom) are more likely to impose restrictive immigration control policies than are countries that have always valued immigration (such as the United States). If there is no tradition of immigration to uphold or respect, fewer constraints are placed on policymakers to imposing harsh restrictions. In such countries (most notably the United Kingdom and Japan), the imposition of restrictive immigration measures is seen as a laudable effort to protect the country from the damaging social and economic effects of population inflows. In countries with traditions of immigration, especially the United States, supporters of continued population inflows have the upper hand in immigration policy making, and policies remain open and less restrictive. Even in these countries, however, the government is under increasing pressure to restrict flows, especially in areas where immigrants are concentrated and in times of economic contraction. Nonetheless, the government's responses to such pressures are not as extreme as those observed in countries that do not traditionally value immigration as part of their national heritage.

A county's approach to immigration policy reform is also related to the degree that its population demands stricter controls—the greater the popular outcry, the stricter the controls. Since the late 1980s citizens in industrialized countries, especially in Europe, are more highly mobilized around immigration control issues, in response to economic downturns and increasing numbers of immigrants in their countries. With the exception of the United States, the case studies show that citizens' demands for greater controls resulted in these countries developing new, more restrictive policy instruments (or, in the case of Japan, choosing not to respond to employers' demands for more foreign labor by relaxing strict controls). The United States is the only country where we observe a gap between public opinion and policymakers' actions, reflecting the ability of interest groups to influence the policy-making process.

We also see the effects of another cultural factor in our examination of these countries' reform efforts. In both France and the United States, liberal political values clearly influenced the policy-making process. In the United States, advocates of continued legal immigration into the country appealed to lawmakers on the grounds that denying immigrants access to the country would violate the United States' fundamental belief in protecting individuals' human rights and would violate the constitutional principle of nondiscrimination. In France, citizens protested the government's attempted implementation of its newly enacted immigration policies on the grounds that they were too harsh and went against the country's republican values. When such political values remain a strong element of the national psyche, they may have a significant impact on the nature of immigration policies.

As seen in the case studies, short-term economic conditions can play an important role in explaining immigration policy reform. Immigration policies tend to become stricter in times of economic difficulty. If a visible proportion of the citizenry blames immigrants for increased unemployment, job loss, and other economic ills, calls for stricter policies or opposition to relaxing policies may arise. For example, in Japan, concerns about declining economic growth and rising unemployment by the early 1990s made the Japanese population unreceptive to any increases in legal immigration to meet employers' demands for low-skilled workers. Restrictions on immigration also may follow significant increases in the number of new entrants, particularly when economic conditions are poor. This explains the German response to a surge in the number of asylum seekers in the early 1990s. Strict immigration control policies seem to be cyclical: They are more likely to be implemented when economic conditions are uncertain; when citizens feel less threatened (economically, culturally, or socially) by the foreign presence in their countries, pressure for stricter policies is less apparent.

In times of economic difficulty (especially when unemployment is high), immigrants tend to be treated poorly by the receiving population and are blamed for an array of social and economic problems, even when foreign workers are needed to maintain global economic competitiveness. This was clearly the case in the United States in 1996. In the European countries, a desire to reduce the size of the social welfare state, especially in an effort to reduce budget deficits in the lead-up to monetary union, also resulted in increased pressure to deny immigrants access to benefits. The tendency to treat immigrants as scapegoats for all of a society's ills creates a strong incentive for policymakers to adopt stricter controls, because a tougher stand on immigration has tended to pay off in electoral terms, particularly in regions where immigrants are concentrated.

Finally, political factors can have an important effect on immigration policy reforms. The existence of far-right parties in industrialized countries has a significant effect on the immigration policy-making process. Such parties may force reforms onto the institutional agenda (as in France), change the policy positions of more moderate mainstream parties (as in Italy or Germany), or both. An institutional factor also is influential here: The ability of right-wing parties to play a role in the policy process is affected by the country's type of electoral system. For example, such parties noticeably affected the policy process only in countries with proportional representation electoral systems. Such systems significantly increase the possibility of electoral success for these parties, which affects their overall credibility in the political system. The multiparty governments that proportional representation electoral systems often produce also create conditions in which right-wing parties may disrupt the policy-making process, even when they are not included in governing coalitions. This situation occurred in Italy, where more moderate members of the governing coalition were forced to agree to stricter policies advocated by other parties in the coalition. These other parties based their positions in part on the appeals of more right-wing parties in the country. In countries where right-wing parties play a role, the entire political climate becomes more anti-immigration, as parties of all political persuasions begin to favor tougher reforms.

The ability of interest groups to influence the political process was a key dimension of the policy decision-making stage only in the United States. Here, the central role of the legislature in U.S. policy decision making was critical. Because congressional decision making provides multiple points of access to policymakers, a well-organized and highly mobilized pro-immigration movement was able to shape policy outputs to fully satisfy their demands. Interest groups may also be able influence the policy process at the implementation stage, as was the French government's experience. In the other countries, interest groups, though they exist, were not integral to the policy reform process, beyond playing a role in agenda setting as part of a general public outcry for reform.

At the same time that the populations of most industrialized countries push for even stricter immigration controls, and political leaders cater to these demands, these countries are faced with many compelling reasons to continue and even increase immigration levels. First, many industrialized countries need immigrant labor to fill jobs their own populations are unwilling to take. Second, the increasing mobility of labor internationally, especially as a result of technological advances in travel and communication, makes it difficult to cut off immigrant flows entirely. International agreements and norms also increasingly compel countries to protect individual human rights, even when state sovereignty may be limited as a result. Finally, most countries also have made explicit commitments, often in their constitutions, to protect individual human rights. Strict immigration controls are argued to interfere with this commitment and often generate significant criticism and public outcry from those who defend human rights and democratic values.

SUGGESTED READINGS

Baldwin-Edwards, Martin, and Martin A. Schain. 1994. *The Politics of Immigration in Western Europe.* Newbury Park, U.K.: Frank Cass.

Bernstein, Ann, and Myron Weiner. 1999. *Migration and Refugee Policies: An Overview.* London: Pinter.

Brochman, Grete, and Tomas Hammar, eds. 1999. *Mechanisms of Immigration Control: A Comparative Analysis of European Regulation Policies.* Oxford: Berg Publishers.

Cornelius, Wayne, Philip Martin, and James Hollifield. 1994. *Controlling Immigration: A Global Perspective.* Stanford: Stanford University Press.

Chapin, Wesley. 1997. *Germany for the Germans? The Political Effects of International Migration.* Westport, Conn.: Greenwood Press.

Douglass, Mike, and Glenda Roberts, eds. 2000. *Japan and Global Migration.* London: Routledge.

Gimpel, James, and James Edwards. 1998. *The Congressional Politics of Immigration Control.* Boston: Allyn and Bacon.

Hargreaves, Alex. 1995. *Immigration, "Race" and Ethnicity in Contemporary France.* London: Routledge.

Hollifield, James. 1992. *Immigrants, Markets and States: The Political Economy of Immigration in Postwar Europe and the United States.* Cambridge: Harvard University Press.

Joppke, Christian, ed. 1998. *Challenge to the Nation-State: Immigration in Western Europe and the United States.* Oxford: Oxford University Press.

Miles, Robert. 1995. *Migration and European Integration: The Dynamics of Inclusion and Exclusion.* London: Pinter.

Papademetriou, Demetrios. 1996. *Converging Paths to Restriction: French, Italian and British Responses to Immigration.* Washington, D.C.: Carnegie Endowment for International Peace.

Spencer, Ian. 1997. *British Immigration Policy Since 1939: The Making of Multi-racial Britain.* London: Routledge.

Ucarer, Emek M., and Donald Puchala. 1997. *Immigration into Western Societies: Problems and Policies.* London: Pinter.

Weiner, Myron, and Tadashi Hanami. 1997. *Temporary Workers or Future Citizens? Japanese and U.S. Migration Policies.* New York: New York University Press.

Chapter 6 **Fiscal Policy**

Fiscal policy is perhaps the most fundamental macroeconomic policy pursued by governments. Fiscal decisions help to frame the national economic environment in which all residents operate. At the same time, decisions about the budget are also driven by policy considerations regarding all other issues considered by governments. Policymakers must make difficult decisions about which policies to pursue, how much to spend in each area, and how to pay for those policies. The sum total of that multitude of decisions is reflected in the government budget. Over the years, elected officials, budget analysts, and ordinary citizens have debated the consequences of running budget deficits. During the middle portion of the twentieth century, budget deficits became increasingly common in industrialized countries. During the 1980s and especially during the 1990s, a variety of public officials, interest groups, and private citizens placed deficit reduction in a highly visible place on the systemic and institutional agendas of industrialized countries.

Common Policy Problems

In the twentieth century, governments (democratic and nondemocratic alike) face a core problem that has implications for all their decisions: Ideally the citizenry as a whole would like to receive more services from the government than they are willing to pay for in taxes. If the assumption about public desires is correct, governments will feel some pressure to run a budget **deficit.** When governments spend more money than they take in, they must borrow money to cover the deficit. In most countries—including the six examined in this book—some degree of deficit spending has been common for decades.

The idea of deficit spending would have seemed ridiculous in the nineteenth century. Government leaders and economic experts of the day preached the importance of running a budget **surplus.** This approach was politically more feasible back then given limited political participation. In most democracies only a minority of the total adult population could vote and many other countries did not have democratic political systems. In the era before radio and television, print news media dominated the coverage of public policy and only a minority of the population was literate. In this context, governments typically intervened in fewer policy areas and in a more limited way. A fiscal surplus was seen as virtually synonymous with sound government. Budget deficits often were incurred during wartime, but surpluses were the order of the day during peacetime.

In the first half of the twentieth century, particularly during the Great Depression, governments ventured into the world of prolonged deficit spending in peacetime. John Maynard Keynes and other economists began to argue that deficit spending was a policy tool that governments could use to help the economy grow out of tough times. **Keynesianism** as a school of economic thought became a watchword for governments for the rest of the century. A core element of Keynesian thought is that no fiscal policy is universally desirable under all circumstances. Instead, fiscal policy decisions should be made to react to the state of the economy as a whole. In general, if the economy is contracting, governments should consider deficit spending as a fiscal stimulus designed to shorten the recession. If the economy is growing so quickly that inflationary pressures may result, governments should consider running surpluses (or at least smaller deficits) to deflate the economy. As a result of the influence of Keynesianism, such **countercyclical fiscal policies** are used to smooth out the performance of the economy.

The rise of Keynesianism also met the pressure of the postwar political environment, in which citizens placed increasing demands on government. Deficit spending could be used to escape hard economic times as well as to resolve the imbalance between demands for government services and people's willingness to pay taxes. Fiscal conservatives tied to the nineteenth-century push for budget surpluses argued that deficit spending would bring national economic ruin. However, when industrialized economies did not collapse in the face of prolonged deficits during the Depression and afterward, opponents of deficit spending seemed less persuasive. The gloom they associated with prolonged deficits of any size did not appear to materialize.

The use of deficit spending to solve these two problems (escaping a recession and handling the political pressure toward deficits) generates a third problem in fiscal policy: How big of a deficit is too big? The whole concept of deficit spending is based on borrowing money to cover the deficit. This need to borrow implies that government deficits cannot get so big that government creditworthiness is lost. If that were to happen, the health of the entire economy—and, hence, the political health of the government—would be seriously challenged.

Another potential problem is raised by the **supply-side school** of economics that emerged to challenge the Keynesian perspective in fiscal policy. Supply-siders argue that prolonged deficits have insidious effects even before a country's creditworthiness collapses. They believe that prolonged budget deficits (and the expansion of government more generally) serve as a drag on the private sector because government borrowing and wasteful government spending soak up financial resources. Supply-siders assert that this money could be used more productively if it remained in private hands.

Major Policy Options

When governments run budget deficits, they must borrow money to cover the excess of expenses over revenues. Like a private citizen, a government can simply go to the bank and ask for a loan. The government can negotiate over the amount of money lent, the length of time over which the loan will be paid back, the interest rate, and other loan provisions.

In addition to contracting loans from banks, governments can also sell **government bonds.** The government offers bonds for sale to cover a certain amount (perhaps all) of its fiscal shortfall. The bond is still basically a loan. Investors pay the government today, and the government agrees to pay back the value of the bond plus interest over a period of time. Bonds have some advantages over loans, however. First, the government can attempt to set a similar set of conditions on its borrowing from multiple sources without engaging in negotiations with each lender. This holds true provided that enough investors are willing to purchase bonds under the terms offered by the government. Second, by selling bonds, the government is able to borrow funds from a variety of sources—large and small—rather than simply from the banking community. Banks, investment firms, foreign governments, businesses, and private citizens are all potential purchasers of bonds. Finally, bonds—in contrast to loans—often postpone all interest payments until the end of the bond term.

The **national debt** is the sum total of future financial obligations incurred by a government (by both loans and bond payments owed). Interest and principal payments on the debt become an additional stream of expenses that the budget must cover every year. In other words, current deficits can lead to future deficits because this year's shortfall becomes next year's **debt service.** Debt service refers to the interest and principal payments made on the debt.

A desire to avoid collecting revenues today to cover yesterday's expenses is a major motivation cited by proponents of a balanced budget. Opponents of deficit spending also claim that government borrowing is a drag on the economy because the government attracts capital that might otherwise go to more productive use. The truth of this assertion rests on two assumptions that may or may not hold true: (1) that this money would indeed have been lent to others and (2) that money lent to the government will be used less productively than money lent elsewhere.

Conversely, others claim that governments can run budget deficits indefinitely with no substantial negative effects on the economy provided that they retain sufficient creditworthiness. In this view, the deficit and the debt are only problems when people believe that the government will not make good on its obligations. When this happens, the government will either be forced to borrow money at exorbitant interest rates in excess of current market levels or, in a worst-case scenario, find it hard to borrow money under any terms whatsoever. To avoid this scenario, governments need to pay their debts on time. See

Box 6-1 **In Depth: A Tale of Two Deficits**

In 1994 the U. S. government ran a budget deficit of $203 billion—equal to 2.3 percent of its gross domestic product (GDP). In that same year, the public debt of $4.6 trillion represented 68 percent of the GDP. In response to these and other financial developments, the U.S. Federal Reserve Bank did not face a run on the dollar. In fact, during 1994, foreign currency reserves in defense of the dollar rose slightly.

That same year, the Mexican government ran a budget deficit equal to 0.1 percent of its GDP. The public debt rose to 58 percent of the GDP. In response to these and other financial developments, the Mexican central bank spent 75 percent of its foreign reserves in defense of the value of the peso. When news of the reserve depletion became public in December 1994, the peso lost half of its value against the dollar.

Why did a smaller budget deficit in Mexico spark a crisis of confidence whereas a larger deficit in the United States caused no noticeable problems? Part of the difference stems from the trends underlying the two deficits. The U.S. deficit in 1994 marked the second straight year of decline following the record $290 billion deficit in 1992. Conversely, Mexico ran a large surplus of 3.1 percent in 1992 and then ran a much smaller one (0.7 percent of the GDP) in 1993. Also, the Mexican government faced greater doubts about its creditworthiness because it had defaulted on several of its financial obligations in 1982.

The moral of the story is that the perception of a deficit is the true driving force that distinguishes a deficit from a deficit crisis. If, for various reasons, many people and firms active in financial markets lose confidence in the government's ability to defend its currency or to meet its financial obligations, the deficit can be considered an indicator of a crisis and trigger a series of problems. Larger deficits, viewed in light of past credit history and other factors, may not be perceived as cause for concern. A crisis is in the eye of the beholder.

Box 6.1 for a look at how the negative impact of budget deficits is tied to perceptions of the government's creditworthiness.

Proponents of fiscal restraint are not as optimistic about the effects of chronic budget deficits and rising national debts. They believe large debts or deficits may lead to higher interest rates—thereby slowing economic growth. A large debt—relative to the size of the economy and the government's creditworthiness—may also generate greater speculation against the national currency. As a remedy to this scenario, supply-side economists recommend dramatic cuts in both government spending and taxes. Supply-siders argue that this course of action should increase economic activity, thereby increasing economic growth (and partially compensating for government revenues lost in the tax-rate cuts).

Although experts differ over the nature of the negative consequences of chronic budget deficits and disagree about the precise threshold at which deficits or debts become highly problematic, few would recommend that governments run chronic deficits in excess of 10 percent of the gross domestic product (GDP). Indeed, many analysts assert that a deficit nearing 3–5 percent of the GDP should serve as a clarion call for greater fiscal restraint. When such fiscal restraint is called for, how can governments reduce the deficit?

Simply put, governments can reduce the deficit by raising revenues, by reducing spending, or by a combination of the two. In the rest of this chapter we examine the dynamics of choices made about spending. In Chapter 7 we take a look at how countries raise revenues.

Explaining Policy Dynamics

In this chapter we focus on the issue of budget deficits. Under what conditions are governments more likely to run budget deficits? The study of budget deficits has relied on a mixture of cross-national statistical analyses (often conducted by economists) and comparative case studies of particular budgetary decisions. Here we review four major sets of potential explanations: cultural, economic, political, and institutional. Along the way you will see the complex web of factors that can influence the final balance sheet of public finances.

Cultural Explanations

Cultural factors have been offered as one explanation for deficit spending choices in the postwar era. One school of thought has been characterized as the something for nothing phenomenon (Sears and Citrin 1985). This notion emerges from public opinion research posing separate questions about government spending and taxation. If we look at polling data on spending, a majority of citizens in most industrialized countries support increased spending for a variety of specific purposes. At the same time, responding to questions on the general level of taxation, majorities oppose tax increases and many assert further that taxes should be cut (Hadenius 1985). The polling data on these sorts of questions have been so stable over the years that they have helped to fuel in the media the notion that policymakers face a nearly impossible task: They must always provide more government services without increasing government revenues.

Another body of research has responded to the something for nothing thesis by arguing that citizens' individual opinions are not as selfishly inconsistent as the general polling trends indicate (Confalonieri and Newton 1995; Peters 1991; Welch 1985). When citizens are asked more detailed questions—for example, asking them to respond to tradeoffs between spending, taxation, and deficits—their answers are not as contradictory as their responses to isolated questions might imply. Peters concludes that "citizens have demonstrated that they are not really as naïve about public finance as is sometimes assumed. Most citizens appear to recognize that if they want more services they will have to pay for them through taxes" (1991: 160). Perhaps the most detailed examination of these issues to date analyzed U.S. opinions on twelve budgetary tradeoffs between deficit levels, domestic spending, defense spending, and taxation (Hansen 1998). Hansen found that 40 percent of citizens had entirely uncontradictory opinions across the twelve fiscal questions, and another 40 percent had only one opinion inconsistent with some of their other answers. Although this finding would need to be supported by similarly detailed research in other industrialized countries, it suggests that the something for nothing paradox emerges because citizens are asked the questions about spending and taxation in isolation from one another. Yes, citizens ideally prefer more services to fewer, and lower taxes to higher taxes. Nevertheless, people can and do recognize the tradeoffs involved when asked to do so in public opinion research.

Economic Explanations

Short-term economic conditions have been central influences on annual budget deficits. Generally speaking, the healthier the economy, the lower the deficit and vice versa. Grilli, Masciandaro, and Tabellini (1991), among others, demonstrated that changes in economic growth rates, interest rates, and unemployment rates all have a significant effect on budget deficits. First, if the economic growth rate increases from one year to the next, this tends to reduce deficits—provided that policymakers did not already anticipate all of the economic expansion in making expenditure decisions and revenue predictions for that fiscal year.

As we noted in Chapter 2, that same dynamic can cut the other way in an economic recession. First, decreases in economic growth tend to increase deficits because the drop in economic activity reduces tax revenues coming into public coffers. Second, if interest rates increase, the cost of financing the existing public debt within the annual budget goes up. This pushes deficits upward unless policymakers account for the increased costs of debt service. The higher the public debt, the more vulnerable annual budgets are to spikes in interest rates. This relationship demonstrates one of the costs passed on by past deficit spending to future governments: Those future policymakers find it more difficult to steer a sound fiscal course. Third, increases in unemployment rates tend to generate higher deficits. Rising unemployment tends to put more demand on a variety of government services—unemployment insurance, poverty relief programs, and the like. This increased demand for government spending due to higher unemployment usually occurs with no compensating rise in economic growth that would generate more revenues to pay for those higher expenditures.

This discussion of short-term economic influences on fiscal policy demonstrates the climate of uncertainty in which fiscal policy decisions are made. Government budget proposals total the expenditures and revenues and project a deficit or surplus; however, it is a projection. Although many of the line items on the public budget are fixed levels of expenditures, the majority are projections of expenditures for varied government activities: debt service, so-called entitlement programs (health care, pensions, poverty relief programs, unemployment insurance), and other areas of public policy where expenditures may exceed projections due to unforeseen circumstances (such as defense policy, environmental clean-up, and relief for natural disasters). As we discuss in Chapter 7, tax revenues are almost entirely projections tied to the level of economic activity in the coming year. If economic growth exceeds projections, deficits will tend to be smaller than projected and vice versa. Accordingly, when we analyze fiscal policy decisions, we must recognize that fiscal policymakers are piloting a sailboat. They can chart a course to certain fiscal outcomes, but unfavorable economic winds sometimes force them to reach their final goal more slowly than anticipated. Conversely, an unusually favorable economic climate can do wonders for fiscal policy fortunes.

International financial markets form another economic influence on fiscal policies. Financial markets have long had a possible influence on fiscal policies because high deficits can create a crisis of confidence in the financial community at home and abroad. Technological changes and rising globalization, however, have caused some analysts to give this factor a higher profile today (Yergin and Stanislaw 1998). During the 1980s and 1990s one can observe a quantum leap in the size of the currency market, in the speed with which it operates, and in the information flows provided by the Internet. In 1986 the normal daily volume of foreign currency transactions was less than $200 billion; that figure increased to well over $1.2 trillion by 1997. Trading is a non-stop enterprise because financial transactions can now be made instantaneously in major trading venues around the clock—beginning with Japan, moving on through European markets, and ending the day in the United States. Worldwide television news and the Internet provide a constant stream of information for financial analysts. Professional traders abroad can track national economic and governmental developments just as quickly as their counterparts in other countries. Even if the prospect of a devastating run on currencies is more remote in industrialized countries than in smaller, poorer economies (such as occurred in the Asian financial crisis of 1997), the governments of industrialized countries strive to maintain the confidence of investors around the globe as part of their overall economic strategy.

Political Explanations

Political factors have also been prevalent in explanations of deficit spending. Some studies (for example, Hicks and Swank 1992) focus on the political ideology of the governing party (or coalition of parties). The partisanship thesis, simply put, is that rightist governments are more likely to run lower deficits than are center-left governments. This difference based on the partisan control of the government has two potential sources. First, rightist parties are more likely to campaign against the expansion of government activity. If followed, this position reduces one potential source of deficit spending—expansion of spending. Rightist parties are also more likely to have leaders (and economic advisers) who are more sensitive to the potential economic problems associated with deficits. Conversely, leftist and centrist parties are more likely to have an ideology and a voting base that support a visible expansion of government action. Although the drive to expand government need not increase deficits (as long as revenues rise accordingly), it creates more potential for deficits than does a steady-state position on expenditures. Support for the status quo on spending will not increase deficits unless revenues drop. Although Hicks and Swank demonstrated a relationship between ideology and public expenditures, Cowart (1978) found no significant relationship between partisan control of the government and budget deficits. Cowart's analysis of the 1960s and early 1970s found that center-left and leftist governments tended to fund government expansion by riding the tide of steady economic growth, by raising tax rates, or both. Similarly, Hahm, Kamlet, and Mowery (1996) found little support for the partisanship argument in their study of deficits in nine industrialized countries from 1958 to 1990.

The unity of the governing party or coalition is another political factor that could influence fiscal deficits. Roubini and Sachs (1989) are most associated with what they call the strength of government thesis (a variant on the party government model discussed in Chapters 2 and 3). They argue that multiparty coalition governments (those with more than two parties represented in the cabinet) tend to run higher deficits because they paper over their policy differences with deficit spending. Conversely, single-party governments and coalition governments dominated by a single major party find it easier to say no to deficit spending because of their greater cohesiveness. The difficulty that multiparty coalitions in Italy faced in reducing the growth in the national debt is often cited as an example of how diverse governing coalitions can come to rely on deficit spending as a means to deal with conflicts over priorities.

Institutional Explanations

Perhaps in an effort to provide some shelter from political demands, some countries have chosen to create institutions that place greater authority for fiscal policy in the hands of the finance ministry. Hahm, Kamlet, and Mowery (1996) focus on three dimensions of bureaucratic strength in fiscal matters: centralization, dominance, and quasi-independence. Centralization refers to the unification of most or all responsibility for fiscal policy formulation in a single ministry. A second, related issue is the power that the finance ministry has after the initial budget proposal is formulated and circulated within the executive branch. A dominant finance ministry can have a veto over additional spending requests from other ministries. Weaker finance ministries might be forced to arbitrate in conjunction with the office of the chief executive. The least dominant finance ministries might simply be viewed as first among equals in the final stages of the budget formulation process. The third dimension of bureaucratic strength lies in the independence of the employees of the finance ministry. The finance ministry's power is enhanced when most of its analysts have permanent civil service protection, which makes firing them difficult. Conversely, the higher the percentage of political appointees in the ministry and the weaker the civil service laws, the weaker the bureaucracy becomes.

The logic of this explanation focuses on two aspects of stronger finance ministries that would tend to reduce deficits. First, centralization and dominance limit access to fiscal decisions. These limits reduce the demands to approve spending above the level of revenues. Second, the greater the independence of the ministry, the more likely that the core employees can distance themselves from the world of political demands faced in other ministries. Although other ministries' prestige is enhanced by a growth in the size of their programs, the prestige of the finance ministry (in the eyes of bureaucrats and the international financial community) is more likely to be enhanced by riding herd over deficit spending demands coming from other sectors of the government (Pempel 1992).

International Policy Making

Three of the six countries examined in this book have made an international pledge to run small budget deficits as a percentage of their GDPs. At present, thirteen of the fifteen member states of the European Union (EU) have committed themselves to considerable fiscal restraint as part of the effort to create a common single currency. The United Kingdom (along with Denmark) retains the option to participate in monetary unification should it decide to do so. Accordingly, France, Germany, and Italy worked hard in the 1990s to meet this fiscal target in order to achieve the stated goal of monetary unification.

The following formal targets were set for admission to the euro zone:

- an annual budget deficit below 3 percent of the GDP
- an inflation rate within 1.5 percentage points of the average rate in the three member states with the lowest inflation
- long-term interest rates within 2 percentage points of the average rate in the three member states with the lowest inflation
- an exchange rate with a fairly stable relationship to the euro
- a public debt of less than 60 percent of the GDP

Box 6-2 **In Depth: The Race to the Euro**

At the beginning of 1996, just two years prior to the selection of participants in the launch of the euro, only one of the thirteen European countries pledged to participate met all five of the economic criteria for inclusion—Luxembourg. Italy had not met any of the targets. Most countries were in compliance with the goals for inflation, exchange rate stability, and interest rates. However, all countries except for Luxembourg and France had public debts in excess of 60 percent of the GDP and all but Luxembourg and Ireland had failed to meet the budget deficit guideline of 3 percent of the GDP.

To make matters even more dramatic, only Germany's budget deficit was fairly close to the target (at 3.3 percent). All other countries' deficits were at or above 4 percent. Finland, Greece, Italy, the Netherlands, Portugal, Spain, and Sweden all ran deficits above 5 percent. All eyes turned to fiscal policy in 1996 and 1997 as countries worked to meet the target in 1997. The race to the euro fueled a visible reduction in budget deficits throughout Europe, including the two EU countries not pledged to participate (Denmark and the United Kingdom). Through a variety of fiscal measures, all countries but Greece managed to meet the target in 1997.

Many of the countries that pledged to join the euro zone had to make tremendous strides to meet these criteria (Box 6.2).[1] Indeed, several came up short in at least one area—usually with a public debt above the target. However, in May 1998, eleven of the thirteen participating EU member states were deemed to have met enough of the macroeconomic targets to adopt a common currency, the euro, in January 1999.

The push toward monetary unification has had serious implications for fiscal policy in EU member states and has had somewhat of a ripple effect on other countries outside the euro zone. During the 1990s the EU's public commitment to monetary unification led countries to take firm steps to achieve the fiscal target of a deficit no higher than 3 percent of the GDP. Because some of these countries had higher deficits than others at the start of the decade, the deficit reduction effort posed serious political and economic challenges. Monetary unification continued to generate pressure for low deficits in the late 1990s and beyond. EU guidelines established in the Stability and Growth Pact (SGP) of December 1996 require countries participating in monetary unification to maintain relatively harmonious fiscal policies and sug-

---

[1]Government expenditure statistics are taken from the International Monetary Fund's *Government Finance Statistics Yearbook 1999* (Washington, D.C.: IMF, 1999). Deficit statistics and macroeconomic statistics on growth, unemployment, and inflation are from OECD (2000).

gest that countries aim to have balanced budgets. In particular, the pact retains the deficit ceiling of no more than 3 percent of the GDP unless the deficit is a product of a recession or an exceptional, unforeseeable event beyond the member state's control. Violation of this policy (or of targets for the public debt-to-GDP ratio) can lead to sanctions. With the SGP in place, the shadow of monetary unification over fiscal policy is not going away in the foreseeable future.

United States

Background: Policy Process and Policy History

More than any of the six countries examined in this book, the United States has a decidedly pluralist fiscal policy process. These procedural differences have their roots in differences in core governing institutions as defined by the constitution; however, the major distinction is not the constitutional provision requiring fiscal policy to be controlled by the legislature. Instead, what makes the ultimate enactment of budget legislation potentially more difficult (and usually more time consuming) in the United States than in the other countries is the presidential system of executive-legislative relations. As we will see in the other five case studies, in parliamentary systems the governing party (or coalition) controls both the executive and legislative branches. This arrangement streamlines the fiscal policy formulation and decision-making processes by giving the executive branch the lead role in formulation and a stronger set of tools with which to negotiate legislative approval of many elements of the draft budget. In the Italian and Japanese systems, the existence of more fractionalized political parties that support the executive branch often leads to a process that involved more negotiation and more revisions than in France, Germany, and the United Kingdom. In the United States, however, the process is even more decidedly decentralized than in Italy and Japan.

As in other countries, the budget formation process in the United States originates in the executive branch, centered in the Office of Management and Budget (OMB). The OMB prepares the budget proposal, after receiving direction from the president and consulting with presidential senior advisers and officials from cabinet departments and other government agencies. After formulating a budget, the president presents it to the legislature. At this point the U.S. process begins to diverge markedly from that found in other countries.

After the legislature receives the budget proposal, the locus of activity shifts markedly to Congress. Members of both houses of the legislature first pass a budget resolution that guides legislative committees as they make their decisions about spending and taxes. This resolution includes targets for expenditures and revenues, and allocations within the spending targets for discretionary and mandatory expenditures. Mandatory expenditures required by existing legislation currently make up about two-thirds of all spending. The rest of the budget's discretionary spending is determined by thirteen separate annual appropriations bills that fund most ongoing government programs that are not formula-driven entitlements. Procedures in place since the 1986 Gramm-Rudman budget reforms put a firm cap on total discretionary spending through 2002. In addition the 1986 law requires legislation that would raise mandatory spending or lower revenues (relative to existing law) to be offset by revenue increases or spending cuts. This requirement (often called pay-as-you-go or paygo) is intended to prevent new legislation from increasing the deficit.

Congress begins to decide on discretionary appropriations bills by examining the president's budget in detail. Committees and subcommittees hold hearings on appropriations proposals under their jurisdiction. These hearings and informal meetings provide opportunities for interest groups and agencies to debate budgetary priorities in different sectors. If the president's budget calls for changes in taxes, the House Ways and Means Committee and the Senate Finance Committee would need to hold hearings on the matter. The budget director, cabinet officers, and other executive branch officials work with Congress to try to maintain what the executive branch views as key elements of the president's initial proposal. In the end, these complex negotiations must produce a budget agreement in both houses of the legislature that will not be vetoed by the president. As we noted in Chapter 4, a presidential veto can be overridden only by a two-thirds majority. Congress has ample opportunity to inject many of its own priorities into the budget, but serious departure from presidential priorities runs the risk of a veto. As a result, although the U.S. legislature plays a much larger role in fiscal policy than in other countries, the presidential veto enables the chief executive to generate a meaningful role in the process even when Congress is controlled by a different party.

The dollar's position as the world's major reference currency gives the United States a comparatively privileged position in the realm of deficit financing. International confidence in the dollar helps to expand the market for dollar-denominated bonds in both domestic and foreign capital markets. The U.S. government traditionally relies predominantly on long-term bonds.

The United States entered the 1990s on an economic upswing. Seven years of steady growth, from 1983 to 1989, combined with restrained spending in the late 1980s (especially in social security and welfare), reduced a budget deficit that had increased to over 3 percent of the GDP in the mid-1980s (for the first time in peacetime). By 1989 the deficit was around 2 percent.

In the early 1990s a combination of diverse factors renewed the focus on deficit reduction in the nation's political debate. Slower growth in 1990 and a recession in 1991 cut into government revenues while government spending grew rapidly in 1991 owing to a combination of Gulf War expenses and a fiscal stimulus designed to speed recovery from recession prior to the 1992 elections. By 1992, deficit reduction had returned to the attention of policymakers.

Contemporary Dynamics

In the 1992 elections, held while the budget deficit was on the rise, business executive Ross Perot ran a popular third-party campaign for the presidency that focused on deficit reduction as the nation's highest priority. The popularity of that position among a substantial minority of voters helped return the issue to the forefront of debate within the Democratic and Republican Parties. Deficit reduction had returned to the upper tier of the institutional agenda for the first time since the mid-1980s.

A variety of fiscally conservative Republicans called for deeper cuts in spending to achieve a balanced budget. Some Republicans argued further that the political will to do so could be achieved via a constitutional amendment requiring a balanced budget. Critics of the measure claimed that such an amendment, if followed, would place the country in an undesirable fiscal straitjacket and, if not followed, would clearly not achieve its objective. Two major efforts to gain legislative approval for the amendment were blocked in the Senate. In contrast, the Clinton administration (victor in the 1992 elections) argued that a few targeted tax increases and a steady monetary and expenditure policy could eliminate the deficit. This message contrasted with the words and actions of many fellow Democrats in the legislature who had numerous (and at times conflicting) programs they wanted to create or expand. Business interest groups tended to line up with Republicans calling for tax cuts, whereas labor tended to side with the Democrats.

In this tumultuous climate, the first Clinton budget barely made it through a Democratically controlled legislature; it passed the Senate only via a tie-breaking vote cast by Vice President Al Gore. Subsequent budgetary decision making grew even more conflictual when the Republican Party won control of both legislative chambers in 1994. Through the rest of the decade, fiscal decision making remained a drawn-out process in which Clinton used his popularity in public opinion polls and the occasional veto threat to influence the Republican majority in the legislature. Clinton made clear his resolve to stay active in fiscal policy when he permitted congressional Republicans to shut down the federal government for lack of funds in the budget battle of winter 1995–1996. The success of that tactic (or, conversely, the failure of the Republican threat once carried out) helped Clinton to remain an important player in fiscal policy making in his second term, even as Republicans retained control of the legislature. The Balanced Budget Act of 1997 represented a series of drawn-out compromises between the Clinton administration and Congress as well as a series of provisions appealing to factions within each party in the legislature.

Fiscal policy in the United States contains more potential implementation problems than in other countries because of the divided nature of government. The executive branch can use its control over the implementation of programs to create a set of priorities more to its liking and less like what an opposition-controlled legislature might have intended. By the same token, legislative appropriations committees have the power to block funds to projects favored by the president or the president's party. These sorts of actions could be carried out in any political system, but they are far more common in presidential systems where the executive and legislative branches may be dominated by different parties.

What is on the fiscal horizon for the United States? In 2000 the country entered its ninth consecutive year of sustained economic growth with comparatively low inflation and unemployment. This circumstance of prolonged growth, combined with the tax increases from the first Clinton term, led to the elimination of the budget deficit in 1998. When a fairly sizable surplus was predicted for 1999, the two main parties returned to familiar themes regarding how to treat the surplus. The Democratic Party called for the strengthening of the Medicare and Social Security programs and a host of small new initiatives, whereas many in the Republican Party spoke of tax cuts and the need to increase defense spending for the first time in over a decade. With a dwindling Republican majority in the legislature and the end of a two-term Democratic presidency, the 2000 elections will constitute a vigorously fought battle. The willingness of either side to give up its major themes in the coming budgets may prove limited. This is perhaps most true for a Republican Party that was strongly criticized within its own ranks for failing to insist on federal tax cuts in the 1998 budget process.

The visible conflict in the U.S. budgetary process demonstrates the impact that a presidential system can have on fiscal policy making. The president tries to set the fiscal agenda but faces a lot of competition: conflicting voices from fellow party members in the legislature and the distinct possibility of a legislature controlled by the opposition. We can see the relative weakness of the president in the extreme difficulty the Clinton administration had in shepherding the majority of its first budget through the legislature, which was controlled by Clinton's own party. The U.S. position regarding the party government model does not clear the path for quick responsiveness in fiscal policy. That difficulty is perhaps an even more telling comment on fiscal policy making in presidential systems than were the highly charged, partisan budget battles of the mid-1990s with a Republican-led Congress.

The elimination of the deficit in the late 1990s is also a testimony to the role of economic factors. Nine years of steady economic expansion, stable inflation rates, declining interest rates, and declining unemployment rates have played a considerable role in paving the way for the current budget surplus. In the future, one should ask not whether the deficit will return during the next economic slowdown but rather how much of a deficit can, should, and will be tolerated by government decision makers.

Japan

Background: Policy Process and Policy History

As in the United States, the budget process in Japan has tended to be more pluralist than in most major European economies in that a wider variety of forces participate actively in the process. While top Ministry of Finance officials generate the framework estimates for the new budget, the Budget Bureau of the ministry examines requests compiled by all ministries and agencies. As the Ministry of Finance puts the finishing touches on the draft budget, representatives from the different ministries and individual legislators from the governing coalition in the Diet begin to lobby the drafters for additional resources. Ultimately disputes are arbitrated in meetings between the Ministry of Finance and the leaders of major coalition partners (and party factions within those partners) to generate support for passage of the budget in the Diet.

Deficit financing was not a major policy issue in Japan in the late 1980s and early 1990s. Japan's comparatively limited needs for deficit financing, combined with a continued strong economic reputation, made it fairly easy to market long-term bonds. The country relies largely on domestic financing.

Japan began the 1990s in an enviable position. From 1985 to 1989, the economy grew at an annual rate of 4.5 percent. Average annual inflation (1.1 percent) and unemployment (2.6 percent) were low. To complete the picture, from 1987 to 1989 the country ran budget surpluses; in 1989 the surplus reached 2.5 percent of the GDP. Although some industrialized countries also experienced several favorable conditions in the late 1980s, none of the other large economies enjoyed such desirable outcomes on all four of these macroeconomic indicators.

At home, this solid outlook fueled a debate over new government programs designed to improve living conditions for those left behind by certain aspects of the Japanese economic miracle. Abroad, Japan's reputation as an economic juggernaut in many international circles continued to grow. In 1990 and 1991, the good times continued as the Japanese economy grew at 4.5 percent annually, even as other major economies entered economic downturns.

In 1992, however, things began to change. An overheated domestic investment market (in both real estate and stocks and bonds) lost a significant amount of its value. In turn, a stronger national currency began to reduce the competitive advantage of many Japanese exporters. Growth slowed to 1.0 percent in 1992. From 1993 to 1995 the economy remained stagnant—growing at around 1 percent per year. This slower growth—which continued despite a fiscal stimulus in 1993 and 1994 that was designed to spark a recovery—ended the run of budget surpluses. By 1995 Japan's budget deficit topped 3 percent of the GDP for the first time since 1983.

In the mid-1990s Japan's economy entered a period of stagnation that it has not fully escaped as of this writing. Although unemployment remains much lower than in most other industrialized countries, it has doubled over the past six years to reach 4.7 percent in 1999. Japan today faces a series of policy tradeoffs that had perhaps faded from view in the late 1980s. The days of Japan's stature as an unstoppable economic machine are at an end.

Contemporary Dynamics

During the boom of the late 1980s and early 1990s, the Japanese government generally succeeded in holding the growth in expenditures below the GDP growth rate. During this period the government managed to bring the budget into balance without issuing special deficit financing bonds for the first time in well over a decade. By 1992–1993 an economic slowdown put a fiscal stimulus back on the institutional agenda. In 1993, when the economy slowed, the government attempted a fiscal stimulus as it increased real spending by over 10 percent. All sectors but defense received substantial real increases; housing and health care experienced the greatest increases. When those actions failed to revive the economy, the debate over what sort of stimulus was needed or desirable was at the top of the agenda.

In 1994 the debate over fiscal policy was conducted in an atmosphere of political and economic uncertainty. A series of unstable coalition governments—the first governments not led by the Liberal Democratic Party (LDP) in nearly forty years—debated how to revive the economy. The new parties in power and the LDP shared a desire to use a mix of spending increases and tax cuts as a stimulus, but they disagreed over the precise mix of the stimulus. With large coalition governments serving as the order of the day (the Hosokawa government initially formed out of an eight-party coalition in late 1993), the budget bargaining was intense as new parties tried to spend money to reward their supporters. The Ministry of Finance (dominated by officials with long-standing ties to the LDP and with a belief in maintaining traditional spending priorities) worried that an excessive spending stimulus would lead to a budget deficit problem. Some elements of the LDP and some of the new parties formed out of the LDP shared this concern and backed the Ministry of Finance in its call for a rise in the consumption tax to back the continued increases in spending being discussed. This tax increase occurred in the face of opposition from the major labor confederations, which argued against any sales tax increase because it would fall disproportionately on low-income people.

The dynamics of the multiparty coalition played a considerable role in the collapse of the Hosokawa government at the decision-making stage: The government passed political reform but broke apart in negotiations over the budget and other economic policy matters. Eventually the Ministry of Finance position won out in the new Murayama government, in which the Social Democrats held the prime minister post but the LDP held the balance of power. Many LDP parliamentary leaders have served in the Ministry of Finance; those who have not still have many close relationships with senior officials. The end result was a compromise tilted toward the position of the Ministry of Finance. Spending increases in public works and a temporary cut in the individual income tax provided a fiscal stimulus. At the same time, a delayed increase in the consumption tax was adopted in the name of fiscal responsibility. The dominance of the LDP in the Murayama government was perhaps most evident in the November 1994 budget vote in which Social Democrats approved a delayed increase in the consumption tax that their party had historically opposed because of its regressive nature (that is, it tends to tax the poor more than the rich). We examine taxation issues in greater detail in Chapter 7.

Upon implementation, these fiscal decisions did not have as immediate an impact as the government might have hoped. In 1993 and 1994 the economy grew at 0.3 and 0.6 percent, respectively. Eventually the initial stimulus, combined with a devaluation of the yen on the international market, helped to restore growth to over 5 percent in 1996. However, when the rise in the consumption tax was implemented as planned in early 1997, the economy sputtered again, achieving negligible growth. The call for more permanent tax cuts and the abolition of the consumption tax hike were visible elements of the public agenda in the late 1990s.

The fiscal policy-making dynamics in contemporary Japan illustrate the difficulties of steering a clear policy path in troubled political waters. The major fiscal policy reform of 1994 produced a mixed bag of contradictory initiatives designed to please different elements of the weak governing coalition. Although a weak coalition government was in place, the government's lack of strength did not produce as large a deficit as one might think. What else was working to influence fiscal policy?

One possible explanation relies on bureaucratic politics. The 1994 reform also demonstrates that the permanent bureaucracy's role can be heightened when governments rise and fall with major shifts in the cabinet. This cabinet instability increased the latitude given to an already powerful Ministry of Finance. Many finance officials feared being forced to sell too many government bonds in a financial system whose bubble burst in the early 1990s. The weakness of the governing coalitions and the strength of the fiscal bureaucracy help us to understand the difficulty elected officials had in moving quickly to increase deficit spending to escape the stagnation of the 1990s.

Germany

Background: Policy Process and Policy History

The German budget formulation process is more centralized than in the United States or Japan. This greater centralization stems partly from more disciplined political parties and partly from more centralized formal government procedures. The chancellor sets a general fiscal target in consultation with a variety of actors. At that point, the chancellor delegates much of the remainder of the formulation process to the finance minister. The finance minister can veto any calls for expenditures that exceed the targets outlined by the chief executive but does not normally act alone in ratifying additional increases. Ultimately any troubling disputes are arbitrated between the chancellor, the finance minister, and senior figures in the governing coalition to ensure passage of the budget in the legislature. The Budget Committee in the Bundestag usually works closely with Finance Ministry officials in reviewing the budget proposal. Legislative activism in the budget-making process is further constrained by two additional procedures. First, any additional spending proposals made in the Bundestag must contain a proposal for a revenue source. Second, the executive branch retains a legislatively mandated veto over any spending increases authorized by the legislature that were not in the government's draft budget. The total effect of these procedures is to limit the role of the legislature to that of a brainstorming second opinion on spending decisions.

In the late 1980s Germany financed its small deficits via a mix of domestic and foreign sources. As Germany's financing needs grew in the 1990s, the country increased greatly the percentage of foreign financing. Throughout the 1980s and 1990s, Germany has managed to finance its shortfalls primarily through long-term bonds. Low inflation rates and a central bank with a long tradition of political independence help to maintain investor confidence in long-term bonds valued in marks. Even as the government rapidly increased expenditures in the early 1990s, the central bank continued to pursue tight monetary policies to hold inflation in check.

German economic policy in the 1990s has been colored by the obligations assumed with reunification. Historically, postwar German economic policy has emphasized fiscal restraint and tight monetary policies in a sustained effort to avoid a return to the hyperinflation of the 1920s. In the 1980s the deficit averaged less than 2 percent of the GDP; in 1989 the government ran a small surplus.

Reunification generated enormous fiscal pressures—particularly in light of the Kohl government's pledge to raise living standards in the east to those of the west as quickly as possible. The decisions to convert East German marks on an even footing and to extend government social programs immediately upon reunification implied a rapid rise in expenditures that pushed the deficit back over 3 percent of the GDP in 1993. Although this deficit level was not as high as the levels faced in France or Italy, it called for an effort at deficit reduction in order to meet the Maastricht guidelines, which Germany had helped design.

Contemporary Dynamics

In the early 1990s spending rose rapidly in Germany to meet the demands of reunification. In 1990, total expenditures increased by 6.4 percent. In 1991 and 1992 the average annual growth in spending was 15 percent. Although the government took steps to increase revenues, the surplus of 1989 became a visible deficit (2.9 percent of the GDP) by 1991. Inflation topped 4 percent for the first time since 1982. In 1993, when the economy spun into a brief recession, deficit reduction had returned to the fiscal policy agenda.

Historically, both major parties have emphasized price stability (and fiscal responsibility) in an effort not to lose voters who might fear the specter of the runaway inflation of the 1920s. The center-left Social Democratic Party has tended to promote the growth of social programs in a fiscally responsible way by raising taxes. The center-right Christian Democrats have tended to shy away from major shifts in either taxes or spending—at least until it became the so-called party of German reunification in the 1990s. German business associations have been vocal in their support of fiscal austerity—in part because many major German firms are owned by holding companies controlled by banks. Banks, as lenders of money over time, are particularly sensitive to inflation. The major labor confederation, the *Deutscher Gewerkschaftbund*, has called for the expansion of social programs but has been willing to compromise on some issues in an effort to keep inflation in check. As the costs of reunification became visible, several small right-wing parties attempted to mobilize voters in the west who complained of the costs of subsidizing the east. Although the Christian Democrats at times talked tough about stern measures to deal with so-called eastern freeloaders, a more important impetus for returning to Germany's fiscally conservative roots was the need to meet the Maastricht guidelines.

Although some spending issues are resolved at the provincial level, most decision making is centered in the national government. Because both major parties rarely have been able to form a government on their own, the role played by junior coalition partners can be crucial. The Free Democrats' role in the center-right Kohl governments of the 1980s and 1990s was another nudge toward fiscal conservatism on several fronts. The center-left Schroeder government that succeeded Kohl's is perhaps less certain of the role the Greens will play as a coalition partner in fiscal policy making.

Few implementation problems cloud the fiscal policy horizon in Germany. Capability concerns are virtually nonexistent. Although the public mood could always change, most of the German public stayed at home when right-wing parties attempted to stir up protests around the issue of subsidizing the east.

Given both the fiscal conservatism of past German governments and the pressures of Maastricht, it is difficult to envision that the 1998 election of a center-left government will lead to a significant expansion of public spending. The Kohl government responded to the 1993 deficit by slowing the rise in spending to a scant 0.2 percent. Since then, the government has tried to keep the rise in spending in line with the rate of economic growth. This approach reduced the deficit to less than 3 percent of the GDP (the Maastricht target) and helped to push inflation back down. However, it also exposed Kohl to criticism for not doing enough either to meet the expectations in the east associated with reunification or to reduce frustration in the west with prolonged unemployment. This frustration (along with Kohl's long tenure as chancellor) helped to produce a narrow center-left victory, but that victory did not seem to foreshadow a move toward major fiscal policy changes. Spending as a percentage of the GDP declined slightly in 1999 and is projected to decline further in 2000 and 2001.

In contemporary German fiscal policy, we see three sets of policy influences in succession. First, the experience of hyperinflation in the 1920s created a cultural norm against inflation that powerfully frames choices about fiscal policy toward an aversion of budget deficits. German citizens and leaders fear inflation more than do people in most industrialized countries. Second, the unexpected event of reunification created a host of economic challenges almost overnight—if the existing government policies were to be applied to this new influx of generally poorer citizens in the east, the government would have to adjust its fiscal policy quickly. In response, the Kohl government launched a rapid expansion of spending that went against the grain of not just national history but also his own party's platform. This situation should serve as a caution against predicting the future of fiscal policy in Germany or any other country. Unexpected global events can and do upset the domestic dynamics of policy making. Finally, an international commitment to European monetary integration played a role in motivating a reduction in the deficit in the late 1990s.

France

Background: Policy Process and Policy History

The French budget process is centered within the executive branch. At the outset of the budget cycle, the prime minister and the finance minister consult to set budget targets for every ministry that has the power to spend. Then the finance minister negotiates one-on-one with each spending minister about adjustments to those targets. The prime minister remains the arbiter of any disagreements between a particular spending minister and the finance minister. This process of negotiation gives spending ministers (and the interest groups who lobby them) an opportunity to influence budget formulation. However, the power to arbitrate disputes, which is held by the finance minister and ultimately the prime minister, puts a noticeable constraint on the extent of adjustments that are plausible during formulation. Once the budget is completed, approval in the legislature is sealed by an agreement brokered among the senior figures in the governing coalition. Interest groups attempt to influence this process in various ways ranging from quiet lobbying to mass demonstrations.

The vast majority of French debt is financed domestically. Traditionally the government has relied primarily on long-term bonds; however, increased financing needs in the mid-1990s pushed the government to market a more even mix of short- and long-term instruments. In addition, the government has turned to short-term loans to finance over 10 percent of its shortfall. This turn to short-term financing has increased the pressure for deficit reduction by shortening the time period in which recent deficits must be repaid to the financial community.

In the 1990s the major economic issue in France was persistently high unemployment. Since 1985 the unemployment rate has averaged slightly more than 10 percent. By the mid-1990s it was around 12 percent.

The budget deficit, in contrast, was under control when the decade began. Years of slow growth in spending in the late 1980s combined with steady GDP growth pushed the deficit below 2 percent of the GDP. However, spending growth in 1992 and 1993 and a recession in 1993 led to a quick increase in the deficit from 2.4 percent of the GDP in 1991 to 6.0 percent in 1993. In light of France's Maastricht commitments, this change moved the deficit to near the top of the policy agenda.

Contemporary Dynamics

Policy problems at the heart of contemporary French spending policy result from a clash between two conflicting imperatives setting the fiscal agenda. On the one hand, the French government has been a solid supporter of the Maastricht Treaty's call for monetary unification—thereby placing fiscal responsibility high on the country's agenda. On the other hand, prolonged unemployment has stirred calls to preserve (or even extend) the social programs that make up the majority of national expenditures.

This turbulent clash of imperatives has made for some high-voltage policy formulation in France. As is the case in most political systems around the world, the major center-right parties (the Gaullists and the Union for French Democracy) have emphasized fiscal austerity, whereas the center-left bloc of parties (led by the Socialists) call for the protection of social spending. Both coalitions have found it difficult to set a durable policy course while in office.

Center-right governments find it difficult to cut spending as much as they promised, and center-left governments find it hard to protect programs as doggedly as they pledged.

The reemergence of the center-right as a large governing majority in 1993 seemed to signal a move toward fiscal austerity. However, as the shadow of prolonged unemployment lengthened seemingly without end, France encountered increasingly visible political opposition to spending cuts. In 1993, as the deficit expanded amid a recession, the center-right Balladur government cut social security and welfare spending by almost 10 percent in real terms. Opposition from many circles and the pressures of the 1995 election campaign led the government to restore much of the spending. After the election of Gaullist Jacques Chirac to the presidency, the new Juppe government proposed a series of spending reductions and privatizations of publicly owned enterprises designed to pull the deficit below 3 percent of the GDP by 1997. These proposals resulted in a massive protest led by organized labor that culminated in a bitter, prolonged general strike in December 1995. The unions were able to mobilize substantial public support for the strike by focusing attention on their desire to protect core social programs. Public support for the strike tended to mute business organizations' willingness to call openly for fiscal restraint (even as many urged it privately). With the election of a center-left government in 1997, it seemed that France's policy course had been set firmly toward the preservation of social spending.

This course seemed particularly well set because the budget process has historically been controlled by the governing coalition in the National Assembly. With a slim, albeit reasonably united, voting majority, it might have seemed unwarranted to expect social spending cuts in the late 1990s from the Jospin government. However, remember the pressure that the Maastricht guidelines placed on participating member states. To meet the target without drastically alienating either center-left voters (by cutting spending) or center-right voters (by raising taxes), the Jospin government pushed through a series of temporary tax increases and reduced the growth of spending. The Jospin government certainly has the authority to choose to restore the growth in spending later, but the SGP constrains its ability to do so in a way that produces budget deficits in excess of 3 percent of the GDP.

Few technical considerations block the implementation of most spending increases or decreases in France. The bigger implementation challenge is decidedly political. As the Balladur and Juppe governments saw when they reversed course on spending cuts, opponents of those cuts were able to place visible public pressure on the government to reconsider its policies. Several cuts that had been announced were pulled back before full implementation proceeded.

In this charged atmosphere, it proved decidedly risky business to make predictions about the future of French spending policy. Many media commentators rushed to judge the election of the Jospin government as the death knell for spending cuts for the foreseeable future. Although a modest economic recovery in 1994 and 1995 helped to reduce the deficit to slightly less than 6 percent of the GDP by the mid-1990s, the Jospin government needed to embrace some spending cuts and revenue increases in order to meet the Maastricht target of 3 percent in 1997. The continuation of the fiscal target as a condition for remaining within the euro zone is likely to continue to place pressure on this and future French governments to keep an eye on the deficit, that is, unless a new wave of popular strikes pushes this center-left government to the wall.

The volatility of French spending policy in recent years reflects the role of cultural and institutional influences on policy making. First, the polarization of the party system reflects deeply felt divisions in French society about the role of government. As a result, national spending priorities are politically explosive. Second, the unitary nature of the French state creates an expectation that governments can implement new priorities quickly—adding to the all-or-nothing flavor of debate over social spending. Notice, however, that the two major parties in the traditionally polarized party system agree on one overarching point that has visible implications for French fiscal politics: France will enter the euro zone and remain there. Until the EU fiscal guidelines for monetary union are revised (or one of several small anti-EU parties in France becomes a major coalition partner), the Maastricht Treaty will continue to constrain policymakers in the major parties. Globalization is a visible force in contemporary fiscal policy making—especially inside the euro zone.

United Kingdom

Background: Policy Process and Policy History

As in France, budget formulation in the United Kingdom is centered around the prime minister and the finance minister (known as the chancellor of the exchequer). They work out a general set of targets, and then the finance minister negotiates with each spending minister. Disputes are arbitrated by a committee of senior ministers who have no power to spend and therefore are not in a position to trade votes for spending increases in each others' ministries. Instead these ministers have tended to reflect the position of the prime minister and, often, the finance minister. The budget then goes to the legislature, where its passage with minimal revision is generally a foregone conclusion—although sometimes the flow of debate in parliament can spark a change in the government's plans. To provide for more debate of major issues before public presentation of the government's draft budget, in late 1997 the newly elected Blair government introduced the practice of having the finance minister present a so-called Green Budget speech in which preliminary economic projections and major policy considerations that guide budget formation could be aired publicly.

The United Kingdom has traditionally relied on a mix of foreign and domestic sources to finance its deficit. However, when the pound's position deteriorated on international markets in the early 1990s, the government was forced to turn more heavily to domestic investors. A long tradition of meeting its obligations—combined with what many observers depict as the risk-averse stance of British investors—has helped the government to finance its now larger deficit in the domestic capital market without hiking up interest rates.

Like Japan, the United Kingdom also began the 1990s with a certain amount of economic optimism. The economy improved on all fronts from 1985 to 1989. GDP growth was steady and comparatively high (3.9 percent annually, on average). Unlike in France and Italy, the growth of the late 1980s helped to reduce unemployment in the United Kingdom from over 11 percent in 1985 to 7 percent by 1989. Inflation also fell from an average of 8.5 percent in the first half of the decade to an average of 5.3 percent in the second half. The steady growth, combined with spending cuts in 1988 and 1989, converted the budget deficit of 2.9 percent of the GDP in 1985 into surpluses of around 1 percent in 1988 and 1989.

The British surplus proved precarious. Flat growth in 1990 and a recession in 1991 and 1992 pushed the deficit back up to 6.5 percent of the GDP in 1992. The newly formed Major government carried out real expenditure increases throughout the recession in preparation for an ultimately successful, come-from-behind general election campaign in 1992. With the election won, the Major government faced the challenge of bringing down the deficit without jeopardizing its slim majority in the legislature. The 1997 elections brought an end to nearly two decades of Conservative governments and ushered in an overwhelmingly large Labour majority. Tony Blair campaigned on a New Labour platform that stressed fiscal responsibility, but with a large, disciplined majority party behind him he did not confront the same political constraints faced by his predecessor. Furthermore, the United Kingdom's option on European monetary unification meant that the British government was under no firm pressure to meet the precise target of a deficit no larger than 3 percent of the GDP.

Contemporary Dynamics

As noted earlier, the British government increased real expenditures in the face of the recession of 1991 and 1992 by an average of 7.7 percent per year. With the elections over and the deficit at a troubling level, the Major government began to hold spending increases down to below 2 percent annually in the mid-1990s. Defense spending (already subjected to substantial cuts in the late 1980s) was reduced by a rate of around 5 percent each year from 1993 through 1995. This so-called peace dividend of the end of the Cold War (along with reductions in housing programs) enabled overall spending increases to remain low without significant across-the-board cuts.

This fiscal restraint combined with moderate growth to reduce the deficit to less than 6 percent of the GDP in 1995 and less than 5 percent by 1996. However, the economic growth did not push unemployment rates below 8 percent by 1996. This economic failure, along with visible divisions in the slim Conservative majority and the legacy of nearly two decades in power, contributed to the overwhelming victory of the Labour Party in 1997.

The new government faced a troubling economic agenda. Macroeconomic conditions in the United Kingdom were better in some respects than in continental Europe; however, economic conditions were deteriorating when compared to the United Kingdom's immediate past. Blair's New Labour program pledged to improve social conditions and reduce unemployment without significantly increasing the budget deficit.

The fiscal responsibility mantra of the Blair campaign was an electorally successful effort to deflect the traditional Tory argument that Labour could not be trusted to govern. From Margaret Thatcher forward, two decades of Conservative politicians had campaigned on the charge that they were more fiscally responsible than Labour. This charge was bolstered by anecdotal evidence that Labour's ties to the trade union movement might lead to a host of expensive social spending should Labour return to power. Many business leaders echoed the call for Conservative leadership in fiscal matters. Given the tendency toward majority party government in the United Kingdom, the challenge for Blair was not to build a unified coalition but rather to win over a disciplined majority within his own party. This process, begun under earlier party leaders, reached a fever pitch under Blair's leadership as he worked hard to use his authority and his public visibility to reshape fiscal policy formulation within the party itself.

These internal party efforts have paid off now that Blair heads the government. As has been the case historically, the presence of a large, disciplined majority in the Westminster model (in which a plurality electoral system is combined with a parliamentary executive) puts decision-making power firmly in the hands of the cabinet. Only a major rift within the party could force the Blair government to make the fiscal policy-making process more inclusive. Similarly, no technical or political implementation problems are on the immediate horizon.

There is no reason to believe that the Labour Party will discontinue its course of modest increases in social spending teamed with the occasional accompanying new tax provision to ensure fiscal stability. This approach converted a 1997 deficit of 2.0 percent of the GDP into small surpluses in 1998 and 1999. The major potential obstacle to the continuation of that approach is the overall economic climate. If domestic or international events lead to a recession, that recession could depress government revenues—thereby leading to deficits if spending is not reduced. A recession would also be accompanied by demands to maintain (or even to extend) social programs. In that scenario, more fault lines may become apparent both in the Labour Party and in the minds of voters than are visible at this time.

This case study demonstrates in practice some of the principles of the Westminster model of parliamentary government: one-party majority governments, two major parties dominating the political scene, and a unitary state capable of making great changes fairly rapidly. With no coalition partners to satisfy, most British governments have faced less political pressure to run deficits. At the same time, the relative unity of British governments is no panacea from a policy outcome perspective. Just because the British government is often capable of making faster decisions and implementing them more quickly does not mean that the United Kingdom is immune to disappointing economic conditions. In fact the responsiveness of the political system may paradoxically raise some people's expectations about government's capacity to work miracles.

Italy

Background: Policy Process and Policy History

The Italian fiscal process during the 1980s and most of the 1990s tended to be somewhat more intricate than the French and German processes—both in theory and in practice. Although a specific Budget Ministry exists, it was not the central arena for annual fiscal policy; the Budget Ministry's principal task was to design medium- and long-term economic plans. The annual budget process centered on the Treasury. The General Accountancy Office within the Treasury drafted the budget within rough guidelines established by an inter-ministerial committee on economic planning chaired by the budget minister. That draft budget needed the approval of both the treasury and the budget ministers; however, because negotiations over details with senior ministry officials and parliamentary leaders were handled by the treasury minister, the Treasury had the central role in the budget formation process.

Since 1978, legislators in both chambers have been able to make amendments to the budget bill. Although some of these changes were last-minute adjustments worked out between leaders of the governing coalitions or their respective major factions, many amendments were members' initiatives from legislators without leadership positions. The inability or unwillingness of the governing coalition to restrain decentralized additions to spending was often cited as a major factor in rising budget deficits in the 1980s and early 1990s. The statutory procedures prevented legislators from spending beyond the revenues and from writing new revenue provisions into the budget bill. Members often skirted these obstacles by basing the funding on changed economic projections or on projections of authorized funds not spent. These less centralized practices at the decision-making stage delayed the timely passage of the annual budget and opened the budget approval process to the participation of a wider variety of actors.

In reaction to these various problems—and with considerable pressure and political commitment to meet the Maastricht deficit target—the Prodi government passed a major reform of the budget procedures in April 1997 (Law Number 94). This procedural reform reduced the number of budgetary categories greatly (to improve control over the administration of spending), streamlined the procedures for parliamentary approval, and expanded the authority of the bureaucracy in monitoring expenditures (as opposed to planned spending). Perhaps the most striking change was a move from the past incrementalist approach to budget formation to a zero-based budgeting approach that requires all spending proposals to be justified on their individual merits. With these tools in place, the Prodi government prepared to meet the challenge of halving the deficit in a single year.

Some of the consequences of perennially high deficits are visible in the Italian experience in the 1980s and 1990s. Italy found it very difficult to market long-term bonds in the 1990s. High deficits decreased investors' confidence in the government's ability to make good on a long-term obligation. More important, comparatively higher inflation rates in Italy (associated in part with higher deficits) decreased the value of Italian bonds relative to other countries' debt instruments. In response, Italy has turned primarily to short-term domestic bonds and changes in cash liabilities to meet its financing needs. It has also been forced to pay higher interest rates in its debt financing. By the mid-1990s interest payments on the debt exceeded one-third of government spending.

Throughout the 1980s Italy ran the highest deficits in the G-7 as the average deficit exceeded 10 percent of the GDP. By 1989, interest payments on the debt constituted nearly one-fifth of all government spending. Among G-7 countries, only Canada faced a similar debt service burden. Many observers cited the political dynamics of perennially vulnerable coalition governments as a major contributor to Italy's seeming inability to cut its deficit. Political reform in Italy in the 1990s—manifested by continued anticorruption efforts and a substantial change in its electoral system—has renewed optimism in some circles that the deficit could be reduced. The Maastricht commitment provided another new tool that Italian governments could wield to build political support for (or at least acceptance of) deficit reduction measures.

Contemporary Dynamics

Although deficit reduction has been on the Italian political agenda for a long time, real spending in the late 1980s increased by more than 5 percent annually. This trend continued from 1990 to 1992. Existing debt obligations are a major constraint on the Italian government's ability to reduce the overall deficit. From 1989 to 1993, about one-third of all expenditure growth each year was accounted for by interest payments on the public debt. This legacy of prolonged recourse to high deficits, combined with the political crisis of the early 1990s, made expenditure cuts difficult even amid widespread concern that deficit reduction was necessary. The Maastricht Treaty and internal Italian evaluations of the explosive growth in the national debt kept returning deficit reduction to the forefront of the institutional agenda.

Coherent policy formulation to tackle the rising deficit was made difficult by the collapse of the old party system—perhaps best signified by the emergence of a new electoral system in 1992. The traditional party of government, the Christian Democratic Party, split into a variety of smaller parties. The other major governing partner, the Socialist Party, was also disgraced by the corruption scandals of the 1980s. In their place, three new parties moved into the spotlight as potential leaders of new governments: the Party of the Democratic Left (PDS) formed by the major center-leftist rump of the old communist party; Forza Italia, a new populist party founded and led by flamboyant entrepreneur Silvio Berlusconi; and the vocally antigovernment Northern League, a coalition of regional parties calling for more local autonomy from the national government. So far, the Northern League has yet to play the lead role in a governing coalition, whereas the two parties that have headed governments have been careful to call simultaneously for the preservation of social spending and for fiscal responsibility. Major business associations and labor union confederations have echoed this dualistic call for having one's cake and eating it, too.

Decision making on fiscal policy arguably has been less centralized in Italy than in most industrialized countries (with the clear exception of the United States). The combination of coalition governments formed by fractionalized parties and the ability of legislators to cast secret ballots to sink undesired spending bills made for complex budget negotiations. The end to the secret legislative ballot and the 1997 budget reforms helped to centralize authority in government; however, the tenuous nature of coalition governments continued to enable many actors to influence policy.

Despite these obstacles, the deficit was reduced substantially in Italy in the mid-1990s. The caretaker government led by banker Lamberto Dini reduced government spending in 1994 and 1995 by a series of across-the-board cuts. The national government's reduction of its health policy commitments in the 1992 reform (see Chapter 8) also began to reduce spending by the national government. By 1995 the deficit was down to just below 8 percent of the GDP. The newly elected center-left Prodi government had a long way to go to push the deficit below 3 percent to meet the Maastricht target. After making minimal progress at further deficit reduction in 1996 (bringing the deficit down to 7.1 percent of the GDP), deadline pressure and the budget policy reform of April 1997 helped the Prodi government to enact a major budget bill that held expenditure increases below the rate of inflation in summer 1997. As in France, the desire to join the euro zone was a powerful force helping the government to reduce the deficit.

The so-called convergence budget of 1997 met the Italian government's immediate goal of sharp deficit reduction through temporary revenue increases, spending increases below the rate of inflation, and changes in the period of spending that brought the 1997 deficit down to 2.7 percent of the GDP. That said, the historical vulnerability of coalition governments and the new volatility of the electorate in the newly forming party system posed potential implementation problems for fiscal policymakers. These problems were of a decidedly political nature. Upon implementation, if a coalition partner decided to increase its leverage, it could threaten to leave the coalition if new spending policies were not adopted to change the ones under implementation. Similarly, electoral volatility, as in France, could push fiscal priorities rapidly in one direction or another.

Unlike the Jospin government, however, the Prodi government did not survive the year. The Refounded Communists, one of the junior partners in the Olive Tree coalition behind the Prodi government, pulled out of the coalition in October 1998 in a dispute over the amount of deficit reduction in the budget under debate. The PDS was able to keep most of the coalition together and formed a new government under PDS party leader Massimo D'alema with the help of centrist parties. Nevertheless, the incident made clear that fiscal policy disputes could still bring down a government quickly in contemporary Italy. Observers would be advised to watch carefully as the Italian government tries to honor its SGP fiscal target in the years to come.

The dynamics of fiscal policy in Italy reinforce the points raised by the strength of government thesis about divided electorates and unstable coalition governments. Although parliamentary governments may prove more responsive when a stable majority or majority coalition emerges in control of the government, the absence of a durable majority can make governing difficult. In short, institutions help to frame policy making, but they do not determine the final outcome. Parliamentary institutions may make fiscal policy easier to conduct but only if the political influences on policy making are not too polarizing.

Reducing a large budget deficit is difficult enough under the best of circumstances. Given the turmoil in the Italian political system in the 1990s, it is perhaps a small miracle that the deficit could be brought down as quickly as it was. That small miracle is a testament to the power of shared political will by major government and nongovernment leaders to enter the euro zone. In this instance, the globalization thesis appears to have triumphed in the face of fragile coalition governments.

Cross-national Trends

Five of the six countries demonstrated a visible trend toward deficit reduction. Although deficit reduction has reduced inflation, in the late 1990s it was rarely associated with a decline in unemployment and faster economic growth. The lone exception to this trend was in the United States. Given that deficit reduction tended to take place amid slow economic growth, it presented these countries with a series of political challenges. As the case studies demonstrated, global economic factors proved crucial in the move toward deficit reduction.

Policy Outputs

At the start of the 1990s Japan and Italy were at the two extremes of fiscal policy among the six countries examined in this book. Table 6.1 shows that Japan averaged budget surpluses from 1985 to 1994. In contrast, Italy had double-digit deficits over the same period.

In all but the United States, deficit pressures remained stable or rose during the first half of the 1990s. The situation changed most radically in Japan as its worst economic slowdown in decades moved the government to adopt deficit spending programs in 1994 and 1995. The days of high growth and budget surpluses came to a halt.

If a deficit of over 3 percent of the GDP is deemed by many to be the litmus test of fiscal problems, then in 1995 none of these countries proved able to meet that overall fiscal target. Among the three European countries pledged to run deficits below 3 percent by 1997, only Germany was close. A desire to

Table 6-1 Deficit Spending Trends, 1985–1999

	Public Deficit, as a percentage of GDP						
	France	Germany	Italy	Japan	United Kingdom	United States	Average
Annual average, 1985–1989	−2.44%	−1.24%	−11.02%	0.56%	−1.18%	−4.28%	−3.27%
Annual average, 1990–1994	−4.04	−2.62	−9.80	0.68	−5.12	−4.76	−4.28
Annual average, 1995–1999	−3.42	−2.40	−4.42	−4.62	−2.18	−0.96	−3.00
Annual average, 1990–1999	−3.73	−2.51	−7.11	−1.97	−3.65	−2.86	−3.64
1990	−2.1	−2.0	−11.0	2.9	−1.5	−4.3	−3.0
1991	−2.4	−2.9	−10.0	2.9	−2.8	−5.0	−3.4
1992	−4.2	−2.5	−9.5	1.5	−6.5	−5.9	−4.5
1993	−6.0	−3.2	−9.4	−1.6	−8.0	−5.0	−5.5
1994	−5.5	−2.5	−9.1	−2.3	−6.8	−3.6	−5.0
1995	−5.5	−3.2	−7.6	−3.6	−5.8	−3.1	−4.8
1996	−4.1	−3.4	−7.1	−4.2	−4.4	−2.2	−4.2
1997	−3.0	−2.6	−2.7	−3.3	−2.0	−0.9	−2.4
1998	−2.7	−1.7	−2.8	−5.0	0.2	0.4	−1.9
1999	−1.8	−1.1	−1.9	−7.0	1.1	1.0	−1.6

SOURCE: OECD (2000).

NOTE: Positive numbers indicate a budget surplus.

GDP = gross domestic product.

reach this target—and to stay there—had a potential impact on every decision made by these governments in the late 1990s, as we saw in the case studies. France, Germany, and Italy all hit the 3 percent target in 1997 through a variety of exceptional measures that were justified politically under the "need for speed" to enter the euro zone. At the time of this writing, with the euro recently launched, the question for the next decade is: Can these countries continue to meet this deficit target over time? Part of the answer certainly lies in the political ingenuity of the governments. Another portion of the answer may be tied to the economic outcomes associated with successful efforts to keep the deficit in check.

Policy Outcomes

The need for spending austerity to meet the deficit target was magnified by markedly slow GDP growth in the 1990s. As Table 6.2 shows, average annual growth for the six countries examined in this book was a paltry 1.77 percent for the period 1990 to 1994. Even after recessions during 1991 to 1993 passed, growth has been minimal. The average annual growth rate from 1995 to 1999 was 2.21 percent. Only the U.S. and British economies managed to grow at rates visibly in excess of 2 percent per year in the late 1990s.

Although growth fell significantly between the periods 1985–1989 and 1990–1994, inflation increased slightly from an average of 3.51 percent to 3.66 percent. In the late 1990s, however, inflation in all six countries fell markedly, to an average of 1.85 percent. Fairly tight monetary policies were used by most of these governments in the mid-1990s to keep inflation in check in the face of persistent budget deficits.

Tight monetary policies helped to check inflation but at the cost of slower growth. Slow growth dampens government revenues—thereby increasing pressures on the expenditure side of the fiscal equation. Slow growth also makes it difficult to escape high unemployment. Although inflation was the major economic problem in many industrialized countries during the 1970s, unemployment has been the bugbear of the 1980s and 1990s. By the mid-1990s only Japan and the United States had low levels of unemployment. Those two countries were joined in the late 1990s by the United Kingdom as economic growth accelerated—particularly from 1995 to 1997.

In contrast, unemployment rose in France, Germany, and Italy during the period 1995 to 1998. Part of the rise in unemployment stems from efforts to reduce the budget deficit rapidly in 1997. Slow economic growth and fiscal austerity are not the entire explanation for these countries' disappointing unemployment outcomes. Other explanations focus on the relative lack of pro-labor legislation in Japan and the United States, in comparison with the European countries.

Although no crystal clear link exists between falling deficits and rising, persistent unemployment in the industrialized countries, the two issues are con-

Table 6-2 Major Economic Indicators, 1985–1999 (in percent)

Country	Indicator	Annual average 1985–1989 (%)	Annual average 1990–1994 (%)	Annual average 1995–1999 (%)	1995 (%)	1996 (%)	1997 (%)	1998 (%)	1999 (%)
France	Growth	2.98	1.16	2.12	1.9	1.1	1.9	3.2	2.9
	Unemployment	10.04	10.58	11.90	11.7	12.4	12.3	11.8	11.3
	Inflation	3.56	2.62	1.26	1.8	2.0	1.2	0.8	0.5
	Deficit/GDP	−2.44	−4.04	−3.42	−5.5	−4.1	−3.0	−2.7	−1.8
Germany	Growth	2.62	2.82	1.54	1.7	0.8	1.5	2.2	1.5
	Unemployment	6.36	5.96	9.02	8.2	8.9	9.9	9.4	8.7
	Inflation	1.26	3.72	1.30	1.7	1.4	1.9	0.9	0.6
	Deficit/GDP	−1.24	−2.62	−2.40	−3.2	−3.4	−2.6	−1.7	−1.1
Italy	Growth	3.06	1.10	1.74	2.9	1.1	1.8	1.5	1.4
	Unemployment	9.32	9.56	11.66	11.6	11.7	11.7	11.9	11.4
	Inflation	6.22	5.36	2.98	5.2	4.0	2.0	2.0	1.7
	Deficit/GDP	−11.02	−9.80	−4.42	−7.6	−7.1	−2.7	−2.8	−1.9
Japan	Growth	4.50	2.16	1.42	1.5	5.1	1.6	−2.5	1.4
	Unemployment	2.60	2.36	3.74	3.1	3.4	3.4	4.1	4.7
	Inflation	1.14	2.00	0.40	−0.1	0.1	1.7	0.6	−0.3
	Deficit/GDP	0.56	0.68	−4.62	−3.6	−4.2	−3.3	−5.0	−7.0
United Kingdom	Growth	3.94	1.18	2.64	2.8	2.6	3.5	2.2	2.1
	Unemployment	9.94	9.22	7.26	8.7	8.2	7.0	6.3	6.1
	Inflation	5.26	4.64	2.78	3.4	2.4	3.1	3.4	1.6
	Deficit/GDP	−1.18	−5.12	−2.18	−5.8	−4.4	−2.0	0.2	1.1
United States	Growth	3.66	2.22	3.80	2.7	3.6	4.2	4.3	4.2
	Unemployment	6.24	6.58	4.92	5.6	5.4	4.9	4.5	4.2
	Inflation	3.60	3.64	2.36	2.8	2.9	2.3	1.6	2.2
	Deficit/GDP	−4.28	−4.76	−0.96	−3.1	−2.2	−0.9	0.4	1.0
Average	Growth	3.46	1.77	2.21	2.3	2.4	2.4	1.8	2.3
	Unemployment	7.42	7.38	8.08	8.2	8.3	8.2	8.0	7.7
	Inflation	3.51	3.66	1.85	2.5	2.1	2.0	1.6	1.1
	Deficit/GDP	−3.27	−4.28	−3.00	−4.8	−4.2	−2.4	−1.9	−1.6

SOURCE: OECD (2000).

GDP = gross domestic product.

nected in the policy debate within the systemic agenda for two main reasons. First, many deficit-cutting politicians raise expectations that a more fiscally sound government could help create a drop in the unemployment rate. Looking across all industrialized countries, that sequence has occurred in only four countries to any visible degree—Denmark, Ireland, the United Kingdom, and the United States. Second, as noted earlier in this chapter, persistent unemployment in many countries (even where it has declined slightly) puts increasing pressure on governments to provide social expenditures to assist people experiencing hard times. The effort to control the deficit amid slow growth and rising demands for some services increases the conflict involved in fiscal policy making.

Understanding Policy Reform

Partisanship may still matter in fiscal policy, but not only did parties of all stripes pledge lowered deficits in the late 1990s, they also delivered deficit reduction. New center-left governments were formed in 1997 and 1998 in France, Germany, Italy, and the United Kingdom. Although these governments included movements historically associated with an expansion of government programs (particularly in health and social policy), all pledged to combine fiscal responsibility with the maintenance of most existing government programs in some form. The Clinton administration in the United States set a policy course along roughly the same lines. The only exception to this trend is Japan, where the deficit rose during most of the decade.

The situation in Japan is a reminder of the role of short-term economic conditions in shaping budget deficits. The weak economy in Japan—including a strong recession in 1997—was a strong pressure toward deficit spending in two senses. First, the contraction in the economy forced government revenues down. Second, that recession and the stagnation that preceded it provided a strong political rationale for engaging in deficit spending to promote economic growth. Although Japan, France, Germany, and Italy all faced some degree of economic stagnation in the 1990s, Japan confronted the greatest number of economic problems.

Further, although some analysts argued for deficit spending to accelerate economic growth and to reduce unemployment in continental Europe, governments of varied political parties in France, Germany, and Italy all pointed to the Maastricht deficit target as a rationale for reducing the deficit. In addition to that international agreement, governments in all five of the deficit-reducing countries pointed to a need to reduce the deficit in order to lower domestic interest rates (to attract foreign capital) and to decrease pressure on the national currency (especially from abroad). In short, global economic factors—both formal integration and de facto interdependence—were the most visible influences at the agenda-setting and decision-making stages of fiscal policy in the 1990s in these countries.

SUGGESTED READINGS

Aghevli, Bijan B., Tamim A. Bayoumi, and Guy Meredith. 1998. *Structural Change in Japan: Macroeconomic Impact and Policy Challenges.* Washington, D.C.: International Monetary Fund.

Baldassarri, Mario, and Paolo Roberti. 1994. *Fiscal Problems in the Single-market Europe.* New York: St. Martin's Press.

Cogan, John F., Timothy J. Muris, and Allen Shick. 1994. *The Budget Puzzle: Understanding Federal Spending.* Stanford: Stanford University Press.

Fitoussi, Jean-Paul, et al. 1993. *Competitive Disinflation: The Mark and Budgetary Politics in Europe.* Oxford: Oxford University Press.

Heilemann, Ullrich, and Wolfgang H. Reinicke. 1995. *Welcome to Hard Times: The Fiscal Consequences of German Unity*. Washington, D.C.: Brookings Institution Press.

Hyde, Albert C. 1992. *Government Budgeting: Theory, Process, and Politics*, 2d ed. Fort Worth, Texas: Harcourt Brace.

Peters, B. Guy. 1991. *The Politics of Taxation*. Oxford: Basil Blackwell.

Sandford, Cedric Thomas. 1992. *Economics of Public Finance: An Economic Analysis of Government Expenditure and Revenue in the United Kingdom*, 4th ed. Oxford: Pergamon Press.

Shojai, Siamack. 1999. *Budget Deficits and Debt: A Global Perspective*. Westport, Conn.: Praeger.

Sturm, Roland. 1999. *Public Deficits: A Comparative Study of Their Economic and Political Consequences in Britain, Canada, Germany and the United States*. Harlow, England: Longman.

Yergin, Daniel, and Joseph Stanislaw. 1998. *The Commanding Heights: The Battle Between Government and the Marketplace That Is Remaking the Modern World*. New York: Simon & Schuster.

Chapter 7 **Taxation Policy**

Contemporary governments need money to carry out the wide variety of activities they pursue. Some of that money is raised by the sale of government-provided goods and services. However, in the six countries examined in this book (and in most countries around the world today), the vast majority of government revenues are generated by taxation.

More is at stake here than the generation of revenue. Governments make countless decisions about whom to tax and at what rate to tax them. These decisions can have important implications for other policy areas. Often governments encourage certain activities (and discourage others) through tax incentives. In this way the tax code—in addition to funding government activity—is itself a policy instrument, used in pursuit of goals on a multitude of issues.

Common Policy Problems

In the nineteenth century, government was much smaller than it is today. Because it provided far fewer services to its citizenry, it needed less money. Many countries managed to meet their revenue needs largely by taxing foreigners—in particular by taxing imports and by selling import licenses. In this way, governments minimized the visible tax burden on their citizens (a less visible tax remained in the form of higher prices for consumers of those imported goods).

During the twentieth century, governments began to provide a wide variety of services to many people and organizations. All things being equal, most people and most businesses would still prefer to pay little or no money in taxes. Expressed in the language of rational choice theory, actors prefer to free ride on the cooperation of others. People want to receive as many government services and subsidies as possible, but they would prefer that those services be paid for by other people's taxes.

This simple truth provides the backdrop against which governments try to achieve the three fundamental goals of tax policy. First, how can the tax code be constructed to ensure that needed revenues are generated? Second, how can the government generate those revenues while generating the smallest degree of discontent possible? Third, how can the government use the tax code to provide tax incentives to encourage desired behaviors and tax disincentives to discourage other behaviors?

People's distaste for taxes gives individuals and firms an incentive to reduce the total taxes paid regardless of the tax system employed. Tax reduction efforts can take the form of **tax avoidance** (managing one's money in a way that minimizes tax liability) or outright **tax evasion** (the illegal refusal to pay taxes owed under the law).

In general, people would prefer to pay few or no taxes; however, they can be persuaded to pay taxes for a variety of reasons. For instance, they may pay taxes because they support the services the government provides with the tax revenue. This concept implies that governments have an incentive to fund popular programs out of funds raised explicitly for that purpose. As an example, old-age pensions are normally funded via payroll taxes earmarked for the pension fund. In an effort to increase tax compliance with many disparate programs, governments will sometimes bundle a popular program with several other initiatives paid for out of a given revenue stream.

People also are sometimes willing to pay taxes out of a sense of burden-sharing. If they believe that most (if not all) people are shouldering a fair share of the load, they may be more likely to pay (and less likely to criticize the government for its tax policies). Thus a major policy challenge for governments is to create a tax code that is viewed as equitable.

A second policy challenge results because people are more likely to pay taxes owed when they face a credible possibility of apprehension and punishment for tax evasion. When apprehension of evaders is likely, taxes are easier to collect. Some taxes are easier (or harder) to collect than others. Unfortunately for governments, many of the taxes that are relatively easy to collect are viewed by many as inequitable—thereby conflicting with the goal of equity.

We earlier alluded to a third problem in contemporary tax policy. The tax code is a major avenue of interaction between a government and its citizenry. As a result, the tax code presents an opportunity to pursue goals in other policy areas by providing preferential (or penalizing) tax treatment to encourage (or discourage) certain types of behavior. These provisions are generally referred to as **tax expenditures**—a term that captures how tax incentives spend revenues that otherwise would have been collected. For example, the tax code can be used to promote savings investment, discourage pollution, subsidize health care and education, provide extra tax relief to the impoverished, and so on.

The potential for using the tax code to promote different policy goals is seemingly endless. Nevertheless, the use of tax policy to meet various ends often runs counter to the challenges of tax equity and ease of collection. Too many tax expenditures may create the impression that some people are not paying their fair share—generating calls for a simpler tax code. Additionally, widespread use of tax expenditures may provide an incentive for tax fraud—the evasion of taxes by understating one's tax burden.

How governments manage this complex and conflicting triad of tax challenges (equity, ease of collection, and tax expenditures)—while still meeting the fundamental goals of generating needed revenues without substantial discontent—is central to government success in many areas. Governments that achieve a working equilibrium in this area can provide a stable economic and political environment. Governments that fail are headed for economic and political trouble.

Major Policy Options

When dealing with the equity issue, policymakers face a difficult series of choices. Sometimes equity is in conflict with other priorities. Moreover, the definition of equity is a question of perspective. For some, equitable burden-sharing entails the rich paying a larger share of total taxes collected; this is deemed fair because the well-off presumably can pay more in taxes and still live comfortably. When a tax system calls on the wealthy to pay a higher percentage of their income in taxes than the poor, the tax system is said to be **progressive** because it is redistributing money from the rich to the poor. For others, equity implies that all persons and firms pay an equal percentage of their earnings in taxes—regardless of wealth and regardless of the source(s) of income. Such a tax system would be **income-neutral;** it would have no impact on the distribution of income. Finally, if a tax system forces the poor to pay a higher percentage in taxes than the rich, it is said to be **regressive** because it redistributes income from the poor to the wealthy. Both notions of equity (the progressive notion and the income-neutral notion) face a difficult technical challenge owing to the multitude of taxes collected. Different sorts of taxes lend themselves better to meeting the dueling concepts of progressivity and income neutrality, respectively.

Tax instruments are usually divided into two major groups. **Direct taxes** are levied as a percentage of income earned by a person or a firm. Personal income tax, corporate income tax, and employee payroll contributions to social security or other government programs (such as health insurance) are examples of direct taxes. Because direct taxes are calculated based on income data, they are a major potential instrument for redistribution. The government can choose to apply increasingly higher tax rates at higher income levels (via the use of **tax brackets**). Alternatively the government can choose to have income-neutral direct taxes and charge all citizens the same uniform rate; this option is often referred to as the **flat tax.**

Although direct taxes provide the government with a ready means for redistribution via progressive tax brackets, they can be harder to collect than indirect taxes. Because direct taxes are based on income levels, the potential exists for the taxpayer's income to be underestimated by the tax collector, the taxpayer (at times intentionally), or both. During the twentieth century, governments worked hard to improve their information about income levels in order to reduce this problem.

Indirect taxes are not based on the taxpayer's income. Employer payroll taxes (based on earnings of employees) represent a major form of indirect taxation found in virtually every country around the world. Another common form of indirect tax is the sales tax—a tax charged on the sale of a good or service. In the United States, sales taxes have tended to be charged and collected at the final point of retail sale. In postwar Europe and in many developing countries, governments have increasingly turned to a value-added tax (VAT) charged on every transaction in the production of a good. A special form of sales tax is the **excise tax**—a tax charged on a particular good (for example, tobacco, liquor, or luxury yachts). Property taxes are also deemed to be indirect taxes because they do not take into account income earned but rather are a percentage of the assessed value of a given piece of property, for example, a house, a vacant lot, or an automobile.

Indirect taxes provided the bulk of government revenues in the nineteenth century because they were easier to collect than direct taxes. During the twentieth century, the sales tax was criticized as regressive because the wealthy spend a smaller portion of their income on consumer purchases than the poor. Efforts to address this problem by charging higher tax rates on luxury items have been problematic in industrialized countries because few products are purchased exclusively by the rich. Instead, the wealthy buy pricier, luxury-brand versions of the same products bought by others: cars, alcohol, food, and the like. Furthermore, the excise and property tax rates needed to address the inequities in the basic sales tax are so high that they are difficult to defend politically.

In industrialized countries during the twentieth century, proponents of both the progressive and the income-neutral notions of equity used the generally regressive nature of indirect taxes to argue for the implementation of progressive income taxes. Late-industrializing countries, however, rely heavily on indirect taxes because of the relative ease of collection. To the extent that indirect taxes in a given country's tax system are regressive, impoverished citizens in many poor nations are caught in a vicious cycle. Government programs to aid the poor are often insufficient, and the means used to fund the programs often place a disproportionate burden on the poor.

One might think that a tax system's effect on income distribution in the industrialized world could be readily evaluated. The information on the progressivity of direct taxes is inherent in the tax structure, and one could estimate the amount of money that people spend in sales taxes each year. Nevertheless, gauging the redistributive nature of a tax system is in practice extremely difficult because of the widespread use of tax expenditures. The estimate of sales taxes paid can be hard to calculate because many goods are subject to different sales tax rates (or, occasionally, no tax at all). Governments charge lower sales taxes on products they want to subsidize—sometimes making the good or service tax-exempt. Things can get even more complicated in the realm of direct taxes because governments can provide income tax expenditures to promote or subsidize a variety of activities. Sometimes governments provide **tax credits,** through which the cost of the activity is counted as a credit toward the taxes owed. For example, charitable donations could conceivably

Box 7-1 **In Depth: Income Tax Expenditures
in the United States**

Tax credits and deductions are used in the United States more frequently than in any other industrialized country. For 1999 the Congressional Budget Office tracked a total 112 specific tax expenditures in the individual income tax code and another 64 provisions in the corporate income tax code. These provisions apply to 131 different specific uses of money or categories of beneficiaries. The estimated revenue loss tied to these tax expenditures totaled $602.5 billion in 1999. By way of perspective, the budget surplus in that year was $98.8 billion. Total government revenues were $1.914 trillion.

Governments engage in tax expenditures to promote specific activities. The ten largest tax expenditures in 1999 (accounting for two-thirds of all tax expenditures) are as follows (the value in parentheses is the amount of revenue loss estimated for each provision):

- net exclusion of employee contributions to employer pension plans ($83.4 billion)
- exclusion of employer contributions to employee medical insurance ($69.6 billion)
- deductibility of mortgage interest on owner-occupied homes ($56.9 billion)
- capital gains exemptions in the individual income tax ($39.4 billion)
- deductibility of nonbusiness state and local taxes other than those paid on owner-occupied homes ($37.7 billion)
- accelerated depreciation of machinery and equipment ($26.4 billion)
- step-up basis of capital gains exemptions at death ($25.8 billion)
- exclusion of interest on public purpose bonds ($22.8 billion)
- deductibility of state and local property tax on owner-occupied homes ($21.2 billion)
- child tax credit ($19.4 billion)

generate a tax credit in an effort to promote giving. Much more often, governments provide **tax deductions**—a reduction in the amount of taxable income. Pursuing further the example of charitable donations, assume that a taxpayer making $50,000 a year donates $1,000 to a charity. If the donation were treated as a tax deduction, the individual's taxable income would be $49,000. If the tax rate were 10 percent, the taxpayer would owe $4,900 in income tax. If the same individual had received a $1,000 tax credit, the income tax bill would be only $4,000. For a look at the major tax expenditures written into the U.S. corporate and individual income tax codes, see Box 7–1.

Once you consider the multitude of tax expenditures written into the tax code, you can begin to appreciate the complexity of evaluating the equity of a tax system based on the concepts of either progressivity or income-neutrality. Why should governments complicate matters by pursuing policy goals via tax expenditures? Tax expenditures are attractive for a couple of reasons. First, governments can subsidize certain activities without collecting money in taxes and then paying out the subsidies to the relevant individuals. This approach can be an effective means of promoting the activity in question as long as the tax assessment process is not subject to fraud. Second, once the use of tax expenditures becomes widespread, they can have political advantages as well. When tax expenditures clutter the tax code, many citizens and firms have a stake in their retention such that the tax expenditures can be used to build political support for tax policy as a whole. Although all countries have a mix of direct and indirect taxes spiced with tax expenditures, various taxation models have proven to be politically viable in the six countries examined in this book.

Explaining Policy Dynamics

The complexity of the tax code provides a series of issues that can promote demands for change in one or more of its major provisions. Some citizens, interest groups, and public officials are concerned about the overall level of taxation. Others mobilize around particular components of the tax code itself. Under what conditions are governments more likely to reform the tax structure? Although the overall level of taxation is amenable to cross-national statistical analysis, the intricacy of the tax structure has made it difficult to study via quantitative analysis. Instead, research has centered on national and comparative case studies of tax policy. In different situations, cultural, economic, political, and institutional factors can shape the emergence of tax reform on the agenda, the particular reform decisions made, and the nature of implementation concerns.

Cultural Explanations

Some research indicates that deep cultural traditions help to shape the tax structures that governments choose. In particular, significant distrust of government can result in a trend toward tax evasion that prods governments to favor indirect taxes over direct taxes because the former are easier to collect. If tax evasion becomes enshrined in the culture, even if its pervasiveness is exaggerated in national folklore, governments may remain reliant on indirect taxation. When new revenues are needed in this context, governments would be more likely to raise rates on existing indirect taxes (or create new ones) than to expand direct taxation. Italy and France have demonstrated this dynamic more frequently than the other countries examined in this book (Haycraft 1987; Peters 1995).

Other research focuses more directly on public opinion regarding the nature of taxation. As we noted in Chapter 6, a stable majority in most industrialized societies would prefer to see taxes decrease, or at a minimum, stay at

Table 7-1 A Model of Citizens' Attitudes Toward Taxation

		Perceived Fairness of Tax System	
		Fair	Unfair
Perceived Justice of Tax System	Just	Tax compliance	Tax formalism
	Unjust	Tax protest	Tax revolt

SOURCE: Modified from Confalonieri and Newton (1995: 126).

current levels. If and when that desire changes from an idle wish into a firmly stated demand, public opinion can tilt toward strident calls for reform that shape the policymakers' environment. Confalonieri and Newton (1995) present a four-scenario typology of public attitudes toward taxation (Table 7–1).

In this model, public attitudes about a tax system are measured along two dimensions—fairness and justice. Fairness concerns people's willingness to accept as fair the tax structure's general, fundamental principles. Justice involves judgments about whether the tax structure in practice calls on all citizens to pay their share in accordance with the tax system's founding principles. Confalonieri and Newton assert that most of the public opinion data do not support a situation of open revolt against taxation but rather a frequently held perception that wealthy citizens are not paying their just share of taxes. If too many citizens' sense of justice has been violated by their perceptions of the tax system's operation, then the prospects for public mobilization in protest of the existing tax structure increases. Confalonieri and Newton steadfastly hold to a distinction between a **tax protest** generated by perceived injustice and an open **tax revolt** in which many citizens find taxation unjust in its execution and unfair in principle. The latter scenario would involve a much more fundamental challenge to governments' very existence.

Economic Explanations

Given the impact of economic growth on government revenues, it should come as no surprise that the health of the economy shapes the climate of tax policy making. A growing economy expands revenues, thereby decreasing pressure for reform. In contrast, a recessionary economy contracts revenues while frequently expanding demand for government services. Governments can consider responding by altering the tax code to meet the fiscal challenges of a recession.

Another economic factor that can build support for reform is sales competition within and across countries. The more open the environment regarding international trade and domestic economic regulation, the more visible tax distinctions that favor some firms or sectors of the economy will become (Hagemann, Jones, and Montador 1988). This logic of reform is another example of pressures posed by globalization. Economic integration in the European Union (EU) has created a variety of reasons to reconsider tax provisions as movement toward a level economic playing field continues within the EU competition policy.

Political Explanations

Political parties will almost always play some role in studies of policy making, and tax policy is no exception. Generally speaking, left-leaning parties tend to speak out for a more progressive tax code as an agent of income redistribution, whereas right-leaning parties tend to call for income-neutral taxation and often favor regressive sales taxes over potentially progressive forms of direct taxation. Research has found that changes in partisan control of government can affect the course of tax policy (Castles 1982b; Morrissey and Steinmo 1987; Steinmo 1993).

That said, the role that partisanship can play is contingent on other factors. Partisanship's effect will be greatest when a single party controls the executive and legislative branches of government along the lines of the party government model. When a single party is in control, substantial tax reform is more likely than in a divided government or in a multiparty coalition government. Steinmo (1993) argues that the United Kingdom has seen greater swings in its tax system over the years as the two major parties alternate in power and have had greater opportunity to realize their visions for reform. Conversely, coalition governments provide the impetus for a more incrementalist approach to tax reform as the coalition partners find it more difficult to work out a shared vision of sweeping tax reform (Rose and Karran 1986).

Interest group politics can also shape the tax system. In more pluralist settings, one should expect to see a greater fight for tax expenditures that benefit a particular segment of the population. Conversely, in more corporatist settings, the encompassing nature of the major interest groups should tend to limit calls for tax provisions that benefit a single firm or group of firms.

Institutional Explanations

Steinmo's work (1993) on the party government model's effects on taxation finds the roots of party government in the electoral and executive-legislative institutions of the three countries whose tax politics he examined—Sweden, the United Kingdom, and the United States. In short, Steinmo believes that party government occurs more frequently in the United Kingdom because of the Westminster model of government, in which a plurality electoral system is combined with a parliamentary executive.

The institutional setting specific to tax policy making can also influence tax decisions. Peters (1991) notes that tax policy making settings can differ in a couple of significant ways. First, the technical nature of tax policy can leave a role for at least three different cultures of expertise: lawyers, economists, and bureaucrats. This approach holds that lawyers are more likely to stress the need for detailed codes, economists are more worried about the incentives associated with taxation changes, and tax bureaucrats are frequently focused on the implementation issues associated with different forms of taxation. This diversity of expert cultures can be a force for incrementalism as the different mindsets make sweeping reform more difficult to deliver in a consensual form.

Second, the division of spending and taxing policy into various executive agencies and legislative committees shapes the context of tax reform. Spending decisions made elsewhere in the government can force the people actively involved in formulating tax policy to create new plans to respond to changed levels of expenditures. The role of government units not charged with forming the tax code is potentially much greater still because legislators, bureaucrats, and lobbyists active in other policy areas may try to place on the institutional agenda specific tax expenditures or particular tax rate changes.

International Policy Making

Few binding international agreements influence the specific tax policy choices individual countries make in an effort to meet the challenges we discussed earlier in this chapter. Countries negotiate a variety of bilateral tax treaties with other countries to determine the tax status of persons and firms spending portions of the year in both countries; however, these negotiations have their own challenges that go beyond the scope of this chapter.

The EU's push for a single market has generated an incentive for national governments to harmonize their tax policies in line with other member countries' tax codes. These pressures have been more informal than formal. The agreement to earmark certain revenues toward the EU may be the lone binding international agreement that directly shapes domestic tax policy in the four European countries examined in this book. Observers of the United Nations can always find news stories about the many member states that are behind on their scheduled national contributions to the organization's shared budget. From its founding in 1957 until 1970, the European Community (EC) faced the same problem. In April 1970 the Luxembourg Agreement called for three sets of tax revenues to be earmarked directly into the EC budget: customs duties on imports coming from outside the EC, special levies on agricultural imports, and a percentage of the VAT collected in each member state (not to exceed 1 percent). Fiscal pressures amid the stagflation of the late 1970s and early 1980s led to reform in this formula at the Fontainebleau summit, where the maximum rate for the EC portion of the VAT was raised to 1.4 percent. In 1992, amid a changed fiscal picture for both member states and the EU, an agreement was reached to lower the maximum VAT rate to 1 percent in 1999.

The decision to dedicate so-called own resources to the EU has achieved its stated purpose. We do not open the newspaper to read a listing of the back contributions owed the EU from its member states every fiscal year. The dedication of certain resources also has a small but visible influence on the taxation options available to EU member states. First, no member state can use tariffs as part of its domestic revenue mix; all such revenues go straight into the EU budget. Second, the decision to earmark a percentage of the VAT collected by member states quietly deepened the trend in these countries toward the adoption of this form of taxation—as opposed to a sales tax at the point of sale or other conceivable options.

A word of caution is in order regarding our treatment of national tax structures. Governments set tax rates, but tax revenues are largely dependent on economic activity. When we discuss tax structure in these six countries, remember that the figures presented can and do change from year to year. When these figures are noticeably out of line with other years, we discuss the difference. In an effort to maintain a similar context across all six countries, the discussion of tax structures below is based on national experiences in 1996. Unless otherwise noted, information on tax rates refers to 1997.[1]

United States

Background: Policy Process and Policy History

The tax policy process in the United States is more centralized than is the country's spending policy process, but these formal and informal procedures remain much more pluralist and open-ended than in other countries. Although tax changes can be written into the annual budget, they can also be proposed separately. As a result, policy formulation does not necessarily originate formally in the executive branch (unlike the budget process). As with most other legislation, the president must find legislative members willing to sponsor proposals that could have originated in executive branch discussions among the Office of Management and Budget, the Treasury, the Internal Revenue Service, the President's Council of Economic Advisers, or from many other sources. Alternatively the tax proposal could originate directly from a legislator.

Although the initiation of formal policy discussions is more decentralized for tax decisions than for spending decisions, the formal review of those ideas in Congress is more centralized. Spending decisions are reviewed by the relevant committees in both chambers, but taxation proposals must be reviewed in the House of Representatives by the Ways and Means Committee and in the Senate by the Finance Committee. Despite this degree of centralization, interest groups have multiple legislative targets to lobby for particular changes in the tax code because ultimate approval depends on passage in both chambers. The open-ended nature of the tax policy process, and a political philos-

[1] Data on the tax structure in 1996 are taken from the Organisation for Economic Co-operation and Development's *OECD in Figures* (Paris: OECD, 1999). Data on tax rates in 1997 are from Coopers and Lybrand's *International Tax Summaries 1998* (New York: Wiley, 1998).

ophy in many sectors that favors tax expenditures over direct transfers, have worked together to produce a seemingly endless list of tax expenditures for both corporate and individual income taxes. The presidential veto is not a useful institutional threat in most cases because tax changes can be attached to legislation that on balance the president supports.

The U.S. tax structure stands out for its reliance on personal income taxes. The United States is the only country among the six examined in this book in which individual income taxes make up well over one-quarter of tax receipts (37.6 percent in 1996). Other direct taxes are also slightly more important in the United States than in other major industrialized countries. The sum of shares represented by employee social security taxes and corporate income taxes in the United States (20.2 percent) exceeded the average for the EU (17.6 percent) by over 10 percent in 1996. The United States relies on sales taxes less than do all countries but Japan. In 1996, sales taxes accounted for 17.2 percent of total government tax receipts in the United States. Sales taxes account for less than 5 percent of tax receipts at the federal level, with excise taxes levied on only a few products and no universal sales tax.

The corporate income tax code has four basic tax brackets, ranging from 15 to 35 percent. A series of surtaxes forces most medium-sized and large firms to pay taxes at close to one-third of taxable income. States and localities are free to establish corporate income taxes. A multitude of systems exist with rates as high as 12 percent (but usually less than 10 percent) and with many different ways of calculating taxable income. There is no capital gains exemption at the federal level, but capital losses can be used to offset capital gains. The individual income tax code has five tax brackets with marginal rates ranging from 15 to 39.6 percent. The top rate on individual capital gains is capped at 28 percent. As with corporations, a variety of state and local income tax systems exist. Employees pay a basic social security tax of 7.65 percent of the first $65,400 in earnings and 14.5 percent thereafter. Employers pay an equal percentage of payroll taxes plus an additional assessment for unemployment insurance, which varies from state to state.

As noted earlier, the United States has no national sales tax. The federal government levies excise taxes on alcohol, gasoline, luxury automobiles, telephone services, and tobacco. Most state governments and many localities levy a sales tax at the point of sale. These combined state and local tax rates vary across the country from 3 to 10 percent. Similarly, the United States has no national property tax, but states and, especially, localities often rely heavily on property taxes. The sort of property taxed, how the property value is assessed, and the rate of tax charged vary across the country.

Contemporary Dynamics

The last major federal tax reform, in 1986, marked the realization of a central piece of the Reagan administration's agenda: the reduction of tax rates. A major element of that reform was a change in individual income taxes. The number of tax brackets was reduced from eleven to four, and the top marginal rate was cut from 46 to 28 percent. Part of the revenue lost was replaced by raising excise tax rates, and another portion was replaced by an increase in the applicability of corporate income taxes. In addition, changes in tax deduction regulations increased many individuals' taxable income.

The 1991 recession helped to push the budget deficit back over 5 percent of the gross domestic product (GDP) for the first time since 1986. In early 1993 the newly elected Clinton administration called for a reduction in the deficit through the promotion of economic growth, a slight reduction in the rate of spending growth, and by some revenue-enhancing changes in the tax code. The president's message contrasted with that of many fellow Democrats in Congress who proposed a series of programs they wanted to create or expand. The major leaders in the Republican Party—backed vocally by many other members—called for a series of tax and spending cuts to promote growth and balance the budget. Business interest groups tended to line up with Republicans calling for tax cuts, whereas labor tended to side with the Democrats.

In the first half of Clinton's first term, the Democratic Party held majorities in both houses of Congress. To push through the so-called recovery budget in his first year, Clinton compromised with several key Democratic members to increase spending in some areas. In the Senate the margin of victory was the slimmest one possible: Vice President Al Gore had to cast the tie-breaking vote in his capacity as president of the Senate. The major tax reform in that budget involved the personal income tax; Clinton fought for and enacted an increase in the highest marginal rate from 36 to 39.6 percent. In 1994, the last year of Democratic congressional control during the Clinton presidency, an additional revenue-enhancing reform took place. Social security taxes were raised by nearly one percentage point in 1994. At the same time, personal income tax brackets were indexed for inflation—avoiding the phenomenon of bracket creep, in which inflation pushes people into higher tax brackets without raising their purchasing power. This loss of revenue was justified by the administration on redistributive grounds because it would limit the share of income taxes paid by low- and middle-income taxpayers.

The Republican Party roundly criticized these two tax hikes in its successful 1994 midterm election campaign—even as the hikes began to spur deficit reduction. The victory of the Republicans initially led to a stalemate on tax policy issues. Continued implementation of the altered tax structure led to the elimination of the budget deficit by 1998 in a context of steady economic expansion and low inflation. This brighter fiscal picture placed a capital gains exemption and several new tax expenditures aimed at families high on the institutional agenda for the 1999–2001 legislative session.

The defeat of the Democratic Party in the 1994 midterm elections shows the political perils of tax hikes undertaken in a country whose citizens are markedly more skeptical of government expansion than residents of most other industrialized countries. The subsequent deficit reduction is a not-so-gentle reminder that politicians aiming at a medium-run objective in a democracy are perhaps particularly vulnerable. The unreversed tax reforms in 1993 and 1994 eventually helped first to lower interest rates and later to eliminate the deficit. However, the Democratic members of Congress who voted for the reforms were not able to take credit for those achievements in November 1994. By the time those achievements were visible in the second half of the 1990s, many of those Democratic legislators had already been voted out of office.

Japan

Background: Policy Process and Policy History

As with spending policy, tax policy formulation in Japan has historically centered around the Ministry of Finance. Proposed changes (which can originate from forces outside the ministry as well) are then reviewed by major coalition leaders and the leadership of affected interest groups. Often the relative power of the prime minister in this process is determined by his or her prior experience (or lack thereof) in the Ministry of Finance.

The Diet's role in tax policy has historically been limited because agreements were normally arrived at among major Liberal Democratic Party (LDP) factions before bills were presented in the legislature. In the contemporary period, however, multiparty coalitions formed by unstable parties have been the rule of the day. As a result, the process of securing passage of tax reforms announced by the government is no longer a foregone conclusion.

Japan's tax structure is different from most other industrialized countries' systems in two notable respects. First, Japan relies far less on sales taxes, which account for only 15.4 percent of tax receipts. Corporate income taxes are much more important. In 1996, corporate income taxes accounted for 16.4 percent of all taxes—almost twice the average share found in the other five countries examined in this book. The portions of the tax structure represented by personal income tax (20.2 percent) and by social security (32.8 percent) are more in line with other countries' tax systems.

Under the 1994 corporate tax law, the basic corporate income tax rate is 37.5 percent; smaller businesses pay a lower rate (28 percent) on the first eight million yen of taxable income. A local corporate income tax code also exists, with three brackets ranging from 6 to 12 percent. Municipalities can increase those marginal rates by as much as 10 percent. Localities also levy a corporate inhabitant tax of 5 to 20.7 percent on the income of businesses headquartered in their jurisdictions.

The personal income tax code has five brackets ranging from 10 to 50 percent in 10-percentage-point increments. Local income taxes have three brackets ranging from 5 to 15 percent with a variety of deductions and exemptions. With the exception of accident compensation insurance, social security taxes are borne equally by employers and employees. Rates vary somewhat depending mainly on occupation. Most employees pay a little less than 13 percent of earnings. Most employers pay a little under 14 percent of payroll.

As we noted earlier, sales taxes are much less important in Japan than in the other industrialized countries. Traditionally Japan had no general sales tax but rather a series of excise taxes. In the late 1980s, after several failed attempts by prior governments, the Takeshita government finally managed to gets its LDP legislative majority to replace the excise taxes with a 3 percent consumption tax (in large part because opposition parties had expressed uniform disapproval of the measure). After considerable debate, the VAT was ultimately raised to 5 percent in a 1996 reform, effective on April 1, 1997. Property taxes are levied at several different rates on buildings and on land—ranging from 0.15 to 1.4 percent.

Contemporary Dynamics

Japan was the one major economy that did not encounter rising budget deficits in the late 1980s or early 1990s. In fact, Japan ran surpluses from 1987 through 1992. When economic growth slowed to 1.0 percent in 1992 and then to 0.3 percent the next year, pressure mounted on the Japanese government to consider a fiscal stimulus.

As we noted in Chapter 6, a series of unstable coalition governments—the first three of which were not led by the LDP, for the first time in nearly 40 years—disagreed about how to reignite the economy. The new parties in power and the LDP discussed using a mix of spending increases and tax cuts as a stimulus, but they differed over the precise instrument mix of the stimulus. With multiparty coalitions backing these governments, the policy formulation process was heated at times. The Ministry of Finance (dominated by officials with long-standing ties to the LDP and with an historical commitment to deficit control) worried that an excessive spending stimulus would lead to a growing budget deficit. Some elements of the LDP and some of the new parties formed out of the LDP shared this concern and backed the Ministry of Finance in its call for a two-thirds increase in the consumption tax rate to back the continued increases in spending under discussion. This increase occurred in the face of complaints from the major labor confederations that a sales tax increase had regressive redistributive implications.

After months of debate and an initial spending stimulus in 1993, stimulative temporary tax reductions were enacted in March 1994 for that year only. Many of the reforms were extended into 1995. In 1996, partly to please the Ministry of Finance, the Murayama government called for a permanent increase in the consumption tax from 3 to 5 percent, effective April 1997. Temporary tax relief for individuals came in a 20 percent reduction in national and local income taxes owed. In addition, taxes on individually held real estate were reduced. Inheritance taxes were also lowered via a mix of deductions and exemptions. Corporations were gladdened by the permanent removal of a special corporate surtax.

Upon implementation of the 1994 tax reform, critics claimed that additional corporate tax relief would have resulted in a quicker recovery in 1994 and 1995. Other observers and many Ministry of Finance officials countered that further tax relief was undesirable because the deficit topped 3 percent of the GDP in 1995 for the first time since the early 1980s. Defenders of the reform claimed that it was just enough of a stimulus to restart the Japanese economy without overheating it. The economy did grow visibly in 1996; however, the consumption tax hike in April 1997, along with continuing domestic financial crises and a burgeoning regional economic crisis, led to economic stagnation that culminated in a recession in 1998, during which the GDP shrank by 2.5 percent.

In reaction to some of these criticisms and the evaluation of subsequent events, the Hashimoto government reduced the corporate income tax rate by 3 percentage points in early 1998, prior to elections for the upper house. In those July 1998 elections (which the LDP lost, resulting in the formation of the Obuchi government), every major party campaigned on a variety of tax cut proposals to lift Japan out of its economic malaise. Tax cuts and other fiscal stimulus proposals seem likely to remain near the top of the institutional agenda as long as this prolonged deflationary economic crisis continues.

The Japanese experience demonstrates a couple of the principles we discussed in Chapters 2 and 3. First, large governing coalitions make it harder to craft a coherent policy. In the eyes of many observers, the weakness of the Japanese government has negatively influenced tax policy making in contemporary Japan. The mix of tax cuts and hikes worked with other factors to snuff out a brief economic recovery begun in 1996. Second, visible failures of the governing party or coalition are often grist for the policy formulation mill of the opposition parties. As soon as the LDP became identified with the failings blamed on the consumption tax increase, other political parties swept in with different plans to reduce the tax burden on individuals.

Germany

Background: Policy Process and Policy History

As with spending policy, tax policy in Germany involves the chancellor consulting with all relevant members of the cabinet in forming a proposal before presenting it to the entire cabinet for approval. Historically, coalition governments in Germany have often split the Economic and Finance Ministries among the coalition partners. As a result, both coalition partners have tended to play a major role in tax policy decisions by heading the two major ministries involved. Ultimately any coalition disagreements are arbitrated by the chancellor, the economic and finance ministers, and senior figures in the governing coalition. Leaders of the major business and labor confederations are usually included in the policy formulation process—although formal, mandatory consultation has not taken place for two decades.

In the German tax structure, the largest share of tax revenues come from social security taxes (38.1 percent). Personal income taxes and sales taxes each accounted for roughly one-quarter of revenues in 1996. Corporate income taxes made up a little less than 4 percent of total tax revenues.

The basic corporate income tax rate is 45 percent, but this rate is reduced to 30 percent for distributed profits. Very limited capital gains exemptions are available to corporations. Individual income tax rates range from 27.3 to 53.0 percent across ten steadily progressive tax brackets. Both corporate and personal income taxes are subject to a so-called solidarity surcharge of 5.5 percent of taxes owed (beginning January 1, 1998). This surcharge raises the highest corporate rate to 47.5 percent and the top individual rate to 55.9 percent. Social security taxes are the same for employees and employers. Each is taxed at 21.15 percent. As elsewhere in Europe, the main sales tax is a VAT. The standard VAT rate since 1998 is 16 percent, although food, plants, books, and a few other items are taxed at 7 percent. Several transactions are exempt from the VAT including banking, insurance, and financial services; property transactions; education; health care services; and some nonprofit activities.

In the late 1980s tax reform focused on rate reduction and simplification. The basic corporate rate was cut from 56 to 50 percent. The number of personal income tax brackets was reduced slightly from eleven to ten; the top marginal rate fell by 3 percentage points, and the lowest rate was raised from 21.4 to 22.1 percent. Amid the steady growth of 1983 to 1989, a small reduction in some tax rates presented no revenue problems.

Contemporary Dynamics

As we noted in Chapter 6, reunification generated substantial fiscal pressures in Germany. By 1991 the deficit neared 3 percent of the GDP for the first time in years. The recession of 1992 to 1993 worsened fiscal pressures by reducing revenues while expanding certain government obligations (such as unemployment benefits). A difficult challenge resulted as two potentially conflicting imperatives reached the institutional agenda: A need to generate more revenues emerged simultaneously with a desire to avoid a significant tax increase (because it might further deepen the recession). The watchwords for the late 1980s had been tax simplification and tax reduction. Now, very quickly, revenue enhancement was added to the agenda.

Vigorous debate ensued within Helmut Kohl's governing coalition of the Christian Democrats and the Free Democrats. Many of the Christian Democratic leaders emphasized the need to raise revenues quickly to maintain Germany's reputation for fiscal discipline and its leadership role in monetary unification. Free Democrats, the junior partners in the coalition, showed more willingness to call for some form of tax cut that could generate jobs, thereby lowering unemployment benefit demands and increasing revenue flows from existing taxes. The Social Democrats—preparing for the coming 1994 general elections (the first they seemed quite capable of winning in over a decade)— were willing to criticize any plan that raised tax pressure on the poor or lowered taxes on the wealthy.

In response to this fiscal shortfall, the Kohl government initially emphasized revenue enhancement, which many Christian Democrats demanded. Tax concessions were eliminated in West Berlin in 1990. In 1991 the government implemented a temporary solidarity surcharge of 7.5 percentage point on top of corporations' and individuals' tax liabilities during fiscal year 1991. In 1992, as the sun set on that provision, the basic VAT rate was increased from 14 to 15 percent to capture revenues in order to stem the rising tide of the deficit.

These measures displeased business associations and Free Democratic leaders, who pointed to predictions of a recession in 1993. As a result of these political and economic developments, the Kohl government crafted a major tax reform in 1993 that addressed the arguments of both coalition partners. In the medium run, the reform was designed to be revenue neutral. With the recession in mind, the government tried to stimulate an escape from recession by reducing the corporate tax rates on retained profits (from 50 percent to its current 45 percent) and on distributed profits (36 to 30 percent). At the same time, the rates on a series of smaller tax instruments were increased, and most important, the solidarity surcharge of 7.5 percent was reintroduced, effective January 1995. This time, the law had no sunset provision; however, the Kohl government declared its intention to revoke the surcharge once the fiscal crisis had passed. The government pushed this reform through fairly quickly in the name of a dual national emergency. First, it needed revenues to meet social spending demands associated with reunification. Second, the tax hike was justified by the need to meet the Maastricht budget deficit target.

These changes were decidedly easy to implement because they involved no new tax instruments. However, easy implementation is not always a guarantee of ready policy success. This is particularly true when the desired outcomes (economic growth and a lower budget deficit) are contingent on many factors beyond a pair of specific taxes. The desired deficit reduction was achieved but amid a climate of minimal economic growth and rising unemployment.

In addition to demonstrating the clear role of international factors in framing contemporary tax policy, the recent German experience illustrates the power of a perceived emergency as a political tool that can overcome opposition to tax increases. In the German case, the dual challenges of reunification and the Maastricht target enabled the Kohl government to pursue an emergency income tax of much greater size than that pursued in other European countries in the mid-1990s. Even with these tax hikes and economic recovery in 1994 and 1995, the deficit did not subside until the final push to meet the Maastricht target in 1997.

Now that these emergencies have faded, tax reduction has bubbled back up onto the systemic agenda. In 1998 the Kohl government reduced the solidarity surcharge from 7.5 to 5.5 percent of tax liability (although to compensate, it raised the basic VAT rate from 15 to 16 percent). In 1999 the Schroeder government quickly enacted a reform that shifted a small portion of the tax structure from individuals to corporations while forming a group to study an overhaul of corporate and individual taxation. The government has announced its willingness to consider reductions in the top rates for corporate and individual income taxes.

France

Background: Policy Process and Policy History

As with spending policy, tax policy in France is centered around the Finance Ministry. Once budget parameters are set using estimates from the Finance Ministry, the finance minister formulates recommendations for tax changes associated with the coming budget. If changes affect sectors of the economy that correspond to other ministries, those ministries are brought into consultations before the prime minister makes a decision to present the changes as part of the budget bill or as a separate measure. The decision to move ahead with the proposal can also be shaped by consultations with relevant interest groups or senior parliamentary leaders, particularly if the government believes the reforms could be controversial. After the public announcement, the Finance Ministry leads the effort to secure passage in the legislature.

In the French tax structure, roughly 40 percent of tax receipts are generated by social security contributions (39.6 percent in 1996). Income taxes are much less important in France than in other industrialized countries. Individual income taxes accounted for 14.1 percent of revenues, whereas corporate income taxes represented just 3.8 percent. Direct taxes constituted just one-third of tax receipts. Sales taxes accounted for an additional 27.3 percent.

Tax rates in France are steeper and more progressive than U.S. residents would be accustomed to seeing. The individual income tax code has six brackets with steeply progressive rates ranging from 10.5 to 54.0 percent. Because of a high income threshold, only half of French households pay income taxes. Residents are assessed an additional generalized social contribution of 7.5 percent of earnings (raised in 1997 from 3.4 percent). The corporate income tax rate is 33.33 percent; a temporary increase enacted in 1997 made the rate 41.67 percent. Short-term capital gains receive no special treatment, but many long-term capital gains are assessed at a lower rate (18 percent). Most individual capital gains are taxed at 19.4 percent. Social security rates vary slightly by occupation. Employees pay around 20 percent, whereas employers pay approximately 40 percent of payroll. The basic sales tax is a VAT with a standard rate of 20.6 (raised in 1995 from 18.6 percent). A lower rate of 5.5 percent is levied on most food products, books, water, and a few other items. On entities with over 90 percent of their production exempt from the VAT, France levies a special payroll tax of between 4.25 and 13.6 percent.

Like many industrialized countries, France simplified its income tax structure and lowered income tax rates during the 1980s and 1990s. Many of these changes came under the so-called cohabitation center-right governments serving alongside French president François Mitterrand. The corporate tax rate fell from 45 to 42 percent under the first cohabitation government led by Jacques Chirac in the late 1980s. After a large center-right electoral victory in 1993, the Balladur government lowered the rate to its present 33.33 percent. Although the individual income tax code remains progressive, the Balladur government slashed the number of brackets from thirteen to seven.

Contemporary Dynamics

Slow economic growth and a recession in France in the early 1990s helped to produce a budget deficit of over 5 percent of the GDP. The rising deficit placed pressure on the French government to defend its currency. This challenge, combined with the Maastricht commitment to monetary unification, generated calls to increase government revenues in order to halt the rising deficit. The government, faced with rising unemployment claims and falling revenues, increased employee social security contributions from around 16 percent of earnings to approximately 20 percent. In 1992 the center-left Rocard government began to levy an income tax surcharge of 1.2 percent of earnings—the generalized social contribution (GSC). The Balladur government doubled this rate to 2.4 percent, effective in 1994. Although this increase was initially described as a stopgap measure, the GSC shows no signs of fading. This is a gentle reminder of how policy decisions generated to deal with one set of circumstances can take on a life of their own.

In an effort to meet the Maastricht budget deficit target of 3 percent of the GDP by the late 1990s, the center-right Juppe government installed with the Chirac presidency in 1995 presented several plans for substantial reductions in spending (see Chapter 6) and some tax increases. Although the spending cut proposals created opposition that received more coverage in the media, the center-right coalition government found it even more difficult to build support at the formulation stage for tax increases. The major reforms called for 1 or 2 percentage-point increases in the corporate income tax, the GSC, and the VAT. Several of the core supporters of Chirac and Juppe (including the major business associations and upper- and middle-class voters) were opposed to tax increases—particularly when the spending cuts were not fully implemented. The center-left parties and the labor union movement criticized the Juppe plan as proposing new taxes that would affect working-class citizens at the very moment that cuts in some redistributive spending were being proposed.

In mid-1995, with a deficit still stubbornly in excess of 5 percent of the GDP and difficulties hampering implementation of the spending cut proposals, the Juppe government enacted the proposed increases. The standard VAT rate rose from 18.6 to 20.6 percent, the GSC rate rose from 2.4 to 3.4 percent, and the standard corporate tax rate rose from 33.33 to 36 percent. In the rarefied atmosphere generated by the late 1995 general strike, the Juppe government found it impossible to push through passage of major tax changes during 1996. In 1997 the government faced a difficult general election, and the center-right government tried to mobilize its core constituency by reducing the top rate for personal income taxes from 54 to 52 percent. Nevertheless, that election was won by the center-left parties that propelled Lionel Jospin to the top of the cabinet.

The Jospin government changed the dynamics of both policy formulation and decision making. The government used the need to meet the Maastricht deficit target by the end of 1997 as a justification for quick action on the fiscal front. In an abbreviated period of new policy formulation, the center-left government tried to maintain the support of organized labor by proposing tax hikes for the wealthy. Almost immediately, the top personal income tax rate was pushed back up to 54 percent. The corporate tax rate paid by large companies was increased from 36 to 41.6 percent. In the name of burden-sharing and in pursuit of the Maastricht target, the GSC was increased from 3.4 to 7.5 percent. To avoid open opposition from the business sector, the Jospin government stressed the need for speed and the business benefits that would come from participating in the monetary unification process. These political tactics proved somewhat successful on both fronts.

The reforms pursued in 1997 were not difficult to implement. Observers do not doubt that France has the technical capacity to execute the policy over time. Instead, some wonder how sustainable the taxes can be. In short, will their implementation lead to calls for major tax reform now that the Maastricht deadline has been met and the euro has been launched?

France's experience demonstrates the potential power of international constraints (and commitments) on domestic policymakers. Although tax increases tend to be divisive, the push to join the euro zone eventually built support for various tax measures to lower the deficit in order to meet the target, once the deadline loomed larger. In 1995 and 1996, the something-for-nothing dynamic won out over globalization pressures. Over the following three years, however, those international pressures and commitments were used to justify a series of tax reforms aimed at reducing the deficit. Time will tell whether these tax changes are pulled back or are as enduring as the so-called temporary GSC surcharge of the early 1990s.

United Kingdom

Background: Policy Process and Policy History

The tax policy formulation process is much more centralized in the United Kingdom than in most other countries. The prime minister and the finance minister (known as the chancellor of the exchequer) work together to discuss potential reforms proposed from within the Finance Ministry. Those reforms are then discussed with relevant ministers and senior officials at other ministries. The prime minister is the arbiter of any disputes. Tax reforms are usually worked into the draft budget. Once the budget is announced, the government is typically confident that it will pass in Parliament. As we discussed in Chapter 6, the Blair government introduced in late 1997 the practice of an annual Green Budget speech in which the Finance Ministry provides a broad outline of possible tax reform initiatives and the economic concerns that motivate them. Some observers have noted that this procedural innovation is a response to Margaret Thatcher's problems with the poll tax initiative (discussed in the next section).

The British tax structure relies more heavily on sales taxes than do the tax structures of the other industrialized countries we examine here. Throughout the 1990s sales taxes have accounted for over one-third of tax receipts (35.2 percent in 1996). In 1996 social security taxes were just 16.8 percent of taxes received, largely because health care is funded out of other revenues and not via an earmarked payroll tax. Shares from individual income taxes (25.9 percent) and corporate income taxes (10.5 percent) are similar to those found in the other countries.

The basic corporate income tax rate is 31 percent. Small firms are taxed at 21 percent, and medium-sized firms receive a small amount of relief from the basic rate. No capital gains exemptions are granted. There are no subnational or local income taxes. The three individual income tax brackets range from 20 to 40 percent. Individuals are granted an exemption up to an updated threshold of capital gains. Employees pay 2 percent of a small initial share of earnings and 10 percent of the remainder up to a moderate threshold (a little over $750 per week in 1997). Employers pay taxes based on a five-bracket scale with marginal rates ranging from 0 to 10 percent; employer social security contributions have no upper limit.

The central sales tax is a basic VAT of 17.5 percent on most goods and services. A lower tax rate of 5 percent is levied on fuel and power for domestic use. Food, books and publications, and passenger transportation are exempt from the VAT, as are many services commonly exempted elsewhere (banking, insurance, and finance; education; health care; and some nonprofit activities). Insurance premiums are subject to a special tax of 2.5 percent. Taxes on residential and business real property are the main source of local government revenues.

Contemporary Dynamics

The Thatcher government came to power on a platform of smaller government and, in turn, lower taxes. Although some tax reduction took place during the Thatcher government's first two terms, a persistent budget deficit and pressure on the national currency in foreign exchange markets made it difficult to pursue major tax reform. In the late 1980s, fresh after leading her party to an unprecedented third consecutive electoral victory in 1987, Thatcher set into motion a series of substantial tax changes placed at the top of the institutional agenda.

Amid the euphoria of another sizable electoral triumph, policy formulation proceeded confidently within the executive branch. The Tories under Thatcher had run three campaigns that emphasized the themes of tax reduction and tax simplification. They enjoyed a large parliamentary majority perceived as strongly supportive of the prime minister's domestic agenda, although the party was increasingly divided over EU affairs. In 1988 and 1989 the government presented a series of reform proposals for national and local taxes that seemed assured of passage in the legislature despite some internal disagreement over the local level reforms.

In the event, decision making in the House of Commons ratified substantial reforms at both levels of government. At the national level, the principal reform was a simplification of the individual income tax code from six substantially progressive brackets down to two brackets. The top rate was lowered dramatically from 60 to 40 percent. The basic corporate income tax was reduced slightly from 35 to 33 percent. In turn, the government looked to recoup lost revenue in these direct taxes by raising the basic VAT rate from 15 percent to its current 17.5 percent.

As for local taxation, local governments in the United Kingdom historically received the largest portion of their revenues in transfers from the central government, the smallest portion from revenues generated by fees for some local government services, and a sizable remainder from a property tax. Under the first two Thatcher governments, transfers to local governments declined and the property taxes (or the rates, as they are called) bore an increasing share of the revenue flow. Thatcher argued that the domestic rates discriminated against property owners by allowing renters to receive local government services without taxation. In their place, the Thatcher government instituted a community charge (based on the number of residents) that could be assessed on all individuals. This measure, which met with some opposition within the Conservative Party prior to passage, was promptly dubbed the poll tax because one of the sanctions for noncompliance was the loss of voting rights.

The poll tax was first implemented in Scotland in 1989 and met with some open public criticism. Nothing prepared the government, however, for the firestorm of public opposition that occurred in England and Wales when the tax was implemented in spring 1990. A wave of public demonstrations ensued that included the worst riot in London in recent history. Visible numbers of citizens openly refused to pay the poll tax in protest. Some Conservative Party members called on Thatcher to support revocation of the tax, but she refused to back down. In some opinion polls forecasting the intention to vote in the next general elections (due no later than 1992), the Conservatives trailed Labour by over 20 percentage points.

The public protests and the discouraging polling results culminated in a challenge to Thatcher's party leadership in November 1990 from Michael Heseltine. When the initial vote was inconclusive (that is, she did not gain a large enough majority to end the leadership contest on the first ballot), Thatcher decided to resign as party leader after consulting with other party leaders—thereby ending her tenure as prime minister. The leadership challenge ended in the selection of John Major as the new party leader. In 1992, the Major government revoked the poll tax—replacing it in 1993 with a slightly altered property tax system. It also decreased the rate for the lowest income bracket from 24 to 20 percent.

The poll tax affair and its subsequent ramifications for the Thatcher government serve as a cautionary tale about the double-edged sword of executive power in the Westminster model of executive-legislative relations. On the one hand, with a sizable majority and the varied resources of the prime minister's post, Thatcher was correct in assuming that she could drive through passage of the poll tax despite some criticisms of the plan both within and outside the governing party. The strength of the government opened a path toward reform.

On the other hand, the ability of the executive to enact with relative ease the poll tax reform left it blindsided by a level of public opposition that was difficult to forecast given the limited public debate over the initiative prior to implementation. This cautionary tale has perhaps not been lost on Tony Blair—currently the leader of an even larger parliamentary majority than Thatcher enjoyed in 1990. The downfall of the Thatcher government is said to have been a motivation for the Blair government's innovation of circulating fiscal reform ideas and proposals months prior to their formal introduction into the decision-making phase of the policy process. Since being elected in June 1997, the Blair government has focused on less visible increases in excise tax rates and a new, onetime 23 percent windfall profit tax on privatized utilities that was earmarked to fund a new initiative to reduce youth unemployment. Although several corporate tax exemptions were eliminated, the government reduced the two basic corporate rates by a few percentage points each.

Italy

Background: Policy Process and Policy History

The Italian fiscal process has differed from most industrialized countries' by formally separating tax legislation from spending legislation. Any changes to the tax code have to be written outside of the budget bill. As with spending policy, the Treasury has taken the lead role in formulating tax reforms. Nevertheless, the greater size of governing coalitions and the weaker party discipline of the participants has made it difficult to negotiate major tax reforms through the legislature. As a result, tax policy has tended to follow the same incrementalist dynamic present in spending policy.

In the Italian tax structure, social security payroll taxes constitute the largest portion of tax revenues (30.5 percent in 1996). Personal income taxes and sales taxes each account for about 25 percent of tax receipts. Corporate income taxes are a significantly greater share of total tax receipts (9.2 percent) than in France or Germany.

The corporate income tax rate in Italy is 37 percent. Until 1998 an additional local income tax was levied by municipalities at 16.2 percent; since 1993 that local tax payment could not be used to reduce the amount owed to the national government. Capital gains exemptions per se are not allowed, but companies are given the option of spreading the gains over a maximum of five years. The individual income tax code has seven brackets with rates ranging from 10 to 51 percent. Like corporations, individuals also paid local income tax at 16.2 percent until 1998; however, a series of deductions and exemptions reduces taxable income for most individuals by over 50 percent. Social security payroll tax rates are among the highest in the world. Most of the responsibility for social security taxes falls on employers, most of whom pay between 40 and 50 percent of payroll depending on the collective contract and the income level of the average employee. Most employees pay around 10 percent of earnings. The self-employed pay, on average, around 5 percent of earnings. Effective in 1998 a new regional VAT of 4.5 to 5.5 percent was instituted to replace the local income tax and the social security payroll tax. This major change increases Italy's reliance on indirect taxes in its quest to reduce tax evasion.

The basic VAT rate is 19 percent. Three diverse categories of goods and services are charged lower rates ranging from 4 to 16 percent. In addition, banking, insurance, and financial services; education and health services; some nonprofit and cultural activities; postal services; and property transactions are exempt. Property transactions, however, are subject to registration taxes ranging from 1 to 17 percent. Excise taxes are charged on several items including furs and luxury automobiles.

Throughout the 1980s and 1990s Italy had the highest budget deficit among the six countries examined in this book. During the 1980s the deficit was consistently greater than 10 percent of the GDP. Following the lead of many other countries, Italy simplified the individual income tax code in the late 1980s by reducing the number of brackets from nine to seven, dropping the top rate from 62 to 50 percent. Many observers called for a greater combination of spending cuts and tax increases to deal with the deficit, but political problems made major reforms difficult.

Contemporary Dynamics

The Maastricht agreement and a run against the lira placed further pressure on the government to fight the budget deficit in the early 1990s. In contrast to France and Germany, Italy had to reduce the budget deficit in a context of tremendous political instability because the old political order was breaking down. The forces pushing deficit reduction and tax reform on the institutional agenda were just as strong (if not stronger) than in the other two countries, but the political atmosphere in Italy made it harder to envision a path to progress.

The climate for policy formulation was rocky. Although the government was committed to the Maastricht guidelines, the coalition government was under tremendous stress. In addition to the problems associated with getting multiple coalition partners to agree on a reform proposal, the situation was complicated in the 1990s by large fluctuations in the Italian party system. Further, the major business and labor confederations refused to take a position on the revenue-enhancing reforms the government discussed.

At the decision-making phase, the government relied on a so-called sunset strategy to tie the proposed new taxes more directly to the need for substantial deficit reduction. To reduce open opposition to the measures, the new tax instruments were instituted for fixed periods of time. A special tax of 0.75 percent on firms' net equity was implemented for a three-year period. A new capital gains tax was introduced on the sale of most land and buildings for a ten-year period. A new minimum tax on business was introduced for a two-year period in 1992. Local governments introduced a new property tax on real estate ranging from 0.4 to 0.6 percent of assessed value; this measure indirectly improved national finances by working to reduce the need to transfer funds to local governments to fund their respective deficits.

Implementation of the capital gains and the minimum taxes met with steep opposition. The capital gains tax went into force as scheduled in 1991 and met with serious criticism in the media and from economically comfortable private citizens. As a result, a wobbly Italian government suspended the measure in 1993. In that context, the minimum tax adopted in 1992 was never implemented fully and was shelved when its sunset clause arrived in 1994. In addition, evasion of social security contributions continued to be a problem; some unofficial estimates top $20 billion per year.

Despite these problems, the other reforms and solid economic growth in 1994 and 1995 helped to reduce the deficit to below 9 percent of the GDP for the first time in over a decade in 1995. That 1995 deficit (7.6 percent of the GDP) was still the highest among the seven largest industrialized countries. Deficit reduction remained high on the systemic agenda in 1995 as the Prodi government took power. The Prodi government pledged a combination of spending cuts (especially via a major pension reform) and temporary revenue rate increases in roughly equal measure to bring the deficit down to the Maastricht criterion of 3.0 percent of the GDP by the end of 1997. Reductions in the top rates for individual and corporate income taxes were compensated for by a broadening of the tax base achieved by the elimination and reduction of several tax exemptions. As in Germany and France, a temporary surtax, the Eurotax, was enacted in 1997 with an eye toward the Maastricht target. The government also created a regional VAT (varying from 4.5 to 5.5 percent) that would pay for health care and some other social services previously funded by payroll taxes; this particular reform combined efforts to reduce tax rates on employers with efforts to reduce tax evasion associated with social security contributions. As we noted in Chapter 6, this program enabled Italy to meet the deficit target at the last minute. As of this writing, it is hard to know whether deficit pressures will return quickly and whether the D'Alema government formed in late 1998 will call for some of these temporary taxes to be extended past their fast-approaching sunset deadlines.

The Italian reforms were pushed through amid trying circumstances via a statutory pledge to limit the application of various tax changes to explicitly medium-run periods of time. Governments often prefer to avoid such clauses because they limit their own discretion (and that of future officials). When faced with a lack of confidence from the public, an expectation of potentially frequent elections, and serious public mistrust in government, however, this sort of government commitment can help to gain the legislative votes needed to enact reform. Policy design is not all about the path from the policy output to the desired outcome. Sometimes the policy designers need to have a keen sense of the relationship between the specific policy instruments and their political feasibility.

Cross-national Trends

A cross-national summary of tax structures in these six countries highlights the greater reliance on indirect taxes in the continental European countries. This distinction was deepened by tax reforms pursued in the push toward monetary unification in the 1990s—most notably by the creation of a new regional VAT in Italy that replaced local income taxes and national payroll taxes for social security. All six countries pursued a simplification of their income tax structures and a reduction in rates for the highest bracket in line with the supply-sider argument, yet the desired policy outcome of higher economic growth rates did not materialize in most countries. Consideration of the dynamics of tax reform in the 1990s leads us to focus on the role of economic and political factors as central to contemporary tax policy making.

Policy Outputs

The tax challenge is lowest in Japan and the United States, where taxes represent less than 30 percent of the GDP. Conversely, France and Italy gather about 45 percent of the GDP in taxes. How do these countries collect taxes?

Several trends and exceptions are visible in Table 7–2. Four of the six countries generate around one-quarter of tax revenues via personal income taxes. The United States generates over one-third of its revenues in this way, and in France personal income taxes account for less than one-seventh of the country's revenues.

Corporate income taxes are a more important source of revenue in Japan than in the other five countries. Corporate income taxes account for over 16 percent of revenues—almost double the average share for the other five countries. Corporate income taxes are least important in France and Germany.

Dependence on payroll taxes (including employee and employer social security contributions) varies even more widely. In the United Kingdom, payroll taxes account for only around one-sixth of revenues. In the United States, they make up almost one-quarter of tax receipts. Italy (30.5 percent), Japan (32.8 percent), Germany (38.1 percent), and France (39.6 percent) are noticeably more reliant on payroll taxes. Table 7–2 also details how payroll tax obligations are divided between employers and employees. In all six countries, employers pay over half of payroll taxes. In most of these countries, employers pay between 60 and 70 percent of the total. At the low end of the spectrum, German employers pay around 54 percent of payroll taxes; at the high end, Italian employers carry a comparatively heavier load (78 percent).

Sales taxes in three of the countries (France, Germany, and Italy) account for just over one-quarter of tax receipts. Sales taxes are most important in the United Kingdom, where they make up over one-third of tax revenues. They are noticeably less important components of the tax structure in Japan (15.4 percent) and the United States (17.2 percent). Remember from the case studies that the United States is the only one of these countries with no comprehensive national sales tax; most sales taxes are collected at the state and local levels.

What drives some of these differences in tax structure? A major force behind smaller payroll taxes in the United Kingdom is the decision to fund government health care programs out of general revenues. This decision is somewhat of a double-edged sword. On the one hand, by funding out of general revenues a basic government program that is popular with many citizens, the government can try to increase popular support for the tax system as a whole.

Table 7-2 Tax Structures as a Percentage of Tax Receipts, 1996

Country	Personal Income Tax	Corporate Income Tax	Employee Social Security	Employer Social Security	Sales Taxes	Other Taxes	Total Taxes per GDP
France	14.1%	3.8%	13.0%	26.6%	27.3%	15.2%	45.7%
Germany	24.7	3.8	17.6	20.5	27.9	5.5	38.1
Italy	25.1	9.2	6.8	23.7	25.9	9.3	43.2
Japan	20.2	16.4	14.2	18.6	15.4	15.2	28.4
United Kingdom	25.9	10.5	7.2	9.6	35.2	11.6	36.0
United States	37.6	9.6	10.6	12.9	17.2	12.2	28.5
Average	*24.6*	*8.9*	*11.6*	*18.7*	*24.8*	*11.5*	*36.7*
EU Average	*26.0*	*7.5*	*10.1*	*16.3*	*31.2*	*8.8*	*42.4*
OECD Average	*26.8*	*8.2*	*7.8*	*14.5*	*32.5*	*10.2*	*37.7*

SOURCE: *OECD in Figures* (Paris: Organisation for Economic Co-operation and Development, 1999).

On the other hand, such an approach makes these programs potentially more vulnerable to a generalized tax protest. If health care were funded in the United Kingdom out of an earmarked tax, it might be easier to maintain support for that particular tax instrument, even in the face of major pressures to cut (or maintain) tax rates.

Income taxes have been least important in France because of the government's suspicion that tax avoidance and evasion are relatively high. In response, French governments have responded over the decades by relying much more heavily on payroll and sales taxes, which are easier to implement. Property taxes have also been an important substitute.

Policy Outcomes

A crucial outcome for tax policymakers is public acceptance of the tax structure. Since the early 1980s, protests calling for tax simplification have emerged in all of these countries. These pressures have helped to increase commonalities across these countries' tax systems. For instance, the major trend in tax reform during the 1990s was the simplification of the personal income tax code and a decrease in the top marginal rate (Table 7–3). In two of the three countries with a tradition of smaller government (the United Kingdom and the United States), the top rate in 1994 was 40 percent or less. The other four countries had top marginal rates for personal income taxes of 50 percent or more.

Lowering of upper marginal rates was expected to increase revenues by stimulating additional economic activity. The added growth would generate new revenue streams to compensate for the tax rate cuts. In most of these countries, however, economic growth slowed during the 1990s in comparison with prior decades. Slower growth stymied the hopes of providing politically popular rate cuts without increasing budgetary pressures. The supply-sider argument we reviewed in Chapter 6 has yet to realize its promised goal in practice.

Table 7-3 Personal Income Tax at the National Level, 1985 and 1994

Country	Top Rate		Lowest Positive Rate		Number of Brackets		Tax Unit in 1994
	1985	1994	1985	1994	1985	1994	
France	65%	56.8%	5%	12%	13	7	Family
Germany[a]	56	53	22	19	N.A.	N.A.	Optional
Italy[b]	62	51	18	10	15	7	Individual
Japan	70	50	10	10	9	3	Individual
United Kingdom	60	40	30	20	6	3	Individual
United States	50	39.6	11	15	14	5	Optional
Average	60.5%	48.4%	16%	14.3%	11.4	5	N.A.

SOURCE: *OECD in Figures* (Paris: Organisation for Economic Co-operation and Development, 1999).

[a]The German system includes a sliding-scale formula and not formal brackets.

[b]Data are for 1986 and 1993.

N.A. = not applicable.

In response, governments often resorted to increases in payroll taxes and sales taxes earmarked for popular government programs (combined with restrained spending) in an effort to reduce the deficit. Despite these changes, real revenue growth trailed economic growth during most of the 1990s in these six countries. Given the commitment to deficit reduction, this situation motivates governments to try to promote growth without raising tax rates or spending significantly.

Understanding Policy Reform

If the 1980s were characterized as the decade of tax protest, tax simplification, and tax reduction, the 1990s might be considered a decade of quiet revenue-seeking. Center-left and center-right governments alike tried to increase revenues in various ways. These hunts for revenue expansion were motivated largely by the desire to reduce (or, in Japan's case, control) the budget deficit. As we saw in Chapter 6, most of the motivation for deficit reduction stemmed from international financial markets and from the monetary unification agreement in continental Europe. To understand the nuances of how governments went about revenue enhancement, we need to consider additional factors.

Prevailing short-term economic conditions clearly played a role in most of these countries. Slow economic growth in all but the United States forced taxation rate increases onto the institutional agenda as a path toward deficit reduction because political considerations made wholesale spending cuts undesirable. Stronger economic growth enabled the United States to zero out its deficit with only one specific tax increase—the jump in the top rate enacted in 1993 at the beginning of the Clinton administration. By the end of the decade, continued economic growth and the budget surplus put tax rate reduction back on the U.S. agenda.

In the other countries, slow growth created pressure for tax rate increases, but the public remained unsurprisingly skeptical. In the case studies, we saw three major strategies used to pursue revenue enhancement in the absence of strong economic growth—increases in indirect taxes, increases in the top rate of taxation for individuals and corporations, and the creation of a surcharge income tax. In the three countries pushing to meet the Maastricht fiscal target by 1997, governments tried to blunt opposition by using the proposed benefits of monetary unification as a rationale for tax increases. To reduce further the vibrancy of opposition, governments often placed sunset clauses on tax increases.

We also observed how political unity within the government provides a force for policy stability, whereas divisions within governing coalitions and visible swings in election outcomes make it difficult for governments to steer a coherent course. In particular, multiparty coalitions and major voting swings made policymakers' jobs more difficult in the 1990s in France, Italy, and Japan. Although these three governments used approaches observed in all six countries, we observed situations in which French, Italian, and Japanese governments had to reverse recent decisions in tax policy. As of this writing, it is difficult to assume that these countries will overcome these political challenges in the foreseeable future.

SUGGESTED READINGS

Conlan, Timothy J., Margaret T. Wrightson, and David R. Bean. 1990. *Taxing Choices: The Politics of Tax Reform*. Washington, D.C.: CQ Press.

Haycraft, J. 1985. *Italian Labyrinth*. Harmondsworth, England: Penguin.

Howard, Christopher. 1997. *The Hidden Welfare State: Tax Expenditures and Social Policy in the United States*. Princeton: Princeton University Press.

Kato, Junko. 1994. *The Problem of Bureaucratic Rationality: Tax Politics in Japan*. Princeton: Princeton University Press.

Leibfritz, Willi, John Thornton, and Alexandra Bibbee. 1997. *Taxation and Economic Performance*. Paris: Organisation for Economic Co-operation and Development, 1997.

Messere, Ken, ed. 1998. *The Tax System in Industrialized Countries*. Oxford: Oxford University Press.

Pechman, Joseph A. 1987. *Comparative Tax Systems: Europe, Canada, and Japan*. Arlington, Va.: Tax Analysts.

Peters, B. Guy. 1991. *The Politics of Taxation: A Comparative Perspective*. Oxford: Basil Blackwell.

Pollack, Sheldon David. 1996. *The Failure of U.S. Tax Policy: Revenue and Politics*. University Park: Pennsylvania State University Press.

Rose, Richard, and Terrance Karran. *Taxation by Political Inertia*. 1986. London: Macmillan.

Slemrod, Joel, ed. 1999. *Tax Policy in the Real World*. Cambridge: Cambridge University Press.

Steinmo, Sven. 1993. *Taxation and Democracy: Swedish, British, and American Approaches to Financing the Modern State*. New Haven: Yale University Press.

Chapter 8 **Health Care Policy**

The most basic element of human welfare is good health. For centuries, governments were largely "off the hook" in this area because most people did not hold government directly responsible for individuals' poor health. Governments tried to slow the spread of infectious diseases but did little else. In the twentieth century, as preventive public health initiatives expanded, governments have also played a growing role in the curative care sector via regulation, funding, and, at times, the provision of care itself.

Common Policy Problems

Health outcomes are the fundamental test of government success in the area of health policy. If many citizens are ill and dying, people would probably say that government efforts are insufficient to deal with the problem—even if government inaction is not the sole (or even principal) cause of these undesired outcomes. The complexity of health outcomes is what makes health policy such a difficult challenge for governments. Should policy focus largely on preventive measures such as vaccinations, clean air and water, and the like? Or is the problem the absence of medical intervention at the right time? Here, too, government can make a difference by sponsoring research to discover new treatments and by providing access to curative care.

Access to curative care is understandably important to most people. People want to protect their most important asset: their lives and those of their families and friends. Perhaps the most fundamental aspect of modern health care policy stems from the widespread belief in the possibility of curing any and all illnesses: Citizens' demands in the health sector are almost unlimited. Once people became confident that even devastating illnesses could be overcome, demands for curative care expanded and many of those demands involved the government as the provider of last resort. As a result, access to curative care is a major public policy issue.

Curative care is often expensive. Specialized health care professionals demand high wages, and new medical technologies and medicines fuel our hope that virtually any illness can be conquered. In many industrialized and late-industrializing countries, the cost of curative care has risen faster than the general rate of inflation. Whether most curative care is provided publicly or privately, governments frequently face pressure to control health care costs.

Major Policy Options

In virtually every country around the world, the government manages and provides an array of public health projects including health education through schools and the broadcast media, vaccination programs, sanitation projects, and the regulation of food and drug quality. In most industrialized countries these projects have covered such a high percentage of the population for so long that one tends to take them for granted despite their crucial importance for health outcomes. In late-industrializing countries, public health programs vary more substantially from one country to the next in several key respects, including money spent per person; the organizational structure of public health; the number of public health professionals per person; and crucially, the percentage of the population reached by public health initiatives. Despite the undeniable importance of these differences in public health around the world, in this chapter we focus on the organization of curative care and cost-control issues because they represent more visible public policy issues in industrialized countries (and in many late-industrializing countries).

National policy models for curative care range from direct provision of care by the government to minimal government activity in providing care or even access to that care. The polar extremes here are not absolutes: Private activity still occurs in government-run systems and government has a considerable role in market-oriented systems. All countries are searching for what they believe is an optimal mix of public and private activity.

In the **national health service** model, citizens are guaranteed access to most curative care services through a system paid for and administered directly by the government. This approach has been prevalent in many communist economies, but it has also been used in some market economies, most notably the United Kingdom. In this model, the government pays hospitals, physicians, and nurses directly to provide comprehensive care to all citizens. Access is guaranteed, but all or almost all costs are absorbed by the government, which has a direct interest in cost-control measures and the authority to carry them out. This can mean, however, that demand for certain services may exceed supply—sometimes significantly. For example, waiting lists for elective procedures can be lengthy. As a result, the national health service approach is sometimes called rationed care.

In many late-industrializing countries, a much more limited national health service is constructed via a system of government-run hospitals that frequently lack the resources needed to meet the demands on their services. Although citizens are legally guaranteed a right to care at these facilities, the quality and availability of care are more often insufficient. A much higher percentage of citizens in these countries seek out private care or forego care than has been the case in the United Kingdom or in most command economies.

The **single-payer** model guarantees all citizens access to health care via a single program in which almost all funds come from the government, but care is provided privately. This approach tries to control costs and guarantee access by pooling all citizens into a single insurance program run directly by the government. The single insurer then negotiates the best rates from hospitals and physicians. Although conceivably all citizens could pay the government a premium earmarked for health insurance, in Canada the single-payer system is funded out of general government revenues. For further discussion of the development of the single-payer system in Canada, see Box 8–1.

Through **mandatory national health insurance,** government guarantees all citizens access to care but with multiple payers and multiple providers. Germany pioneered such efforts in the late nineteenth century, and many other countries followed this model during the twentieth century. In this approach, many citizens receive health coverage through private insurance (often tied into their jobs), but government regulations guarantee certain benefits or control costs and fees. The government provides health insurance to the unemployed, the self-employed, and retired citizens through various programs.

In the **market-maximized** model, the government provides no guarantee of access through either public hospitals or mandatory health insurance. In this approach, the government might provide access for some categories of people but not all. This approach assumes that access to health care is not a right of citizens but rather a choice each citizen makes. Government regulation of private health insurers, while still significant, is not at the level found in the mandatory national health insurance model. The United States has been a proponent of the market-maximized model. Health care in the market-maximized model is also rationed—not by the availability of services relative to the urgency of their need but rather by one's ability to pay.

In addition to policy options dealing with access, policymakers have an array of alternatives for dealing with cost-control concerns. Some cost-control measures try to limit costs by altering the behavior of certain individuals in the health care system. For example, one way to reduce health care costs is to make patients pay at the time care is delivered. Even if private or public insurance will pay the lion's share of the bill, forcing patients to make a **copayment** may make them monitor their use of medical services more carefully. Conversely, if care is free at the point of service, patients may be more likely to pursue care even if, in the long run, it will result in higher health insurance costs for them. Critics of this cost-control approach argue that patients' decisions to pursue treatment should not be constrained by economic considerations.

Other cost-control measures try to influence the behavior of physicians. Many countries employ a **fee-for-service** system, in which doctors are paid a fee for each service performed. If the number of services that can be provided is not constrained, physicians can provide additional services to rule out certain diagnostic possibilities or to enhance their incomes. In contrast, doctors are sometimes paid on a **capitation** basis; they receive a fee based on how many patients they treat, not on how many services they provide. In the United States, **health maintenance organizations** (HMOs) provide most services based on

Box 8-1 **In Depth: Canada's Single-payer Model**

For the first half of the twentieth century, Canadian health policy generally resembled the situation in the United States. The desirability of publicly mandated or financed health insurance was debated several times, but no such policies were adopted. In the middle of the century, a series of five provincial governments created universal hospitalization programs—beginning with Saskatchewan in 1947. The popularity of these programs put national health insurance back on the institutional agenda, and in 1957 the government passed the Hospital Insurance and Diagnostic Services Act. The law required all provincial governments to provide hospitalization insurance for their residents under financing shared jointly by the federal and provincial governments.

As this policy was being implemented in the 1960s, its popularity raised the issue of providing a comprehensive insurance plan that would also cover outpatient services. Despite opposition from private insurers and the Canadian Medical Association, the 1968 Medical Care Act expanded the system to its present scope. The Canadian Medicare system—in which each provincial government serves as a single payer for covered services in its jurisdiction—was in place in all provinces by 1971.

Under this single-payer system, each provincial government provides universal health coverage to its residents. The federal legislation dictates the basic coverage of the Medicare system; provinces are allowed to provide additional coverage should they choose to do so. Coverage is portable from province to province, although citizens generally must reside three months in a new province prior to joining its plan. The Medicare system features fee-for-service billing in accordance with a fee schedule worked out between provincial governments and physicians' associations. Physicians who choose not to obey the fee schedule cannot treat Medicare patients; this aspect of the Canadian system expands greatly the number of physicians in the system. As a result, citizens are able to choose their physicians from virtually the entire medical community. Covered physician services include general medical and maternity care, surgical and laboratory services, and other specializations. Medicare covers all basic hospitalization services. Hospitals in Canada are nonprofit organizations, and most are privately run. However, the government controls the annual public budget associated with the Medicare program as well as the technology acquisition decisions made by hospitals.

Under the terms of the single-payer system, private insurance companies are not permitted to write policies for benefits provided under Medicare. However, private insurers are allowed to provide supplemental medical insurance to cover benefits not provided by the government. Over 80 percent of all Canadians have some form of private supplemental health insurance often are paid in whole or in part by employers. Since 1984, when the 1984 Canada Health Act virtually outlawed patient copayments, the system has been free to the user at the point of service. The vast majority of program funding comes from general government revenues at the federal and provincial levels (rather than from premiums or from payroll taxes earmarked for health care).

capitation reimbursement. In the capitation system, physicians presumably will restrain themselves in providing services to strictly necessary care in order to remain within the bounds of their per-patient budget. Again, critics of this approach do not want economic considerations front and center when treatment options are being decided.

Another cost-control measure that focuses on the behavior of the medical community involves **limits on technology acquisition.** Studies have shown that making expensive technologies more available increases the likelihood that they will be used. Although this seems logical enough, cost-control advocates charge that much of this technology is overused—especially in countries that operate on a fee-for-service reimbursement system. They also argue that placing limits on the acquisition of medical technology by hospitals and private physicians can help keep costs under control. Limits on technology acquisition are associated with lower costs but also imply waiting lists to use certain technologies for which demand exceeds supply.

An organizational measure that tries to change cost dynamics in the health sector involves the use of a gatekeeper. Some health plans give patients the freedom to go to not just the general practitioner (GP) of their choice but to any physician of any specialty. In contrast, in a **gatekeeper system,** patients must see a GP and get a referral before going to see a specialist. In this way, the GP serves to control costs by trying to make the appropriate referral or no referral when the diagnosis or treatment does not require the participation of a specialist. This is the cost-control measure most widely used across countries—whether the health insurance plan is public or private. In the United States, **preferred provider organizations** (PPOs) use gatekeepers. PPOs also limit patients to the selection of doctors who agree to the insurer's fee schedule. The notion at work here is that the physician is a better judge of where the patient should go than is the patient. GPs are often preferred as gatekeepers because in most countries they make significantly less money than more specialized physicians. The gatekeeper approach is not without its controversies. In some countries, gatekeeper physicians at times complain that they are under pressure to keep costs low by keeping referrals under a certain budgetary limit.

The most frequent criticism of these cost-control alternatives stems from a desire to make health care decisions without reference to economic considerations. We cannot present ironclad evidence about the optimal amount that a country (or an individual) should spend on health care; it is a choice that must be made. Choices in health policy, as in other policy areas, are made by government officials who are responding to a variety of constituent groups.

What is the average citizen concerned about in the health sector? Everyone needs medical attention from time to time, and people know that they could incur serious medical problems (and expenses) due to illness or injury. That said, not everyone is equally risk-averse in his or her approach to health care. Some people want to spend as little as possible on health care, and others want complete coverage almost regardless of cost.

These different individual perspectives on health insurance are related to different approaches to medical insurance: the principle of **actuarial fairness** and the principle of **risk-pooling.** Actuarial fairness calls for people to be grouped by risk factors—enabling healthy individuals in low-risk occupations to join health insurance plans with other similar individuals. Thus high-risk patients (including those already diagnosed with chronic health problems) would be forced to pay higher health insurance premiums in recognition of the greater likelihood that they will require care. The principle of risk-pooling calls for solidarity of citizens based on a recognition that everyone is at risk of needing care because of chronic illness or accidents. That risk is then pooled across a large body of currently healthy and unhealthy individuals to provide maximal coverage at a lower cost. Advocates of actuarial fairness criticize risk-pooling because they claim that it asks the healthy to subsidize the unhealthy when they have no responsibility for the illnesses involved. Advocates of risk-pooling counter that even narrowly self-interested individuals should pool risks together to lower the costs of illness to the sick because today's healthy could become tomorrow's ill.

Explaining Policy Dynamics

Health policy has become an increasingly visible issue on the systemic agenda during the 1980s and 1990s. That visibility has motivated a new wave of research on the dynamics of health policy making. Most research has consisted of national case studies, but several analysts have conducted cross-national comparisons. Although in past decades primary attention was paid to cultural, economic, and political factors, a series of studies in the 1990s brought new attention to the role of institutions.

Cultural Explanations

Cultural factors have been used most frequently in analyses of U.S. health policy making. A series of studies have emphasized the role of an individualistic and antigovernment culture in blocking the emergence of legislation that ensures universal access to medical care in the United States (Anderson 1972; Jacobs 1993; Patel and Rushefsky 1999; Starr 1982). As we noted in other chapters, cultural differences are frequently used to explain countries' use of government authority in responding to various policy challenges.

This approach, however, has proven more problematic in building an explanation of health policy making that holds up to cross-national examination. When we look at the rest of the Anglo-American family of nations, we see a delay in the adoption of some form of universal access policy (especially in Australia and Canada). That said, we also see that two of those countries developed health policy models that are among the most government-intensive in some respects: the first national health service (in the United Kingdom) and the first single-payer system (in Canada). In fact, during the twentieth century, health care was one of the policy areas in which most countries actively debated fairly similar policy options (Immergut 1992:11–12). Perhaps a more nuanced version of the cultural argument merits consideration. Citizens in the Anglo-American family of nations tend to prefer a limited government role and private responsibility. These attitudes can conceivably be exploited by organized groups and political parties seeking a smaller role for government (Morone 1995).

Economic Explanations

The convergence thesis (Wilensky 1975) introduced in Chapter 2 has played a role in comparative studies of health politics. Recall that Wilensky argues that as countries become industrialized—usually measured by gross domestic product (GDP) per capita—they are likely to experience similar social and political pressures. These pressures culminate in the adoption of a wide range of similar welfare policies—in part because those greater economic resources provide more breathing room for the expansion of government spending and activity. Roemer (1977) applied this logic to explain the expansion of government activity and spending in health care across the industrialized world during the postwar era. In addition to Wilensky's emphasis on affluence, Roemer noted that advances in medical technology developed in industrialized countries provide an additional force driving toward convergence of spending levels. This logic has been less useful, however, for explaining differences among industrialized countries regarding the specific choice of policy models and the ongoing reform of those models since the 1980s.

   A central feature of contemporary reform debates, as we noted at the beginning of this chapter, is a desire to control costs. These pressures continue to intensify as the populations of industrialized countries age, owing to the observed connection between age and demands of health care services (Abel-Smith 1994). These demographic changes are particularly relevant in the area of health policy. Senior citizens are more likely than younger citizens to want and need medical attention. Accordingly, as the elderly constitute a rising percentage of the population, health care utilization tends to rise while the amount paid into the overall system tends to decrease (especially in countries with the **employer-mandate** model in which premiums are tied to wages). This graying factor, as we noted in Chapter 2, is projected to intensify further through the 2010s as the postwar baby boom generation reaches retirement age (Raffel 1997).

Political Explanations

Interest group politics approaches have also been used to explain health policy making. In fact, health care constitutes the one policy area discussed in this book in which a single interest group—the medical profession—has been argued to hold a defining role all by itself. As we note throughout this book, many interest groups work to influence policy making, and their effectiveness is tied to a variety of factors such as financial and organizational resources, personal connections to policymakers, and strategies for mobilizing public opinion in favor of their positions. Several analysts of health policy making have asserted that physicians' associations have a special form of political power not found in other spheres: They are the only group licensed to provide most forms of curative care (Anderson 1972; Starr 1982). This power is deemed greatest when health policy concerns touch directly on physicians' professional domain, for example, regarding the form of payment: "As producers of a crucial service in industrial countries, and a service for which governments can seldom provide short-run substitutes, physicians have the overwhelming political resources to influence decisions regarding payment methods quite apart from the form of bargaining that their organizations employ" (Marmor and Thomas 1972: 436–437). Stated in its most extreme view, this assertion implies that physicians' associations hold a veto power over varied policy proposals not to their liking.

Over the years, however, a series of studies has demonstrated that doctors do not always have the ability to block reforms they oppose (Eckstein 1960; Glaser 1978; Immergut 1992; Klein 1995; Stone 1980). Instead, medical associations' policy-making influence varies in accordance with the constellation of other influences on policy making. For example, a study of health policy reform in ten industrialized countries concluded that a variety of factors—including internal divisions in the profession, the political cost of being labeled as obstructionist in prior reform debates, and the increasing importance of cost-control concerns—diminished medical associations' political influence during the 1990s (Raffel 1997). As more people perceive health care activities as affecting their own sectors of the government budget or the economy as a whole, other stakeholders (for example, government officials, business leaders, and diverse interest groups) become more reluctant to defer to physicians' associations in disagreements over health policy.

Other political explanations focus on the positions of the major political parties. When one steps back to consider the role played by political parties from a broader cross-national perspective in the welfare state literature, leftist political parties played an important role in stimulating the emergence and evolution of the welfare state in most industrialized countries, whereas rightist parties worked to slow its development (Castles 1982a). Health care proved no exception to this trend as the countries with the least important leftist parties—Canada and the United States—were the slowest to devote active consideration to some form of national health insurance. In the contemporary period, center-right and rightist parties have played a visible role in promoting reforms deemed to reduce government's role in health policy by providing more discretionary behavior by health care providers and patients alike (Marmor 1997), whereas left-leaning parties have tended to be more critical of many of those measures. The ability of reform-minded political parties is contingent not only on the size and unity of its governing majority but also on a variety of factors beyond the parties' direct control (Tuohy 1999).

Institutional Explanations

Cultural, economic, and political factors traditionally received the most attention in studies of health politics. Since the 1980s, however, scholars have attempted to highlight the role of institutional influences that past studies understated (or, in some cases, ignored entirely). Perhaps the most widely read institutionalist study is Immergut's (1992) analysis of the evolution of health policy in France, Sweden, and Switzerland. Immergut focuses on how distinctions in government organization (federal versus unitary), the nature of executive-legislative relations (parliamentary versus presidential systems), and the ability to call a binding referendum shape health policy making by determining the number of veto points available across the policy-making process. In this analysis, the Swiss system characterized by federalism, a multimember chief executive, and frequent use of referenda in politics makes large reforms more difficult. Conversely the unitary Swedish government, in which the prime minister frequently enjoyed a firm legislative majority with no threat of a referendum, provided a path toward party government. The number of veto points in France during the twentieth-century evolution of health policy lay between those two extremes. Although Immergut emphasizes the role of institutional factors in preventing a straight line from groups' stated positions to policy making, she concludes her study with a call to remain open to a variety of influences (1992: 242–244).

International Policy Making

No binding set of international agreements guides the curative care policies of the six countries examined in this book. As we discuss in more detail in Chapter 9, the Maastricht Treaty includes a series of social policy goals (the so-called social chapter) that the United Kingdom refused to sign. The other European Union (EU) member states agreed to form a Social Community with a qualified majority voting system that excludes the United Kingdom. The language of the social chapter itself contained no specific references to curative care initiatives in the health sector. The language emphasized public health policy instruments and outcomes—as was the case subsequently in the health component (Article 151) of the Treaty of Amsterdam that entered into effect in 1999. Despite the EU's focus on public health, one of the social chapter's major themes—a call for harmonized social policies among member states—coincides with the pressures associated with the single market initiative in the EU. The move toward more open competition among the member states makes businesses more sensitive to varying costs associated with health care expenses. The cost pressure implied by economic globalization affects countries in and outside of the EU and its Social Community.[1]

United States

Background: Policy Process and Policy History

Throughout this book we keep turning to different policy sectors to discover a shared truth: The policy process in the United States is usually the most decentralized among the six countries. With the possible exception of appropriations decisions, this is most true of contemporary health policy making. In part, the diffuse nature of health policy making stems from the absence of a unified national health policy. The United States has multiple segments to its health care policy:

- a government-mandated and managed health insurance Medicare program for the elderly
- a Medicaid program for the poor with basic guidelines set by the federal government but with most specific standards and benefits determined by the state governments
- a majority of the population covered by private insurance providers regulated by both federal and state legislation

As a result, health care reform initiatives can emerge from a variety of public arenas. The decentralization of Medicaid and insurance regulation means that any of the state governments can make health policy. The field is even broader in terms of federal policy. A variety of executive agencies are engaged in health policy formulation, including the Health Care Financing Administration (in charge of Medicare implementation), the Department of Health and Human Services, and the Surgeon General's office. In addition, presidents can convene working groups to formulate policy recommendations. The number of congressional committees holding hearings on one or more aspects of health policy is mind-boggling. From 1980 to 1991, ten House committees and seven Senate committees held hearings on health care reform. The percentage of congressional hearings held by the presumably dominant health committees approximated a paltry one-quarter of all hearings held on health care. These estimates do not track the flurry of hearings held when health care reform was thrust toward the top of the institutional agenda in 1993–1994 at the start of the Clinton administration.

---

[1] The statistics presented in the case studies on benefit levels and funding are taken from the Social Security Administration's *Social Security Programs Throughout the World 1999* (Washington, D.C.: U.S. Government Printing Office, 1999).

The United States is the only industrialized country that has no form of national health insurance. During the twentieth century, a series of (mainly Democratic) legislative efforts to generate some form of national health insurance failed as government focused instead on providing tax incentives for the provision of private insurance as a job benefit. This approach left many elderly and low-income citizens without health insurance. Criticism of this large block of uninsured people eventually resulted in the 1965 establishment of the Medicare and Medicaid programs as part of Lyndon Johnson's New Society initiatives. Medicare is a federally managed insurance program that covers pensioners over age 64 (later extended in 1972 to cover the disabled). The Medicaid program provides care to different categories of low-income citizens.

The basic Medicare program (Part A) provides up to 90 days of hospitalization coverage (and up to 100 days of nursing home care) to pensioners over age sixty-five, to those who have been disabled for over two years, and to patients suffering from chronic kidney disease. A supplemental program (Part B) covers general and specialist physician services, laboratory services, and physical therapy. Medicaid covers many inpatient and outpatient services for uninsured pregnant women and children whose family incomes are below a specified minimum. In the 1990s roughly one in seven citizens at any point in time had no health insurance. Uninsured individuals who do not qualify for Medicaid benefits must either pay for services out of pocket or seek care from a limited number of nonprofit clinics.

Most citizens have some form of private insurance (often, but not always, linked to employment). These plans have traditionally featured fee-for-service billing; however, during the 1980s and 1990s the portion of the insured population covered by HMOs rose to over 20 percent. These comprehensive health care providers try to limit the utilization incentives associated with fee-for-service billing by hiring an array of GPs and specialists on a salary or capitation basis. Another 50 percent of the insured population are in managed fee-for-service plans. More than one-third of the population are enrolled in standard PPO networks, and another one-fifth are in **point-of-service** (POS) plans that are a hybrid of managed care and unrestricted fee-for-service insurance. In POS health plans, patients can participate in a managed care system in an HMO or in a preferred provider network headed by a gatekeeper. However, they retain the option to see physicians outside of the network at a lower rate of reimbursement from the insurer.

Most hospitals are privately owned. Since the 1980s a visible shift has occurred from nonprofit to for-profit private hospitals. In recognition of the substantial number of uninsured citizens, the law requires all hospitals to provide emergency treatment to all citizens; in practice, violations of this principle occur. In both Medicare and Medicaid, inpatient and outpatient services are paid for on a fee-for-service basis.

Medicare Part A is funded by payroll taxes. Employees pay 1.45 percent of earnings; employers pay an identical percentage of payroll. The self-employed pay the full 2.9 percent themselves; pensioners pay a flat-rate monthly premium (almost $46). Medicare participants can pay a monthly premium to gain access to Part B, which covers outpatient care. The vast majority of participants choose to do so. The federal government covers the balance of expenses for the supplemental plan out of general revenues. The Medicaid program is administered at the state level; funding is shared between the federal and state governments out of general revenues. Federal contributions now take the form of block grants, in which states have greater freedom to determine how to spend the federal funding.

Medicare rules include a variety of deductibles and copayments. Similarly, Medicaid patients can be held responsible for billing above the relevant Medicaid reimbursement schedule; however, they are not responsible for copayments. In the private sector, deductibles and copayments are also a substantial component of the system for most people. Out-of-pocket payments account for around one-fifth of the country's health expenses.

Contemporary Dynamics

Since the 1980s the U.S. health reform debate has been dominated by two issues. The first, cost control, is quite familiar to other industrialized countries. The second issue is unique to the United States: the large number of uninsured residents. Some political forces have approached coverage for the uninsured as a moral imperative. Others, especially many business groups, have focused on how the cost of covering the uninsured is passed on to the insured by overbilling by private providers to compensate for losses stemming from services for which uninsured patients failed to pay.

In short, some proponents of national health insurance linked unequal access to the other major reform issue: high and rising health expenditures. Despite the notion that market competition among insurers and providers would lead to quality care at low cost, the United States spends more money per capita (approaching $4,000 in 1997) and as a percentage of GDP (around 14 percent) than any other industrialized country. In addition to overbilling, predominant reliance on fee-for-service reimbursement, administrative costs associated with the multitude of payers and providers, and so-called defensive medicine (that is, tests conducted to rule out unlikely scenarios in an effort to avoid malpractice lawsuits) have been associated with high U.S. health care spending. The willingness and ability of many providers to purchase the latest technology also lends itself to greater utilization of expensive services.

In the 1980s the government attempted to control rising costs through fee schedules. A uniform fee schedule based on diagnosis-related groups was introduced unilaterally in 1983 to try to brake the government's rising obligations under the Medicare supplemental program. Over the rest of the decade, the government kept a keen eye on fee structures in the Medicare and Medicaid programs in an effort to cut costs. However, higher utilization rates per insured in Medicare and an extension of the covered population in Medicaid kept expenses on the rise. In 1988 Congress tried to reduce the strain on Medicare by passing the Medicare Catastrophic Coverage Act. However, the negative reaction of many prominent interest groups for the elderly and others moved Congress to repeal much of the measure in 1989.

Against this agenda-setting backdrop, in 1993 the newly elected Clinton administration pledged to create a national health insurance system to deal with the twin problems of high costs and unequal access. President Clinton appointed a special task force led by his wife, Hillary Clinton, to develop a health reform proposal. Given the high-profile commitment of the presidency and the many business leaders who had spoken in favor of reform, many observers felt that some major reform would take place. However, once policy formulation began in earnest, the Democratic majority in Congress was visibly divided on which model to adopt, and most Republican legislators bitterly opposed the managed competition plan favored by the presidency. In addition, the Health Insurance Association of America launched a biting media campaign aimed at reducing popular support for the president's plan by asserting that the proposal would reduce patients' choice, increase their costs, and decrease the quality of services provided.

The decision-making stage in this push for health care reform was a long summer of non-events in 1994. No fewer than six major health reform bills circulated from across the policy and political spectrum. The Wellstone-McDermott bill called for a move to the single-payer model and was backed mainly by liberal Democrats. The Cooper-Grandy bill called for a less comprehensive managed competition plan driven by employer-mandate insurance and was backed by a partisan group of moderates centered in the House. The Moynihan bill, backed by a bipartisan group of moderates in the Senate, sponsored a hodgepodge of specific initiatives designed to pay for expanded insurance access for most citizens. The Chafee bill called for a diluted managed competition plan with a more limited employer mandate that found support among other moderates and some conservatives in both chambers. The Gramm bill, which proposed to change tax codes to expand access to some additional citizens, was favored by many conservatives in both chambers. The Clinton proposal (calling for managed competition with federal budget controls under an employer-mandate plan) was not even formally introduced by moderate Democratic members until late in the session. The diversity of positions made it difficult to envision how to craft a voting majority in support of a major proposal. At the eleventh hour, Senate majority leader George Mitchell led a series of bipartisan discussions trying to find a path toward a more limited reform. In the end, none of the handful of major health care bills proposed during the 1993–1995 session received a floor vote.

In 1995 the Republican Party, which opposed major health care reform, took majority control of both houses of the legislature. In 1996, amid continuing criticism from some corners for failing to deal with the problems of the uninsured, Congress passed legislation requiring insurers to extend coverage to employees between jobs for up to one year. It remains to be seen whether this is a first step toward an employer-mandate system or another in a long series of limited government initiatives in the health insurance sphere. Most contemporary observers find the latter scenario more probable.

Meanwhile, the implementation of cost-control efforts in the private-sector-dominated health care sector placed new issues higher on the systemic and institutional agendas. The expansion of HMO activity and the extension of PPOs and other utilization-controlling efforts by traditional insurers were effectively implemented in the 1990s. In 1988 only 30 percent of the insured population was in some form of managed care; by 1998 that figure had risen to 86 percent. In the mid-1990s, the rate of health care spending growth slowed (along with inflation more generally). However, these cost-control measures drew complaints from both physicians and patients, who complained that necessary tests and treatments were sometimes not provided in the effort to control costs. These public discussions of perceived decreases in the quality and freedom of care, implied by curtailed utilization, placed insurer regulation on the agenda. As the decade came to a close, legislators in both parties and the president began to shift their attention toward the enactment of legislation that would create something along the lines of a patients' bill of rights.

The health care reform experience under the Clinton administration demonstrates a series of obstacles that make major expansion of government activity difficult in this sector. Many citizens are skeptical of government intervention. Interest groups are able to mount private and public lobbying campaigns on behalf of their preferred policy positions so that reformers find it difficult to see their vision rise to top of the systemic agenda unchallenged. The federal system dictates that policy can be made (and blocked) at multiple levels of government. The presidential system of executive-legislative relations permits not only the possibility of divided government but also the daily reality of a decentralized legislative process in which multiple poles of power exist in both houses of Congress. Remember, the Clinton health care proposal did not fail in a Republican-controlled legislature. It failed to get a floor vote in a session in which the Democratic Party held majorities in both houses. This is a telling reminder about the ability of the president to generate major legislation in the U.S. political system: It depends largely on the president's success at persuading both the public and individual legislators to support a presidential initiative.

Japan

Background: Policy Process and Policy History

National policy making in Japan has a corporatist element. The government interacts with sickness funds established by individual businesses and sectors of the economy. These sickness funds are in constant contact with the relevant health care provider organizations. The fee schedule is set in formal negotiations between the Central Social Insurance Medical Council and the Ministry of Health and Welfare. The central council has twenty members that represent various groups, including health care payers (sickness funds, management, and labor), the general public (represented by lawyers and economists), and health care providers (who have eight seats). Surprisingly, hospitals have historically been excluded from the council. It should not be surprising, then, that hospital physicians have tended not to fare as well as outpatient physicians and clinic heads in fee negotiations. Major reforms have been brokered historically not just in negotiations between the council and the Ministry of Health and Welfare but also in negotiations between various factions in the Liberal Democratic Party (LDP).

In contrast to the U.S. experience but in line with developments in Europe, Japanese health policy was built on a foundation of occupationally grounded government-mandated insurance plans, which began in the industrial sector in 1922 and gradually expanded to cover most employee groups. A separate, government-run National Health Insurance (NHI) program was established in 1958 by the LDP government to provide care for those not covered by employee health plans; every locality was required to have an insurance plan for such residents by 1961. Approximately one-third of the population is currently covered by this program.

The sickness funds and the NHI program often have health care providers under contract. The system calls for outpatient physician services to be paid on a fee-for-service basis; fee schedules are negotiated by physicians and insurers. In many cases, the NHI fees are lower than the employer-mandate fee schedules. Both the employee plans and the NHI cover physician services, hospitalization, prescription drugs, and dental care. The employee plans often provide additional benefits or require smaller copayments.

Most hospitals are privately owned. Hospital physicians are salaried employees; however, reimbursements for hospital procedures are made on a fee-for-service basis. Many physicians own small clinics that provide inpatient treatment and, often, long-term care. Furthermore, many physicians are also pharmacists—enabling them to profit from the medicines they prescribe. Japan has tended to have the highest per capita pharmaceutical consumption in the world.

Funding varies considerably across different employee plans. Most employees in such plans pay between 3 and 4.25 percent of their base wage plus 0.3 percent of bonuses. Most employers pay between 4 and 5 percent of the base wage payroll plus 0.5 percent of bonuses paid to employees. Government subsidies from general revenues cover 13 percent of most benefit costs and 16.4 percent of costs for elderly employees and covered retirees. In the main NHI system, the insured pay a flat-fee premium that varies somewhat by locality. The government bears the brunt of the costs out of general revenues because it pays for half of all medical care provided and all administrative costs and provides additional subsidies to certain localities. In 1982 the government introduced a separate NHI for the elderly that limits government obligations to 30 percent of benefit costs. The remainder is paid for by contributions from the sickness funds.

Copayments are a major feature of the Japanese system. In the employee plans, the insured employee pays a 20 percent copayment on all care up to a monthly out-of-pocket maximum, which varies by family income, up to a ceiling of about $450. Workers' dependents pay a 20 percent copayment for inpatient services and a 30 percent copayment for outpatient care. Hospitalized patients also pay a per diem, earmarked for food services, that is tied to income and ranges from around $5 to $7. In the NHI, patients pay a 30 percent copayment on all services; they also pay the same hospital per diems as those insured by the employee plans.

Contemporary Dynamics

Most of the copayment provisions described in the preceding section were initially adopted in 1984. In 1994 a multipartisan consensus (shared by business leaders) led to a 50 percent increase in the monthly copayment, up to the current levels noted in the preceding section. Apart from that debate, in the late 1980s and 1990s reform discussions centered primarily on the elderly and, in particular, on the issue of long-term care. Historically Japan has had high hospital occupancy rates (above 80 percent) and a long average length of stay (often over 50 days) in large part because hospitalization has been used to provide long-term care.

These trends generated serious debate within and between the major factions of the LDP regarding how to address the need for long-term care. Rising costs in the 1980s were viewed as the first wave of a much larger problem, given the demographic trend toward an increasingly older society. As was often the case during the LDP's heyday, the policy formulation process involved extensive consultation between party faction leaders, civil servants, business leaders, health professional associations, and (to a lesser extent) labor unions. Nearly a decade of debate culminated in the presentation of the LDP's Gold Plan for long-term care.

Given all of that work at consensus building and the LDP's dominant position in the legislature at the time, the passage of the Health Care for the Elderly Home Visit legislation in 1992 did not surprise observers. The plan provides benefits for nursing home care and home care in order to shift the elderly away from prolonged hospitalization for chronic health problems. Membership in the long-term care program is for people over age 70 (or over 65 if bedridden). To ensure funding, the legislation requires the various sickness funds to pool their financial resources as if each fund had a percentage of elderly members equal to the national average. Ultimately 70 percent of the new funds come from the sickness funds, 20 percent from the national government, and 10 percent from local governments.

Despite the government's effort to gain prior support for the legislation from a variety of interest groups, the Gold Plan has run into serious implementation problems. As of this writing, implementation of the plan has not met the desired goal of expanding the utilization of nursing and home care. Some analysts have asserted that cultural norms work against nursing care because the institutionalization of one's elderly parents is often equated with the ancient custom of leaving one's parents in the mountains to die. In 1995 the government estimated that only 2 percent of the 836,000 people in need were covered by the new system.

The difficulties faced by the Gold Plan demonstrate another facet of the complexity of policy implementation. During the policy formulation and decision-making stages, the interaction of government officials and interest groups dominates our attention. In many policy areas, including health care, their activities are crucial to effective policy implementation as well. However, when the realization of policy goals also depends on the behavior of individual citizens, substantial cooperation between organized interests and government may not eliminate all implementation problems. In this case, generalized cultural norms form a barrier to full implementation. Culture—as we discussed in Chapters 2 and 3—is a factor that can be slow to change.

Germany

Background: Policy Process and Policy History

In contrast to other countries, Germany's health policy process has been more inclusive and more decentralized. An 1883 statute called for the establishment of labor-management boards to administer the sickness funds. Government played the role of the honest broker in disputes—but it was a broker with the power to alter the rules and provide subsidies. Over time, physicians began to form associations specific to each sickness fund through which to bargain over budgets and fees.

Since 1977, health policy making in Germany has been even more formally corporatist in its approach to interest group participation. Legislation established the federal Concerted Action process to oversee the government-mandated health insurance program. Twice a year representatives from over seventy groups meet to review the state of the health care system and to negotiate budgetary, fee, and utilization guidelines for the next six months in a variety of health subsectors including hospitals, outpatient services, pharmaceuticals, and dental care. These measures were taken to provide an inclusive setting from which to deal with the inflationary problems of the late 1970s. The Concerted Action group sets guidelines—often based on recommendations formed by its permanent professional staff—intended to shape subsequent formal negotiations between the regional sickness fund associations and the corresponding regional physicians' associations.

Germany adopted the first government-mandated health insurance program in 1883. A series of German governments gradually extended the mix of sickness funds tied to job categories until arriving at truly nationwide coverage during the postwar era. After reunification into a single Federal Republic of Germany (FRG), residents of the former German Democratic Republic (GDR) (who retained GDR pension and disability benefits in many instances) became participants in the FRG health insurance system.

As in Japan, Germany has a patchwork of government-mandated sickness funds with special systems existing for miners, seamen, public employees, and self-employed farmers. Almost all other employees, the unemployed, pensioners, and the self-employed are required to join the government sickness fund system if their annual income does not exceed a threshold level determined by the government. In 1999 the threshold was over $37,000 in the former GDR and just under $45,000 elsewhere; about one-quarter of the population has been above the threshold since reunification. Those earning more than the threshold can choose to join the sickness fund system voluntarily; around two-thirds of such Germans are in voluntary sickness funds. Most of the other third have private insurance; however, citizens who choose private insurance cannot return to the sickness fund system. A little less than 1 percent of the total population is above the income threshold and chooses not to have health insurance. All sickness funds are required to cover physician services, maternity, hospitalization, and prescription drugs. A 1994 reform added a series of long-term care provisions (along with a boost in the payroll tax earmarked for that purpose). Semiprivate rooms and eyeglasses are not covered, but many Germans have supplemental private policies for these services.

Outpatient physician services are provided on a fee-for-service basis in accordance with fee schedules negotiated at the national and regional levels. Hospital physicians, however, work on salary. Hospitals are paid an all-inclusive per diem by the insured's sickness fund. The per diem varies by region and, since 1996, by illness. The government controls the acquisition of capital equipment by hospitals.

A majority of sickness fund revenues is generated by payroll taxes charged up to the annual income ceiling used to determine mandatory participation. As in Japan, funding varies across different sickness funds. Employees pay between 4 and 8 percent of earnings, depending on the sickness fund; most people pay between 6 and 7 percent. Employers usually pay an identical share as a percentage of payroll. However, employers pay the full share for low-income employees (those earning less than $373 monthly in 1999). The government contributes subsidies for maternity benefits and to help cover pensioners, the unemployed, students, and apprentices; these subsidies constitute around one-quarter of sickness fund revenues. Patients make flat-fee copayments for prescription medicines, and they must cover the difference in price between a brand-name drug and a generic. In addition, they pay a supplemental per diem for the first two weeks of hospitalization.

Contemporary Dynamics

Most contemporary health policy reform efforts in Germany have focused on cost control, beginning with the aptly named 1977 Health Care Cost Containment Act, which established annual spending targets for physician services and the current mechanism for fee negotiations. When the government squeezed the fee schedules, physicians often provided more services. In 1986 the government replaced the targets with annual caps; once the cap is breached in a region, the sickness fund pays out less than 100 percent of the normal fee. Because physicians submit fee vouchers to physicians' associations that are reimbursed by the sickness funds, the move to a cap gave physicians an incentive to police themselves. If a doctor bills for too many services, he or she is eating into the fee schedule of all other physicians in the regional association. In 1988 the government responded to rising expenditures on prescription drugs by moving to the current system of requiring the use of generic drugs. It also implemented many of the copayments visible in today's system.

These measures were largely successful in controlling costs during the 1980s. In the 1990s reunification placed renewed fiscal pressure on the government (as we saw in Chapter 6). Health care cost containment rapidly returned to a visible place on the systemic and institutional agendas.

A variety of possible solutions were brought forward from different elements of the policy network. Some members of the Concerted Action group's permanent staff called for copayments in order to curtail utilization. The rise in pharmaceutical expenses proved particularly troubling to some group participants. Concerted Action participants with ties to the Social Democratic Party (particularly labor representatives) opposed most measures that would limit utilization as well as proposals to raise contribution rates to cover rising expenditures. Other participants detailed the pressures placed on the health care system by an aging population that was opting for more expensive hospitalization when other long-term options were conceivable—albeit not clearly covered in the existing system.

In the end, the Kohl government negotiated a brokered set of reforms over three years that embraced elements of all of the major proposals in circulation. The 1992 Structural Health Reform Law increased copayment levels for drugs and for hospitalization. The Concerted Action process was basically overridden for three years by this legislation's provision to freeze contribution rates—a clear attempt to meet concerns from the center-left. In addition, in spite of the vocal objection of physicians' associations, the government tied fee increases to others' wages and took steps to reduce the supply of doctors. In 1994, in an effort to reduce the impact of an aging population on the sickness fund system, the government created a long-term care program that is mandatory for all insured persons. An additional payroll tax of 0.5 percent is charged to employees and employers (in one province it reaches 1 percent) to pay for the plan's cash and in-kind benefits to cover long-term home and nursing care. The reform intended to meet real human needs but also to limit overuse of the basic sickness fund system owing to previously limited long-term options.

Upon implementation, these reform measures slowed the growth in health care costs. However, the changes did not eliminate cost pressures in the system. With the Maastricht deadline approaching, by 1996 the German government was proposing additional measures to limit rising expenditures on medicines, dental care, and patient transport. The hospital sector (with its firm global budgets, salaried physicians, and technology acquisition limits) remains the only part of the health care system that has kept expenses at a stable level.

The response to cost pressures in contemporary health policy demonstrates the consensus-seeking nature of German political dynamics. However, seeking consensus by producing a multifaceted compromise does not ensure that all (or even most) major constituencies are satisfied fully. In this situation, most participants consoled themselves (and their constituents) with the knowledge that concessions were probably essential to face the difficult fiscal challenge of reunification.

France

Background: Policy Process and Policy History

Health policy making takes place largely at the national level in France. The action centers around two agencies—social security and finance. Historically, major proposals for reform have emerged out of the social security agency and are then reviewed by the Finance Ministry staff. At times, however, the initiative for reform has stemmed from the Finance Ministry in response to pressure to cut costs.

The ongoing debate over budgets and fee schedules also takes place at the national level. The association of sickness funds negotiates with the three major physicians' associations over fee schedules. These agreements must then be approved by both the finance minister and the social security minister. The sickness funds can use the central government's veto power in disagreements over fee schedules in two ways. First, the funds can try to reduce demands from physicians by claiming that the government will simply reject them later. Second, if the funds want to appear conciliatory, they can go along with physicians' demands when they are confident the government will reject that portion of the agreement. In both cases, the strength of the sickness funds' negotiating position is determined in part by having open communication with the relevant ministries. The funds' position is enhanced further because they need consent from only one of the three physicians' associations in order to form an agreement. The physicians' bargaining strength lies in their predominant role in establishing the relative values among different service groups such as the ratio of the cost of open heart surgery to the cost of a heart stress test.

Government intervention in the curative care sector in France began in earnest with the 1930 Social Insurance Act, which provided health insurance to low-income workers. After World War II, a series of laws expanded the system until it covered virtually all citizens by 1978. The resulting patchwork of programs, comprising a variety of plans directed toward different occupational groups, is a government-mandated insurance system. The system is dominated by the general health insurance plan, which covers over 70 percent of all employees. Special systems exist for occupations including the agricultural and mining sectors, public employees, and the self-employed. Pensioners are covered in the general system, and people not covered through their employers may affiliate voluntarily to the main health insurance system. Because the majority of French citizens are covered in the general system, our discussion focuses on that plan.

The general system covers all eligible employees with 60 hours of paid employment in the previous 30 days (or 120 hours in the previous 90 days) with contributions duly paid into the system. Because it is a national health insurance system, coverage is portable across the country. Physician services are provided on a fee-for-service basis. The insured usually pays for services first and is then reimbursed by the local sickness fund for a percentage of the cost (usually around 70 percent, but reimbursements vary from 30 to 100 percent). Reimbursements are calculated in accordance with negotiated fee schedules for the fund; the patient is responsible for excess fees. Covered services include general medical and maternity care, surgical and laboratory services, other specializations, dental care, and medicines.

Hospitals are a mix of public and private institutions. Although fewer than one-third of all hospitals are public, they account for over two-thirds of the available beds in the system. French public hospitals are run on fixed global budgets (introduced in the mid-1980s by the Mitterrand government in response to cost-control concerns). Private hospital care is also covered by the sickness fund system. The insured pays a flat per diem (almost $14 in 1999) for hospital room and board. Disabled children, soldiers injured in war, and employees injured in job-related accidents are exempt from the per diem. All inpatient medical services are handled as part of the insurance program and reimbursed as described earlier. The system as a whole provides comprehensive coverage for everything but semiprivate rooms and, in some instances, eye care and chiropractors. Patients enjoy unrestricted access to specialists; the system has no gatekeeper provisions. Approximately four-fifths of the population has supplemental private insurance to cover copayments and additional services not covered in the general plan.

The bulk of sickness fund revenues comes from payroll taxes. Employers pay 12.8 percent of total payroll into the general system. Employees pay 6.8 percent of total earnings. Pensioners and persons collecting unemployment benefits pay much smaller percentages of their income in health insurance taxes (ranging from 1 to 2.4 percent). The government contributes subsidies into the system taken from a 12 percent surtax on automobile premiums and from excise taxes on pharmaceutical advertising, tobacco, and alcohol. State subsidies have historically made up around one-quarter of program revenues. The government also provides funds for hospital construction.

The French system is not free to the user at the point of service. As we noted earlier, patients generally pay for services and are then reimbursed by the insurance program. In addition, most services call for a 30 percent copayment on the part of the patient. In fact, copayments for many users tend to exceed 30 percent annually because more services are reimbursed at less than 70 percent (either by regulation or in practice because of fee differences) than the few reimbursed at over 70 percent. Treatment for serious prolonged illnesses (including cancer and diabetes) is exempt from copayments. These twin funding measures—initial payment in full by the patient and a substantial copayment—are cost-control aspects of the system that try to limit utilization by influencing patient behavior. The effectiveness of copayments as utilization control is uneven because over 80 percent of the population buys supplemental insurance to cover the copayments. The availability of supplemental insurance leads to a stark division in coverage and utilization between low-income citizens and the rest of the population.

Contemporary Dynamics

The French system has not been subject to a major legislative reform since the 1978 extension of coverage to its current levels. Subsequent reform efforts have tried to control costs by focusing on providers. In 1983, public hospitals were placed on fixed annual budgets in a largely successful effort to control average lengths of stay. In subsequent years the government has taken a stronger stance in negotiations with physicians over the national fee schedule. As in Germany, many physicians responded by billing for additional services. An increasing percentage of physicians were permitted to bill for certain services in excess of the established fee schedule; by the late 1980s nearly 30 percent of all physicians could do so. That extra billing had to be paid out of pocket by the patient (or, in turn, by private supplemental insurance). Rising health expenditures (along with the publicized behavior of physicians) placed the issue of controlling costs firmly on France's systemic agenda in the 1990s.

Socialist governments had called for responsible fee negotiations, whereas parties on the right criticized the left for being soft on labor. In 1992 the Socialist government negotiated a convention with private hospitals to establish a ceiling on inpatient expenditures, but the convention fell short of calling for a cap on outpatient services. This rhetorical difference led to a change in policy formulation during the conservative Juppe government. In 1996 the government proposed placing a firm cap on physician services expenditures. If breached, no fee increases would be granted for the next period. The government also proposed sanctions for individual physicians who exceeded their personal utilization targets. The 1996 proposal called for government administrators to oversee care in private and public hospitals and to coordinate spending across both sectors.

At the decision-making stage, however, the major physicians' associations were able to publicize claims that patients could lose necessary care through what they termed draconian caps on physician services. The debate on this point would sound familiar to those in the United States who have followed doctors' arguments that utilization controls implemented by HMOs and health insurers reduce the quality of patient care. This criticism of the initiative—leveled at a government already under assault in the media and through the general strike of December 1995 as lacking a concern for social issues— was sufficient to block the proposal from coming to a vote during the Juppe government.

Some implementation concerns are related to the use of firm caps for physician services. The plan would call for the collection of more detailed information on physician practices than is currently required. Physicians would have to dedicate more resources to generate those reports, and the government would need to expand its activities as a monitor of utilization. In Germany (a country of comparable size that has had a cap on physician services in place for over a decade now), implementation demands were met by directly charging the physicians' associations with both utilization monitoring and payment of physicians. The French division between outpatient payments made by the sickness funds and utilization review shared by physicians and the government suggests that the French caps may be more difficult to implement.

The ability of physicians to block the Juppe reform proposals demonstrates a situation in which the policy network privileged the physicians' position. The formal inclusion of physicians' unions in bargaining over fee schedules enabled physicians to play the labor card despite their historical emphasis on free-market principles in the health sector. The physicians' associations depicted themselves as unionized workers attempting to protect the other unionized workers jeopardized by the threat of inferior care that doctors claimed would result from the cap. Divisions among doctors had weakened their bargaining position in fee negotiations in the past, but the threat of a firm cap enabled the three major physicians' groups to speak with one voice on this particular issue, further enhancing the doctors' ability to mobilize opposition to the cap from elements of organized labor and from the public at large.

United Kingdom

Background: Policy Process and Policy History

The National Health Service (NHS) plays a major role in policy formulation in the health care sector in the United Kingdom. The senior administrators are charged with setting fee schedules and global budgets in consultation with the health minister, the Treasury, and relevant health providers' associations. Because services are provided directly under NHS supervision, the agency also provides the vast majority of data suitable for program evaluation. For three decades after its inception in 1948 the NHS was largely autonomous—at least once it demonstrated an ability to meet most of its core functions with limited annual funding increases from the national government. Prime ministers and their health ministers tended to view the NHS as a popular government program that had proven itself relatively free of the cost pressures evident in other countries in the 1970s. This set of assumptions gave the NHS more freedom to determine how to allocate limited resources, but it also made it difficult for the NHS to generate political support for increasing its funding. Nevertheless, this historical autonomy was neither unlimited nor formally guaranteed. The executive always retained the capacity to consider reshaping not just the flow of NHS funding but also its basic mode of operation. The potentially activist role for the prime minister in health care policy was realized by the Thatcher government in the 1980s.

The United Kingdom's first national health insurance legislation in 1911 provided incomplete care to a limited number of low-income citizens. During the next three decades, dissatisfaction with the system increased despite efforts to expand the percentage of citizens covered and the range of services provided. The Beveridge Report in 1942 recommended sweeping reforms. Shortly after the end of World War II, legislation led to the creation of the NHS—which mirrored many of the Beveridge recommendations. Three decades later the Thatcher government began a series of attempts to inject competitive dynamics and financial incentives into the NHS system, culminating in the 1990 National Health Service and Community Care Act, which created the NHS system as we know it today.

The NHS provides a comprehensive range of services to all citizens. All patients must enroll with a GP who serves as a gatekeeper for referrals to specialists. Capitation reimbursement is the key aspect of GP compensation: It constitutes half of their income. A base salary (40 percent) and fees charged for vaccinations and some diagnostic tests (10 percent) provide the rest. Under the 1990 reform, GPs with over 9,000 patients (later lowered to 5,000 patients) can operate autonomously as self-governing clinics that can keep any surplus for capital improvements. The NHS covers all physician services, hospitalization, dental and eye care, long-term care, and prescription drugs.

Most hospitals are publicly owned and managed by one of twelve district health authorities in the NHS system. Public hospitals receive fixed global budgets from the NHS based on actuarial trends in their area. The 1990 reform enables large hospitals with over 250 beds to become self-governing trusts with the freedom to raise their own capital and to set staff pay levels. Such trusts (now constituting 95 percent of all hospitals) can also keep any surplus for capital improvements. Long-term care is provided by the Community Care Sector of the NHS, which also administers pubic health initiatives.

The system is paid for out of general revenues. This funding from the central government covers more than 90 percent of NHS expenses. Although the Beveridge Report called for services to be free at the point of service, copayments have been introduced over the years that support around 5 percent of NHS services. Patients pay 80 percent of the first $567 of dental care. Checkup consultations require a flat fee of around $6. Patients are charged a sliding flat-fee copayment for prescription drugs, up to a maximum of about $9. The dental and prescription copayments rose by around 40 percent under the conservative Major government in the mid-1990s. Low-income citizens, children, and pregnant women are exempt from dental and pharmaceutical copayments. The elderly are exempt from prescription drug copayments. Around 12 percent of British citizens have some form of private health insurance. Most have supplemental coverage for nonemergency care to escape waiting lists in the NHS.

Contemporary Dynamics

Eliminating waiting lists was a watchword for the proposed Thatcher reforms. In contrast to most other industrialized countries, the major British health reform issue has not been cost control. Of the six countries examined in this book, the United Kingdom spends the smallest percentage of its GDP on health care. In the years preceding and following the 1990 reform, this spending figure has remained fairly stable. With its fixed global budgets, minimal fee-for-service reimbursement, salaried physicians, and limits on technology acquisition, the NHS has possessed from the outset many of the cost-control measures discussed in other countries. Instead, the market-oriented Thatcher government used formal program evaluations and anecdotal patient complaints to try to build support for reforms focused on improving the quality of services and the speed with which they were provided. A January 1989 slogan pledged to "put the interests and wishes of the patients first" (White 1995, 124).

The policy formulation stage was dominated by the well-known perspectives of the two major parties' platforms at the time. Thatcher promised to reform the system via competition. Two major market-oriented paths were actively discussed within Conservative ranks during the 1980s. Some Conservatives called for internal reforms of the NHS that would inject market mechanisms into the system. Others called for the replacement of the national health model with a system of competing private insurers in a government-mandated national health insurance program. This approach would also entail shifting the funding mechanism from general government revenues to the institution of insurance premiums. The Labour Party responded that most of the publicized problems (NHS waiting lists and lack of specialty treatment and professionals in some areas) were the result of systematic underfunding by the Thatcher government. Given the clear Tory majority, this partisan debate was largely an effort to jockey for position for the coming 1992 general elections. The real action centered on less public negotiations with the NHS and with private health care professionals who managed to persuade the government not to eliminate the NHS. They did not succeed, however, in convincing Thatcher to take the Labour-backed approach of reducing waiting lists via funding increases. Instead, in January 1989 the government issued a White Paper outlining a call to inject some market dynamics into the NHS. This report was publicly criticized by many physicians, but neither those criticisms nor the outrage associated with the implementation of the poll tax in April 1990 (see Chapter 7) stalled Thatcher's plans.

In passing a comprehensive reform in June 1990, the government highlighted guaranteed maximum waiting periods for different procedures. This guarantee dovetailed with the Tories' prior strategy to build public support for change by focusing on patient-level outcomes. Guarantees aside, the principal thrust of the reform adopted was the introduction of competition for resources inside the NHS system. In addition to granting autonomy to large primary practices and to large hospitals, the 1990 reform enabled district health authorities (the basic administrative unit of the NHS) to purchase necessary care from an array of public and private care providers. In theory, this is the most profound aspect of the reform because the district health authorities can choose to punish inefficient public providers by replacing them with public or private competitors.

The effects of this and other 1990 reforms on cost efficiency are difficult to assess for a variety of reasons (especially the sketchy information on NHS costs at the point of service). Instead, evaluation of the implementation of the reforms centered initially on the analysis of the same sorts of waiting lists that had been highlighted at the agenda-setting stage of the 1980s. John Major's government, formed in late 1990, trumpeted the reduction in waiting lists over the first half of the 1990s as evidence of the success of the market mechanisms in improving outcomes. However, it is virtually impossible to know whether Thatcher's claim that market pressures could generate those outcomes was validated because the Major government gave the NHS its largest budgetary increases in over a decade during 1991–1993. In addition, it is difficult to know what percentage of the reduction was due simply to the increased political and administrative attention on the waiting list as a crucial policy outcome.

Like the poll tax, the NHS reform was an area where the third Thatcher government forged ahead with a controversial measure in the face of visible opposition. The presence of the party government model made this a political possibility as we have seen in several policy chapters. However, in NHS reform, unlike the poll tax, the Thatcher government had spent quite a few years building public support for its reform by hammering away at the waiting list issue. This political strategy—maintained during the implementation stage by the Major government—helped to generate adequate support for the reform. At the very least, the reduction of waiting lists sufficiently minimized the level of public opposition.

Italy

Background: Policy Process and Policy History

In Italy the process for health policy making differs from the process for other policy areas. In other areas the lead role is played by the central government within a unitary state. Since passage of the 1979 National Health Service Law, however, the locus of health policy making shifted to the twenty regional governments. Those governments set global budgets and arbitrate fee schedules and other matters for the local health units (USLs) in their respective territories. The USLs administer services via contracts for a combination of public ambulatory clinics, public hospitals, and private providers. At their creation in 1979, the USLs became public enterprises governed by boards appointed to represent the partisan balance of forces in the regional government. The central government sets the basic parameters for services that must be provided, but the regions can determine whether to provide additional services. Policies are largely implemented (and reforms discussed) between the regional governments and the boards of their respective USLs.

The health sector was the first major function transferred from the central government to the regions. Health expenditures, funded by transfers from the central government and by revenues raised at the regional level, constituted a majority of regional government budgets throughout the 1980s. Some proponents of decentralization at the national level trumpeted the passage of the 1979 law as the first step toward the creation of meaningful regional governments. In contrast, as time passed, critics grumbled that regional administration of the health sector was more politicized and less professionalized than it had been at the national level. In particular, some observers questioned the professional credentials of not just the boards governing the USLs but also of the general managers charged with directing the USLs' activities. Others pointed out that the central government's pledge to cover revenue shortfalls at the regional level gave little incentive to both the regional governments and the USLs to administer their services efficiently.

Italy also developed a government-mandated system during the twentieth century. If anything, the Italian system of numerous sickness funds organized by occupational groups was more complex than its French and German counterparts. By the 1970s over 90 percent of the Italian population was covered. As the system expanded, many observers came to criticize the disparities in care across occupations, the duplication of effort and services across public and private care providers, and the continuing exclusion of the unemployed and several other categories of citizens.

In 1978 the so-called national solidarity government—a heterogeneous coalition that included the support of the traditionally excluded Communists—tackled these criticisms by adopting the national health service model. The reform, passed in January 1979, promised to provide universal coverage free to the user at the point of service. In 1992 a major organizational and financial reform modified the system into its present form.

Italians are currently guaranteed access to the National Health Service (SSN). Similar to the British NHS after the Thatcher reforms, the Italian system is a patchwork of public ambulatory clinics, public hospitals, and private providers contracted by the USLs responsible for providing care mandated by the national and regional governments. Coverage is portable across localities and regions. Some regions cover items not included in the national mandate. The system covers general and specialist physician services, hospitalization, prescription drugs, maternity, and dental care.

Most of the hospital sector is public. Under the 1992 reform, large public hospitals can separate administratively from the USL. Such hospitals must run balanced budgets and can spend surpluses on additional capital acquisitions or staff compensation incentives. About 10 percent of the population has some form of private insurance—to cover copayments, to extend coverage to additional services, and in some cases to provide comprehensive insurance.

Traditionally, a slim majority of funding came from payroll taxes (of which employers paid a larger share than employees). Government subsidies from general revenues filled in gaps in revenues and provided coverage for the unemployed. In 1998 the D'Alema government moved to fund the entire system out of general government revenues at the national and regional levels. In particular, a new value-added tax collected by regional governments will bear primary responsibility for funding the health service. This financing change toward the use of general revenues mirrors the system already employed in the United Kingdom.

From its inception, the SSN has been subject to a series of reforms of its copayment provisions. By the mid-1990s, a wide variety of copayments were in place. Patients pay a deductible on the first $60 for all diagnostic tests and specialist care billings. They pay a 50 percent copayment for most prescription medicines up to $60, as well as a flat-rate fee of $2 to $4 for all pharmaceuticals. In addition, they pay an annual surcharge of roughly $53 for GP services. Several categories of persons are exempt from the copayment and deductible requirements: children (6 years and under) and persons over age 65 with annual family incomes below $42,000, cancer patients, invalids, pregnant women, poor retirees over age 60, and unemployed individuals with incomes below $9,500.

Contemporary Dynamics

The Italian SSN has been the subject of reform efforts almost annually since its inception in 1979. As we noted earlier, copayments have been introduced on an increasing number of services. In some cases, governments revoked major copayment hikes, only to reinstate them (often at higher levels) later. Copayment increases and a reduction in the number and nature of exempt pharmaceuticals have reduced prescription drug use per capita. These decisions helped to control costs by controlling utilization, but they also helped to place the efficiency of the SSN on the institutional agenda. Critics of copayments did not always succeed in defeating the introduction of (or increase in) copayments on certain services, but they did force the major parties to consider reform measures.

In the early 1990s, amid the disintegrating political dynamics that had prevailed in Italy since World War II, both the Northern League and Forza Italia became voices for market-oriented reform in the health care sector. Beset by the political stalemate and serious budgetary woes, elements of the Christian Democratic and Socialist Parties began to consider serious reform of the SSN's internal dynamics and funding mechanisms. Advocates of limited use of market mechanisms were further strengthened at the policy formulation stage by events in the United Kingdom and the Netherlands, where governments were introducing similar reforms.

This policy debate culminated in comprehensive reform legislation in 1992. In addition to further adjustments in copayments, a decision was made to adopt major changes in the administrative structure of the SSN. This "reform of the reform" empowered the national government to set more specific nationwide coverage and planning guidelines and to apportion funding to regional governments based on population and additional criteria. The regional governments must now generate revenues to cover expenses in excess of the national government contribution. Before the reform, the national government had pledged to cover all unforeseen health expenses. This reform made SSN funding similar to the Canadian health care system in that regional governments have an incentive to control costs in order to avoid raising taxes and imposing fees on their constituents. Furthermore, the 1992 reform made the USLs autonomous public enterprises no longer controlled by boards appointed to represent the partisan balance of forces in elected government. The USL general managers are chosen based on professional qualifications and receive five-year contracts with a possibility of renewal.

This last change has helped to reduce perceived and real problems associated with the politicized boards of the past. The move toward a more professionalized management has made it easier to implement other elements of the 1992 reform. Fiscal reforms were designed to ensure that—at the implementation stage—managers and regional politicians would have an incentive to comply with the cost-control goals that helped to motivate the legislation. Not all implementation problems were overcome, however. One of the most controversial aspects of the 1992 legislation has not been implemented. The reform called for allowing citizens (and occupational groups) to opt out of the SSN—thereby reducing much of their SSN payroll tax—beginning in 1995. In 1993 the major rump of the old communist party, the Democratic Party of the Left (the PDS), lobbied hard for the abolition of this clause. Meanwhile, the Northern League began to collect signatures to hold a referendum to abolish the legislation that established the SSN. In early 1995 the Constitutional Court ruled against the possibility of holding this referendum. With the 1996 election of the Olive Tree coalition led by the PDS, the possibility of opt-out provisions became remote. However, the major center-right parties have platforms calling for the ability to withdraw from the system or, in some cases, for the abolition of the entire system.

The reform of the SSN demonstrates how concerns over implementation problems can also motivate major policy reforms. As we have seen in other policy areas, the fluid nature of contemporary Italian politics enables the absence of a visible consensus—among both elected officials and voters—to give rise to wide-ranging proposals that have more perceived feasibility than they would in a more settled political climate. In this atmosphere, the primary universal aspects of the Italian SSN are more vulnerable than Canada's single-payer system or the United Kingdom's NHS.

Cross-national Trends

In the 1990s we can observe considerable convergence in the content of health policies. All six countries have enacted reforms designed to control costs. In addition, there has been some convergence toward a mixed approach to health policy as a whole. The most market-oriented country, the United States, has increased government involvement, whereas the two countries employing the national health service model (the United Kingdom and Italy) pursued reforms designed to inject some market mechanisms into their health care systems. In terms of health policy outcomes, the United States is exceptional in that it has the worst outcomes on several major indicators, despite spending visibly more money than any other industrialized country. Consideration of the contemporary dynamics of reform on this policy issue highlights cultural and economic factors as central to agenda setting whereas political and institutional influences prove important to the decision-making process.

Policy Outputs

Most industrialized countries pursue one of two options: a national health service or mandated national health insurance via a mix of public and private providers. The latter option is by far the most common. Among the six countries examined in this book (and in comparison to other countries, as well), the United States has opted for minimal government activity in the health sector. Italy and the United Kingdom have adopted the national health service model; and France, Germany, and Japan have adopted the prevailing model in the industrialized world—mandatory national health insurance.

During the 1990s these countries instituted reforms aimed at curtailing costs in one or more sectors of their respective health care systems. Copayments have been adopted in new areas and increased in existing areas in all six countries. Copayments represent an attempt to reduce costs in two senses. First, they transfer a portion of the cost from the government-funded or government-mandated plan to the patient. Second, they can influence patients' choices about utilization—provided that patients do not have a supplemental insurance policy to cover the copayments.

These countries' governments have taken a harder stance, to varying degrees, in negotiating fee schedules for physician services. This is particularly true in Canada and Germany, where the climate for negotiations has been more publicly bitter than in years past. This same dynamic of increased tension has occurred in the predominantly private U.S. system as physicians complain about tighter fee schedules and utilization reviews conducted by private insurers.

Policy Outcomes

Although the reform concerns are fairly similar in some senses, visible differences remain in the health policy models and in the levels of health care expenditures in the six countries. A key question is, are these policy differences associated with any differences in policy outcomes? We examine briefly here outcomes in the three main policy problems discussed at the beginning of this chapter: health outcomes, access to curative care, and cost control.

It is difficult to assess the role of government policy in promoting good health outcomes across individuals or across countries. One might think that average life expectancy is a good health indicator because it measures the basic threshold of health: continued life. However, life expectancy is problematic as a measure of how well the health care system is performing because life span is affected by a variety of factors including diet, exercise, surroundings,

Table 8-1 Infant Mortality and Life Expectancy in Six Countries, 1986 and 1996

Country	Infant Mortality in 1986 (% of live births)	Infant Mortality in 1996 (% of live births)	% Change in Infant Mortality (1986–1996)	Life Expectancy at Birth in 1986 (years)	Life Expectancy at Birth in 1996 (years)	% Change in Life Expectancy (1986–1996)
France	0.80%	0.49%	−39%	75.6	78.0	3%
Germany	0.86	0.50	−42	75.1	76.8	2
Italy	1.02	0.58	−43	75.5	78.1	3
Japan	0.52	0.38	−27	78.1	80.2	3
United Kingdom	0.95	0.62	−35	74.8	76.9	3
United States	1.04	0.80	−23	74.7	76.1	2
Average	*0.87*	*0.56*	*−35*	*75.6*	*77.7*	*3*

SOURCE: *OECD in Figures* (Paris: Organisation for Economic Co-operation and Development, 1999).

genetics, stress, and health care. For this reason, studies of comparative health policy often rely on infant mortality statistics (the number of infants who die prior to age 1) as an indicator of health system performance. Even though factors other than access to care and its quality influence infant mortality rates, this measure has fewer additional intervening factors than does life expectancy. Table 8–1 provides infant mortality and life expectancy statistics for the six countries.

In 1996 the United States had the highest infant mortality rate and the lowest life expectancy at birth among the six countries. The United States also experienced the least improvement in its infant mortality rate from 1986 to 1996. These outcomes have often been used in the policy debate to criticize the effectiveness of the market-maximized model. The lowest infant mortality rates (albeit by a small margin in some cases) are found in the countries with mandatory health insurance: France, Germany, and Japan. The countries with national health services (Italy and the United Kingdom) are in the middle of the pack.

On the access issue, the United States also does not compare favorably to the other six countries. In the United States, 35 to 40 million people lack health insurance at any given time. A few other countries allow citizens above a high income threshold to opt out of health insurance, but most choose not to do so. Thus, about 15 percent of the U.S. population has no health insurance, whereas in the other five (and most other) industrialized countries less than 1 percent of citizens lack access to a comprehensive health care program and those who do tend to be wealthy.

One might assume, then, that the United States's relatively poor performance in health indicators and in access to health care is simply the result of a societal choice to spend fewer resources on health care. Such a scenario would certainly be congruent with the view that a private sector approach (1) enables people to choose precisely how much health care they want and (2) provides for greater efficiency via the operation of the free market. Nevertheless, pre-

Table 8-2 Health Care Spending in Six Countries, 1986 and 1996

Country	Total Health Spending in 1986 (percentage of GDP)	Total Health Spending in 1996 (percentage of GDP)	Change in Spending (1986–1996)	Government Health Spending in 1986 (percentage of GDP)	Government Health Spending in 1996 (percentage of GDP)	Change in Spending (1986–1996)
France	8.5%	9.7%	14%	6.5%	7.8%	20%
Germany	9.2	10.5	14	7.1	8.2	15
Italy	7.0	7.7	10	5.3	5.3	0
Japan	6.6	7.2	9	4.8	5.7	19
United Kingdom	5.9	6.9	17	5.0	5.8	16
United States	10.8	14.0	30	4.4	6.5	48
Average	*8.0%*	*9.3%*	*16%*	*5.5%*	*6.6%*	*20%*

SOURCE: *OECD in Figures* (Paris: Organisation for Economic Co-operation and Development, 1999).

cisely the opposite pattern of events has occurred. The United States spends significantly more than these other countries on health care (as a look at Table 8–2 indicates), yet it performs poorly relative to those thriftier countries.

In 1996 the United States spent 14 percent of its GDP on health care. Germany was the only other of the five industrialized countries that spent over 10 percent (10.5 percent). Furthermore, expenditures as a percentage of GDP rose from almost twice to over three times as much as they did in the other five countries. Another way to look at these trends is in terms of spending per person. In 1996 the United States spent $3,898 per person on health care. Germany ($2,278), Canada ($2,065), and France ($2,002) were the only other industrialized countries in the world spending over $2,000 per person. Among the six countries examined in this book, the United States spent a higher percentage of GDP on government funded health care programs than all but France and Germany, despite covering a smaller percentage of the population in public programs. Further, the increase in government expenditures for health care rose two to three times as quickly in the United States than in the other countries. Efforts to explain higher health care spending in the United States point to several factors including:

- higher administrative costs due to the variety of insurance plans (estimated by some analysts to constitute as much as 20 percent of costs)
- fee-for-service reimbursement of both outpatient and hospital physicians
- the absence of firm global budgets for hospitals
- defensive medicine (that is, multiple and expensive tests to protect against potential malpractice lawsuits)
- cost-shifting from the uninsured and underinsured to the insured

Putting talk of different statistical measures of health care system performance aside, how do citizens view their health care systems? In a 1990 public opinion survey of citizens in ten industrialized countries (including the six countries examined here), U.S. respondents were the least content with their health care system (Blendon et al. 1990: 188). Over 90 percent of U.S. respondents called for either fundamental changes or a complete overhaul of the system; only Italians were similarly unhappy (88 percent). Japan and the United Kingdom had substantial minorities of content respondents combined with majorities who were critical of the system. France and Germany had noticeably fewer unsatisfied citizens.

Understanding Policy Reform

Thinking back to the case studies, you can see how popular discontent (or its absence) has shaped the reform agenda. In France and Germany, reform proposals have focused on maintaining the current system while restraining costs in various ways. In Japan and the United Kingdom, major reforms have been discussed in both countries; the same can be said for Italy and the United States.

However, discontent with the system alone does not imply that sweeping reform is on the way. As we have seen in other policy areas, decision making and implementation are subject to a variety of influences beyond general public opinion trends. For example, with its solid, one-party legislative majority, the Thatcher government was able to pass reforms similar to proposals that failed in Sweden, where they were advocated by many leaders of a shakier, four-party coalition government. The collapse of the political party system in Italy and the structural decentralization of decision making in the United States made it easier for opponents of reform to block new proposals that had considerable public support in some sectors. In the realm of implementation, professional patterns and loyalties limited the adoption of some market-oriented behaviors in the British reform, whereas cultural obstacles slowed the Japanese provision and utilization of long-term care called for in 1992 legislation.

Although widespread concern over health care as a priority does not guarantee that government action will be taken (much less predetermine its nature), it does guarantee that health care will remain on the agenda. This is especially true given that the percentage of elderly citizens is on the rise in all six countries. Senior citizens incur the largest health care expenditures per capita of any age group. They also are the one category of citizens that receives government health care in some fashion in all six countries. Health policy will continue to attract attention on the systemic and institutional agendas in the 2000s and 2010s as the baby boom generation reaches retirement age.

SUGGESTED READINGS

Abel-Smith, Brian. 1994. *The Reform of Health Care Systems: A Review of Seventeen OECD Countries.* Paris: Organisation for Economic Co-operation and Development.

Altenstetter, Christa, and James Björkman, eds. 1997. *Health Policy Reform, National Variations and Globalization.* New York : St. Martin's Press (for the International Political Science Association).

Campbell, John Creighton. 1998. *The Art of Balance in Health Policy: Maintaining Japan's Low-cost, Egalitarian System.* Cambridge: Cambridge University Press.

Graig, Laurene. 1999. *Health of Nations: An International Perspective on U.S. Health Care Reform,* 3d ed. Washington, D.C.: CQ Press.

Ikegami, Naoki, and John C. Campbell, eds. 1995. *Containing Health Care Costs in Japan.* Ann Arbor: University of Michigan Press.

Immergut, Ellen M. 1992. *Health Politics: Interests and Institutions in Western Europe.* Cambridge: Cambridge University Press.

Jacobs, Lawrence. 1993. *The Health of Nations: Public Opinion and the Making of American and British Health Policy.* Ithaca: Cornell University Press.

Klein, Rudolf. 1995. *The New Politics of the National Health Service,* 3rd ed. New York: Longman.

Morone, James A., and Gary S. Belkin, eds. 1994. *The Politics of Health Care Reform: Lessons from the Past, Prospects for the Future.* Durham: Duke University Press.

Raffel, Marshall, ed. 1997. *Health Care and Reform in Industrialized Countries.* University Park: Pennsylvania State University Press.

Roemer, Milton. 1991. *National Health Systems of the World.* New York: Oxford University Press.

Skocpol, Theda. 1996. *Boomerang: Clinton's Health Security Effort and the Turn Against Government in U.S. Politics.* New York: Norton.

Tuohy, Carolyn. 1999. *Accidental Logics: The Dynamics of Change in the Health Care Arena in the United States, Britain, and Canada.* New York: Oxford University Press.

White, Joseph. 1995. *Competing Solutions: American Health Care Proposals and International Experience.* Washington, D.C.: Brookings Institution Press.

Wilsford, David. 1991. *Doctors and the State: The Politics of Health Care in France and the United States.* Durham: Duke University Press.

Chapter 9 **Social Policy**

In many countries the largest portion of the government budget is spent on social policy, the dizzying variety of government efforts to boost citizens' standards of living. Social policy initiatives include pension programs, unemployment and disability benefits, subsidies to support families with dependent children, and assistance to families and individuals with low incomes. Because of the diverse nature of social policies, these initiatives are referred to collectively in many ways. Policy experts also use the terms income maintenance policy or family policy, yet not all such policies maintain incomes or deal explicitly with families. In the United States, one often hears the term welfare policy, although social security and many other social programs are frequently excluded from the welfare debate. In this book, we use the term social policy because it captures the many ways in which government tries to protect and directly improve people's standards of living.

Common Policy Problems

Prior to the late nineteenth century, government social policies were a patchwork of emergency initiatives and a few standing programs whose implementation was dominated by favoritism. As increasing numbers of citizens gained the right to vote and to organize freely, many began to pressure the government to provide a social safety net in the economic sphere for people who suffered visible misfortunes and to try to alleviate poverty more generally. These dynamics in democratic governments often led nondemocratic governments to create programs to avoid disappointing their citizens. As governments devoted more and more resources to these efforts, other citizens became concerned about the rising cost of social policy. In the late twentieth century, governments sought to fine-tune social policies in response to the increasingly visible globalization of domestic economies.

Four major groups of citizens—children, the elderly, the infirm, and the recently unemployed—have been at the center of social policies in industrialized countries for a century now. These groups include people who for one reason or another can make a claim that they cannot support themselves at the moment. Children are too young to work, senior citizens might be too old, the infirm are too ill, and the recently unemployed were working but happened to lose their jobs. Because these are situations that most citizens can visualize facing, public pressure for government programs to deal with these **situationally poor** citizens has been considerable. Social policies began in earnest in this area as governments responded to demands to alleviate these common problems.

Over time, governments moved to respond to another challenge: alleviating poverty among the **chronically poor,** that is, people who are of working age but are having a hard time escaping poverty. Obviously, alleviating poverty among the economically active can be attacked through many sorts of policies. In Chapter 6, we saw how macroeconomic policies try to create an economic environment propitious for economic growth and job creation. Later, in Chapter 10, we will see how government tries to promote economic opportunity for individuals via education policy. In this chapter we deal with government efforts to alleviate poverty by providing economic benefits directly to individuals.

Dealing with poverty is a difficult problem for all governments, although policymakers confront fewer impoverished citizens in industrialized countries than in poorer countries. In industrialized countries, 5 to 20 percent of the population lives in poverty. In late-industrializing countries, the percentage of people living in poverty ranges from about 15 percent to more than 50 percent. There are more poor people in these countries and governments typically dedicate far fewer resources to social policy. This resource gap has three major dimensions. First, the total economic resource base is smaller—as measured by gross domestic product (GDP) per person—in late-industrializing countries. Second, governments in late-industrializing societies are smaller: Taxes as a percentage of GDP are around half as high as taxes in industrialized countries. In other words, the government has a smaller share of what was already a smaller economic pie. Third, social policy represents a much smaller portion of government expenditure in late-industrializing countries. Instead of spending 20 to 50 percent of the budget on social policies, the average late-industrializing country spends around 15 percent; the median late-industrializing country spends less than 10 percent (IMF 1995: 44–45).

As social policies have expanded in industrialized countries, another policy issue has emerged: concern about the present and future costs of those government initiatives. These cost-control concerns spring from a variety of sources. First, political support for dealing with poverty has been uneven— particularly for programs dealing with chronic poverty. In some industrialized countries in northern Europe, particularly during the economic boom of the 1950s and 1960s, programs dealing with the chronically poor faced limited opposition. In the 1980s and 1990s (amid slower economic growth), opposition grew. In other countries, particularly the United States, a visible group of citizens has opposed these efforts from the outset. Second, the single largest set of social policies in most countries relate to old-age pensions; however, as societies age the proportion of active workers to retirees continues to fall. For example, in the United States in 1960 there were 6.5 people of working age for every person over age sixty-four. By 1990 that ratio had fallen to 5.3 to 1;

by the year 2040 it is projected to be 2.7 to 1 (OECD 1994c: 100). If current pension benefits are to be defended, then ever smaller numbers of workers will be called on to pay more into the social security system. The United States is not an exception here; the percentage of the population that is elderly is rising in all of the industrialized countries. This demographic pressure has placed cost-control even higher on the policy agenda. Assistance programs in the social policy sphere are the single largest component of government spending in the industrialized countries. These governments face a true political dilemma: Should they decrease benefits to control costs, or should they protect those benefits by either cutting other programs or raising taxes?

This difficult decision is made more complicated by the impact of economic globalization. Globalization presents two major sets of challenges for social policy. First, as global economic competition expands to include firms from more and more areas of the world, many unskilled and semiskilled workers in industrialized countries face the prospect of losing their jobs to similar employees in late-industrializing countries who are working for lower wages. This situation forces domestic governments into a bind regarding social policy. On the one hand, the dislocation associated with greater competition increases demands on existing social policies to pay out benefits to unemployed workers. On the other hand, because some of that unemployment is blamed on high compensation levels in the industrialized world, the dislocation creates political pressure to reduce social policy benefit levels in an effort to avoid losing these jobs to foreign competitors. Critics of this approach often call for renewed emphasis on education and on-the-job training so that vulnerable citizens can obtain the skills needed to produce more competitive products and in turn to merit higher wages.

The second impact of globalization on social policy stems from economic integration efforts. As nation-states enter binding agreements to remove barriers to economic exchange, they not only reduce tariffs but also often call for an end to restrictions on the movement of investment capital and labor. The free flow of products, labor, and capital creates the possibility that workers will strive to move to countries with better social policy benefits while investors will attempt to move production to low-benefit countries. Domestic governments in high-benefit countries fear that this puts them in a lose-lose situation, often referred to as **social dumping,** in which workers with low skills will move to high-benefit countries to enjoy greater social policy benefits while employers will move abroad to avoid the higher tax burden associated with those programs. As a result, economic integration can lead to calls for international coordination on social policy in an effort to create a more level playing field within the association. From Ross Perot's charge that a "great sucking sound" would pull U.S. and Canadian firms to Mexico within the North American Free Trade Agreement (NAFTA) to calls for a greater social policy coordination in the European Union (EU), economic integration is placing

---

Box 9-1 **In Depth: Social Security Contributions, Social Dumping, and Unemployment**

In media discussions, social dumping usually refers to the possibility that workers might move to countries that have higher benefit levels embedded in social policies while employers might move their firms to countries with lower levels of government-mandated social security contributions. Some analysts have challenged this presentation of the issues because it implies that workers and firms each have high mobility. Several studies have demonstrated that individual employees are less likely to move than firms. In addition, because most firms are small and medium-sized businesses, they are also unlikely to move.

Working from this perspective, some analysts have argued that high social security contributions may not result in a visible influx of foreign workers nor in a highly visible flight of businesses. Instead, social security contributions may serve as a factor that decreases both people's willingness to form new businesses and existing firms' willingness to take on new workers. These sorts of studies try to highlight the relationship between high social security contributions and national unemployment rates. Although many factors influence unemployment, the ability of social policy reformers to construct tables similar to the one shown below forms an important part of the contemporary debate over social policy:

Country	Average Employee Social Security Payroll Tax Rate in 1996	Average Employer Social Security Payroll Tax Rate in 1996	Unemployment Rate in 1996
France	20%	40%	12.4%
Germany	19	19	8.9
Italy	10	45	11.7
Japan	12	13	3.4
United Kingdom	7	10	8.2
United States	8	9	5.4

SOURCE: Tax rate data are from Messere (1998); unemployment data are from OECD (2000).

---

international social policy coordination on the agendas of many industrialized countries. Box 9–1 illustrates the visible differences in social security taxation in the six countries examined in this book, on the eve of European monetary unification.

Major Policy Options

Once the government decides to provide economic assistance directly to individuals, how might this goal be accomplished? Social policy design involves three basic choices: (1) How does one determine who qualifies for this assistance, (2) how redistributive is the program, and (3) how will the assistance be provided?

Two major approaches can be taken to determining who qualifies for social policy benefits: the **public assistance** model and the **social insurance** model. In the public assistance approach, sometimes called social assistance, eligibility for benefits is **means-tested.** Recipients must demonstrate economic need in order to qualify for benefits. Advocates of this approach argue that means-testing enables governments to target resources to the truly needy—thereby alleviating extreme poverty without spending government resources on self-supporting individuals. This logic has proven powerful in countries with an individualist heritage such as Australia and the United States; both countries' social policies are predominantly means-tested. Critics of public assistance charge that this approach poses logistical and political problems. On the logistical side, critics note that the truly needy often struggle to prove their eligibility while others cheat the system by using fraudulent documents to qualify for benefits they should not receive. On the political side, critics assert that reliance on means-tested programs makes it difficult to build public support for social policy because few people want to envision themselves as poverty-stricken individuals. This attitude can stigmatize recipients of public assistance and can make such programs more vulnerable to political attacks.

Critics of public assistance favor a social insurance approach to social policy. In this model, all citizens in a given circumstance are eligible for assistance regardless of their degree of economic need. For example, all families with minor-aged children might receive benefits, all senior citizens might receive pensions, or all unemployed persons might receive income supplements. Because of the absence of means-testing, this approach creates **entitlements.** Citizens pay taxes to support these programs with the knowledge that they cannot be denied benefits. Because many citizens can imagine themselves having children, growing old, or temporarily losing a job, the social insurance approach helps to build support for social policy by ensuring taxpayers that they will get back some of their taxes in government benefits. Critics of social insurance charge that this political appeal creates new problems not faced by public assistance programs. Because citizens are sold on these programs through the promise of future benefits, they do not want to see benefit levels cut. However, as the number of active workers per dependent citizen (the young and the aged) decreases, it becomes harder and harder to protect benefits without increasing the taxes paid by working citizens.

A second policy choice involves determining how redistributive each social policy should be. That is, how much money should be taken from some taxpayers to pay for others' benefits? The public assistance approach is explicitly redistributive: Everyone pays taxes to support the program, but many people may never meet the relevant poverty test to qualify for benefits. In contrast, the social insurance approach leaves open the possibility that all citizens may benefit. As a result, governments can choose to limit the redistributive element in social insurance programs. This means that programs can be based on either the principle of **individual equity** or the principle of **basic needs.** According to the individual equity principle, citizens can expect to receive benefits in accordance with their level of contributions: You get back what you paid in. According to the basic needs principle, the government sets benefit levels at a certain standard and then pays each citizen a common benefit. The basic needs approach combines an entitlement with some redistribution: Everyone benefits, but wealthy contributors help to subsidize the benefits paid out to the needy. Social insurance pensions are also redistributive over time. The contributions of younger citizens fund pensions for current senior citizens; however, the younger citizens contribute to the pension system with the knowledge that their retirements will be funded by future generations. Distrust over the feasibility of maintaining current benefit levels in countries with aging populations is a major political problem in contemporary public pension policy in industrialized countries.

A third choice faced by government is determining how to provide economic assistance. That is, what policy instruments should be used? Often benefits are provided via government **transfers** to the individual. These transfers could be cash payments or they could involve in-kind benefits—for example, food or government services. Another instrument of social policy involves government **subsidies** for certain basic needs. For example, government could spend money to make food, public transportation, or housing available at abnormally low prices. A third option consists of the use of **tax expenditures,** which, as we discussed in Chapter 6, reduce citizens' tax obligations when they spend their money for certain purposes. Lower sales taxes on food and income tax deductions for dependents and for owning a home are examples of the tax expenditure approach to social policy.

Explaining Policy Dynamics

What contextual factors influence policymakers as they try to meet the varied challenges of social policy? Similar to research on health policy, most studies of social policy making have been national case studies complemented by several comparative case studies. Cultural forces are particularly visible in this research, but economic, political, and institutional factors can also influence the path of social policy.

Cultural Explanations

Cultural traditions form one of the most widely discussed influences on social policy making. Much of the policy analysis in this area takes the family of nations approach introduced in Chapter 2. Anglo-American countries have had a greater tendency to emphasize the role of the individual than have societies from different cultural traditions. As a result, some scholars (Castles and Mitchell 1993) assert that Anglo-American traditions serve as a brake on social policy (or as a force for contraction). Conversely, the Scandinavian family of nations is seen as more collectivist in its cultural norms, which helps to fuel more support for government expansion in social policy.

Studies of the emergence and development of the welfare state in advanced industrial societies note that the liberal tradition of individualism had deeper roots and more political impact in the Anglo-American countries than in other industrialized countries. This cultural obstacle of a strongly liberal tradition is said to have slowed the initiation of major welfare policies (Flora and Alber 1981), lowered transfer spending levels (Castles 1982b), and created distinctive welfare policies (Esping-Andersen 1990) in the Anglo-American countries.[1] The logic of this deeper cultural explanation is that individualism simultaneously reinforces both a reluctance to provide government programs for able-bodied working citizens and a distrust of government solutions to societal problems. The United States is often said to be the most individualistic of the Anglo-American countries in terms of its approach to social policy issues (King 1973).

Economic Explanations

As we noted in Chapter 2, the convergence thesis (Wilensky 1975) argues that as countries become industrialized countries (usually measured by GDP per capita) they are likely to experience similar social and political pressures that culminate in the adoption of a wide range of similar welfare policies—in part because those greater economic resources provide greater breathing room for the expansion of government spending and activity. The convergence thesis can be used to explain the timing of welfare policy initiation and the level of welfare spending in various countries around the world (Flora and Alber 1981). It has been less useful, however, for explaining differences among industrialized countries.

Some studies of public opinion support for social spending in industrialized countries show a negative relationship between public support for increased welfare spending and national economic fortunes in the 1980s. First, the greater the national wealth (measured again by GDP per capita), the lower the support for social spending tends to be. Second, the greater the income equality across a society, the lower the support for social spending (Roller 1995). This alternative vision—specific to the study of industrialized countries alone—turns Wilensky's convergence thesis on its head. As industrialized countries become more affluent, it may be harder for most citizens to support reaching out to less fortunate citizens via social policies because they may feel that such policies are no longer necessary.

Short-term economic conditions also shape decision making. As we noted in Chapter 6, rising unemployment tends to put more demand on a variety of

---

[1] For an effort to draw finer distinctions among the welfare practices in the Anglo-American countries, see Castles and Mitchell (1993).

social policy services—unemployment insurance, poverty relief programs, and the like. This increased demand for social spending due to higher unemployment usually occurs with no compensating rise in economic growth that would generate more revenues to pay for those higher expenditures. Writing on European social policy developments, Vic George asserted in the mid-1990s that the "most obvious and most powerful economic pressure for increased welfare spending today is unemployment" (1996: 184). In addition to the direct impact that rising unemployment rates can have on demand for social spending, chronic unemployment can indirectly increase demand for social spending over the medium run. Long-term unemployment has been associated with higher rates of mental and physical illness and with the dissolution of families (Sinfield 1984), thereby increasing demands for other social policies.

Another economic influence on social policy stems from the impact of the international economic environment. Scholars focusing on contemporary economic globalization assert that increased economic competition is a factor that motivates a reconsideration of social policies (Gould 1993). This competition occurs both among industrialized countries and between industrialized countries and newly industrialized countries (characterized by lower wages and less expensive social policies). Some analysts have argued that the pressures of globalization have motivated a move away from universalist social insurance policies in search of an "affordable welfare state" (George and Miller 1994: 17). In this context, the path toward a more affordable welfare state involves reducing the role of entitlement programs or replacing such programs with programs based on fixed annual budgets as a means of capping social expenditures.

Political Explanations

From a cross-national perspective in the welfare state literature, political parties are frequently cited as an influence on social policy. Leftist political parties played an important role in stimulating the emergence and evolution of the welfare state in most industrialized countries, whereas rightist parties worked to slow its development (Castles 1982b). Schmidt (1982) demonstrated that leftist prime ministers were visibly associated with the expansion of public revenues from 1950 to 1975. In contrast, the few countries without powerful leftist parties—Canada, Switzerland, and the United States—manifested the slowest growth in government and in welfare spending.

Another political factor that influences social policy decision makers is the nature of interest group competition. In most policy areas, several groups of economically comfortable citizens or firms are organized participants in the policy network, with a vested interest in protecting and enhancing the scope of government activity. Consider, for example, the role of economic sectors that employ immigrant laborers in immigration policy making, the teacher and parent associations active in education policy, the conservationist and environmental watchdog groups working on various ecological issues, the physician associations and retiree organizations active in health policy formulation, and so on. In contrast, the primary constituencies of social policy are among the least affluent and least organized portions of any country. This situation has given rise to what former U.S. budget director David Stockman dubbed the weak clients thesis. Stockman observed that amid a search to reduce government spending, well-organized interest groups were better able to defend their portions of the budget (even for expenditures that public opinion generally opposed) than were scattered voices calling for the preservation of social spending (Greider 1981).

Institutional Explanations

A broad cross-national literature explores the relevance of institutional distinctions for welfare state policies and for government decision making more generally. Several cross-national studies of the evolution of the welfare state note that federal states have tended to have lower levels of welfare spending than unitary states (Cameron 1978; Wilensky 1975). Federalism's mix of responsibilities provides more opportunities for opponents of welfare spending to intervene in the political process and slow the growth of the welfare state. This pattern holds for both large and small federal countries and when one controls for population size.

Another often-discussed institutional obstacle to sweeping policy change is the use of presidential executive-legislative relations. Weaver and Rockman (1993a) provide a useful summary of the advantages for major policy enactment said to be provided by parliamentary executives "with parliamentary systems featuring stronger party discipline, greater recruitment of ministers from the legislature, greater centralization of legislative authority in the cabinet, and greater centralization of accountability" (p. 11). This excerpt from Weaver and Rockman is taken from the framing introductory chapter to their edited volume on the relevance of executive-legislative distinctions for a variety of domestic and foreign policy issues in industrialized countries. Near the end of that same volume, Weaver and Rockman (1993b) conclude that the relationship between parliamentary and presidential systems and policy making has proven more contingent on factors other than its straightforward presentation would imply. As we noted in other policy chapters, institutional factors help to frame opportunities and obstacles for policymakers, but they do not always determine which policy outputs are chosen.

International Policy Making

Although the case studies that follow focus on domestic policy efforts, economic integration involving five of these countries have placed international coordination on the political agenda. The NAFTA debate in the United States highlighted concerns that the freer movement of products and of investment among Canada, Mexico, and the United States might lead employers to move firms to Mexico in order to avoid taxes associated with more generous social policies. Although this debate has not led to a binding NAFTA-wide social policy, it did lead to a side agreement on labor policy in which the Mexican government pledged to increase the enforcement of existing protections for unionized and nonunionized workers. In turn, Canada and the United States pledged to provide financing to assist in those efforts.

Given the longer history of the EU, it should not be surprising that social policy coordination has been on the agenda in Europe for a longer period of time than in the United States. Although Article 123 of the Treaty of Rome called for the creation of a European Social Fund (ESF), member states initially put this action on the back burner as they focused instead on reducing tariff and nontariff barriers to trade. However, after northern European countries began to experience increased social problems with foreign guest workers in the 1970s (see Chapter 5), the ESF was finally created in 1974. During the 1970s and 1980s, as the European Community expanded to include several relatively poorer countries, ESF spending rose to provide job training but also unemployment benefits to workers in Greece, Ireland, Portugal, and Spain who were harmed by the initial transition to freer competition with the major European economies. When the 1987 Single European Act called for steps to realize the Treaty of Rome's call for free movement of labor, pressure for a coordinated social policy rose to minimize the possibility of widespread social dumping.

These concerns led to the adoption of a European Charter of the Fundamental Social Rights of Workers (or Social Charter) in 1989 by eleven of the then twelve member states; the United Kingdom, under the vocal opposition of the Thatcher government, refused to sign the agreement. The Social Charter is a proclamation of principles that did not lead to many concrete initiatives because of the need for unanimity under traditional EC voting rules; even the eleven countries in the Social Charter found it difficult to agree on specific community-wide social policies. The Maastricht Treaty included a social chapter of similar goals that the United Kingdom again refused to sign. The other EU members agreed to form a Social Community with a qualified majority voting system that excludes the United Kingdom. To date, the social chapter has not been associated with any major EU-wide policy directives, but its existence points to the possibility of greater coordination should the signing countries come to greater agreement. At this time, social policy remains dominated by domestic governments; the major impact of globalization has been felt in greater demands for some benefits and in calls for cost control.

Because social policy is such a diverse area, it would be impossible to cover all aspects of this policy area in the case studies. For that reason, we have chosen to focus on family policy, that is, government social programs designed specifically for children and their parents.

United States

Background: Policy Process and Policy History

The political process for family policy is more complex than it is for most of the other policy areas treated in this book. By complex we mean that policy formulation and decision making occur in many arenas and that a multitude of interest groups tend to participate actively. The only other policy area that perhaps approaches this level of complexity is spending policy. However, even in spending policy, in most countries the broad outlines of policy formulation and decision making are usually shaped through the leadership of one or two government agencies.

Why is the family policy network more complex in the United States and elsewhere? First, the diversity of individuals whose pocketbooks are visibly affected by family policies is greater than in most policy areas. Second, the variety of conceivable policy instruments opens the path to meaningful contributions from many agencies, legislative committees, and interest groups. Finally, the multitude of policies in place gives many government agencies and legislative oversight committees jurisdiction over different elements of family policy. The result is a diffuse process such that the nature of family policy making tends to resemble fairly closely the major dynamics of policy making in the country as a whole.

In the decentralized world of policy making in the United States, family policy exhibits the most complex policy network of all. Some aspects fall under the Department of Labor; most others are handled by the Department of Health and Human Services. The nature of the federal policies is such that many crucial decisions are made by state governments. Major reforms need to gain not only executive approval but also the approval of both houses of Congress. A host of subcommittees within various committees in both chambers play an active role in policy formulation and decision making. In the House, the Ways and Means, Economic and Educational Opportunities, and Appropriations Committees have been central. In the Senate the Agriculture (because of the Food Stamp program); Finance; Appropriations; and Health, Education, Labor, and Pensions Committees have been crucial. Interest group involvement is varied. By some estimates, nearly one-sixth of registered interest groups are active in health and social policy formation.

The United States relies more than any other industrialized country on a means-tested approach to family policy. Nothing on the political horizon indicates that a shift will occur toward greater use of a social insurance approach. In fact, the United States has tightened eligibility requirements—embarking on what may prove to be the most substantial welfare reform in a generation. To put the 1996 Personal Responsibility and Work Opportunity Reconciliation Act into perspective, it will be useful to look at family policy prior to that legislation.

The United States, like Japan, has never had a universal child allowance. Instead, the United States has used means-tested transfers and universal tax deductions to supplement incomes for families with children. The main means-tested program during most of the twentieth century, Aid to Families with Dependent Children (AFDC), had its origins in the 1935 Social Security Act—a major element of the Roosevelt administration's New Deal initiatives in response to the Great Depression. Although the program originally provided cash benefits only for children with deceased or incapacitated fathers, since the 1950s it has also provided support to single parents (usually mothers). To be eligible for AFDC, the family must have a gross income at or below 185 percent of the state's needs standard, and the family must also meet an assets test. In this federal system, standards vary considerably from state to state as do benefit levels. Benefits are taxable, and many states have work or education requirements for adult AFDC recipients (we discuss federal reform of these requirements in the next section). The federal government pays, on average, for about half of the AFDC program, and the state government pays the rest. In addition, many states receive federal matching funds for forming an Emergency Assistance program within AFDC for specific purposes (for example, burial costs, first and last month rental housing payments, and utility payments).

In addition to these means-tested transfers for families with children, the United States provides various tax concessions for children. For generations, the U.S. tax code has permitted tax deductions for adult and minor dependents. In 1976 the earned-income tax credit was initiated for families with children under nineteen years. The tax credit is to be used for child care and other family-related expenses. This refundable, means-tested credit was created in response to criticism that the dependent tax deduction transfers more money to middle- and upper-income families than to poor families.

Child care policies provide another example of the emphasis on means-testing and tax expenditures in U.S. family policy. The United States provides a tax deduction for parents who put their children in licensed child care facilities. About half of all state governments provide additional tax deductions and tax credits for child care expenses. In addition to these universal tax expenditures, a variety of federal programs try to subsidize child care for low-income families that meet relevant eligibility criteria (for example, the Child Care Food program, Head Start, and the Social Services Block Grant program). Despite these subsidies targeted at low-income families, such families spend a disproportionate amount of their income on child care. The average U.S. family using day care spends 11 percent of its income for that service; low-income families spend over 20 percent, and high-income families spend less than 5 percent (Hofferth and Phillips 1991).

Just as in the area of child allowances, the United States is a policy outlier in its maternity and parental leave policies. Among the six countries examined in this book, the United States is the only one that does not require employers to provide paid maternity leave. In fact, only with the 1993 Family and Medical Leave Act did the government require employers to provide twelve weeks of unpaid leave for childbirth, adoption, or care for dependent family members. This unpaid leave (which many workers cannot afford to use) is mandatory only for employees in firms with fifty or more workers. Less than half of all women are employed in such firms.

Other forms of social policy are available. Poor families with gross incomes less than 133 percent of the Office of Management and Budget standard and less than $2,000 in disposable assets can receive vouchers to purchase food-stuffs via the Food Stamp program. Finally, families that receive AFDC benefits are also eligible for medical benefits under the Medicaid program. Medical benefits are a crucial issue in family policy in the United States because — unlike all other industrialized countries — the United States has no universal health insurance program (see Chapter 8). Somewhere between 35 and 40 million U.S. citizens lack health insurance.

Contemporary Dynamics

The context of family policy making in the United States is different from that found in other countries in several respects — perhaps principally in the area of public attitudes. Many people in the United States believe that transfer programs breed sloth and should be limited. In public opinion polls from 1975 through the late 1980s, less than half of the respondents supported government intervention on behalf of the poor (Schlesinger and Lee 1994). In the same stagflationary economic environment in which Margaret Thatcher won the executive in the United Kingdom, Ronald Reagan placed welfare reform firmly on the national systemic and institutional agendas in his successful 1980 election campaign.

From 1980 into the 1990s, the United States engaged in a prolonged period of policy formulation and debate. As was the case in several other policy areas in the United States, the environment was decidedly pluralist. Not only did interest groups from across the political spectrum weigh in, but each of the two major parties was divided on how to proceed. In the Democratic Party, major factions called for, respectively, the expansion of the current family policy into new areas and new benefit levels, the protection of the existing system with minor changes, or the wholesale reform of most programs. Republicans were also divided — principally between those calling for minor reform and those advocating sweeping changes. The expansions discussed by some Democrats involved the reduction of means-test levels (or, occasionally, their elimination). The major reforms advocated were the addition of work requirements (dubbed workfare) and the creation of a sunset period for the provision of benefits. From January 1981 through January 1993, this debate took place in the context of a divided government in which Republican presidents called for welfare reform while Democratically controlled legislatures zigzagged between expansion of benefits in some programs and contraction of benefits in others. The majority of the few program expansions in this conflictive atmosphere were un-funded mandates in which the federal government could agree to pass an ini-tiative—but only if state governments were responsible for funding.

In this federal system, implementation of funded and unfunded federal so-cial programs took place largely at the state level. The uneven implementation across states provided grist for the publicity mill of advocates of program ex-pansion and contraction alike. The wave of unfunded mandates also created room for considerable program innovation at the state level as many states successfully appealed to the federal government to explore many of the reforms discussed at the federal level for years—denial of benefits to certain categories of citizens, varying means-test and asset-test levels, work requirements for benefits, and, ultimately, a time limit on the benefit period.

Against this political backdrop, the Republican Party in January 1995 gained control of the legislature for the first time in well over a generation. The reduction over time in the proportion of the Republican caucus protective of the status quo, and the presence in the White House of a Democratic presi-dent who was committed to some forms of social policy change, opened the door to a new decision-making stage under a changed balance of forces at the federal level. The result was the passage of the 1996 Personal Responsibility and Work Opportunity Reconciliation Act, the biggest change in federal so-cial policy since the 1960s.

The intent of this law is clear: The federal government wants to limit fur-ther both the number of people receiving welfare transfers and the time pe-riod of benefits. The legislation proposes to meet these goals through a vari-ety of means. The federal guarantee of AFDC funds has shifted to block grants to the states that are contingent on state policies meeting reform guidelines. These block grants under the new Temporary Aid to Needy Families (TANF) program cover not only the former AFDC expenses but also initiatives previ-ously funded as the JOBS and Emergency Assistance programs. TANF benefits are limited to a maximum of five years (although states could conceivably ex-empt 20 percent of families for hardship). Adults are required to go to work within two years or lose benefits. The formula for food stamps was changed to reduce benefit levels almost 20 percent by the year 2002. Legal immigrants are now denied welfare benefits during their first five years of residency.

The eventual impact of this legislation is difficult to predict because it en-tered into force only recently. The act decentralizes even further cash assistance to needy families via the move to federal block grants. In turn, the federally mandated work requirements and time limits present state governments with a real challenge—to provide meaningful work opportunities for their poor cit-izens. The path to successful implementation is unclear. In particular, it is not clear whether state governments will be willing to refuse benefits to people once the ceiling on benefits is reached in 2002. Time will tell whether the 1996 reform will be an enduring piece of legislation or the impetus for even more substantial reform—in either direction.

The saga of contemporary social policy reform in the United States is a microcosm of several fundamental features of U.S. politics since the 1980s — divided government, weak party discipline, an important role for state governments, and a wide open field for interest group politics. These factors make it difficult for the federal government to make sweeping policy changes. That said, major reform is not impossible in this political system. The passage of the 1996 legislation bears witness to the fact that change is possible — albeit time-consuming.

Japan

Background: Policy Process and Policy History

The central ministry for social policy in Japan is the Ministry of Health and Welfare. The lead agency for family policy is the Children and Family Bureau, which is responsible for family allowances, child care, and public assistance policies. Family leave and unemployment insurance are supervised by the Ministry of Labor. The Ministry of Finance has played a crucial role as well in determining the fiscal parameters for family policy. Major reforms have tended to involve prolonged negotiations between the relevant ministries, the leaders of coalition partners or party factions, and heads of major employer organizations and labor unions.

Although a few social policy measures were initiated during the Depression and World War II (including the establishment of the first Ministry of Welfare), the bulk of contemporary family policy has its origins in legislation passed after the war. The 1947 Child Welfare Law was followed by a variety of other measures designed to provide a minimum standard of living for children; the 1947 law calls on all Japanese citizens "to ensure that all children have basic economic security" (Ozawa 1991: 2). Despite the universal standard that this implies, the policy instruments chosen to meet that goal have tended to be means-tested. As Japan faces a new century, the challenge of devoting sufficient resources to meet that goal has increased amid a wave of economic and political crises from which Japan seemed immune just a few years earlier.

Compared with other industrialized countries, Japan was late to adopt child allowances as part of the country's social policy. The 1971 Children's Allowance Law initially provided allowances only for third and subsequent children. The law currently provides means-tested allowances for all children, and higher benefits are paid for third and subsequent children. Recipients must have a family income below a ceiling that varies according to the number of dependents. All parents receive a lump-sum childbirth allowance. In addition to this program, single mothers not receiving benefits from the Old-Age, Survivors, and Disability Insurance program are also eligible for a child support allowance that has a less stringent means-test and pays benefits until children reach age eighteen (age twenty if the children are disabled). Parents with mentally or physically disabled children are also eligible for a means-tested special child dependent's allowance. The tax code provides a deduction for children and other dependents.

Since 1947, child care for preschoolers has been provided for all children whose parents or relatives cannot provide care (due to work responsibilities or disability). Fees in both public and private child care centers are based on a single, universal sliding scale tied to income. The government subsidizes the difference between the fee charged and a universal per-child fee collected by the centers; the local and central governments share the funding burden equally.

Maternity leave is provided for a maximum of fourteen weeks under the 1947 Labor Standards Law. Compensation is at 60 percent of the relevant reference wage. The issue of parental leave for child (and elder) care has entered the Japanese legislative agenda only recently. In 1992 the government passed the Child Care Leave Law, which requires most firms to provide either parent (not simultaneously) with unpaid leave during a child's first year. Since 1992, leave policy has been a topic of repeated legislative debate.

The impoverished are potentially eligible for public assistance under the 1950 Livelihood Protection Act. All other income supplements (including child allowances) are counted as income in the means-test standard. For those who qualify, the program pays a benefit designed to bring people up to roughly 62 percent of the median family income in their region. Because of social stigma and ignorance, far less than half of those eligible for public assistance have applied for benefits during the entire history of the program.

Contemporary Dynamics

Japan is arguably the only one of the six countries examined in this book in which an expansion of family policy was under serious discussion at the start of the 1990s. Japan engaged in electoral system reform in the 1990s to deal with discontent about one-party domination and corruption scandals. In Japan's newly more fluid political environment, the major postreform political parties all publicly contemplated some expansion of the family welfare system.

The most visible example of this expansionist tendency is perhaps found in family leave policy. Some of the newly formed political parties helped to put this issue on the public agenda by pointing out how Japan—despite its rapid ascent to economic heights at or beyond European standards—had yet to enact this basic element of European family policy. In 1992 Japan passed its first parental leave legislation—calling for unpaid parental leave during a child's first year of life. As nearly half of all mothers moved to accept this leave, pressure increased to provide some form of paid leave. Rather than dulling attention on the issue, the implementation of this initial reform worked to raise the profile of the issue once the Liberal Democratic Party (LDP) lost its control of the executive in 1993.

All of the major parties staked out positions on the issue as the policy formulation process continued. The Japan New Party (at the helm of the first post-LDP coalition government) called for some form of paid leave as did the Social Democratic Party. The New Frontier Party backed Rengo, the major labor confederation, in its call for one-year paid leave for either child or elder care with the possibility of multiple leaves. The LDP, in its effort to regain the political initiative, upped the ante by calling for a comprehensive review of the entire social policy framework to ensure that citizens' needs were met in all areas—including leave policy.

As the new parties strove to win over voters, the decision-making process produced a series of new initiatives. In 1994, the Unemployment Insurance Act was amended to provide a leave benefit at 25 percent of previous earnings. The Hashimoto government, a coalition led by Liberal Democrats and Social Democrats, passed in 1995 a compromise expansion of the leave system, which called on all firms to provide at least three months of child or elder care leave per family.

When vigorous debate began over family policy at the beginning of the 1990s, Japan was riding the crest of a seemingly unending economic expansion that had made it one of the richest countries in the world. By the time several leave reforms had been enacted in the mid-1990s, however, Japan was on the cusp of an economic crisis from which it has yet to recover fully. Although agenda setting, policy formulation, and decision making had taken place in a context of prosperity and self-confidence, the implementation and evaluation of these new family policies are taking place in a deflationary environment in which Japan has suffered its worst economic contraction in the postwar era. To date, no subsequent government has terminated the new leave programs—in part because of a fear that lower government spending would simply further decrease demand amid a protracted period of stagnation and recession.

The debate over family leave in Japan in the 1990s demonstrates that in a fluid political environment, examples from abroad may be used more powerfully. New and changing political movements attempt to stake out positions to attract (what they hope are) uncommitted voters by calling for policy innovations previously ignored on the public agenda. The presence of the family leave policy in so many other industrialized countries made it a safer issue on which to call for expansion of government activity. Its use in other countries gave it credibility that it might have otherwise lacked.

Germany

Background: Policy Process and Policy History

The central elements of family policy in Germany are currently managed by two major ministries. The Ministry of Labor and Social Affairs is in charge of the social security system, family allowances, and means-tested poverty assistance. The Ministry of Family Affairs, Senior Citizens, Women, and Youth supervises child care programs and other family social services. These ministries work with the Economics Ministry, Finance Ministry, and the chancellor in formulating new family policy initiatives. As in other policy areas, the interest group structure is less freewheeling and more centralized in Germany than in France. The two major employers' associations—the Federation of German Industry (BDI) and the Confederation of German Employers' Associations (BDA)—and the German Federation of Trade Unions (DGB) have been of particular historical relevance in family policy making.

The German pattern of caring for families has been a combination of means-tested programs and universal benefits that provide cradle-to-grave protection. The German constitution requires the government to establish and maintain basic social welfare rights, and family policy has fallen under this umbrella. Several contemporary family policies (maternity benefits and unemployment insurance, for example) trace their roots to the late nineteenth and early twentieth centuries. However, most legislation designed to protect families has been adopted since 1949. The German political parties' attempts to outbid each other for moderate votes have resulted in the steady expansion of these programs by conservatives as well as socialists. The partisan debate has concerned the nature of government activity—a debate that in recent years has gained significance in a changing German economic environment.

Germany has traditionally adopted **pronatalist family policies** that reward parents for having additional children and encourage increasing family size. The first German pronatalist policies date back to the Weimar Republic and were continued with racist rather than pro-family intentions in the Nazi era. Since 1949 the German government has continued in the pronatalist tradition. The family allowance has varied with the political climate in the country; Social Democratic governments have created more universal benefits, and Christian Democratic leaders have based these allowances more often on means-testing. Presently all German parents receive the same benefit for their first child, but larger allowances are paid for second and subsequent children based on a sliding scale tied to income. Poorer families receive greater benefits, and the poorest families are eligible for a supplemental benefit.

Taxation in Germany is designed to encourage women to focus on their role as mothers. The tax system rewards married couples by taxing them at a much lower rate than unmarried individuals, and German couples with a financially dependent spouse also receive generous tax credits. In combination, these policies create a powerful incentive for married women to remain at home with their children.

Although Germany currently offers a wide array of child care options, this was not always the case. The German government traditionally viewed child care as the responsibility of parents, relatives, and neighbors. However, since the 1970s, day care has been heavily subsidized by government. Ninety percent of the cost is shared equally by state, regional, and local governments, and parents supply the remaining 10 percent (Baker 1995: 216). Limited government funds are available for parents who arrange for child care in their homes. The 1991 Child Care Act states that all children, but especially preschoolers, have a right to develop fully through private and public organizations.

Maternity leave is provided through a social insurance program that dates back to 1883. This program is funded through employer, employee, and government contributions. Employed women who have worked for a designated period of time are entitled to fourteen weeks of maternity leave at 100 percent of previous earnings up to a cap of $15 per day that was instituted in the mid-1990s. Parents may also take up to five days of leave each year for each sick child under age eight. Since 1986 a parental leave program has operated in Germany, allowing one parent to take job-protected leave for child rearing. This leave could extend to a maximum of thirty-six months. The relatively long leave period reflects, in part, a desire to decrease the unemployment rate by creating job openings.

Relatively few direct benefits are targeted toward the poor in Germany. This dearth of benefits has traditionally reflected the small number of Germans living in poverty and that many of the poor have been foreign guest workers with few guaranteed rights. For poverty-stricken Germans, direct payments for food, housing, clothing, and other necessities are available, but these expenditures are a small proportion of the national budget. To receive public assistance, individuals must have no income or assets and cannot receive assistance from relatives. They are required to seek employment unless it would endanger the raising of children. Parents of children under age three who receive public assistance are not required to work, and those with children ages three to six must work only part-time. A child-rearing benefit was introduced in Germany in 1986 for parents who are unable to work full time because they are taking care of their children. The child-rearing benefit is available to parents in the labor force and homemakers and cannot be received simultaneously with unemployment benefits. In addition to central government programs, some state governments also provide assistance to families. Finally, parents may claim family assistance under a young family program for children born on or after July 1, 1989. This is a one-time payment upon the birth or adoption of a child. These family allowances are all means-tested.

Contemporary Dynamics

The support and expansion of social policies in Germany was not a problem in times of economic growth. In recent years, however, an economic downturn has focused attention on reducing the cost of social programs. This was especially true as rising unemployment and an economic slowdown reduced payments into social insurance funds at the same time that demands for unemployment benefits and worker retraining programs increased. Germany also faces new challenges in family policy. Many observers today comment on the potential for the emergence of a permanent underclass of welfare recipients living in areas of urban decline, with little prospect for improving their standard of living. Among those constituting this new underclass are the long-term unemployed, single parents, low-income pensioners, and refugees seeking asylum. Several indicators highlight the increasing severity of this problem: In 1985 the proportion of jobless Germans who had been unemployed for more than one year was 20 percent, by 1995 the proportion had risen to over 30 percent. Further, it was estimated in 1980 that 2 percent of the population lived below the poverty line; by 1995 about 4 million Germans, or 5 percent of the population, were living in poverty (Conradt 1996: 284). These new poor place tremendous pressure for benefits on the political system in an environment of shrinking economic resources. In the 1990s the prospect of budget deficits for the first time in the postwar era resulting from the underestimated costs of unification further focused attention on cost reduction.

It is one thing to put social policy reform on the systemic agenda and quite another to adopt concrete measures. Much of the German public strongly supports existing family programs and is unwilling to see the programs eliminated or severely cut back (or to see their contributions in the form of taxation increased). At the same time, many policymakers on the center-right and the major business associations argue that Germany has reached the point at which high levels of social spending endanger the long-term health and competitiveness of the economy. At the policy formulation stage, advocates of cuts have tried to tie social spending reductions to the issue of reducing unemployment.

The decisions adopted by the Kohl government in the 1990s called for modest cost reduction and not for a wholesale attack on the welfare state. Maternity leave benefits were capped, and many other benefits (such as child allowances) were not increased in real terms. This understated approach to social policy reform proved easier to adopt and to implement than was the case in France. Reductions in benefits have also been made easier to implement by the Kohl government's ability to play the inflation card. The long-standing aversion to inflation in Germany faced its most serious challenge in over a generation because of the expenses associated with reunification. In that context of a once-in-a-lifetime event—reunification—it was difficult for labor unions or the Social Democrats to mount vigorous opposition to slight spending reductions.

The German experience demonstrates that similar proposals can be politically feasible in one country even as they fail in others. Both the way that reform is presented and the overall cultural, economic, and political context can work to make proposals that might be rejected in some countries politically feasible elsewhere. The Kohl government's reputation for earnestness in dealing with reunification (and other issues) was a political resource that could be used to blunt opposition to proposals that might have faced more criticism had they come from another government.

France

Background: Policy Process and Policy History

As we noted in Chapter 3, the precise number and nature of cabinet ministries is not fixed in France. Each cabinet minister has the ability to form ministries over existing permanent agencies and bureaus as a reflection of his or her priorities. For example, the family allowance program in France is administered by the National Fund of Family Allocations (CNAF). This means that CNAF could be placed under the bailiwick of the economic or finance ministry. Nevertheless, in most situations it falls to an employment or labor ministry or to a welfare ministry. In the cabinet established by Lionel Jospin in 1997, the CNAF came under the supervision of the Ministry of Employment and Solidarity. The CNAF has a permanent bureaucracy and a permanent advisory council. Although the notion of an advisory council is a potentially corporatist one, the pluralist nature of French interest groups creates a variety of representatives for each set of interests. Representatives of the same basic interest often have decidedly different ideological perspectives. This diversity of interests at the table has given French governments some political space to maneuver as governments of different political stripes can appeal to different groups to gain support for pet initiatives.

Besides the CNAF, other agencies and ministries are influential in family policy decisions. Often the pressure for changes in spending levels emerges out of the budget, economic, and/or finance ministry, which then consult with the supervisory ministry or ministries to set parameters for family policy that the relevant agencies need to meet. Support of these executive decisions in the legislature tends to depend on perceptions of public reaction to the proposed changes.

France provides to its citizens an extensive array of universal and means-tested family subsidies. Government assistance to families began in the early twentieth century with policies such as an unemployment insurance program (1905), maternity leave (1913), and a child allowance program (1932). Family programs were improved and expanded after World War II. Building on this tradition, the 1958 constitution of the Fifth Republic declares a national responsibility for families. The prominence of left-wing movements, the activities of labor unions, the influence of Catholic social teachings, and concern over a declining birth rate have been important factors promoting a generous system of family supports in France.

As in Germany, France has a pronatalist child allowance policy. This policy is a clear response to concerns about low birth rates and population decline. France introduced a child allowance program in 1932 to provide assistance to employees with dependent children. This program was modified in 1939 to eliminate support for first children and increase payments for subsequent children, to a maximum of three children. Currently all parents with two children under age seventeen (age twenty if the children are students) receive the allowance. The family allowance is not considered taxable income and is financed through payroll taxes. Low-income families are also eligible for a means-tested supplement to the child allowance.

Taxation policy in France also reflects a pronatalist orientation because parents significantly reduce their income tax burden when they have more children. In contrast to most other countries, taxation in France is based on the family rather than the individual. Tax concessions to parents for third and subsequent children are twice the amount allowed for the first and second children. Further, French parents do not pay income tax until their income reaches nearly 1.8 times the income of the average production worker. As a result, only half of French households pay income taxes (see Chapter 7).

France has one of the most comprehensive child care systems in the industrialized countries. The government provides a system of tuition-free preschools for all children ages three to six through the public education system. These preschools are funded through employer and employee contributions. Publicly financed and operated day care centers are also widely available, as are before- and after-school care facilities. These facilities are funded largely at the local level and involve some form of direct contribution from parents. In addition to the universal availability of child care, parents are also given tax concessions for children in public day care and for the cost of private day care in their homes. The child care system, despite its breadth, is criticized because demand for public day care outpaces supply and because of apparent inequities from region to region.

Government-sponsored maternity leave has been available in France since 1913. The program has some restrictions based on family size and length of employment, but generally speaking the French have universal access to paid maternity leave. Female employees now enjoy leave from work for at least sixteen weeks and up to twenty-six weeks with a guarantee of return to their same positions. As with other family benefits, the length of the maternity leave and level of benefits increases with the number of children in the family. Fathers may take three days of leave when their children are born. French parents are also entitled to cash maternity benefits for birth and adoption. Employers are required by law to accommodate nursing mothers by providing nursing rooms and additional breaks for one year after childbirth. In 1984 a new benefit was introduced for families with more than three children, one of whom is under age three. The benefit provides partial compensation for lost earnings to parents who choose to stay at home with their children rather than return to work. As of 1987 this benefit could be claimed for up to three years. These benefits are financed through a social insurance fund based on payroll taxes and government contributions.

Public assistance is available in the form of means-tested relief for both single and married parents. For low-income families with children, this benefit consists of housing, medical care, and help in finding employment. This assistance is intended to provide the minimum level of income necessary to help people get back on their feet. The extent of this benefit depends on income and household size. Another income-based program provides a basic income level to single parents who have a child under age three or for one year after the individual becomes a single parent.

Contemporary Dynamics

When Jacques Chirac captured the French presidency in 1995, he inherited a large center-right majority in the legislature. His election ended a period of cohabitation between opposing political forces in the executive and gave Chirac a platform from which to call for a series of boldly presented conservative initiatives. Social policy was perhaps the most volatile of the issues pressed by Chirac when he put together the Juppe government. Chirac and Juppe tried to use Chirac's triumph as further evidence of an agenda-setting mandate for a reduction of the government's role in social policy. This initiative also could be presented as part of the general effort to cut costs and to reduce the budget deficit (particularly in response to pressures to meet EU budgetary standards). Chirac and Juppe argued that social reform could reduce the size of the public workforce and the flow of transfer payments to individual citizens—thereby improving the macroeconomic climate.

At the policy formulation stage, such efforts were widely opposed by organized labor and by French citizens more generally. Unions participating in the general strike launched in December 1995 were quick to refer to these twin efforts at privatization and social reform as evidence that the Juppe government was callously indifferent to the needs of the common person. The initial announcements of cuts in social spending prior to the strike were repeatedly attacked in the press and in person-on-the-street media interviews that demonstrated popular support for many of the strikers. The Juppe government appeared to be caught off guard by the adherence to the strike across different sectors of the economy. Perhaps more important, the government was dismayed to see the widespread support for the strikers among the citizenry at large. It became clear to the government that social policy was a sacred cow in the minds of many citizens.

The wave of protests and criticism led the Juppe cabinet to withdraw most of its social policy reforms at the decision-making stage because the Gaullists and the Republicans feared the possibility of an electoral backlash that could threaten to reduce their large majority in the legislature. As it turned out, this retreat on social policy reform came too late to meet this concern. The early attacks on social policy by the Juppe cabinet helped to fuel the electoral defeat of Juppe's center-right coalition in 1997.

Family assistance programs remain very popular and neither the Socialists nor the Gaullists have been willing to risk the political backlash that a serious reduction of benefits would likely generate. This climate calls into doubt the willingness of governments of either political stripe to implement fully reductions in social policy over time. For example, when the center-left Jospin government called for several cost-cutting measures in fall 1997, it faced a host of opposition—most visibly a major truckers' strike.

The dynamics of social policy in France in the 1990s demonstrate just how effective interest groups can be when they can mobilize vocal public support for their stated position. Although we often consider interest groups as agents of backroom politics and quiet lobbying, they are perhaps most powerful when they win the war for public opinion to put pressure on cabinets and legislators. In a democracy, the visible threat of an electoral backlash against an unpopular policy decision is a powerful political tool. In France during the mid-1990s, the weak clients thesis did not hold because advocates of social spending succeeded in mobilizing visible public opposition to the proposed cuts.

United Kingdom

Background: Policy Process and Policy History

Although the dynamics of family policy in the United Kingdom are more centralized than in the other countries examined in this book, a greater decentralization of the policy network exists in the family policy area than in other British policies. Family leave and child care policies fall under the Employment Ministry, which is currently contained in the Department of Education and Employment. Most other elements are supervised under the Department of Social Security. The ministries work closely with the prime minister and the finance minister (the chancellor of the exchequer) in formulating potential policy reforms. Although formal and informal consultation with interest groups is ongoing, most major reforms have tended to take the shape of the electoral campaign platforms that led to a new party forming the government.

By the early 1900s, the British had introduced policies to provide old age pensions, unemployment insurance, and public housing. A widely read plan for postwar reconstruction, the 1942 Beveridge Report, resulted in policies that now provide a series of government-sponsored services. Nevertheless, apart from the National Health Service (see Chapter 8), the United Kingdom has few comprehensive, universal social programs. With the exception of family allowances, the majority of family policies are means-tested. During the 1980s and 1990s, Conservative governments emphasized the importance of market mechanisms. In family policy, this ideological thrust was associated with a significant reduction in the level of benefits in most areas.

Family allowances have been distributed in various forms in the United Kingdom since the end of World War II. Whatever their form, these allowances have always been intended to equalize the incomes of parents and individuals without children, as well as to acknowledge the additional costs of child rearing. As such, the child allowance program is a universal benefit financed through general government revenue. Since 1976 the child benefit has been a weekly nontaxable payment to mothers and legal guardians. It is universal for children under age sixteen (age nineteen if the children are students), but the highest benefit is paid for the first child. The child benefit is not subject to automatic cost-of-living adjustments. Its value declined in real terms during the 1980s and then recovered part of that loss in 1992. A means-tested supplement to the child benefit, the family credit, is also available to low-wage parents who work more than twenty-four hours weekly.

Taxation in Britain has been based on the individual since 1989, with each taxpayer entitled to one exemption. When the universal child benefit was introduced in 1976, existing tax deductions for families with dependent children, which had been in place since 1909, were eliminated. Child care expenses are not tax deductible.

The United Kingdom clearly has a shortage of child care options, especially publicly funded care. In a departure from the European model, the standard for day care in the United Kingdom is private provision. In part this reflects a traditional reluctance by both the public and the government to encourage mothers to participate in the workforce. The vast majority of children under age three are cared for by parents or other relatives, with class being an important determinant of the type of child care arrangement used. Middle- and upper-class parents tend to employ nannies. Publicly funded preschools and kindergartens are used by only 10 percent of eligible children (Baker 1995: 224). Although employment for lower- and middle-class women has become more of a financial necessity, a corresponding movement toward direct public provision of day care services has not followed. Government day care centers have tended to be for children who are considered disadvantaged. Public day care is typically provided by local authorities, but these services vary widely and are generally not of high quality.

Maternity leave has been provided for British women since 1911. Currently the first six weeks are compensated at 90 percent of earnings. An additional twelve weeks of leave are subsidized by a modest flat-rate weekly benefit. After meeting certain conditions relating to wages and length of service, women can opt for up to an additional twenty-two weeks of unpaid maternity leave with a guarantee of reinstatement. Under the Thatcher government (1979–1990), the requirements for maternity leave were tightened for employees and relaxed for employers. Many women do not take the full leave because less than half of the period is covered by benefits and only the first six weeks provide substantial compensation. There is no official provision for parental leave.

The British approach to poverty relief has historically lacked generosity in comparison with most European countries. Prior to 1948 the British government assisted the poor under the provisions of the 1834 Poor Law, which created poorhouses for so-called paupers, who were forced to relinquish their citizens rights upon entry. Most assistance to the poor came from religious and charitable organizations. In 1948, national public assistance programs were initiated that were expanded in the 1960s and 1970s. The 1986 Social Security Act provides the standards that currently apply in the area of poverty relief. The new standards were intended to reduce the available level of benefits; keep spending down; and encourage the voluntary, informal, and private sectors to cover the difference. Poor people are now entitled to three means-tested benefits: income support, family credits, and housing. Income support is available for unemployed individuals and those who work less than twenty-four hours weekly. A family credit is also provided to persons with dependent children who work more than twenty-four hours per week. Finally, those who receive public assistance are also eligible for housing benefits that cover 100 percent of public or private rental, or interest on mortgages, and 80 percent of local taxes.

Contemporary Dynamics

Margaret Thatcher sought to move government out of the social welfare business by placing increasing emphasis on personal responsibility and the market. Winning the executive in the stagflationary 1970s—amid a period of prolonged British economic decline—Thatcher chose to place welfare reform (and the reduction of government activity more generally) in the context of making the United Kingdom economically competitive again.

Although Thatcher's electoral victory propelled social reform to the heart of the public agenda, it did not necessarily guarantee its medium-run success. The policy debate during the first Thatcher government was particularly high-voltage. Labour called the Thatcher program something just shy of economic terrorism on the common man, and the Tories all but labeled the Labour platform a road to full communism. However, when Thatcher's parliamentary majority was expanded comfortably by the 1983 elections (held after the victory in the Falklands War with Argentina), the Conservative government moved to consolidate its reduction of the dole.

Given Thatcher's large parliamentary majority, the unitary nature of the state, and the general professionalism of the bureaucracy, there were few hurdles to the enactment of social policy reform and its subsequent implementation once the specter of a Labour-led backlash was put to rest in 1983. Thatcher's governments achieved considerable success in reducing the state's role in providing for families. Most of the major institutions charged with providing family assistance saw their powers curtailed and functions changed. Although public polls showed that support for universal family assistance did not decline significantly, Thatcher built support for her program by convincing many voters that the old benefits and services could be maintained only by increasing taxes. A willingness to pay more to maintain or increase social services was not visible among the majority of British citizens at the time. Ironically, a later misstep on taxation led to Thatcher's ouster as prime minister (see Chapter 7, regarding the 1990 poll tax scandal).

This lesson would not be lost on Thatcher's successors, John Major and Tony Blair. Both leaders called for stable or increased social spending but promised to provide it without raising taxes significantly. Blair's New Labour program—the centerpiece of his huge victory in the May 1997 elections—even trumpeted a visible dose of Thatcher's emphasis on personal responsibility. Thus far, the most visible initiatives calling for new spending in the Blair government have not been in family policy but rather in education and job training.

The United Kingdom's experience with family policy making in the 1980s and 1990s demonstrates two central features of British political dynamics. First, the combination of strong party discipline, a unitary state, and plurality elections paves the way for governments to pursue bold reform initiatives. Second, this increased reform capability is not limitless. Governments that steer too far away from the voters do so at their own risk. The Major government moved to the center to avoid furthering the perception that the Conservative Party had become overly callous under Thatcher. At the same time, Tony Blair finished a fifteen-year-long effort to demonstrate that the Labour Party would not simply rush to restore every social program brought down during the Thatcher era.

Italy

Background: Policy Process and Policy History

Most family policy issues in Italy currently come under the jurisdiction of the Ministry of Labor and Social Welfare. The core agency is the General Directorate for Welfare, which supervises family allowances and other public assistance programs. Many of these other programs are designed and implemented at the local government level. The finance minister has always been a part of the family policy process, but this role grew during the 1990s as Italy struggled to bring down its budget deficit. As in other areas, compromises worked out among different party leaders represented in and across the relevant ministries have not always translated smoothly into new legislation.

Italian family policy has undergone an evolution similar to social policy in Germany. First, a variety of unemployment, disability, and pension programs were initiated at the turn of the century. Then, between the world wars, new family programs responded to both the Great Depression and the fascist rhetorical emphasis on solidarity. After World War II, Italy experienced the greatest economic growth in its modern history, and some of the resulting resources were devoted to an expansion of family policy funding and programming—often via universal social insurance policies.

Child allowances were introduced for all workers under Benito Mussolini. In the postwar era, allowances initially varied by region and by occupation, but by the 1970s Italy had moved to a universal flat-rate monthly benefit per child. Over the next decade, amid burgeoning government deficits, successive governments inserted means-tested restrictions: Families earning more than twice the national average receive no child allowances, whereas those earning between 150 and 200 percent of the average receive partial benefits. At the local level, several additional means-tested transfer programs exist for needy families with children, including a benefit for single-parent families. The tax code provides additional support for families. Tax deductions exist for children and other dependent family members. In addition, a tax credit for children pays out an equal benefit per child. Several public assistance programs exist at the local government level with funding from the central government.

Since the 1970s universal child care for preschoolers has been provided via child care centers and kindergartens. The centers are run by local governments with funding support from the central government. Since 1950, female employees have been entitled to five months of paid maternity leave (beginning two months prior to delivery). The maternity leave program provides benefits at 80 percent of previous earnings. Either parent can also opt for an additional six months of leave, at 30 percent of earnings, during the child's first year. Female employees are also entitled to paid parental leave to care for sick children under age three.

Contemporary Dynamics

During the 1990s, efforts to reform Italian social policy were shaped not just by fiscal pressures visible in several other countries but also by widespread disaffection with the national government. The political dynamic of two generations of Italians—coalition governments dominated by the Christian Democrats—collapsed during the 1980s in the midst of corruption scandals that damaged the traditional governing parties. The ensuing chaos made it extremely difficult to fashion political coalitions willing to tackle substantial policy reform in any major area. In this volatile climate, social policy reform emerged on the public agenda in the 1990s amid a climbing budget deficit and increasing attacks on the exchange rate.

Following the political reforms of the early 1990s (perhaps most notably the changes in the electoral system), many people spoke of the possibility of major changes in various policy areas as well. In 1994 the newly elected Berlusconi government proposed a 1995 budget that called for a substantial reform of the pension system as well as reductions in family policy benefits in several areas. The labor unions aligned with the once-communist Democratic

Party of the Left (PDS) stridently opposed the proposed cuts. That opposition gained strength when Berlusconi became embroiled in a series of corruption scandals (and associated legal problems) that reduced his ability to mobilize support for his policy agenda as part of the path to a new Italy. Instead, the scandals highlighted Berlusconi's ties to the old Italy and made him an easy target for critics.

At the decision-making stage, the social policy reform efforts were blocked initially. However, when Berlusconi was removed by a no-confidence vote after less than a year in office, a nonpartisan successor, Lamberto Dini, was named prime minister, with an unclear majority in the legislature. Dini presented himself as a technocrat concerned about the ability of Italy to meet its obligations under the Maastricht agreement on fiscal policy. Using that justification, he shepherded through a budget that reduced the rate of increase for family spending but made no major family policy reforms.

The long-term implementation of a strategy of slow or even zero growth in social spending was called into question by the results of the next election (after the fall of the Dini government). The 1996 election produced a center-left victory led by the PDS, the major faction of the once-communist party. The new government under Romano Prodi pledged fiscal and social responsibility. Prodi's governing platform called for a welfare state compatible with fiscal responsibility, which he deemed essential given Italy's need for sharp deficit reduction to meet Maastricht Treaty criteria for European monetary unification (see Chapter 6). Through some temporary spending freezes and tax increases, Italy met its obligations in 1997 and 1998, but at a price. The Refounded Communists (the other faction of the old communist party) pulled their support away from the Prodi government in October 1998 on the grounds that Prodi had not done enough to protect social spending. It remains to be seen whether the new center-left coalition government under Massimo D'Alema will restore growth to social spending. It is clear, however, that some retrenchment of family policy was on the stated agendas of all of the largest political parties in Italy in the late 1990s.

The Italian experience demonstrates some of the special difficulties faced by multiparty coalition governments. When the executive needs the support of several parties with different ideologies and different core constituencies of voters, policy reform of any magnitude can be decidedly difficult to conduct. Both the Berlusconi and the Prodi governments were toppled because of disagreements among coalition partners with different regional or ideological constituencies. The success of the Dini and Prodi governments in pushing through social policy spending reforms despite such divided coalitions is more of a testament to the consensus of the major parties in support of adhering to the Maastricht guidelines (and to the EU more generally) than it is evidence of a stronger parliamentary coalition. In other words, the pressures of globalization appear to have created a rationale for common action across diverse political forces.

Cross-national Trends

As in tax policy the general social policy approach of the three continental European countries (France, Germany, and Italy) differs from that found in the other three countries. The continental countries tend to have more universalist policies whereas the other three pursue means-testing measures more frequently. In general, universalist policies tend to be associated with lower rates of relative poverty. Despite the superior performance of universalist policies (and of higher social spending) in reducing relative poverty, in the 1990s all six countries enacted reforms that rely more frequently on means tests (or tightening existing means standards). Furthermore, all six countries have frozen or, more frequently, reduced welfare benefit levels. Although this contraction of social policy efforts is compatible with cultural traditions outside of Europe, it represents a new development in France, Germany, and Italy. Efforts to explain this change have tended to focus on the impact of globalization and, in particular, the push toward deficit reduction implied by monetary unification.

Policy Outputs

A clear division appears to exist between countries that have tended to rely more on means-tested policies (Japan, the United Kingdom, and the United States) and those that have opted more often for universalist social insurance policies (France, Germany, and Italy). In making such a generalization, however, we are referring to differences of degree in the mix of instrument choices.

The mix of public and private responsibility and of means-tested and universal policies is summarized in Table 9–1. No country relies exclusively on means-tested policies. For example, all countries employ a social insurance approach to unemployment benefits (and to public pensions). At the same time, even the three countries with the predominantly universalist approach (France, Germany, and Italy) employ several means-tested programs for poverty relief.

Policy Outcomes

Given this variety of policy mixes, which countries have been most successful at limiting poverty? Poverty can be defined in a multitude of ways. The notion of **absolute poverty** implies some basic needs standard beneath which citizens are said to be poor. This threshold varies substantially from expert to expert and from government to government. This lack of agreement on a common standard makes meaningful cross-national comparison of absolute poverty statistics difficult.

Poverty can also be defined in a relative sense. Perhaps the most thorough attempt to conduct a comparable, cross-national study of **relative poverty** in industrialized countries has been the Luxembourg Income Study (Atkinson, Rainwater, and Smeeding 1995). The study attempts to create comparable

Table 9-1 Social Policy Models, 1980–1998

Country	Child Allowances	Child Care Funding	Paid Family Leave Policy	Unemployment Insurance
France	SI	Public > Private	Maternity and parental (1984–1998)	SI
Germany	SI (1980–1982) Mixed (1982–1995) SI (1996–1998)	Public > Private	Maternity and parental (1986–1998)	SI
Italy	Mixed	Public > Private	Maternity and parental	SI
Japan	MT	Private > Public	Maternity and parental (1994–1998)	SI
United Kingdom	SI	Private > Public	Maternity	SI (1980–1994) Mixed (1995–1998)
United States	MT	Private > Public	None	SI

SI = social insurance; MT = means-tested; Mixed = mix of SI and MT.

Table 9-2 Relative Poverty Statistics

Country	Year of Observation	Percentage of Population in Poverty[a]
France	1984	7.5
Germany	1984	6.5
Italy	1986	10.4
Japan	1984–1985	10.0
United Kingdom	1986	9.1
United States	1986	18.4

SOURCE: Data for Japan reflect the average for the years listed based on data from the official Family Income and Expenditure Survey. Data for the other countries are from the Luxembourg Income Study (Atkinson, Rainwater, and Smeeding 1995).

[a] Percentage of the population earning below 50 percent of the median income.

data sets on income for seventeen Organisation for Economic Co-operation and Development member countries. Japan was among the countries excluded from the study because official income data are based on a household survey system that systematically excludes several of the poorest segments of the population such as agricultural workers.

Table 9–2 presents data on relative poverty for the six countries examined in this book. The poverty rate is defined here as the percentage of households that earn less than 50 percent of the median household income (adjusted for family size). Keep in mind that the poverty figure for Japan is likely to be somewhat higher than shown here. Two of the three countries that have opted

Table 9-3 Child Allowance Benefits, 1998

Country	Annual Minimum Child Allowance (for qualifying one-child families)
France	$1,591
Germany	$1,775
Italy	$144
Japan	$495
United Kingdom	$1,152
United States	None

SOURCE: U.S. Social Security Administration: *Social Security Programs Throughout the World* (Washington, D.C.: U.S. Government Printing Office, 1999).

NOTE: All figures are in U.S. dollars. Foreign currency conversions were done using the average U.S. dollar exchange rate for 1998. Japan and the United States have means-tested allowances; figures provided are for the minimum benefit provided to all who fall below the means test. Japan pays only for families with children under age 3. Italy pays benefits on a sliding scale tied to income; the figure listed is the lowest possible benefit. The other three countries provide benefits regardless of the family's income level.

more often for social insurance policies have noticeably lower poverty rates (France and Germany); the exception is Italy. The three countries with the greatest reliance on means-tested programs have higher poverty rates. The U.S. poverty rate is considerably higher than that found in the other countries.

Why do the countries with more universalist policies tend to have lower relative poverty rates? At least two interrelated explanations are possible. First, social insurance policy advocates would argue that the universalist approach helps to prevent many potentially poor citizens from experiencing prolonged poverty by allowing families at the lower end of the middle-income range to save during good years. In contrast, means-tested policies (especially those involving assets tests) often require citizens to become desperately poor before receiving government assistance. As a result, by the time government help arrives, citizens are in a deeper hole that is harder to escape.

Second, social insurance policies tend to be more politically viable because they guarantee benefits to all. This approach makes it easier to build political coalitions that will protect and raise the benefit packages associated with the programs. In contrast, means-tested packages are more vulnerable to political attack because the beneficiaries—the impoverished—are often not well organized politically. This supposition that social insurance policies lead to higher benefit levels generally holds true for child allowances in these six countries in 1998. As Table 9–3 demonstrates, the three countries with universalist child allowances (France, Germany, and the United Kingdom) have the highest benefit levels. The data for the United Kingdom represent a particularly compelling example of how social insurance programs can generate support for funding even in a comparatively hostile political environment.

Understanding Reform Dynamics

One might assume that all countries—because they certainly share a desire to reduce poverty—would move over time toward increasingly greater use of social insurance policies. However, in reviewing the six case studies, one sees the trend line in the 1980s and 1990s moving toward a contraction rather than an expansion of government activity in social policy. This contraction is taking place on two different levels: policy instruments and funding levels. First, there is a visible trend toward greater means-testing in the area of child allowances (see Table 9–1). In 1980 only Japan and the United States had means-tested child allowances. By the mid-1990s Germany experimented with means tests and Italy stepped up the role of means-testing in its mixed approach to child allowances. Further, shifts to means-testing and tightening of existing needs standards are on the systemic agendas of all of these countries. Second, in all six countries, benefit levels over the 1980s and 1990s have tended to increase more slowly than the rate of inflation. This lag has resulted in spending cuts in real terms in several programs in these countries.

As we have discussed throughout this chapter, reforms aimed at limiting government responsibilities in social policy have taken place amid more generalized efforts at deficit reduction. This is not mere coincidence. Social policy broadly defined is the largest single category of government spending in industrialized countries. As long as deficit reduction remains high on the political agenda, we can expect social policy to be a spending category under the microscope. It is no accident that Japan—the only one of these countries with an annual average budget surplus from 1990 to 1994—was also the only country whose major political parties were discussing an expansion of the welfare state at that time.

How long should one expect this contraction to last? The Anglo-American countries have long been skeptical about universalist social policies. For those countries, the contemporary contraction in government intervention in this area is part of an ongoing debate in society and among the major political parties. In the continental European countries, with citizens and major parties historically more supportive of welfare initiatives, this contraction represents a novelty. The 1990s marked the first decade since the end of World War II in which government intervention in social policy decreased. In the case studies, French, German, and Italian politicians placed a heavy rhetorical emphasis on the budgetary demands of monetary unification as a rationale for a contraction of the welfare state. Is the Maastricht target the primary plausible explanation for welfare spending decisions within the EU in the contemporary era? It certainly played a major role in the late 1990s. Time will tell whether governments will continue to rein in social spending over the next decade as part of an effort to stay within the budget deficit guidelines of the Stability and Growth Pact (see Chapter 6).

SUGGESTED READINGS

Ambler, John S. 1991. *The French Welfare State: Surviving Social and Ideological Change.* New York: New York University Press.

Baker, Maureen. 1995. *Canadian Family Policies: Cross-National Comparisons.* Toronto: University of Toronto Press.

Clasen, Jochen, ed. 1999. *Comparative Social Policy: Concepts, Theories and Methods.* London: Blackwell.

Cochrane, Allan, and John Clarke, eds. 1993. *Comparing Welfare States: Britain in International Context.* London: Sage.

Cousins, Christine. 1999. *Society, Work and Welfare in Europe.* New York: St. Martin's Press.

Esping-Andersen, Gøsta. 1990. *The Three Worlds of Welfare Capitalism.* Cambridge: Polity.

Esping-Andersen, Gøsta, ed. 1996. *Welfare States in Transition: National Adaptations in Global Economies.* London: Sage (for the UN Research Institute for Social Development).

Flora, Peter, ed. 1986. *Growth to Limits: The West European Welfare States Since World War II.* New York: De Gruyter.

George, Vic, and Stewart Miller, eds. 1994. *Social Policy Towards 2000: Squaring the Welfare Circle.* London: Routledge.

George, Vic, and Peter Taylor-Gooby, eds. 1996. *European Welfare Policy: Squaring the Welfare Circle.* London: Macmillan.

Gould, Arthur. 1993. *Capitalist Welfare Systems: A Comparison of Japan, Britain, and Sweden.* London: Longman.

Karger, Howard J., and David Stoesz. 1998. *American Social Welfare Policy: A Pluralist Approach,* 3d ed. New York: Longman.

Lewis, Jane. 1993. *Women and Social Policies in Europe: Work, Family and the State.* Aldershot, England: Edward Elgar.

Melhuish, E. C., and P. Moss. 1991. *Day Care for Young Children: International Perspectives.* London: Routledge.

Mishra, R., ed. 1990. *The Welfare State in Capitalist Society: Policies of Retrenchment and Maintenance in Europe, North America, and Australia.* New York: Harvester Wheatsheaf, 1990.

Chapter 10 **Education Policy**

Since the end of World War II, education expenditures have represented the fastest growing area of public spending. In countries in the Organisation for Economic Co-operation and Development (OECD), education spending absorbs on average 6 percent of the gross domestic product (GDP) and 10 to 12 percent of total public expenditures. Education is prominent on national political agendas not only because of its budgetary prominence but also because of its integral role in society. The most basic interests and values of a society are represented in education policy. Often the definition of what constitutes such basic interests and values is a matter of great controversy.

Common Policy Problems

The most striking feature of the education debate today is the nearly universal and perpetual call for national education reform. Better education has become the prescription for creating individual success, social harmony, and international competitiveness. Political leaders often argue that the solutions to their nations' most pressing problems are to be found in the schools or, more specifically, in reformed schools. When citizens feel that their country is faltering in some fundamental respect, they, too, often blame the schools. Dissatisfaction with economic development and progress is increasingly likely to take the form of a backlash against schools and educators. For example, the chairman of IBM maintains that the failure of U.S. schools is pushing the country into a perilous situation. He believes schools have not produced "a labor force that is prepared to solve problems and compete on a global level" and that this shortcoming requires a "national strategy for resurgence that reaches every school in the country" (Passow 1990: 11).

An important education policy problem concerns the question of who education is for, or **access to schooling.** A nation's position on this issue is generally considered to be an important indicator of the **equality of opportunity** in a society. The equality of opportunity perspective assumes that school systems can compensate for existing social and economic inequalities in a society. The assumption is that universal access to schooling will serve as a leveler, as opposed to less open education systems that perpetuate existing social or economic divisions. Opponents of this view of education access believe that individuals differ innately in their capabilities and are not equally capable of benefiting from an education. Thus efforts to equalize education access squander resources. Supporters of the latter perspective advocate access to education systems based on achievement, especially in secondary schools and universities.

Concerns about whether all students are receiving the same type of education and about the substance of education also involve a debate over **liberal versus vocational education.** This is a debate between an orientation in which education is aimed at reducing social and economic inequalities and a market orientation that emphasizes education to promote global competitiveness.

The definition of education policy objectives has evolved over time and remains an unsettled issue: What should students learn? The list of potential objectives raised in the political debate is almost endless. Possible objectives include basic literacy, critical thinking skills, a well-rounded grounding in many fields of study, building of a shared national history and values, and technical training for a particular career—to name just a few. This problem area frequently raises questions about courses of study, national standards, and national testing or assessment programs.

The issue of who controls the education system is another education policy problem. Different countries create more or less centralized administrative structures. For example, federal political systems such as the United States tend to be more decentralized, delegating responsibility for education to the local level. In contrast, unitary political systems such as France and Japan are traditionally characterized by centralization of education decision-making authority at the national level. In most industrialized countries, the trend in recent years has been toward greater decentralization. Another dimension of the control over education is the issue of **public versus private schooling.** This dimension often involves the question of whether to permit religious schools to exist and of the appropriate allocation of public funds to these schools, where they exist. Nonreligious private schooling also raises concerns over control, in particular through pressures for more parental control and choice relative to local schools.

In considering the most pressing public policy choices encountered in the education arena, we focus on three areas of concern: (1) Who will be educated, (2) what will that education entail, and (3) who will control the education system? All three issues are typically controversial, and in most countries a widely accepted view of schooling continues to be elusive.

Major Policy Options

Policies that emphasize equality of opportunity are not the norm in most education systems. Many countries determine access to secondary and postsecondary education by means of competitive exams or other evaluations of an individual's **merit.** Because such mechanisms tend to reward those who were better off prior to entering the system, such policy choices tend to reinforce rather than reduce existing inequalities. For example, European systems, which rely on competitive exams, have traditionally reinforced rather than overcome class distinctions, with only a small percentage of university students coming from the middle and working classes. In systems that have adopted equality of opportunity policies, such as in the United States, the emphasis on promoting equality has declined. In short, although the implication of a universal right to education is access for all, education policies in most countries stress merit over egalitarianism, thereby reinforcing existing inequalities.

The debate over liberal versus vocational education also results in policy controversy. Proponents of liberal, or general, education advocate traditional training of students in the classics as well as reading, writing, and arithmetic to provide for the full development of the individual. Supporters of vocational, or technical, training emphasize the development of useful skills that translate directly into specific occupational opportunities. This latter policy orientation raises questions about which skills are most needed to produce a well-trained, competitive global labor force and who should receive which skills. For example, who will be trained as workers, who as executives? Who will make these decisions? And what will this training entail?

Related to the question of what students should learn, a continuing matter of controversy in education policy concerns the content of the **curriculum,** or the course of study that education institutions offer. Should the curriculum be governed by **equality of provision?** That is, should the curriculum ensure that all students in an education system receive the same type of education, particularly with respect to subject matter? The content of the curriculum is not merely a question of liberal versus vocational education; rather it involves debates over adopting western, non-western, multicultural, feminist, or religious perspectives. Because both economic outcomes and societal values are at stake, curricular reform is the source of considerable controversy. In recent years, pressures to adopt national curricula have increased in most industrialized countries. Adoption of such curricula entails the creation of a national standard for what students should know and be able to do in order to ensure equality of provision throughout the country.

Pressures to adopt a national curriculum often are accompanied by a move to create comprehensive standardized testing systems to assess student achievement and to measure equality of outcomes. Such tests also can be a matter of intense debate. Many critics of standardized tests argue that these exams are biased in favor of advantaged students and that they penalize students from diverse socioeconomic, ethnic, and racial backgrounds. Others question the ability of standardized tests to measure learning at all, particularly when it comes to assessing writing or the ability to reason or argue. Thus calls for curriculum reform are extremely contentious and meet with vehement opposition from educators, who often disagree with new education goals, reject restrictions on their academic freedom, and resent the reduction of education to "teaching to the test."

The locus of education decision-making power has a number of important implications for the nature of education policy. For example, where education funding is decentralized (meaning education funds rely on local revenue-raising capabilities), inequalities in expenditures per pupil are much more likely to occur among a nation's schools. In systems where education is controlled centrally, spending per pupil is likely to be equalized from locality to locality, and from student to student. As a result, increased centralization is a common response to calls for greater equality of provision. Centralization also permits the development of more common curricular goals and facilitates the pursuit of such goals by increasing the state's power over comprehensive policy implementation. Further, centralization of decision making also enables better monitoring of outcomes, particularly in regard to national education goals.

In decentralized systems, education policy is made at all levels of government—national, state, and local—resulting in a less focused policy agenda and greater access to this agenda. These systems exhibit a marked absence of national education policy. Decentralization also translates into somewhat greater potential for effective protest against controversial decisions (for example, textbook or curriculum choices), because the responsible policymakers tend to be more accessible and susceptible to pressure than are remote national politicians. Further, the initiation of policy change and participation in the decision-making process by educators tends to be less difficult in decentralized systems because educators tend to be more autonomous and to have developed their own power and financial resources. Local administration also allows for greater participation by local community members in these processes. Meaningful involvement in education decision making by both educators and citizens is far less likely in centralized systems where change is instituted by national politicians and bureaucrats. For these reasons, many observers believe that decentralized systems are more democratic.

A recent version of the decentralization approach to education reform emphasizes the need for parents to be able to choose among the schools in a system. School choice programs are intended to give parents more control over their children's education. Such programs involve financial assistance for education that is provided directly to individuals, not schools. Parents would be free to spend these funds at the school of their choice. The assumption of such an approach is that by giving parents the ability to take their "business" elsewhere, government would create a more competitive environment among schools and improve education quality overall. Under such a system, each school would presumably focus its efforts on attracting the greatest number of students (and additional funds) by improving the services it provides. The idea of school choice typically includes a variety of approaches: tuition tax credits, privately financed tuition reimbursement programs, an increased number of public charter schools, and tax-funded **vouchers** (Box 10–1).

Striking an appropriate balance between public and private education providers is a difficult and controversial task for political leaders. The desire of some parents to educate their children as they see fit creates conflict with national education policies. Countries differ in their approach to resolving this conflict. Some countries, such as the United States, allow religious schools to

Box 10-1 **In Depth: The Voucher Movement in the United States**

A recent policy innovation in education is the voucher. This option involves the government issuing parents a voucher, or coupon, representing tax dollars they would use to pay tuition at the school of their choice, public or private (presumably only a partial payment for private schools). The assumption is that such a system increases parents' ability to evaluate and choose the educational styles and curriculum best suited to their children. Such a system, it is argued, relies on competition to improve schools as parents avoid poor quality schools, which then forces public schools to improve in order to compete with the presumed higher-quality of private schools.

Public support for school choice in the United States has grown since the early 1990s. Public opinion polls indicate that a majority of the population favors allowing parents to send their children to the school of their choice (public, private, or religious) with government funding. Support has risen across socioeconomic groups for the general idea of school choice, but especially for vouchers, as those living in economically disadvantaged areas have come to view vouchers as their best chance for improving the educational opportunities available to their children.

Some of those who oppose the use of vouchers claim that their advocates want these vouchers to be available to all income groups, however, not just low-income families. To date, most voucher proposals and programs in the United States involve an income cap, but many opponents claim that the ultimate goal is universal vouchers. Were these to be implemented, the country's educational systems would become even more unequal, opponents claim, because private schools can accommodate only a small percentage of the country's students.

Opponents of the voucher system argue that such a system would reinforce and encourage existing social and economic divisions and would not improve most schools. Instead, dual education systems based on socioeconomic factors would emerge, with private schools improving and public schools worsening. For these reasons, they argue, the use of vouchers would serve the interests of a privileged few and remove their interest in the overall quality of public education. Those opposed to such a system further maintain that it reduces the diversity of experiences that public schools provide by serving students with different backgrounds.

exist but deny government funding to these institutions. This approach usually results in a marked inequality in the provision of education in that private religious schools are less well equipped (or are better equipped but at tremendous cost to parents).

The public versus private schooling issue also encompasses nonreligious private schools. These institutions are most controversial in countries where private school students enjoy a distinct advantage over public school students, especially in university admissions or in seeking employment, thereby allowing the wealthy to maintain their privileged status. The controversy tends to surround the right of these institutions to exist and may be manifested in abolition campaigns. Such campaigns usually maintain that those who can afford to do so should not be allowed to purchase a better education at private schools. Controversy in this policy area intensifies to the degree that successful private schools highlight the deficiencies of public schools. That is, where the quality of public schools is poor, people are more likely to resent private institutions.

Explaining Policy Dynamics

The study of the education policy-making process is often described as being more descriptive than theoretical. Scholars tend to describe the processes surrounding education reform in the industrialized countries (particularly beyond the United States) rather than place their studies within some wider or explicitly theoretical framework. Although the atheoretical nature of this field has changed somewhat in recent years, our understanding of policy processes in this area is often based on descriptive case studies, primarily focusing on the United States and the other Anglo-American countries.

Cultural Explanations

Cultural factors are commonly used to explain education policy reform. Researchers note the importance of public attitudes both for setting the reform agenda and for policy outputs. More specifically, contemporary movements for reform are argued to have emerged from widespread public perceptions that education systems had lowered their standards and were failing to prepare students to function in a more competitive economic environment (Ambler 1987). These attitudes resulted in reforms that stressed a return to basic education; emphasized discipline and effort; and focused on training students to serve more internationalized, high-technology, knowledge-based economic systems.

Another cultural explanation for contemporary reform involves the prevailing ideology in a country. Researchers note a shift in values in industrialized countries relative to education. From the 1930s to 1980, education policy in many countries focused on equity and social justice, whereas since the early 1980s, education policy has stressed freedom and excellence. This value shift is argued to reflect the resurgence of classic liberal ideology—favoring deregulation, decentralization, and varying degrees of privatization (Eliason 1996; Lauglo 1996). This return to a liberal ideology results in education reforms that stress economic efficiency, choice, and market mechanisms (Iannacone 1988). More specifically, this ideological shift is apparent in the move from an emphasis on equality and access to education to an emphasis on education excellence, selectivity, and choice (Boyd 1996; Boyd and Kerchner 1987). In the Anglo-American countries, resurgent liberalism in the 1980s and early 1990s led reform advocates to argue that schools should be subject to regulation by market forces rather than by the government—and thus be forced to respond to parental demands (Ambler 1987; Chubb and Moe 1990). These reform advocates argued that school choice would achieve three goals: higher average academic achievement, lower costs, and greater equality of opportunity.

Cultural perspectives also point to the importance of culturally based education traditions in defining a country's approach to reform. This literature stresses the importance of deeply imbued cultural attitudes about the most desirable kinds of knowledge, the best ways of transmitting it, and the means for deciding who will benefit from education. These values are shared across cultures and influence education policy decisions. Thus the emphasis on individualism and equality of opportunity that characterizes Anglo-American countries, as opposed to the more collectivist and social equality cultural norms found in France or Germany, have significant implications for questions about education access, content, and control (Fowler, Boyd, and Plank 1993; McLean 1988, 1995; Rust and Blakemore 1990). In the United States, for example, important cultural values include an emphasis on freedom, quality, efficiency, and equity, with education policy outputs reflecting, at least in part, the country's positions on these values at the time (Marshall, Mitchell, and Wirt 1989). Conversely, in Japan, the cultural importance of group identity, uniformity, hierarchy, and centralization result in very different policy outputs (Wray 1999).

Economic Explanations

Many researchers argue that education reforms can be explained by concerns about globalization and increasing international economic competition. Reform efforts are viewed as having been stimulated in part by worries about more intense global competition and the need to develop a better educated workforce to enable countries to compete effectively and enhance their global economic position (Boyd 1996; Boyd and Kerchner 1987; Wirt and Harman 1986). As industrialized countries increasingly are defined by interdependent, postindustrial, and knowledge-based economic systems, their demands for more effective schooling escalate. In this context, existing approaches to education are viewed as slow, outdated, and incapable of producing necessary improvements in student preparation. These perceptions result in pressures on the government to design and implement centrally controlled standards and accountability schemes for their school systems (Boyd and Kerchner 1987; Cibulka 1996; Coombs 1985; Eliason 1996; Ginsburg et. al. 1990; McLean 1995; Wirt and Hartman 1986).

Political Explanations

The partisanship thesis introduced in Chapter 2 can be important for understanding education reform, particularly when examining cross-national differences in education spending. As expected, left-wing governing parties are more likely to favor and achieve increased government spending on education. However, as Ambler (1987) notes, although changes in partisan control may affect education spending levels, the inherent complexity and relative autonomy of education institutions create particularly strong resistance to other types of education reforms. He argues that sometimes, even when a party that comes to power is intent on major reform (such as the Conservatives under Thatcher in the United Kingdom or the Socialists under Mitterrand in France), the nature of the education system itself (its size, complexity, and tendency toward bureaucratic inertia) may interfere with that party's capacity to achieve its goals.

A multitude of scholars, examining the full range of industrialized countries, point to the influence of highly mobilized, powerful, and entrenched interests in affecting education reforms. In all countries, interest groups (especially teachers' unions but also parents associations, education administrators, business groups, and religious groups) place limits on the ability of governments to initiate and implement widespread education reforms. In pluralist systems, interest group activities are seen as a prime driver of education decision making, but such movements also are argued to play a strong role under more corporatist arrangements. In the education policy area, interest groups are frequently argued to be strong enough to override the distinction between unitary and federal political systems regarding the access they provide such groups. Even in unitary political systems, groups representing the various sectors of the education establishment have been highly successful in shaping reforms (Ambler 1987; Elmore 1997; Kogan 1971; McLean 1988; Rust and Blakemore 1990; Spring 1998).

Institutional Explanations

Institutional approaches to understanding education policy reform focus on the degree of centralization of political authority. In most policy areas, centralization of decision-making authority is regarded as being advantageous for reform. In examining education reforms, however, researchers take issue with the centralization thesis. They note that centralization is most effective in policy areas in which power is centralized in the hands of relatively few individuals. In education policy, this is usually not the case, even in more centralized political systems. The size and complexity of education systems—as well as their relative autonomy—is the problem here (Ambler 1987). Education systems may create a powerful set of vested interests. For example, in France (a highly centralized country) successful education reforms require broad support in public opinion as a means of getting the system moving because of the strength and inertia of the education establishment. Such public support is necessary to put pressure on teachers and their unions to accept change. In the absence of such public support, the education establishment often is able to block or delay new policies proposed by government, with centralization giving government no great advantage (Duclaud-Williams 1988). Along these same lines, however, decentralized systems are argued to fare no better in enacting education reforms because of the multiple points at which these same opponents of reform can block change.

International Policy Making

When it comes to education policy, little in the way of international policy making exists. Education policy is a domain in which countries are very protective of their national sovereignty and in which a high degree of policy flexibility and independence is maintained. There are no major international agreements that establish norms or practices for education, nor do we find such policies at the regional level. Beyond national sovereignty issues, the lack of international cooperation on these matters may also reflect the fact that in many countries education policy making is highly decentralized. Lower levels of government often are reluctant enough to surrender authority over education policy to their own central governments. As a result, it is even more difficult to envision them transferring their decision-making powers to some even further removed external body.

Education is a policy area in which the European Union (EU) has exercised considerable restraint. This is true regarding its present policy position and its plans for the future. Under the Maastricht Treaty, the EU's education mandate is to play a supporting role to the member states. The treaty does not authorize the union to issue directives or regulations pertaining to education that are legally binding on members. Instead, the EU's role is to encourage cooperation by member states on education issues and to supplement and support their education efforts. To this end, the EU currently administers several education programs, including one on vocational training (called Leonardo da Vinci) and another on transnational cooperation (called Socrates). These programs represent the full extent of the EU's education initiatives. Beyond these activities, we currently find no other major international education policies at work.

United States

Background: Policy Process and Policy History

The United States, with its multiple centers of decision-making power, has no comprehensive national education policy. Specific education goals and spending levels vary across both states and localities. Because the financing of education at the local level usually is based on property taxes, funding differs markedly across school districts. Typically students who live in more affluent districts attend better quality schools than do children living in poorer areas. To address this inequality, states and the federal government have created policies aimed at equalizing education provision across districts. The most recent policy innovations in this regard require states and localities to comply with federal education mandates to receive federal education funds. In this sense, U.S. policies are becoming somewhat more similar to the centralized approach common in other industrialized countries.

Constitutionally, education is a state responsibility, although most states have delegated authority to operate and finance schools to local education authorities, or school districts. The federal government plays a limited role in the governance of education but provides funding to states and school districts, mostly to support programs for students with special educational needs. The government also provides financial aid to students in the form of scholarships and loans to support their participation in postsecondary education. State and local school districts provide the vast majority of funds for public elementary and secondary education. Because no state has taken responsibility for financing public schools, nor do any seem likely to do so, the tradition of local autonomy is likely to live on.

This diffusion of jurisdiction has fostered a profusion of uncoordinated policies. The United States has over 15,000 school districts (governed through school boards by more than 95,000 citizens), and in recent years a shift to greater federal and state regulation of local districts has been made in order to create greater equality and effectiveness. The United States is unique with respect to the number of issues and responsibilities that these local school boards confront: everything from budgets to maintenance to the curriculum. These boards are burdened with many responsibilities that in other countries are dispersed among many levels of government and bureaucrats. Local school boards also tend to be highly politicized.

The issue of school choice has been on the political agenda in the United States since the 1980s, first in the form of an unsuccessful effort to create a national system of vouchers (although some states and localities have introduced the use of vouchers), and currently with a charter school plan that many states have adopted. Charter school laws create independent public schools that are largely free from government control but are held accountable for education results agreed upon in each school's charter.

The United States has traditionally endorsed the view that all citizens have a right to an education. This belief reflects the notion that a key element of effective democracy is an educated citizenry. Thus education is regarded as important not only for the improvement and success of the individual but also for molding democratic citizens. Reflecting this emphasis, the U.S. education system expanded during the twentieth century, and the average level of education attainment rose.

Compulsory education begins at age six or seven in the majority of states, but most children enter kindergarten in a public elementary school at age five. Compulsory schooling ends at age sixteen in over half the states, but a large majority of young adults (73 percent in 1990–1996) continue their education and receive regular high school diplomas at age seventeen or eighteen. Full-time primary schooling begins at age six and ends at age twelve or thirteen. Students then enter middle school (grades 6–8) or junior high school (grades 7–9) and then proceed to secondary school for grades 9–12 (or 10–12). This pathway results in a single-track system. Secondary schools in the United States provide a choice between general, college preparatory, or vocational tracks (the latter do not provide comprehensive vocational training of the sort found in Germany, however). About two-thirds of students enroll in the college preparatory and general tracks, and just under one-third enroll in the vocational track.

The United States does not have a national curriculum or curriculum framework, although most states have developed curriculum frameworks and performance standards. Specification of the curriculum and selection of textbooks are usually delegated by the states to local school districts. Currently the federal government is sponsoring the development of curriculum standards in numerous subject areas and is encouraging states to implement voluntary standards that promote improved student performance. Most states have some form of mandated statewide testing program to assess individual student performance against state-established performance standards. Twenty states also have mandatory promotion or graduation tests. Most of these tests are geared to ensuring minimum standards.

Recent efforts at education reform have placed increasing emphasis on the provision of vocational alternatives at the secondary level. One area of controversy with respect to vocational education has concerned the type of training that should be provided. For example, should students be trained for one specific job, should they be provided with more general skills that can later be refined through on-the-job training, or should they receive a comprehensive education combined with specific job skills? Because this question generally remains unanswered, the United States has advanced in the provision of vocational education far less than have the other industrialized countries.

Contemporary Dynamics

Contemporary education reform in the United States began in the early 1980s. Since then two reform trends have influenced U.S. education systems: the imposition of uniform standards and a push for greater accountability. Reforms in the United States are based on an assumption that academic achievement will be improved by establishing rigorous education standards, uniform curricula, and assessment tests. The goal of such reforms is better quality, not greater equity. Early criticisms of the U.S. education system emerged from within the business community; these criticisms in turn tapped into growing public concerns about the deteriorating quality of public schools.

Concerns about education related to international competitiveness arrived in 1983 with the publication of a federal commission's report, *A Nation at Risk*. The report claimed that the United States was losing its ability to compete in an increasingly competitive global marketplace. The loss of the country's competitive edge was blamed on an education system that had failed to do its job, as evidenced by almost two decades of decline in student achievement levels. *A Nation at Risk* launched what is commonly referred to as the excellence movement in the United States. This movement argues that the United States must intensify its education approach to increase rigor, raise graduation standards for students and teachers, and reemphasize the importance of education overall. The business community and public opinion quickly galvanized around the report's findings, and education reform became situated firmly on the country's institutional agenda. In a clear example of the outside initiation agenda-setting model, reaction to this report almost single-handedly placed education reform on the institutional agenda for nearly two decades.

The Reagan administration initially responded to this agenda by devolving a great deal of education decision-making authority to states and reducing the federal government's role overall. Beyond this, the administration did not develop any comprehensive response to calls for change. In the first real attempt at policy formulation for education reform, President Bush convened in 1989 an education summit of business leaders, government officials, politicians, and educators. The goals developed at this summit were translated into policy proposals that were submitted to Congress in 1991 as the America 2000 plan. The plan focused in large part on government funding for parental choice between public and private schools, although national standards and testing also were addressed.

At the decision-making stage, the America 2000 plan illustrated the problem of divided government at the national level; Congress was under Democratic control, and the president was a Republican, thus presenting a major obstacle to reform. The Democrat-controlled Senate rejected a Bush administration spending proposal, largely along party lines, to spend $30 million on school choice programs (to which the Democrats were for the most part strongly opposed). Another aspect of the Bush proposal, for national standards and a national assessment system, ended up in a nondecision, as a result of primarily Republican opposition (although some Democratic legislators also opposed these policies). A subsequent Democratic reform initiative, the New American Schools proposal, also ran into deep-seated opposition and produced a nondecision. Thus the end result of this stage of reform was gridlock and inaction. Subsequent efforts at reform did not occur until after the 1992 presidential elections, in which education was a prominent campaign issue.

After the 1992 elections, education reform efforts returned to the policy formulation stage. By 1992, many reform advocates argued that education problems required more comprehensive reform involving state and national curricula and testing geared toward developing world-class standards rather than the incremental approach pursued by the two previous administrations. The Clinton administration embraced this view and developed a sweeping reform agenda that resulted in its Goals 2000 proposal. The Clinton plan dropped the Bush school choice proposals and instead pursued charter school plans. These schools were new or reorganized independent public schools that would be held accountable for results agreed upon in charters authorizing their creation. Clinton also proposed national standards and testing.

Despite the end to divided government in 1992, partisan conflict on education reform continued in this second decision-making stage. Because the Goals 2000 bill was similar to the America 2000 plan, congressional debate on the bill involved many of the same disputes. Both Democrats and Republicans opposed various aspects of the plan. Republicans feared national standards would result in federal control of education, abandoning the country's long tradition of 15,000 local districts choosing their own curriculum and assessment methods. They also argued that such standards would violate prohibitions against the federal government dictating a national curriculum. Further, they noted that ninety-three cents of every education dollar came from state and local governments and that greater federal interference would be nothing more than a power grab. More liberal Democrats, especially the African-American and Hispanic congressional caucuses, opposed national tests, arguing that poor results might be used to cut funding to children in already underfunded, low-performing schools and that such tests would be unfair to disabled and non-English-speaking students. At the same time, public opinion polls indicated that Americans overwhelmingly favored national standards and tests. In 1991, by a margin of 68 to 24 percent, Gallup poll respondents favored "requiring the public schools in this community to use a standardized national curriculum."

Eventually the commitment of some influential Democrats to education reform, as well as favorable public opinion and the influence of powerful business lobbying groups, resulted in the passage of the Goals 2000: Educate America Act in 1994. The act established national education goals and voluntary national standards for what students should know. The legislation authorized financial support for states that agree to comply with the act's standards. These funds are passed on to school districts in the states that commit themselves to these reforms. The act also created a number of national panels and boards that were to create and oversee these standards.

The implementation difficulties surrounding the Goals 2000 Act are legion. In many localities, the religious right has exerted pressure on or gained control of local school boards and blocked many changes related to the act (especially concerning curriculum control and outcomes-based education). Public school bureaucrats, as well as teachers, have complained bitterly and worked to block reforms, especially involving curriculum control and testing. The federal nature of the U.S. political system also has obstructed the implementation process: Local control over education makes it difficult to enact the kind of comprehensive change the act envisions. Further, the deep partisan divide that emerged after the 1994 congressional elections also spells trouble. Since 1994, congressional Republicans, as opponents of greater federal control, have seized on every opportunity to eliminate the Goals 2000 program entirely—or at least to block national standards and testing. In 1995 a bill to eliminate Goals 2000 passed in the House of Representatives but stalled in the Senate. At the same time, however, education reforms conforming to the act's requirements were endorsed in most of the fifty states, led by governors of both political parties. Further, the business community remains committed to the need for these, and even larger, reforms, and public opinion remains in their corner as well.

Comprehensive education reform in the United States, both the decision to engage in reform and the nature of the reform itself, resulted from a set of interrelated factors. Fears about the country losing its ability to compete in the global marketplace drove public attitudes on education reform. These concerns were echoed by the business community, which sought to shape education systems to meet its employment needs. The perception that U.S. students did not measure up to their peers in other industrialized countries—and that this shortcoming was detrimental to the country's future economic strength—was sufficient to drive large-scale reform. Further, the return to classic liberal political values that began in 1980 (especially an emphasis on smaller government and greater local control) led the public and the business community to fully support reform proposals to give schools and parents greater control over education decisions. Although policies creating greater control did not succeed at the national level, many localities in the United States have moved to more market-based mechanisms for school choice. Some observers would argue that it is only a matter of time before such plans return to the national policy agenda.

Politically the power and activism of business interests strongly influenced the policy-making process from the early 1980s onward. As we noted earlier, business interest groups hoped to set the education policy agenda, largely to serve their own purposes. Many analysts argue that the influence of these groups is the most important explanation both for reform occurring and for the content of that reform. In addition, the government's difficulty in passing reforms was related directly to the nature of executive-legislative relations. In the Bush years in particular, divided government and policy gridlock prevented enactment of the government's planned reforms. Finally, at the implementation stage, many aspects of those reforms stagnated because political leaders were unable to muster the necessary levels of support from the education establishment. At this stage, education interests obstructed policies they had been unable to influence at the decision-making stage. The ability of the education bureaucracy to obstruct the implementation process also was related to the country's federal structure, which leaves the bulk of education powers in the hands of state and local governments. Under these conditions, large-scale reform was far more difficult to achieve.

Japan

Background: Policy Process and Policy History

The national government administers education in Japan through the Ministry of Education, Science, Sports, and Culture (known as the Ministry of Education). The Ministry of Education creates guidelines for the curriculum and courses, and approves textbooks. National government education expenditures include direct expenditures for national education activities (for example, operating national universities and schools); specific subsidies for the education activities of other institutions (that is, prefectures, municipalities, private schools, and research organizations); and local allocation of a tax grant, part of which is for education. Boards of education exist at the prefectural and municipal levels. Prefectural boards administer schools (upper secondary and special education) established by the prefectures, whereas municipal boards administer mainly elementary and lower secondary schools established by the local authorities.

A commitment to the widespread provision of education in Japan can be traced to the nineteenth century. A Fundamental Code of Education was promulgated in 1872 that established literacy as a national goal. After World War II, the Japanese education system was reorganized in line with the U.S. model. Until 1987 the plan for Japan's education system was laid out in the 1947 Fundamental Law on Education. This system experienced reform for the first time in the late 1980s and early 1990s.

The primary education policy objective in Japan is declared to be the provision of equal access to a high quality of education to all students in the country, regardless of where they live. Compulsory education is from ages six to sixteen, with upper secondary schools serving those aged fifteen to eighteen. Nearly 97 percent of students graduating from lower secondary schools go on to upper secondary schools (which are not compulsory). Japan has a single-track school system comparable to that found in the United States.

Upper secondary schools admit entrants based on a selection process that considers student credentials, scholastic test records, and other factors. This selection process determines the distribution of students among upper secondary schools, not access to education, which is universal. For university admissions, however, students take a standard commercially developed test as well as tests administered by each university. University admissions are based almost exclusively on performance on these entrance exams; this system has produced what is widely viewed as an excessively competitive examination process.

About 25 percent of students go on to universities and 30 percent to other forms of postsecondary education. In principle a student may apply to any university from any upper secondary school, but in practice a strong link exists between the status of the upper secondary school attended and university admissions. In seeking admission to a particular university, Japanese students are more likely to have based their choice on the placement and status of an institution's graduates than on the quality of its education program. Reflecting these conditions, efforts have been developed to reduce the single criterion of a standard exam score in career guidance, and schools have been encouraged to diversify their selection criteria.

The national government sets curriculum standards for elementary, lower secondary, and upper secondary schools. The Ministry of Education has issued a document called the Course of Study, which defines Japan's general education standards for curricula, textbooks, and entrance exams. These standards provide the basic framework for curricula including the aims of each subject and school activity, the content of teaching at each grade level, and the basis for teacher training. The most recent curriculum revisions (made in 1989) were enacted from 1992 to 1994. These curriculum revisions emphasize independent learning activities and students thinking for themselves rather than the traditional one-dimensional transmission of knowledge and skills from teacher to student. Each school is left to organize its curriculum as it sees fit to reflect these guidelines and to take into account the conditions of the community and the school as well as the characteristics and development levels of its pupils.

Student performance in meeting the objectives of the national curriculum is assessed by individual teachers on a case-by-case basis rather than through national examinations. At the secondary level, studies have traditionally been focused on academic subjects; an extensive vocational education program does not exist. Reforms are planned in this area but have yet to be implemented. In postsecondary education, technical and junior colleges provide technical and vocational education.

Contemporary Dynamics

As in the United States, Japan is concerned about international competitiveness and education reform. Since the mid-1980s many Japanese have been critical of the country's education system for failing to create the sort of workers that employers need in an increasingly competitive global marketplace. More specifically, the public became concerned that the system was failing to encourage creativity and individualism and that this had serious ramifications for the abilities of Japan's future workforce. Unlike most of the countries examined in this book, however, Japan has been less successful in moving its education system in dramatically new directions. In particular, little movement has been made away from a highly centralized system of control. Rather, the small-scale reforms ushered in during the 1990s have focused on changing the internal aspects of education, such as reducing the stress of the competitive exams or changing the manner in which teachers are trained.

Education reform appeared on the institutional agenda in the mid-1980s. At that time, newly elected prime minister Nakasone, after having campaigned on a general reform platform, called for comprehensive education reform. He created an Ad Hoc Council on Education Reform that was charged with reviewing the existing system and making recommendations for changes, especially in the direction of liberalization. The council worked outside the Ministry of Education, and its membership consisted of business representatives, bureaucrats, and Nakasone's own intellectuals but no education representatives. By 1987 the council had issued four reports that described several areas of reform, including high schools, tertiary education, curricula at all levels of education, lifelong learning, and teacher education and certification. The council suggested three major principles on which to base future education reform: emphasizing the individual; encouraging lifelong learning; and adapting to changes in society, especially internationalization and information technology.

The policy formulation and decision-making stages of education reform occurred not in the Diet but in a consultation process organized by the Ad Hoc Council. Among the many proposals debated by the council were several that called for liberalization. These reforms involved reducing the power of the Ministry of Education, introducing private sector mechanisms as a means of education control, establishing more private schools, and making private "cram" schools alternatives to regular high schools. As these proposed reforms moved through a series of consultative groups and meetings, they were frequently criticized for being too individualistic. Ideas about liberalization and privatization were unpopular across the board, even within the governing Liberal Democratic Party. As expected, strong opposition came from the Ministry of Education and from *Nikkyoso*, the teachers' union, both of which would see their authority weakened by greater liberalization and decentralization. Public opinion also lined up against the reforms.

As a result, the council's recommendations geared toward liberalization were weakened substantially as the consultations progressed. In 1987, when the council made its education policy recommendations, they had been reduced to weak and insubstantial efforts that made only scant reference to liberalization. The council's final policy recommendations merely noted that Japan should consider the idea of privatization and taking into account parents' wishes; the council did not suggest that the country should move toward a system of school choice. These decisions reflected a reluctance to move to market-oriented education, based on the rejection of a more individualistic approach to education.

Since 1987, education reform in Japan has proceeded inconspicuously. Education reform is a policy area in which change comes as a result of bureaucratic consultation and decision making rather than through legislative debate or law making. Based on the Ad Hoc Council's recommendations, the Ministry of Education pursues reform through administrative guidance, which eliminates opportunities for debate, opposition, or the exertion of external influence. This is a process of incremental change within existing frameworks that leave little space for opposition. Thus policy change occurred and continues but through administrative rather than legislative action. As a result, few implementation concerns surround education reforms. The direction of these changes since 1987 is consistent with the basic philosophy of the Ad Hoc Council, addressing social changes such as globalization, the information-based society, aging, and the low birth rate.

The drive for education reform in Japan can be explained largely by economic factors. Although the Japanese economy was strong in the 1980s, the Japanese became increasingly concerned that their education system was not training students adequately to be creative and innovative—two qualities recognized as essential to future economic success. The nature of education reform in Japan, in particular the rejection of moves toward greater privatization and liberalization, may be explained by cultural factors. The Japanese education system does not emphasize individuality and freedom, reflecting the traditional Japanese value system. Consequently, reform efforts that stressed individualism, choice, and school autonomy were rejected because they contradicted accepted cultural norms. The Nakasone reform experience also supports the view that in education policy it is often not enough to simply have a party in power that wants change. In Japan's case, the influence of the education bureaucracy, especially the Ministry of Education, was sufficient to ensure that Nakasone's primary goal—liberalization—was not achieved.

Germany

Background: Policy Process and Policy History

The control of education in Germany reflects the country's federal structure. According to Article 7 of the Basic Law, the entire school system is under the control of the state governments, but this responsibility in practice is shared by federal and state governments. In each state, schools are usually maintained by either municipalities or the state, whereas higher education institutions are state-level institutions. Education legislation and its administration is developed and adopted largely by the states. States and municipalities carry over 90 percent of education expenditures. Each of the sixteen state governments enjoys full control over the organization and structure of their education systems. Since 1971 the states have been legally bound to maintain comparable basic structures in their school systems and a Standing Conference of Ministers of Education and Cultural Affairs meets regularly to provide for greater harmonization of policies across school systems.

The German education system is seen by many as the envy of the world. It is distinguished by the high quality of its graduates and the considerable attention paid to vocational education at the secondary and postsecondary levels. As a result, citizen dissatisfaction and subsequent calls for education reform are not as strong in Germany as in many of the other countries we are considering. However, German policymakers have addressed questions of reform in recent years, particularly with respect to higher education, although not on the scale observed in some other countries.

German education structures involve a multitrack system offering general, technical, and vocational options. Compulsory schooling lasts for twelve years, from ages six to eighteen. Students start with nine or ten years of full-time education (depending on the state) and then complete their compulsory schooling on either a part-time or a full-time basis. Part-time education takes place in vocational schools in a dual system that combines practical on-the-job training with in-school theoretical instruction. Secondary school students receive one of three qualifications: a lower secondary school qualification after eight or nine years of schooling (with or without vocational training), an intermediate school qualification after ten years (vocational or nonvocational), or an upper secondary qualification after twelve or thirteen years. Students who leave school with lower or intermediate secondary qualifications are likely to enter vocational training in the dual system or serve a two- to three-year apprenticeship.

Higher education in Germany consists of either professional colleges or universities, entrance to which requires an upper secondary school qualification. A reform process is currently under way in this sector in an effort to improve institutional efficiency and address problems of insufficient space. An identified problem in higher education is the length of time it takes students to complete their education, which averages around seven years. Insufficient space has forced the government to introduce admissions restrictions in some subject areas. Until recently, tuition was free at public institutions; some states now impose tuition fees in their higher education institutions.

State ministries of education develop their curricula to reflect guidelines developed at the national level. These guidelines were last revised in 1989. To ensure some degree of uniformity in curricula and standards across states, a standardization process has been developed. The Standing Conference of Ministers of Education and Culture oversees state education systems to ensure a baseline of provision across the states while respecting state autonomy. The process of incorporating the five new eastern states has raised some concern over whether such a balance will be sustained in the future or whether the federal government will have to intervene to ensure the maintenance of such standards.

Reflecting a decentralized education system, Germany does not use national testing or large-scale assessments of students. In particular, state governments are resistant to any movement toward cross-state comparisons. The German government monitors the performance of the education system by paying strict attention to teacher training, establishing compulsory curricula for all sixteen states for all subjects and areas of study in all types of schools, and ensuring that textbooks comply fully with the curriculum.

Among the industrialized countries, Germany has one of the most well-developed and extensive systems of vocational schools. A clear goal of the government is that no young person should begin his or her working life without some form of vocational training. Currently, about 1.6 million students are receiving some form of vocational training, and vocational schools are required for all young people under age eighteen who attend no other type of school. This training is a joint effort between private business and industry and the public sector. In addition, at the postsecondary level, two- to three-and-a-half-year internships are available that provide a paid training allowance that increases for each year of service. More than 500,000 German firms participate in the apprenticeship program.

Contemporary Dynamics

Given the generally strong state of the German education system, education reform is not a perennial political battle in this country. Overall, quality and efficiency is not an education concern. The one exception to this pattern applies to the higher education system. By the late 1980s, common complaints about the higher education system included too-long periods of study (some lasting as long as ten years), overflowing lecture halls, too little contact between teachers and students and between researchers and industry, and a lack of comparability between German and international qualifications. In June 1995 Foreign Minister Klaus Kinkel called for reform of higher education based on his feeling that such reforms were needed in order to make Germany more competitive in foreign trade. As a result, pressures began to mount for government action, particularly among students but also within the German business community and among some conservative politicians. As their concerns increased (in particular as the German economy began to falter in the early 1990s), the federal government moved to develop a policy response.

In late 1996 the conservative government introduced plans for fundamental higher education reform—aimed at improving performance, giving universities greater autonomy, and making them more competitive at the international level. This was a somewhat unusual approach to education reform for Germany, where education policies are not usually introduced at the federal level because states are individually responsible for their own education systems. The decision-making stage of these reforms was not particularly heated, but it was notable in that the federal and state governments were able to reach an agreement in this policy area. When these reforms were introduced into the parliament, many observers were skeptical that they would come to fruition. Historically the federal and state governments had been unable to agree on higher education policy in this manner (which in part explains the real need for reform because nothing had been done for quite a while). Because education is constitutionally a matter for the states, the opinions of the party controlling the Bundesrat matter a great deal, especially because the Bundesrat can reject any federal policies. At the time of this decision, the opposition Social Democratic Party (SPD) carried greater weight in the Bundesrat, and a strong possibility existed that the party would block federal efforts to impose controls over higher education standards. Several factors helped this particular decision to break from the usual pattern of disagreement and difficulty.

For one, the timing of the decision was critical: The reforms were being decided during the lead-up to a general election, which meant that all the actors involved had strong political motivations surrounding the reforms. In the months preceding this decision, the two major parties, the Christian Democratic Union (CDU) and the SPD, had been struggling to position themselves for the election, which meant that decisions about most reforms had been debated intensely, with gridlock often occurring, especially between the Bundestag and the Bundesrat. However, at the time of this decision, politicians of all stripes were aware that the German public was tiring of the seemingly endless legislative standstill, which spurred a compromise. It was also widely recognized that the higher education system was in serious disarray and needed to be repaired, which created a strong incentive to act. Further, the German student population was strongly mobilized around the issue, making the reform decision highly visible. Finally, unlike other areas of education policy, interest group activity surrounding higher education is fairly limited in Germany, and no powerful organizations strongly opposed (or, for that matter, advocated) the overall reforms.

Thus an historic higher education agreement between the federal and state governments was reached to simplify governance, increase flexibility and autonomy, raise standards, and promote greater competition. Initially some implementation difficulties were associated with the reforms. German students were dissatisfied with what they viewed as the too-tame nature of the new policies. Following the CDU-SPD agreement, a series of student strikes and protests were held in fall 1997 in an attempt to focus national attention on the need for even more substantial reform. In November 1997, in one of biggest student demonstrations since 1968, some 40,000 students marched on the German government in Bonn to protest deteriorating university quality and inadequate funding. German president Roman Herzog delivered a harsh message to the country's universities saying the German higher education system was too bureaucratic, too time-consuming, and too provincial. Students demanded that more money be spent on improving facilities and that a comprehensive review of government support for students be undertaken (especially the issue of student fees, which some states had recently introduced). The movement did not remain mobilized for long, however, and many of these issues, though not resolved, have ceased to be the focus of attention. Since this unrest has dissipated, there have been no implementation concerns concerning the reforms. The limited nature of the higher education reforms introduced in 1997 means, however, that a continuing cause for concern in the country's education system is the ability to produce Germans who are well equipped to compete in the global economy.

The German government's decision to place higher education reform on the institutional agenda, after years of neglect, reflected the influence of economic factors. Problems in higher education had been pointed out by German students and others for many years; however, the government did not respond until concerns became based on arguments about the country's loss of international economic competitiveness. Once the German economy faltered in the early 1990s, concerns that the country was losing its competitive edge became widespread. These economic concerns—combined with continuing complaints that German universities had no standards, were outdated, and were inefficient—provided an opportunity for government to address two problems with one reform package. The government could say it was doing something about the deteriorating quality of higher education, while affirming its commitment to safeguarding the country's position in the global economy. The federal nature of the German political system partly determined the political path of these reforms—the dispersion of authority over education decision making meant that widespread reform could not be imposed from the center because universities are the states' responsibility. Instead the proposed reforms required the cooperation between the states and the federal government—which was not easily achieved because the states were traditionally protective of their constitutional right to determine higher education policy. The direct involvement of the states in this decision-making process also meant that policy implementation proceeded relatively smoothly.

France

Background: Policy Process and Policy History

Since 1985 the French government has been engaged in the process of transferring some education decision-making powers to regional administrations and decentralizing education responsibilities to elected local authorities. Each level of government has been made responsible for a tier of education: communes for nursery and primary school management, departments for maintenance and construction of lower secondary schools, and regions for upper secondary schools and for education planning. Secondary schools and universities have been made more independent, although postsecondary education is still largely centrally controlled.

Despite such changes, however, a good deal in the French education system remains largely under the domain of the national government, including the recruitment and pay of teachers, the framing and implementation of general education policy, the national curriculum and the national exam, and the right to confer university diplomas. National government also continues to fund two-thirds of total expenditures on education. By the late 1980s education expenditures made up the largest part of the national budget.

The French education system has been public, uniform, compulsory, and centralized since the late nineteenth century. Education in France continues to be widely considered the foremost national priority, both to impart knowledge and to transmit a sense of national identity. Education also is seen as a democratic right and is viewed as an important mechanism for creating equality of opportunity.

Among the industrialized countries, France has one of the highest levels of education activity: French students spend longer in school (an average of 18.9 years) and are more likely to go on to higher education. Education in France is compulsory for ages six to sixteen and is divided into primary, secondary, and upper secondary levels. General, vocational, and technological education is provided at the secondary level. Higher education is open to all holders of secondary degrees (the *baccalaureat*).

The 1989 Education Act makes a clear commitment to creating equality of education opportunities, with an emphasis on equal access and outcomes. The French education system was expanded substantially in the 1980s in an endeavor to ensure that 80 percent of eligible students would complete upper secondary level education and obtain the *baccalaureat*. As a result of this expansion, in the 1990s approximately 70 percent of eligible students entered upper secondary education, twice as many as in 1980. This increase has also resulted in a significant increase in higher education enrollments—2.1 million enrolled in universities in 1996, compared with just over 1 million in 1980.

Under the 1989 Education Act, new standards for the country's common curriculum were adopted. This curriculum, set at the national level, defines both subject matter and the number of hours to be devoted to each subject; it may not be modified at the regional level. At the secondary level, students are offered some optional courses, such as a foreign language, but must also complete the national curriculum.

France has a national assessment procedure. The Ministry of Education examines students on a regular basis to note their level of achievement. National assessment tests are given at the third year of elementary education, the end of lower secondary education, and the beginning of upper secondary education. Assessment is also achieved through monitoring of students' progress through the education system and their learning skills and social behavior in school.

The French education system has increasingly moved to some form of secondary level vocational education (from a system traditionally focused exclusively on academics). Recent education reforms resulted in the extension of the *baccalaureat* to cover a wide range of vocational options in addition to the traditional general and technical subjects. France also offers an apprenticeship program for students over age of sixteen, in which they learn a trade partly in employment under an apprenticeship trainer and partly in education institutions. Nearly all students who do not go on to university enter some form of vocational training.

Contemporary Dynamics

The French government's efforts in education reform in the mid-1980s focused on questions of school choice and the public funding of private schools. These efforts represented an earlier attempt to address such issues than were made in the other five countries. In France, private (and especially religious) schools historically have had an unusual relationship with the government. Since 1951 the government had made scholarships available to private school students and offered subsidies to private schools through parents' associations. The Socialist government that came to power in 1981 was intent on changing that situation, after having campaigned heavily on education reform issues. A key aspect of the Socialist education reform program was the creation of a unified and secular education system. Following the Socialist party's victory in 1981, the new education minister, Alain Savary, put this commitment directly onto the country's institutional agenda.

The policy formulation process to achieve this goal was long and deliberative. Savary spent two years consulting, negotiating, and compromising with Catholic and other private school leaders and other educators to develop a policy proposal acceptable to all parties. Private schools were reluctant to surrender too much control to government. On the other side of the discussion were those individuals and groups wanting full integration of private schools into the public system. Supporters of full integration eventually withdrew from the policy negotiations once it became clear that their goals were not going to be realized.

The resulting Savary bill was introduced in 1984 into the National Assembly. The plan introduced in the bill was far reaching and involved substantial reform to the existing relationship between private schools and the government. Under the plan, subsidized private schools (almost all of which were Catholic) would be included in the government plans for opening and closing schools. Further, the bill created mechanisms for parental choice among public as well as private schools and hoped to incorporate private school teachers into public school teaching corps. The proposal did not conform to any of the wishes of those who hoped for a fully integrated and secular school system, which proved significant at the decision-making stage.

As a result of the extensive consultations that occurred at the policy formulation stage, the Savary bill had the full support of Catholic school leaders and other private school educators, as well as the government. Unfortunately for Savary, however, this is where the policy consensus ended. At the decision-making stage, the bill faced fierce opposition from those who hoped to create a truly secular and unified school system. The opposition, whom we might describe as the secularists, felt that the proposals made too many concessions to the private schools. This secular opposition came from within a large portion of the Socialist Party in the National Assembly, from the largest teachers' union, and from interest groups (for example, the National Committee of Secular Action).

The National Committee of Secular Action and the largest teachers' union campaigned ardently for simple integration during parliamentary debates on the bill. The secularists had many allies in the Socialist Party's members of the parliament, who presented a strong offensive to the bill at the committee stage. At this stage, the secularists suggested several amendments intended to promote greater integration. Savary and the government strongly opposed these amendments, however, recognizing that Catholic leaders would accept no further concessions. Once the government rejected the amendments, the issue further polarized the National Assembly and the governing Socialist Party itself. The Socialist leadership in the National Assembly indicated to Prime Minister Mauroy that if the amendments were not accepted, there would be massive resignations from the party and possibly an open split in the government's parliamentary majority. As a result, the amendments were endorsed by the government and the bill passed.

This decision was not well received. As is often the case in France, large public demonstrations against the legislation were held following its passage by the National Assembly. Over a million supporters of private schools took to the streets of Paris in protest. These demonstrations, when considered in tandem with public opinion polls indicating that over 70 percent of the French population favored a separate and subsidized system of private schools, resulted in President Mitterrand withdrawing the bill from consideration in the Senate. Prime Minister Mauroy and the government resigned. As a result, the government's attempt to revise fully the country's approach to private schooling resulted in no change to the status quo and a lost opportunity for an historic compromise.

The policy reform process in this instance clearly reveals the problems of enacting widespread reform in the face of significant divisions within the governing party. The absence of a strong, unified, and disciplined party at the time of this decision enabled the opposition not only to oppose effectively the reforms but also to bring down the government itself. In the face of significant divisions within the governing coalition, reform could not succeed. This experience also points to the ability of interest groups to block reforms that they oppose—first within the legislature (the secularists), and then on the streets (the private school supporters). Finally, the failure of this comprehensive reform effort demonstrates the importance of political support within the parliamentary majority as well as among the electorate at large. In the end, French citizens indirectly cast the deciding votes.

United Kingdom

Background: Policy Process and Policy History

The principle of decentralization is an important dimension of British education policy. Under the 1944 Education Act, a high degree of autonomy was given to local education authorities (LEAs) and school principals. Under the 1988 Education Reform Act (and subsequent reform acts in the early 1990s), reform has been comprehensive and systematic and has simultaneously increased and decreased the degree of decentralization. More specifically, power has been decentralized in that individual local schools have been given more authority, and it has been centralized in that this reform has taken place within a framework of national evaluation and curriculum control. Both the Thatcher and the Major governments supported a process of moving education authority from producers (that is, teachers and administrators) to consumers (that is, parents and students).

Under a plan known as Local Management of Schools, individual schools in the United Kingdom are now free to make their own choices about how to realize nationally defined education goals, accompanied by a high degree of parental involvement. These schools have been given control over their own budgets, with parental determination of the goals and organization of the schools. Parents also have choice over which school their child attends, with the stated intention being that schools will have to compete for students within a so-called education market. Although most schools remain under the control and funding of LEAs, these authorities are funded by the central government, not local taxes, thus reducing the degree of local control.

Power in certain areas of education policy also is centralized through a mandatory national curriculum for core subjects and a set of nationally administered and determined tests. Another form of centralization and weakening of local authority was the creation of a new category of schools, the so-called grant-maintained schools. These schools have chosen to opt out of their LEAs to become self-governing and centrally funded. A 1992 education bill made it even easier for schools to opt out; currently there are roughly 1,100 grant-maintained schools. Their numbers are expected to increase, especially because the 1992 law introduced measures for identifying failing schools whose problems will presumably be addressed by moving them to grant-maintained status.

The national Department of Education and Employment sets and administers the statutory framework of the education system and establishes national education policy, working with other central and local government bodies. The public sector predominates in British education (with attendance by over 90 percent of children), although the diversity of providers is growing. About 7 percent of children attend a variety of tuition-charging independent schools (or public schools). Independent schools are privately funded and are permitted to opt out of the national curriculum, although many conform to at least some of its guidelines. A government-funded Assisted Places Scheme, designed to increase choice, enables around 35,000 secondary students from low-income families in England and Wales to attend selected independent schools. Reforms in September 1996 increased the program to accept 70,000 students and extended eligible choices to all compulsory education. The scheme has been criticized widely, however, as a private sector subsidy that comes from the public purse.

The bulk of resources for education are generated at the central level, but expenditures generally take place at the local government level through LEAs. These authorities are required to pass 85 percent of the funds they receive directly on to the schools. Higher education councils are responsible for directing funds to higher education institutions.

Since the late 1980s the education system in the United Kingdom has been subject to some of the most comprehensive and stringent reforms experienced in the industrialized countries. During the 1980s, education change was identified as an important component of economic progress and growth. As a result, a significant overhaul was embarked upon. The British experience with reform has been somewhat distinctive, in that although a decentralizing trend is observed similar to that seen in other industrialized countries, this trend was combined with a marked tendency toward centralized control in some key areas, most notably funding and curriculum.

Education in the United Kingdom is compulsory from ages five to sixteen. In most localities a two-tier system of primary and secondary schools operates, but some areas have a three-tier system of first, middle, and upper or high schools. Although the majority of schools are comprehensive, some areas also have grammar and secondary modern schools that cater specifically to children in the higher and lower ability ranges, respectively. Secondary schools specializing in particular subject areas, such as technology or languages, have developed in some areas as well.

At the end of compulsory schooling, students may either enter a one- to two-year course of study in what is known as the sixth form of a school, or study at one of more than 450 further education colleges. These institutions offer three types of certificates: in education (A levels), broad-based vocational qualifications, or job-specific vocational qualifications in one- to two-year programs. Nearly one-third of students then go on to higher education.

All compulsory-age students in government-run schools follow a national curriculum that is at the heart of a recent drive to improve standards and to provide a minimum entitlement for students. The curriculum was established under the 1988 Education Reform Act and was revised and scaled back in January 1995 in response to complaints that it was far too comprehensive and consequently unmanageable. Prior to the creation of this curriculum, the British education system was not based on a system of national standards, although some LEAs offered optional guidelines for basic subjects.

Formal assessment of students with national testing begins at age seven and is followed up at ages eleven and fourteen. These assessment points correspond to the end of key stages in the national curriculum. At ages sixteen and eighteen, several public examinations (the General Certificate of Secondary Education and the A levels) are the main assessment instruments. The government also planned to introduce nationwide baseline assessment and testing for five year olds in 1997. The introduction of such tests has been highly contentious, with the tests criticized for a lack of integrity and their hurried introduction. The government has since reviewed and modified the testing process, although the policy of nationwide tests has not been abandoned.

Vocational education has yet to be addressed in a comprehensive manner in the United Kingdom. The country offers no vocational alternative to the academic course at the secondary level. Government education policy also plans for all sixteen and seventeen year olds not in full-time education to be in training or in a job, preferably with training. A system of youth credits gives all sixteen- and seventeen-year-old dropouts access to a Modern Apprenticeships and Youth Training program. Limited attention has also been paid to making vocational courses available to students who choose not to pursue academic courses after age sixteen, but this is not yet a systematic effort.

Contemporary Dynamics

Education policy reform arrived on the institutional agenda in the United Kingdom as a result of pressures similar to those observed in the other industrialized countries. In particular, the move to reform reflected a belief that the education system was not up to challenges presented by increasing international economic competition. Such competition from abroad generated a belief in the need for increased education system effectiveness to be achieved through greater centralization of authority of the system, as well as an emphasis on standards and performance. Efficiency, performance, and quality became important reform keywords.

The British government introduced a series of reforms between 1986 and 1993 in response to these pressures. The policies introduced in four separate Acts of Parliament (1986, 1988, 1989, and 1993) were formulated by the government and the Ministry of Education to strengthen local and parental management of schools, increase parental choice, make schools more accountable to external standards, reorganize school funding on an almost market basis, create a national curriculum, and develop a national assessment system linked to performance standards. These reforms simultaneously centralized and liberalized the education system.

The decision-making process surrounding all of these reforms, but especially the 1988 act, involved an intensely partisan debate. The Thatcher government fully embraced conservative, free-market principles in designing these policies, which triggered strong opposition from the Labour Party. The fusion of powers between the executive and legislature (as well as control of the legislature by a disciplined majority party) meant that this opposition bore little fruit; the four separate pieces of legislation that put the United Kingdom's new education system in place between 1986 and 1993 all passed easily through the House of Commons with few changes made.

With respect to the most important of these policies, the 1988 Education Reform Act, many critics charged that legislation had been steamrolled through Parliament with too little opportunity for debate. Evidence indicates that this was the Conservative government's strategy: The government believed that the reforms would not have passed had extensive consultations taken place. In particular, the government was unwilling to consult with any groups perceived as potential adversaries in the education reform process. The resulting policies thus were not the product of a bargaining or consensus-building process. Instead they were purely partisan in content, fully reflecting only the government's intentions.

As the 1988 act was implemented, the dangers of such a policy decision-making process became apparent. In developing this policy, the government had failed to consider the many issues involved in introducing a national curriculum and national assessment system, both in terms of complexity and costs. Also the decision to avoid an in-depth consultative process in designing these reforms meant that the policies had no clear advocates among key education players when they were being put in place. In particular, the government had failed to pay any attention to teachers in this process—either at the decision-making stage or as implementation proceeded. As such, teachers became formidable obstacles to effectively putting in place some aspects of the reforms. For example, the National Union of Teachers undertook organized public protests and strikes to oppose the implementation of national assessments. Similarly, educators of all political stripes vehemently criticized the national curriculum.

Ultimately the 1988 act did not result in the changes expected, creating the impetus for further reforms. The subsequent adoption of a new education act in 1993 was intended to address many of these implementation issues—not by scrapping the 1988 reforms but by modifying many of its provisions. However, the state of the education system did not improve appreciably in the wake of this new act. In 1994, opinion polls revealed increasing public skepticism about the government's ability to accomplish the ambitious goals it had promised. These reform difficulties eventually resulted in the Tory government scaling back its education reform ambitions, thus illustrating what frequently occurs when radical reforms run into political realities: Such reforms inevitably become moderated.

As elsewhere, the drive for education reform in the United Kingdom in the 1980s and early 1990s began with a sense that the education system was failing to prepare students for new economic challenges. These concerns began in the business community and moved to the public at large, creating substantial pressure for the government to act. Further, the United Kingdom's dominant political ideology stressed individualism, privatization, and market-based mechanisms; hence, its education reforms focused on local control and parental and school choice. The British government's experience with education reform, however, points to the difficulties a party bent on comprehensive education policy reform can encounter. The United Kingdom does not strictly conform to the model of a centralized, unitary form of government in education policy; instead the decentralization of some authority to local levels of government meant that the country appeared almost federal in nature, in that opponents to reforms were able to intervene in the implementation process at multiple points. The multiple actors involved in the provision of education and their relative autonomy turned out to be a serious obstacle to reform at the implementation stage. Despite the ease with which these policies were adopted (in a manner consistent with the strong government thesis discussed in Chapter 2), once they were in place, the government had great difficulty in mobilizing sufficient political support to overcome the resistance of these vested interests.

Italy

Background: Policy Process and Policy History

The Italian government's central Ministry of Education supervises and coordinates all education activities carried out in the country by public and private institutions. The ministry governs curriculum and syllabus changes and administers budgetary activities and school staffing decisions. Regional governments oversee school building and maintenance, the management of vocational education, the provision of training, specialization and teacher requalification, and counseling and guidance services. Provinces provide equipment, services, and non-teaching staff to schools; and local councils manage services necessary for running schools in their own areas. Education is funded primarily at the central level (80 percent of education expenditures). The remainder is covered by regions, provinces, and municipalities.

This pattern of control reflects the traditional Italian view that education is a national responsibility that should be controlled and financed by national government. Since the early 1990s, however, the issue of control has been debated. There has been a strong movement for local autonomy and increased input in running schools by those most involved in education—parents, students, and teachers. Although most Italians still want education to be funded at the central level, a more clearly defined and rigorous curriculum is desired, and many Italians believe that this goal can be achieved only through more local control. This perceived need for a more open and participatory structure has been the subject of tremendous debate, yet nothing has been resolved. Italy may eventually move to a greater, but not complete, level of autonomy in which the central government funds education and sets standards for and monitors outcomes, while local schools adapt national mandates to local needs and take advantage of local resources.

Education in Italy is compulsory for all children aged six to fourteen. An increase in the length of compulsory education is currently being considered. Compulsory education is divided into primary and lower secondary schools, with 98 percent of the relevant age groups enrolled. More than 80 percent of students continue their education for four to five additional years in a variety of secondary school types: general education, elementary teachers' training schools, technical education with different specializations, vocational education for various working activities fields, or fine arts institutes and schools. Nearly three-fourths of secondary school graduates go on to some form of postsecondary education, either in vocational programs or some form of university. Graduates of general education and five-year vocational schools are qualified for university entrance.

Italian students are given the option of enrolling in any Italian school, even in a district in which they do not live or pay property taxes. To inform students and parents' choices, individual schools are asked to make available information about their education programs. The issue of vouchers recently made it onto the education policy agenda in Italy, with some supporters advocating their use for Catholic and private schools. Not surprisingly, the Catholic schools and other private schools have been especially strong advocates of vouchers, rather than Italian parents more generally, given that Italian students already have the option of choosing to attend any public school.

The Italian government supports a common national curriculum in the interest of promoting a common national culture and providing education equity for all students. The national minister of education enacts national curricular programs approved by the parliament and gives approval for experimental curricula in selected schools. In elementary schools a new curriculum was implemented in 1990 that emphasizes new teaching methods and more disciplinary-based teaching and the teaching of a foreign language from grade 3 onward. The middle school curriculum has been in place since 1979.

In elementary school, assessment is carried out through teacher reports. At the end of grade 5, students take an examination to enter middle school. In the middle school, a council of teachers for each class sets objectives to be reached by students in each subject and conducts an analytical evaluation at the end of each term and at the end of the school year using a descriptive form about each student's achievement. A final national exam at the end of the third year of middle school consists of three written tests and an oral interview. The final diploma awarded to students who pass the exam is an indispensable document for entry to further education or vocational training or to obtain a job.

At the end of each school cycle, all students take a national examination to ensure a certain level of education equity. In upper secondary education, marks are awarded for each subject at the end of each year and students who do not have the minimum marks are required to repeat the year. By law the final exam gives access to all universities. When deciding on a student's final exam mark, an external committee considers reports from the student's teachers and the student's school career documents. The Ministry of Education creates the written exams, which are the same nationwide for any one subject.

Important reforms were made in technical and vocational education in Italy in the 1990s. Significant reform has been made in the technical institutes to prepare young people adequately for future employment. Post-diploma courses were introduced for higher professional qualifications, and vocational institutes also underwent curriculum reform. In the last two years of the five-year vocational course some teaching hours are now devoted to job-training activities under the responsibility of the regions. This reform is intended to result in a broader basic education for students that is then followed by vocational training. In addition, a diploma in all languages of the EU was created for students who successfully complete a three-year course after compulsory schooling to increase their job mobility.

Contemporary Dynamics

Among the six countries examined in this book, Italy has spent the least time engaged in education reform in the contemporary era. Before 1997, two landmark education reforms were enacted in Italy, the 1859 Casati law, which created the existing education system, and a major reform undertaken in 1923, the Gentile reform. Other important but smaller reforms have been undertaken since then, such as the introduction of a single middle school in 1962 and the opening of higher education to universal access in 1969. Although calls for more substantial reforms were issued, consensus about how to approach such reforms was consistently lacking, so much so that most Italians talked about the impossibility of reform when it came to education matters.

The basic shape of the education system in Italy remained largely unchanged throughout most of the twentieth century. This lack of change should not be taken as an indication of widespread satisfaction, however. On the contrary, during the 1980s and 1990s in particular, Italians were increasingly recognizing that their students were performing at lower levels than students in other industrialized countries. As a result, external pressure mounted for the government to create new standards to raise the skill levels of students about to enter the workforce. These concerns were strongly related to concerns about Italy's ability to increase its economic competitiveness both within the EU and internationally.

In May 1996 the newly formed Prodi government merged the Ministry of Education with the Ministry of Universities and Scientific Research and Technology and appointed Luigi Berlinguer as minister. Berlinguer immediately made clear his intentions to strengthen the tie between education and the workplace and devoted his energies to the most comprehensive education reforms ever envisioned for the country. The Ministry of Education formulated new policies under Berlinguer's direction and in consultation with educators and other interested parties. As in our other countries, these proposed reforms stressed decentralization and school autonomy, although they went far beyond these two themes. The reform eventually proposed by the Prodi government in 1997 was comprehensive. Its coverage included an extension of compulsory schooling, modifications to the secondary school leaving exam, improvement of vocational and technical education, creation of a national system of evaluation to go along with greater school autonomy, and administrative reform.

In a somewhat unusual approach to decision making, before submitting a reform bill to the legislature, the government published a policy document designed to create the opportunity for public debate and to build consensus around the need for reform. The government argued that education reform was not the concern of one particular party or interest group but was a matter of national concern that warranted widespread public discussion. This strategy proved effective. A wide range of criticisms and suggestions were made at this discussion stage that were subsequently incorporated into the proposed bill. Not only did this approach open up the policy formulation process to all interested parties, it also raised public awareness of education issues and helped to create a broad national consensus about the need for change. In the process, the government converted many of the key players in education reform into strong advocates for its policies. As a result, in the subsequent reform decision-making stage, debates about the bill never questioned the need for reform, although intense discussion about specific provisions of the reforms occurred. This strategy resulted in public support for the reforms as well as the strong endorsement of most educators.

Regardless of how much underlying support exists for a policy, implementing reform on the scale Italy was attempting is a problem in and of itself. This is especially true in Italy, a country notorious for its policy implementation problems. To circumvent its traditional inability to achieve political consensus on comprehensive projects, the Prodi government opted for an incremental approach to implementation, arguing that its planned reform was on such a vast scale that a range of legislative, regulatory, and contractual options, developed over time, were needed to cover all aspects of the reform. The government also argued pragmatically that it was more realistic to seek agreement and consensus on parts of the plan as they progressed, rather than on a comprehensive package of reforms. This approach, when combined with a far more stable political landscape than has existed for most of Italy's recent history, has enabled the government to take more time to undertake and implement these far-reaching changes. This is not to say, however, that the government has solved all of its problems, particularly those concerning its ability to mobilize and sustain the support of an array of education policy stakeholders: teachers, parents, students, employers, trade unions, the general public, and local and regional authorities.

In Italy the movement for education policy reform was driven by concerns about global competition and demands for a more flexible and highly skilled workforce and by a belief that students were less well educated than in the past. Arguably, education policy reform has proceeded more smoothly in Italy than we observed elsewhere. In part, this reflects the government's efforts to incorporate the views of all stakeholders. By including members of the education establishment in the policy formulation process, and by incorporating their criticisms and concerns into the policy proposal, the government avoided much of the opposition of strong education interest groups that hindered the effective implementation of reforms in other countries. Finally, we see in this policy approach a marked break from Italian-style politics. This approach was not a reflection of an unstable multiparty coalition or a deep divide between the executive and the legislature, but rather serves as one of the few examples of consensual decision making in the Italian political system.

Cross-national Trends

In reviewing the broader cross-national trends in these six countries, we consider the choices these countries make with respect to education provision as well as how well their education systems have performed with respect to access to education and student achievement. All six countries have engaged to varying degrees in education policy reforms in recent years, with a pattern of mixed results regarding students' access to education and their education achievements.

Policy Outputs

Among the industrialized countries examined in this book, most have been engaged in an ongoing process of education reform since the 1990s or earlier. Cross-national variation exists in the degree of interest in changing the control, administration, financing, and evaluation of education systems, but generally all countries have addressed at least some, if not all, of these issues. These countries have made a variety of choices, ranging from creating more centralized control systems to ones that are highly decentralized to a mixture of the two, and from systems based on loose education standard frameworks to rigid systems of national curriculum control. In most countries, the reform process also has included a focus on evaluating and creating education standards and improving assessment tools to respond to the public's demand for greater education accountability and productivity.

In these countries, education reforms have been directed toward some or all of the following: improving quality and efficiency, monitoring students' progress more comprehensively and systematically, closing the gap between standards and actual learning, and, for some countries, improving the vocational training of the workforce and managing the transition from work to school. Included in their reforms in the 1990s have been curriculum revision, standardized and centralized testing, and new approaches to school governance, with an increased emphasis on market-based mechanisms. The most comprehensive reforms have been undertaken in the United Kingdom and Italy (through the introduction of new policy instruments in nearly all of these areas). The other four countries have tinkered with various aspects of education provision but avoided dramatic, wholesale change.

Another area of policy outputs involves education spending in these six countries. In many areas of education, the United States spends more than most other industrialized countries. At the primary and secondary levels, U.S. expenditures per pupil are among the highest of the OECD countries. As Table 10–1 indicates, the United States outspent the other five countries at both public and private primary and secondary levels per pupil in 1995, especially for primary education. If we consider government education expenditures as a percentage of GDP (Table 10–2), the United States spends more than all the other countries, with the exception of France. From 1990 to 1995, public spending on education rose in the United States, France, Japan, and the United Kingdom but dropped dramatically in Italy (Center for Educa-

Table 10-1 Expenditure per Student on Public and Private Institutions, 1995

Country	Annual Expenditure per Student (in equivalent U.S. dollars)		
	Primary Education	Secondary Education	Tertiary Education
France	$3,379	$6,182	$6,569
Germany	3,361	6,254	8,897
Italy	4,673	5,348	5,013
Japan	4,065	4,465	8,768
United Kingdom	3,328	4,246	7,225
United States	5,371	6,812	16,262

SOURCE: Center for Educational Research and Innovation: *Education at a Glance: OECD Indicators 1998* (Paris: Organisation for Economic Co-operation and Development, 1998).

Table 10-2 Educational Expenditures as a Percentage of Gross Domestic Product (GDP)

Country	Direct Public Expenditure for Educational Institutions (percentage of GDP)		
	1980	1990	1995
France	5.0%	5.1%	5.8%
Germany	N.A.	N.A.	4.5
Italy	N.A.	5.8	4.5
Japan	5.8	3.6	3.6
United Kingdom	5.6	4.3	4.6
United States	6.7	N.A.	5.0

SOURCES: For 1980, World Bank: *Entering the 21st Century: World Development Report 1999/2000* (New York: Oxford University Press, 2000); for 1990 and 1995, Center for Educational Research and Innovation: *Education at a Glance: OECD Indicators 1998* (Paris: Organisation for Economic Co-operation and Development, 1998).

N.A. = not available.

tional Research and Innovation 1998: 18). Given these figures, it is logical to question whether higher spending on education translates into better results, which we address in the next section.

Policy Outcomes

How do countries compare with respect to education outcomes? If one were to assume that higher spending translates automatically into better quality education, then one would expect the quality of U.S. education to be especially high. On the issue of access to education, the United States is performing fairly well. Enrollment in primary education in the United States in 1991 was at the median level for high-income economies; enrollment is basically universal as it is in most industrialized countries. Upper secondary education is now the norm in the industrialized countries examined in this book. Although some variation exists in provision among countries, this difference has continued to be reduced over time. Of the six countries we considered, only Italy had an upper secondary graduation rate for the twenty-five- to thirty-four-year-old age group that fell below the 87 percent range (47 percent in 1995, compared with 90 percent in Germany). Enrollment in secondary education in the United States in 1991 was slightly below average due to higher dropout rates.

In higher (postsecondary) education, the United States's emphasis on access has shown the most tangible results: Enrollment rates in the United States were about twice the median level found in other industrialized countries (Center for Educational Research and Innovation 1998: 217). Although higher education is also accessible to increasing numbers of people in all industrialized countries, considerable variations in participation rates are observed from country to country. The greater use of postsecondary education in the United States stems from an emphasis on general education at the secondary level. The one-track system used in the United States leads to higher enrollments in postsecondary education in two ways. First, more U.S. students meet the entrance requirements to go to universities and colleges. Second, because high schools have fewer vocational programs, students who want a vocational degree or certificate often pursue that training at the postsecondary level. Italy again performs poorly relative to the other countries in higher education participation.

Although the United States has done well in providing access to education, the performance of the system (as measured by student scores on achievement tests) has been decidedly mixed. In a 1991 study of reading levels among nine and fourteen year olds in eighteen industrialized countries, reading literacy in the United States was considerably above average in the age nine group and slightly above average in the age fourteen group. However, the improvement in reading literacy between age nine and fourteen was lowest in the United States (24.9 percent); average improvement among all eighteen countries was 55.2 percent. In other words, students in the United States appear to have better reading skills at an early age but then do not improve those skills very rapidly (Center for Educational Research and Innovation 1998: 207–208). In science and mathematics, students from the United States have not fared well in cross-national studies. In a variety of studies from the 1970s through the 1990s, the average U.S. student performed at or, more often, considerably below the median for other industrialized countries. Also, in most studies, the top U.S. students did not perform in math and science as well as the best students in other countries (Ravitch 1995: 83–89). The most recent confirmation of this trend is found in the results of the Third International Math and Science Study, on which U.S. students placed twenty-eighth and seventeenth in math and science, respectively. Japanese students placed third in both math and science, and in math the United States placed behind the other countries examined in this book. Significantly, students with the best exam performances were from countries that tended to have education systems based on mandatory national curricula and testing.

Cross-national comparisons suggest that increased spending on education is not a foolproof solution to improving education outcomes. Money can help, but it is not a cure-all. The United States, like other countries, finds itself pressed to engage in education reform in an environment characterized by declining resources, rising expectations, and limited consensus. In all countries, such factors are simultaneously incentives for and barriers to meaningful reform.

Understanding Policy Reform

Reflecting on the case studies, we see that these industrialized countries have come to recognize that they no longer can maintain their global economic status through mass production because low labor costs in late-industrializing countries allow them to engage in mass production for a fraction of the cost in industrialized countries. Thus, for these richer industrialized countries, the primary remaining economic niche is found in employment sectors that require highly skilled, well-educated workers. In large part, recognition of this economic situation initially pushed the movement for education reform in these countries. This recognition especially fueled the shift in emphasis from academics to vocational education, the return to the basics, and the increased emphasis on curriculum content. These reform efforts reflect a widespread interest in producing a more highly skilled and technologically competent workforce. Because these driving forces for reform remain, policymakers likely will continue to be confronted with pressure for significant education change, regardless of the results of their ongoing reforms.

Citizens in industrialized countries have increasingly come to view education systems, correctly or incorrectly, as being ineffective. A widely held opinion in many settings is that education standards have either fallen or have not been set sufficiently high. As a result, the focus of concern in education reform has switched from an emphasis on inputs (such as level of finance) to outcome control (especially through greater emphasis on curriculum and testing). Levels of popular concern and dissatisfaction with the education system have been highest in the United Kingdom, France, and the United States, with a more muted cry for change being sounded in Germany and Japan. The differences in the observed degree of citizen concern are related in part to the education performance of students in these countries from a cross-national perspective (usually based on standardized exam results). For example, German and Japanese students have tended to score much higher than students from other industrialized countries on such exams; consequently, a sense of education failure has been far less widespread in these countries. Likewise, the pressure for comprehensive education reform has been relatively less intense in these countries. Strong pressure for reforms also is related to economic conditions: Countries facing economic difficulties are more likely to pursue significant education restructuring than are those in relatively good economic shape. This relationship was particularly evident in the United Kingdom, where economic downturns produced significant impetus for intensive education reform.

Education reforms also are related to a return to market-based mechanisms and individualistic orientations in many industrialized countries. As governments began to emphasize the virtues of privatization, decentralization, deregulation, and market forces, these principles began to be applied outside the sphere of economic systems. As dissatisfaction with education performance emerged in these countries, these more liberal political values provided ready solutions to many areas of concern. In the United States and the United Kingdom, we see a clear example of this pattern of influence, as school choice policies were ardently pursued.

Education policy implementation was no easy task in any of the countries examined in this book, but it proved especially difficult in the less centralized political systems. In all six countries, implementation was impeded by the broad number of participants involved and the power of entrenched education bureaucracies. Education systems offer multiple points at which opponents of prior policy decisions can attempt to change the course of those policies. This is especially true in political systems where the control of education remains firmly in the hands of lower levels of government, as in the United States, Germany, and the United Kingdom. In these countries, the passage of reforms was not enough to effect widespread change because powerful interests at the implementation stage were able to exercise their clout. In contrast, in Japan, where the entire education system is controlled tightly by the education bureaucracy at the center, implementation was of far less concern. The experience of these six countries implies that dramatic policy changes are more difficult to achieve in this policy area because an extensive array of interests (many of whom control the systems that are the targets of reform) have a stake in preventing innovation from occurring and had the means to do so. This is not to say that change is impossible, however. In this regard, the Italian experience, in which consensus on reform among the major actors involved was emphasized early in the policy-making process, may yet teach the industrialized countries a valuable lesson.

Our focus in this chapter has been on ongoing efforts to reform education systems. Given where most countries are in the reform process, the next step for these countries is to evaluate the effects of these reforms and proceed from there. The industrialized countries will continue to face pressures for further reform because of an ongoing concern about remaining or becoming more competitive in the global economic system. Many parents, students, politicians, and business people continue to feel that their countries' education systems are not capable of addressing new economic challenges—in particular, the demand for better educated and more highly skilled workers.

SUGGESTED READINGS

Chapman, Judith, et al. 1996. *The Reconstruction of Education: Quality, Equality and Control.* London: Cassell.

Corbett, Anne, and Bob Moon, eds. 1996. *Education in France: Continuity and Change in the Mitterrand Years, 1981–1995.* London: Routledge.

Chubb, John, and Terry Moe. 1990. *Politics, Markets and America's Schools.* Washington, D.C.: Brookings Institution Press.

DiConti, Veronica. 1996. *Interest Groups and Education Reform: The Latest Crusade to Restructure the Schools.* Lanham, Md.: University Press of America.

McLean, Martin. 1995. *Educational Traditions Compared.* London: David Fulton Publishers.

Phillips, David, ed. 1995. *Education in Germany: Tradition and Reform in Historical Context.* London: Routledge.

Roesgaard, Marie. 1998. *Moving Mountains: Japanese Education Reform.* Aarhus, Denmark: Aarhus University Press.

Shavit, Yossi, and Hans-Peter Blossfeld. 1993. *Persistent Inequality: Educational Attainment in Thirteen Countries.* New York: Westview Press.

Spring, Joel. 1998. *Conflict of Interests: The Politics of American Education.* New York: Longman.

Tsuchiya, Okano. 1999. *Education in Contemporary Japan.* Cambridge: Cambridge University Press.

Wray, Harry. 1999. *Japanese and American Education: Attitudes and Practices.* Westport, Conn.: Bergin and Garvey.

Chapter 11 **Environmental Policy**

Since the early 1980s environmental issues have become increasingly promi-nent on policy agendas in all the industrialized countries, including the six examined in this book. These issues are important for policymakers in political terms (as reflected in the effort of political parties and political leaders to appear "green"); in terms of the dimensions of the problems, which include global warming, global destruction of the ozone layer, global deforestation, and global overpopulation; and in terms of the sheer number of issues—for example, air, water, ground, and noise pollution; radioactivity; toxic waste; pesticides; and endangered species—and the possible solutions. Although substantial envi-ronmental gains have been achieved in most industrialized countries, the pro-cess of environmental protection has been more difficult, costly, and frustrat-ing than policymakers initially foresaw, and much remains to be done.

Common Policy Problems

Industrialized countries make choices regarding environmental policies in a number of important areas. A relatively clearly defined and shared set of en-vironmental issues confronts policymakers in each of the industrialized coun-tries examined in this book. In this section and in the case studies we focus on problems related to air pollution, one of the first environmental issues that industrialized countries recognized and addressed. The process of postwar in-dustrialization and a general reliance on fossil fuels for energy meant that by the late 1960s most industrialized countries began to experience significant air pollution problems and by the early 1970s the first air pollution control poli-cies began to be implemented. As a result, each of the six countries has a sub-stantial environmental protection record.[1]

The term *ambient air quality,* which refers to air in our immediate sur-roundings, is common in discussions about the air we breathe. Deterioration in ambient air quality generally results from an increase in the number of con-taminants present in the atmosphere—largely the result of the burning of fos-sil fuels in industrial and transport activities. These contaminants are produced at far greater levels than can be processed naturally and are absorbed into the air relatively easily.

---

[1] For more detailed discussions of environmental issues in these countries, see the series *Environmental Performance Reviews,* published since the early 1990s by the Organisation for Economic Co-operation and Development. Included in this series are in-depth treatments of environmental problems and policies for each of the coun-tries examined in this book.

317

Air-polluting contaminants include both particles and gases. The term *particulate matter* refers to solids—including ash, soot, and lead—that are released into the atmosphere in industrial emissions and exhaust gases. The most important polluting gases include carbon monoxide (CO), which is emitted primarily from gasoline engines. Sulfur oxides (SO_x), such as sulfur dioxide (SO_2), are produced by burning sulfur-containing fuels (when combined with water vapor, SO_2 forms sulfuric acid and falls as acid rain). Volatile organic compounds (VOCs), which include many compounds that are known carcinogens or that have climate-changing properties, contribute to the large-scale formation of ozone and smog. Nitrogen oxides (NO_x), especially nitrous oxide, are byproducts of fossil fuel burning at high temperatures; these oxides combine with VOCs to produce smog. Finally, chlorofluorocarbons (CFCs) are compounds with a chemical composition such that part of the molecule, when released in the atmosphere, is highly destructive to ozone molecules.

Scientific studies demonstrate that both short- and long-term exposure to emissions containing these gases or particulates causes serious health problems in humans. Air pollution also endangers people indirectly by causing significant harm to plant and animal life. The threat from these emissions is compounded by the interaction effects of these pollutants, which can be more hazardous than exposure to each of the compounds separately.

The existence of such air pollutants in recent years also has created growing concern about ozone layer depletion. Increasingly, scientific evidence has supported the argument that the earth's ozone layer has gradually become depleted or developed holes as a result of polluting human activities. Such damage is thought to be an environmental danger because of the ozone layer's role in shielding the earth from dangerous wavelengths of ultraviolet rays. When this layer is depleted the level of ultraviolet radiation that reaches the earth increases significantly. Increases in levels of ultraviolet radiation are linked to increases in skin cancer rates, possible weakening of the human immune system, crop loss, and forest damage. The most significant factor in ozone layer depletion is believed to be the production of CFCs in commercial activities.

Air pollution also creates another area of government concern with respect to the problem of global warming. This problem is caused by substances known as trace gases (so named because they make up less than 1 percent of atmospheric gases). They are also known as **greenhouse gases,** because they allow heat from the sun to enter the earth's atmosphere and then trap it, creating a greenhouse effect. These greenhouse gases are usually vital to the earth's ecology: They ensure that average temperatures are suitable to sustain life. However, human activities cause a harmful buildup of these gases, and the excess cannot be processed through the earth's natural capacity to recycle these gases. As these gases (such as carbon dioxide, or CO_2) build up, the atmosphere's capacity to capture heat radiated from the earth's surface increases, which raises the average temperature of the earth's surface. Should global warming increase, it is generally held that higher temperatures would likely produce a range of harmful effects—including rising sea levels, changes in agricultural production patterns, and warmer weather patterns. Although evidence for global warming is considered to be strong, environmental scientists disagree significantly about the degree to which this phenomenon is the direct result of human-produced greenhouse gases.

Finally, indoor air pollution, resulting from the presence of compounds such as formaldehyde and asbestos, is increasingly recognized as an environmental hazard. These substances are documented as posing serious human health risks requiring a public policy response.

Major Policy Options

In all industrialized countries, environmental protection policies usually are designed with one of two goals in mind. Policies such as those regulating automobile emission standards may be intended to prevent additional environmental contamination from occurring. Alternatively, policies may be aimed at eliminating existing contamination, for example, through a policy of planting forests to absorb excess gases already in the atmosphere. Public policies designed to achieve either, or both, of these objectives may take several forms.

The most widely used environmental protection policy instruments are **direct regulations** (or **command and control policies**) imposed by governments. Regulatory policies tend to look very similar from country to country. They typically are either framework policies, which allow latitude in their interpretation and implementation, or detailed laws, which permit little discretion in their application. Environmental regulations usually define permissible levels of pollutants and place limits on their discharge in the interest of reaching established target levels.

Although the content of these policies tends to be similar from country to country, a significant degree of difference in direct regulation policies is observed in the sanctions for noncompliance. Penalties for noncompliance may include criminal liabilities with fines as a penalty and the possibility of personal liability for responsible individuals. Alternatively, sanctions may include modifying, suspending, or revoking a license to operate. Governments may also be given the power to clean up after a pollution incident, with the costs paid by the polluter. Polluters also may be required to pay significant damages for civil liability. The enforcement of such penalties may generate costly adverse publicity for the polluter. In most industrialized countries these noncompliance penalties have become stricter and more vigorously enforced than in the past.

Industrialized countries may also develop **voluntary agreements** between the government and producers to reduce pollution levels. These agreements are usually used in conjunction with other policy instruments. They typically are negotiated directly between government and industry or are developed independently by industry (reflecting a genuine environmental concern, a concern about positive public relations, or both). These agreements are not legally binding but instead involve mutually agreed upon goals and target dates. Their use is limited in most industrialized countries because of perceived difficulties related to monitoring and enforcement, sanctions for noncompliance, and unclear objectives.

In some industrialized countries, policymakers have begun to address environmental problems by stressing the importance of market mechanisms through the use of **economic incentives.** These incentives include tax breaks for corporations that implement pollution controls, pollution charges or taxes, deposit-refund systems, and tradable discharge permits. These policies involve what are known as **polluter pays principles,** in which individuals are charged for their environmentally harmful activities, or **user pays principles,** which involve additional costs for consumers of environmentally hazardous products.

An economic incentive policy with respect to waste disposal practices might, for example, use a deposit-refund system that requires producers to pay a deposit on hazardous materials produced (say, per gallon). This policy increases production costs, which are passed on to the consumer. This scenario is expected to discourage consumers from using the product. To encourage the safe disposal of materials that nonetheless are bought, consumers receive a deposit refund when they safely dispose of the product. Such a policy uses market-based incentives to incorporate the true environmental costs of the product into its production and consumption value.

Although such policy instruments are increasingly being discussed by policymakers, many industrialized countries continue to be reluctant to use such incentives to control environmental pollution. This reluctance is probably a reflection of a natural bureaucratic preference for regulatory policies. In addition, opponents of incentives argue that these policies are too complex to be administered and that they offer less certainty that specific pollution reduction goals will be achieved. Others argue that economic instruments can be effective only when polluters, both producers and consumers, accept a notion of shared responsibility and have accurate information about the effects of their activities, conditions that are difficult to achieve.

An important environmental policy instrument for industrialized countries, particularly in the face of the globalization of many environmental problems, is the use of international environmental agreements. Since the late 1980s a number of international agreements have been developed that set pollution reduction targets for individual participant countries. One of the earliest of these agreements was the 1987 Montreal Protocol on Substances That Deplete the Ozone Layer, which forty-nine countries ratified. Other international agreements include the 1992 United Nations Framework Convention on Climate Change (FCCC) and the Convention on Biological Diversity, also drafted in 1992. One of the more controversial international agreements is the 1997 Kyoto Protocol on global warming. The use of such agreements is expected to become even more common in the future. Box 11–1 provides a more in-depth look at these agreements regarding climate change.

Box 11-1 **In Depth: Climate Change Agreements**

The first international agreement to address the climate change problem was developed at the 1992 Earth Summit in Rio de Janeiro, Brazil. This document, the United Nations Framework Convention on Climate Change (FCCC) was intended to stabilize, not eliminate, greenhouse gas concentrations in the atmosphere. Under the FCCC, the industrialized countries made voluntary commitments to reduce their levels of greenhouse gas emissions to 1990 levels by 2000. By June 1993, the FCCC had 166 signatory countries, and it went into effect in March 1994. The United States was one of the first countries to ratify this agreement. It was estimated in 1999 that roughly half of participating countries would meet the FCCC targets by 2000.

In the face of rising concerns about continued increases in CO_2 and other greenhouse gas emissions, a consensus emerged that further international action was needed. As a result, the Kyoto Protocol to the UN FCCC was adopted in December 1997. The protocol sets more ambitious goals for reducing greenhouse gas emissions and involves binding commitments (though it lacks effective enforcement mechanisms). The Kyoto Protocol commits the industrialized countries to specific, binding emission targets for six key greenhouse gases, especially CO_2, methane, and NO.

By June 1999 the Kyoto Protocol had received only eighty-four signatures, including the European Union, Canada, Japan, and China. Few countries have ratified the protocol thus far, and they are not subject to its commitments until they do so. The United States signed the protocol in November 1998 but has yet to ratify it. The Kyoto Protocol would commit the United States to a target of reducing three greenhouse gases by 7 percent below 1990 levels between 2008 and 2012. The Clinton administration has indicated that it will not submit the protocol for ratification in the Senate until developing countries also act to reduce their greenhouse gas emissions. This position in part reflected a 1997 Senate resolution that the United States should not become a party to the agreement until developing countries also submit to binding targets.

The fact that the United States has failed to take mandatory and legally binding steps to reduce its carbon emissions makes it difficult to persuade industrializing countries to slow their rate of greenhouse gas emissions and begin to use alternative technologies. The developing countries are widely opposed to the Kyoto Protocol's binding commitments. These countries argue that because existing greenhouse gas problems were largely the result of industrialization in wealthy countries, those countries must take primary responsibility for the ensuing problems.

Explaining Policy Dynamics

The existing research on environmental policy reform rests largely on a case study approach; thus large-scale theorizing about these issues is generally lacking, and most work in the area is highly descriptive. Existing analytical work points primarily to the importance of institutional factors in explaining both policy reform and outcomes.

Cultural Explanations

A cultural factor that may influence environmental policy reform involves citizens' definition of their rights and freedoms with respect to the environment. Widely held social values, such as the right to own and drive an automobile, the importance of the open road, the freedom to drive at high speeds, or the freedom to fish and use waterways, are argued to influence a government's ability to impose more restrictive environmental policies. Where such things are viewed as right and proper, they are rarely challenged when it comes to making decisions about environmental policies (O'Riordan and Jordan 1996).

Not surprisingly, environmental policy reforms often reflect public opinion and priorities. In countries where environmental policy has yet to arouse public concern, governments face greater difficulty in enacting reforms. Conversely, in countries where populations are more mobilized on certain environmental issues, reform may be easier to pursue (depending on whether a match exists between public opinion and the government of the day). This pattern is especially relevant for understanding the policy reform process when the policy agenda has been determined by external rather than internal pressures (Collier and Lofstedt 1997; Crepaz 1995; Jansen, Osland, and Hanf 1998; Vernon 1993).

Economic Explanations

Environmental policy reform may also be affected by economic pressures arising from globalization and increased international competitiveness. For example, reforms involving environmental taxes have been difficult to adopt in industrialized countries. These reforms are often rejected on the grounds that they impede international competitiveness. In such cases, policy reform is affected by a perception that the policies will reduce the chances of making national industry profitable in a globally competitive environment (Jansen, Osland, and Hanf 1998).

Cost considerations also influence the environmental policy reform process. For example, the economic costs of achieving CO_2 emission targets are viewed as either the most critical factor for national decision making or one of the most influential factors. Where estimated costs of a particular policy are low, support for the policy will be more readily forthcoming; where the policy involves tremendous expense, cost becomes a decisive factor in mustering opposition to reform. Thus cost is a critically influential factor when great expense is required to achieve the target but is less influential when the cost is small or uncertain or when environmental improvements may be economically beneficial (Kawashima 1997).

Political Explanations

As we noted in earlier chapters, the ideology of the governing party in a country often determines the nature of policy reform. This relationship often holds true with respect to environmental policy. In particular, because organized environmental interests are usually allied with the political center or the left, we expect centrist or leftist governments to be more likely to pursue substantial environmental policy reform (Scruggs 1999).

Researchers also observe that the extent to which citizens participate in environmentalist movements or parties varies greatly from country to country. Not surprisingly, wider and more frequent reform efforts occur in countries where such movements are active than in those where they are conspicuously absent. Some countries have highly active interest organizations that continually demand more environmentally oriented policies and more effective environmental administration. In other countries, the government is subject to no significant political pressure concerning environmental policy, from either specific groups or the population at large.

Institutional Explanations

Many scholars argue for the importance of institutional arrangements in accounting for environmental policy reform (Hanf and Jansen 1998; Jager and O'Riordan 1996; Jansen, Osland, and Hanf 1998; Scruggs 1999; Weale 1992). Some scholars emphasize a lack of coordination and cooperation between different levels of government as an important influence. They note that although environmental problems offer substantial scope for action at lower levels of government and most countries have taken a good deal of initiative at these levels, central governments often pay little attention to such efforts when drawing up national environmental programs. This lack of cooperation frequently results in duplications of effort, squandering of resources, and, overall, ineffective policy reforms (Jansen, Osland, and Hanf 1998).

Another important institutional factor may be the nature of a country's electoral system. Proportional representation electoral systems are argued to create the possibility for greater success in environmental protection, because they encourage the representation of smaller and more particularized interests. Under such a system, green parties are more likely to gain policy influence either by gaining access to elected office themselves or by compelling the more mainstream parties to accommodate those interests (Scruggs 1999).

Researchers also have pointed to the importance of interest representation systems for explaining policy reform. Corporatist political systems are widely held to be more amenable to broader environmental policy reforms because they are more consensual and amenable to compromise. Pluralist systems are argued to allow for the blockage of such reforms because of their adversarial and competitive nature. Because environmental policies involve collective goods and action, they are argued to be more difficult to achieve in pluralist systems, which allow various interests to intervene in the policy process to defend their own interests. In particular, environmental policies impose costs on private economic interests, which are highly motivated to prevent the adoption of such policies. Although these policies are generally of aggregate benefit, particular sectors and individuals may lose out, resulting in considerable opposition to some measures—opposition to which pluralist systems are more likely to respond (Crepaz 1995; Enloe 1975; Lundqvist 1980; Vogel 1986).

O'Riordan and Jordan (1996) point to policy networks as important institutional factors that influence the direction and development of environmental policies. They argue that policy networks provide both an enabling and a constraining filter to policy development. Stable policy communities become an effective constraint to radical policy change because they tend to change slowly, if at all. Where policy networks exist, governments faced with new policy problems are forced to negotiate with and gain the support of relevant and important communities if they want their policies implemented. In such settings, these networks can place significant constraints on large-scale reform.

Lundqvist (1974) argues that the highly technical and standards-based nature of environmental policy makes policy development and implementation more difficult in a federal system. A federal structure may interfere with the technical connection between the national government, which sets standards, and those agencies responsible for monitoring and implementation at lower levels of government. As a result, effective policy making in federal political systems takes more time (because policies need to be articulated more fully) and requires consensus building (because multiple actors are involved). In unitary political systems, the existence of more immediate connections between various governmental actors concerned with standards typically reduces the need for consensus building or policy elucidation. Lundqvist further argues that federal systems may also result in the development of more lenient standards than policymakers prefer, as well as a greater ability to delay actions because policy making in federal systems involves multiple decision-making points. At the same time, he notes that unitary political systems often result in reforms that deprive lower levels of government of the flexibility needed to cope with local problems when implementing reforms.

Scruggs (1999) argues that the relationship between the executive and the legislature is important to the degree that these two government branches are divided. In a unified legislative-administrative structure, policy continuity, consensus, and accountability will be enhanced. Where significant divides exist between the executive and the legislature, government will be less capable of providing consensual decisions about public goods and thus will be even less successful in achieving substantial reform.

International Policy Making

Policymakers in industrialized countries increasingly acknowledge that the environment in one country is not distinct from the environment in another and that environmental problems do not respect national territorial boundaries. Instead most environmental issues have an international dimension or at least a regional or transborder component. This phenomenon is commonly known as the **globalization of the environment.** In policy terms, this globalization has meant that although effective environmental policies can be developed at the national level, identifying and addressing the regional and global dimensions of these problems also is necessary. This awareness has resulted in the development of a substantial number of international environmental agreements.

Environmental protection policies in the United States, Canada, and Mexico may be affected by some provisions of the North American Free Trade Agreement (NAFTA), which has a clear environmental component. NAFTA's environmental provisions are intended to ensure that environmental conditions in the agreement's three signatory countries do not hamper trade or give one country a comparative advantage over the others. Under the agreement, none of the three countries may lower its environmental regulatory standards to attract investment. In addition, the agreement encourages the integration of environmental policies and a raising of environmental standards in these countries while protecting each country's right to set its own level of environmental protection.

NAFTA was also accompanied by a supplemental agreement on environmental cooperation that was drafted in 1993 at the encouragement of the Clinton administration. The supplemental agreement came in response to unprecedented pressures from many U.S. environmental groups with respect to trade issues. The agreement was intended to foster environmental cooperation and to improve enforcement of national environmental laws; however, it does not require the signatory countries to adopt any new environmental laws. It established a North American Commission on Environmental Cooperation, which has some powers to impose fines or trade sanctions for the failure to enforce existing environmental laws. Thus far, NAFTA's strongest impact on environmental policies has been seen in Mexico.

Environmental protection is one of the best developed policy areas within the European Union (EU). Approximately 300 environmental laws have been adopted since 1957, and roughly 200 are currently being implemented by member states. The majority of these laws are directives to be adopted by individual member states and transposed into national laws. The EU has developed some of the most comprehensive and innovative environmental policies found among the industrialized countries, reflecting a strong commitment to environmental protection that is supported by the EU member states and the majority of European citizens.

The European Community (EC) did not include among its original objectives environmental protection. The 1957 Treaty of Rome did not address environmental issues, and the EC did not address multinational environmental concerns until the 1970s. A series of environmental action programs was introduced in 1973, with four subsequent programs through 1993. These programs had no legal basis and were intended primarily to eliminate barriers to a common market rather than to focus on environmental issues. Environmental protection was not recognized as a formal obligation of member states until the Single European Act in 1987, certain provisions of which defined the EC's environmental policy goals and established a legal foundation for its actions. Beyond simply defining environmental protection as a priority, the environmental sections of the 1986 act called for the EC to consider environmental protection to be an integral part of all EC laws, whatever their primary focus. These commitments were reinforced and extended in the 1991 Maastricht Treaty. The majority of environmental policies are now adopted through qualified majority voting in the Council of Ministers and approval by the European Parliament. The Treaty of Amsterdam does not extend the EU's environmental goals but does commit the EU to further consolidate the progress that has already been made by stating that environmental concerns be integrated into all EU policy making.

The EU member states generally have transposed EU environmental directives into national legislation. As in other policy areas, however, subsequent implementation and enforcement of these policies has not been uniform across the member states. In particular, the lack of EU enforcement mechanisms and resources, as well as cross-national differences in administrative structures (and differences within countries), have produced uneven policy effectiveness. States with well-established environmental protection records, a strong philosophical commitment to the environment, and existing environmental policy administrative infrastructures are more likely to have implemented EU directives effectively (although implementation in these countries also is less than perfect).

In 1994 the European Environment Agency was established at the supranational level. The agency primarily has an information-providing, integrationist role rather than being responsible for environmental regulation or monitoring enforcement of EU laws. As such, many analysts view as limited the prospects for more successful enforcement of EC environmental directives. These difficulties with implementation and enforcement notwithstanding, EU environmental policy making is viewed widely as having encouraged environmental improvements that would not otherwise have occurred and as one of the best examples of cross-national policy integration.

In the case studies that follow, we focus our consideration of contemporary policy dynamics on the countries' most recent attempts to meet their international commitments in preventing climate change under the FCCC and the Kyoto Protocol. These attempts typically involve efforts to reduce CO_2 concentrations in the atmosphere by reducing consumption of fossil fuels in both the energy and transport sectors.[2] In all six countries, these efforts have been a primary focus of attempts at environmental policy reform since 1990, with the systemic agenda having been set largely through external influences.

United States

Background: Policy Process and Policy History

The development and administration of environmental policy in the United States can be very complex because it occurs at multiple points in the government system. Responsibility for the development of environmental policies lies with a variety of executive branch offices, departments, and agencies, including the Environmental Protection Agency (EPA), the principal environmental bureaucratic agency. Congress, under its constitutional jurisdiction to regulate interstate commerce and control activities on federal lands, also passes specific, detailed (rather than framework) environmental policies. These laws may be implemented by either the executive branch or the states, depending on their specific provisions. Further, both criminal and civil actions may be used in the U.S. judicial system for implementing and enforcing environmental legislation, and many environmental cases are heard in federal courts. Strong compliance and enforcement are notable features of federal environmental management in the United States.

Although primary responsibility for environmental protection traditionally is placed in the federal government's hands (to harmonize regulations nationwide and to equalize the protection burden), individual states also may develop their own environmental policies that extend, or possibly supersede, federal mandates (albeit under strict federal oversight). Other states have laws that prevent them from toughening federal standards. Many states also have created their own bureaucratic structures to develop and implement environmental policies. A general policy of shared authority and cooperative arrangements exists between federal and state governments to implement and enforce national environmental laws. The federal government may authorize states to issue permits and take enforcement actions that are consistent with national-level policies. Local governments also have the authority to address environ-

---

[2]Although all six countries have signed the Kyoto Protocol, none has ratified it, meaning that the countries are not yet legally bound to meet the protocol's commitments. Nonetheless, current environmental policy reform efforts in each country have begun to address the issues that conforming to the protocol raise.

mental problems in their areas. Increasingly, states and localities have sought more independence in their environmental protection efforts and have objected to federal programs that require action without supplying the necessary funds.

The United States has pursued air quality improvements since the early 1970s. Environmental policy on air quality in the United States primarily takes the form of direct regulations that set strict standards. More than in other industrialized countries, air quality standards in the United States are enforced through stiff penalties and noncompliance fees. The United States also use economic instruments and voluntary agreements to control air pollution but to a much lesser degree than direct regulations. The focus of air quality management policies is primarily on removing existing contaminants rather than pollution prevention. The United States is a strong advocate of and participant in international environmental policy making to improve air quality.

Air pollution control in the United States occurs under the 1970 Clean Air Act (amended in 1977 and 1990), which calls for the creation of a set of national ambient air quality standards. Under the 1970 act, technology-based emission levels were set for eight compounds classified as hazardous air pollutants. This list of air contaminants was extended to 189 compounds in 1990, with a requirement for technology-based control standards to be developed for each (these standards replaced the quantitative, health-based risk assessments introduced in 1977). Ambient air quality is not monitored on a national basis but is checked at various points throughout the country.

Emission controls for mobile sources of air contaminants have been in use in the United States since the 1960s. Stringent exhaust limits for passenger cars were instituted in 1981, following fuel-efficiency standards in 1978 that were progressively strengthened until 1985. Unleaded gasoline was introduced in the United States in 1975, and the complete phase-out of vehicles running on leaded gasoline was concluded in 1996. To reduce CO emissions, the use of oxygenated gasoline, particularly in winter, is required in thirty-one U.S. cities, and the use of reformulated gasoline with lower hazardous emissions is being introduced in select areas. The 1990 Clean Air Act amendments further tightened and introduced new controls. These controls include standards for cleaner fuels, new vehicle emissions' limits, inspection programs (many of which already exist at the state level), and changes in transportation policy to encourage van pooling and carpool lanes.

The United States makes only limited use of voluntary agreements in air quality management, mostly to promote energy-efficiency improvements but also to reduce emissions. The Climate Challenge, a recent voluntary agreement between the Department of Energy and major utilities, involves a pledge to limit or reduce greenhouse gas emissions in the most cost-effective way possible under strict performance measures. More than 80 percent of U.S. electric utilities are party to the agreement. The use of these agreements is expected to increase in the future.

Economic instruments, especially those based on user pays principles, are not an important air pollution control mechanism in the United States. The one strict use of tax incentives involves a significant tax on CFCs to facilitate their phase-out. Some market-based mechanisms, such as the use of emission trading systems, particularly for SO_2 allowances and CFC emission permits, are used to help reduce air pollution at minimum cost. Under such systems, a company that reduces emissions below a required level can receive credits usable against higher emissions elsewhere; companies may also trade emission credits. Under the SO_2 program, allowances for SO_2 emissions may be bought, sold, or traded among utilities or industrial plants with the intention of reducing compliance costs to industry. The goal of these trading systems is to balance combined emissions within an aggregate limit. The United States also makes limited use of environment-specific subsidies and has created some tax programs aimed at funding damage compensation or clean-up activities performed by government.

The United States is party to both regional and international agreements to reduce air contaminant emission levels. In the 1991 Air Quality Agreement with Canada the United States committed to reducing SO_2 emission levels between 2000 and 2010 with a 40 percent decrease from 1980 levels. The United States also has agreements with Mexico, such as the 1992 Integrated Border Environmental Plan and the 1996 Border XXI Program, and participates in agreements on long-range transport of air pollutants, such as the acid rain program and the NO_x and VOC protocol. The United States was the first industrialized country to ratify the FCCC. Like most industrialized countries, the United States has signed but not ratified the Kyoto Protocol. The United States also is on the leading edge of the development, implementation, and encouragement of global environmental agreements, particularly with respect to air quality.

Contemporary Dynamics

Having ratified the FCCC and as a signatory to the Kyoto Protocol, the United States has placed the problem of how to reduce CO_2 emissions on its institutional agenda. CO_2 emission levels in the United States are expected to rise because of the continuing increase in motor vehicle use, despite the implementation of strict emission controls. Overall, CO_2 accounted for 85 percent of net greenhouse gas emissions in the United States in 1995, and in the period 1990–1995 the country experienced a 6 percent increase in overall CO_2 emissions. In this policy area, we find a consolidation model of agenda setting, in which the government has placed the question of global warming on the agenda but in so doing relies on the support of scientists and environmentalists who share the government's views on the issue.

The country's CO_2 emissions continue to rise as a result of heavy increases in motor vehicle use. Since 1970 the annual distance traveled by the average driver in the United States increased by 51 percent, motor vehicle traffic doubled, and passenger transport increased 86 percent. Further, between 1960 and 1995 the number of cars and trucks on the road more than doubled— more than offsetting any improvements in air quality achieved through vehicle emission reductions. In 1993, transport accounted for 29 percent of CO_2 emissions from fossil fuel burning, and transport was expected to be the fastest growing source of CO_2 emissions through 2000.

Problems of increased motor vehicle use are particularly vexing in the United States because of a pattern of low-density land use that necessitates motor vehicle use. In addition, public mass transportation in the United States is less efficient for many people than is the use of personal motor vehicles. The heavy use of motor vehicles in the United States also is encouraged by the very low cost to use them. Unlike most other industrialized countries, the United States does not require individual motorists to bear much of the real costs of road transportation (such as road construction, maintenance, parking, and even gasoline—the real cost of which is now lower than in 1950) or of the environmental costs. At 27 percent, the fuel tax in the United States is just over one-third of the average rate among European member countries of the Organisation for Economic Co-operation and Development (OECD).

Although there is general support in the United States for environmental protection, policymakers are not inclined to use increased fuel taxes in an attempt to reduce motor vehicle use (and thereby reduce CO_2 emissions). This reluctance is clearly a function of political expedience. The vast majority of the U.S. population is in no way predisposed to seeing fuel prices rise or to using their vehicles less because of global warming. Many people think fuel prices are already too high, which, when combined with a strong dependence on motor vehicles for the economy and mobility, makes the future use of such measures unlikely.

In its attempts to achieve CO_2 emission stabilization, the U.S. government has developed both regulatory policy instruments, such as mandatory vehicle inspections, vehicle fuel consumption standards, and development of climate change guidelines, and economic policy instruments, such as government subsidies to encourage development of alternatively powered vehicles and fiscal measures to promote sales of fuel-efficient vehicles and to encourage use of public transport by commuters. A voluntary agreement (Clean Car/Super Car) between government agencies and the three largest automakers, and involving suppliers and research institutions, has been established to develop new energy-efficient vehicles.

Thus far the U.S. government has not formulated policies that involve specific CO_2 emission targets because of the perceived negative influence such targets will have on the domestic economy. Here we are referring to the cost factor—namely that increasing energy efficiency in the country overall will have real economic costs in both the short and long term. Although the public demonstrate some interest in climate change issues, they are not overly alarmed and are especially persuaded by arguments that targeted emission reductions clash with their right to move about freely and cheaply and that such reductions will involve greater expense to them individually (in terms of both energy and transport). Without pressure from the public and with intense opposition from industry, political leaders have had only weak incentives to place on the institutional agenda CO_2 emission targets or economic instruments for controlling emissions.

Significant opposition to setting specific targets for CO_2 emissions (and other greenhouse gases) comes from industrialists who argue that they are hurt by more stringent emission standards and increased costs of transport and that such costs affect their international competitiveness and result in lost jobs. Industry has encouraged the use of voluntary standards, which most supporters of environmental control argue will achieve little. Businesses also fear that emission targets will result in higher energy prices. Echoing the concerns of industry, many Republicans charge that the Kyoto Protocol imposes costly environmental controls on U.S. businesses while giving developing countries an unfair competitive advantage by easing restrictions facing them—all in an effort to address an environmental problem they believe does not exist.

In this political context, the Clinton administration, under its 1993 Climate Change Action program, formulated new guidelines for reducing emissions. The program proposed a considerable expansion of the United States's abatement efforts but relied largely on voluntary action by industries—most of whom reject the scientific evidence about global warming. The program resulted in only limited actions, particularly related to transport, because of policymakers' inability to develop a consensus between public and private sector interests on their suggested guidelines.

The combination of Republican control of the legislature, strong business opposition, and the close relationship between the Republican Party and industry has meant that efforts to set CO_2 reduction targets and new emission standards have failed. Since the Republicans took control of Congress in 1995, few new environmental policy proposals have become law. Overall, opposition to climate change policy is so strong that the Clinton administration has yet to submit the Kyoto Protocol to the Senate for consideration and ratification. This opposition was made clear in 1997 with the passage of a Senate resolution blocking the Kyoto Protocol's ratification until the developing countries submit to binding emission targets. Congress also barred the EPA from doing anything related to implementing the Kyoto Protocol and tried unsuccessfully to prohibit the administration from even holding public educational seminars on global warming.

Supporters of more stringent efforts to control CO_2 emissions in the United States include, not surprisingly, environmentalists, the EPA, and scientists. Environmental organizations are highly critical of the Clinton administration for not pursuing the reduction of CO_2 emissions more aggressively. Given the recent pattern of partisan control of Congress and the fact that none of these groups enjoys the support of (or access to) the Republican Party, they have had little influence of late on environmental policy making.

In 1997 the EPA introduced a number of new regulations concerning ground-level ozone and particulate matter that were intended as a start in emissions reduction. A broad coalition of industries immediately mobilized against these new standards as too costly and of unproved scientific benefit. Republican members of Congress accused the Clinton administration of attempting to achieve the Kyoto Protocol standards by stealth. The new regulations were challenged in a federal appeals court, and in May 1999 the court sided with industry and reversed the restrictions. This action has opened the door to speculation that the courts may be increasingly willing to challenge the EPA's authority to issue environmental regulations. Throughout 1999, Congress repeatedly responded to White House requests for climate change programs with deep cuts. Finally, efforts to gain public support for new standards, and particularly for fuel taxes, have been unsuccessful.

Despite past gains in emission control in the United States, CO_2 emissions, especially from the transport sector, are expected to rise again after 2005. Such expectations have negative implications for the country's ability to meet its commitments under the FCCC and the Kyoto Protocol. Reducing such emissions requires the United States to introduce policies similar to those found in other industrialized countries. Such policies would be aimed at further developing public transport systems, educating and informing the public to help change their transport behavior, funding research and development in new technologies, and introducing economic instruments that transfer the burden of taxation from car ownership to car use. Given the status of public opinion on motor vehicle use and global warming, as well as the strength of organized interests opposing such measures, however, such changes do not appear likely in the short term. Most observers expect little executive or congressional action on climate change in the near future.

The U.S. government's failure to set emission reduction targets or introduce economic instruments to reduce CO_2 emissions, especially from the transport sector, reflects the presence of several formidable obstacles to reform. First, cultural influences play a role in this reluctance, in that Americans are strongly attached to their right to own and operate a vehicle. The culture of the open road is an important part of the national psyche, and policies that increase the cost of motor vehicle use are politically risky. Second, public opinion in the United States is only weakly mobilized about global warming, creating little pressure for immediate action. Third, industry and consumer advocacy groups have been effective in lobbying against the adoption of economic instruments to reduce emissions, claiming that the costs are too high and that the country's economic competitiveness will be threatened. Several political factors also play an important role. The lack of an environmental party in the United States (in part reflecting the country's single-member district plurality electoral system) reduces pressure to address environmental issues in Congress.

More important, the existence of a divided government since 1994 has presented a formidable reform obstacle. In particular, the Republican Party's opposition to any discussion of global warming issues has meant executive-legislative gridlock on this issue since 1994 as congressional Republicans consistently blocked the Clinton administration's efforts to address the issue.

Japan

Background: Policy Process and Policy History

In Japan, primary responsibility for the development of environmental policy lies with the national Diet. Japan's forty-seven prefectures and the municipalities organized below them also are permitted to draft policies that are in line with national laws. Such policies typically are aimed at toughening national standards or responding to specific prefectural problems. Thus all prefectures, as well as many municipalities, have their own pollution control policies. Further, where air pollution levels are particularly high, prefectural governments are required by the national government to develop integrated pollution prevention plans.

The relationship among national, prefectural, and municipal governments generally is well coordinated through the ministries of the Japanese bureaucracy. Environmental issues are coordinated by the Environment Agency, in cooperation with other government ministries, at the central level. Implementation and enforcement of environmental laws is passed on to the prefectures and sometimes municipalities, with close supervision from the national government, resulting in a high degree of policy effectiveness.

The Japanese government has vigorously pursued air quality management since the late 1960s and has made considerable progress in reducing air pollution levels. This reduction was accomplished through a combination of strong direct regulation and widespread use of voluntary agreements with industry, with only limited use of economic instruments. An important environmental policy emphasis in Japan is on air pollution prevention, especially through improved pollution control technology and strict standards. Since the 1990s Japan has been a strong advocate for and participant in global environmental agreements.

Environmental quality standards and emission standards are strictly controlled in Japan through direct regulations. The 1968 Air Pollution Control Law put in place limits on both stationary emissions (that is, from industrial and combustion facilities) and motor vehicle exhaust. Subsequent restrictions on emissions have made Japan's requirements among the world's strictest. Emission targets were established for the major air contaminants in the early 1970s and are revised as new scientific data are gathered. For areas with more serious air pollution, the Area-wide Total Pollutant Load Control System was introduced in 1974 through amendments to the 1968 law. This policy determined the maximum tolerable emission levels for SO_x in these areas to conform with environmental quality standards; the policy was extended to NO_x in 1981. Accompanying these emission controls in Japan is one of the most extensive and effective air pollution monitoring systems found among the industrialized countries.

Japan also has introduced some of the world's strictest measures to control motor vehicle emissions. Passenger car and heavy vehicle emission standards and NO_x standards gradually have been strengthened, emphasizing the use of best available technology. From early on, the Japanese government emphasized the development of technological improvements for new vehicles, favoring the use of catalytic converters. Vehicles are subject to emission inspections at one- to three-year intervals. Fuel quality improvements accompanied new vehicle technology. All gasoline was lead free by 1978, and sulfur levels in diesel fuel were reduced. Vehicle emissions are further controlled through a 1992 NO_x law to accompany more restrictive vehicle emission standards with special measures in designated areas to reduce NO_x emissions.

Voluntary agreements are an important component of environmental policy making in Japan, probably to a greater extent than is found in the other industrialized countries. Local governments and citizens' groups have signed a number of voluntary agreements with industry to control both emissions and fuel use; these agreements encourage the use of best available pollution control technology and energy-efficiency measures. In 1994, close to 40,000 agreements between government and industry were in effect (OECD 1994b: 103).

The use of economic instruments in Japan is limited primarily to incentives (in the form of tax relief or low-interest loans) for investment in air pollution prevention and control equipment, mostly for industry, but also to encourage the replacement of older vehicles with newer, less polluting ones. For example, companies that install or improve their air pollution control equipment receive tax exemptions and may depreciate this equipment at special rates.

Since the 1980s, the Japanese government has placed increasing emphasis on international environmental issues and has become a strong advocate of international cooperation in this area. Japan is an active partner in international attempts to control air quality as supporters of the Montreal Protocol and the FCCC. Japan also has increased its financial support and technology transfers to less developed countries to assist in their efforts to improve their environmental conditions. Further, Japan was one of the first countries to create a national government structure (the Global Environmental Department in the Environment Agency) specifically to address global environmental issues.

Contemporary Dynamics

Japan ratified the FCCC in 1993 and committed itself to stabilizing CO_2 emissions at 1990 levels by 2000. The country is also party to the Kyoto Protocol. In Japan, as in the other industrialized countries, CO_2 emissions from the transport sector continue to present an important obstacle to meeting these goals, despite substantial gains in the 1980s and 1990s. Although Japan's CO_2 emissions remain the lowest of the industrialized countries, they are increasing steadily (CO_2 emissions increased 40 percent from 1970 to 1990) and are projected to be 3 percent higher than 1990 levels in 2000 (OECD 1994b: 115–117). The number of vehicles in use has risen sharply in Japan (tripling from 1970 to 1990—although car ownership remains low relative to other industrialized countries). Further, consumer preference for larger, more powerful vehicles has recently resulted in a decline in the fuel efficiency of passenger cars in use. These two phenomena have led to increases in CO_2 emissions resulting from transport, which accounted for 19.2 percent of total CO_2 emissions in 1994. Emissions of CO_2 from the road transport sector will continue to present a difficult environmental problem for Japanese policymakers, particularly as they attempt to meet the more stringent binding targets of the Kyoto Protocol. In this context, the government has placed further CO_2 emission reductions on the country's institutional agenda.

The Japanese government has formulated policies primarily under the guidelines of the 1990 Action Program to Arrest Global Warming. These guidelines are largely economic instruments such as government subsidies to public transport, traffic management, and alternatively powered vehicle programs as well as fiscal measures to promote sales of fuel-efficient vehicles. The government has also used regulatory policies that set vehicle fuel consumption standards and implement measures to promote combined transport. Voluntary agreements have played a small role in CO_2 emission management—involving voluntary fuel-efficiency targets for autos and light trucks.

The most notable policy reform controversy relating to CO_2 emission reductions surrounded the adoption of the 1993 Basic Law for the Environment. This law was notable not so much for what it accomplished but for what it failed to achieve. The policy formulation stage of this legislation took place through close consultations between industry and the bureaucracy. The Environment Agency advocated the introduction of an environmental tax as a means of reducing CO_2 emissions. This proposal brought strong opposition from several other government ministries, especially the Ministry of Construction and the Ministry of International Trade and Industry, both of which are closely connected to industry. In addition, the country's most powerful business organization, the *Keidranen*, strongly opposed the proposal. By 1993 the Japanese economic bubble had burst, and business was focused on blocking stricter environmental regulatic.is perceived as economically detrimental. Thus these ministries and industry argued that economic expansion should take precedence over environmental concerns. Because the Environment Agency is much less influential than the ministries that opposed the environmental tax, the proposed legislation was weakened considerably, and the tax was omitted entirely. In this instance (and as is often the case), industry's close connection to the bureaucracy was highly effective in influencing policy development.

Although environmental groups were unhappy with the 1993 law, they had no say in its formulation, nor were they able to influence the decision-making process. Environmental groups exist in Japan, but there is not a strong national-level movement and a green party has not emerged. The strong industrial-bureaucratic linkage in Japan, combined with relatively few access points to the highly centralized decision-making process, meant that interest groups were weak and ineffective overall. In addition, because policymakers are unreceptive to citizen involvement on environmental issues (indeed most issues) at the national level, public opinion made no difference on the 1993 decision.

There are no significant implementation concerns for policies in this area at present. The implementation of all environmental policies remains under strict bureaucratic control. Environmental policies receive ample bureaucratic attention and are implemented efficiently. As Japan's government continues to develop policies to meet its existing commitments, it likely will be forced to create new sorts of policy instruments in this area, many of which may be more controversial among the general public and industry. For example, the government has yet to develop a taxation system for vehicle ownership and fuel use that would provide incentives for the use of more fuel-efficient passenger cars, commercial vehicles, and ships that emit less CO_2. The use of economic instruments such as taxes and charges may be the next policy approach to be adopted by the national government.

The reform process in Japan is explained by two key factors: economic concerns and the existence of a closed policy network in this policy area. The Japanese government's CO_2 emission control policies have thus far failed to include economic instruments (most notably, taxes) that could make significant inroads toward the country's emission reduction goals. This situation reflects the ability of industry to prevent the adoption of measures that involve significant costs, based on arguments that such measures will reduce international competitiveness. Because environmental policy formulation and decision making occur through a pattern of close consultation between business and industry, with no room for environmental groups or public opinion in the policy formulation or decision-making process, policy outputs reflect the wishes of industry and the bureaucracy. The absence of a strong environmental interest group at the national level in Japan, coupled with little public interest in the problem of global warming, results in little pressure being placed on the government to open up this policy network for more debate and discussion.

Germany

Background: Policy Process and Policy History

The German constitution does not allocate legislative responsibility for the environment to different levels of government. As a result, the distribution of environmental responsibility has differed among environmental areas. In most cases, federal environmental law supersedes state law. Air quality management has fallen predominantly under the domain of the federal government. Federal environmental policy is managed by the Federal Ministry for the Environment, Nature Conservation, and Nuclear Safety, created in 1986.

The German constitution makes state governments responsible for implementation of environmental protection laws. Once environmental standards are set, the federal government's authority ends and the states are responsible for enforcement. State governments are usually free to establish the specific institutional arrangements for carrying out these laws, thereby creating the possibility for notable differences at the implementation stage. With respect to air quality management, state governments may grant permits; set penalties, fines, or sanctions; monitor ambient air pollution; and identify so-called investigation and smog areas. They are also responsible for developing emission inventories and air pollution abatement plans for these areas. Finally, the states are permitted to develop their own policies for locally specific air pollution problems, such as traffic control in smog-prone areas.

Successful environmental policy implementation in Germany requires a significant degree of cooperation between the federal government and the states. To facilitate this process, a number of highly effective committees and working groups exist, comprising both federal and state representatives, that facilitate coordination and cooperation. For example, the Conference of Environment Ministers includes ministers from both levels of government. These bodies are generally successful in harmonizing environmental policy enforcement in the states.

The Schroeder government plans to draw all of Germany's existing environmental regulations together into a single environmental code. Regulatory reform will take place as part of this process. In addition, the government has indicated a desire to move away from a regulatory approach to environmental problems and toward a greater emphasis on economic incentives. To date, however, little action has been taken in this regard.

Concern over air quality has been a central focus of German environmental policy making since the early 1970s. The German approach to air quality management relies primarily on direct regulation involving strict standards and limited use of economic instruments. German policy especially is focused on pollution prevention, emphasizing the development of technology-oriented standards and new methods for eliminating air pollution. Germany has transposed the EU's environmental directives into national law and is party to all international agreements on air quality.

The primary mechanism for controlling air pollution in Germany is direct regulation adopted at the federal level. Such regulations involve emission standards, the use of best available technology, fuel quality standards, and product standards. The foundation of air management policy in Germany is the

1974 Federal Immission Control Act.[3] The 1974 act provides an overarching framework for licensing of industrial facilities, air pollution monitoring, and enforcement. More than twenty ordinances are involved in the implementation of the act. In addition, three administrative regulations, the most important of which is the Technical Instruction on Air Quality Control (TI Air), are uniformly implemented throughout the country and have addressed numerous pollutants from a variety of sources. Overall, the German air quality management program is one of the strictest and most successful among the industrialized countries.

Many of the air quality regulations that Germany has implemented are targeted to control production facilities. In particular, the government has focused on limiting emissions from large combustion installations. The Ordinance on Large Combustion Plants set stringent emission standards based on best available technology for dealing with SO_x and NO_x emissions. Industrial sources of air pollutants are regulated under the TI Air that calls for the adoption of continuously evolving state-of-the-art controls. The TI Air is invoked on the premise that the higher the potential risk of a pollutant, the more stringent the controls or emission limits should be. This regulation thus involves best available control technology requirements and emission limits specific to individual industries. Emission limits are set for all industrial pollutants. Since coming to office in 1998, the new center-left government has indicated its intention to strengthen enforcement of the best available technology standard, although mechanisms for doing so have not been introduced.

This emission control approach is accompanied in Germany by the setting of ambient air quality standards (or as the Germans call them, *immissions values*) under TI Air. These standards are linked directly to the process of licensing polluting facilities. To obtain a license, industries must demonstrate that they will keep their immission values within acceptable levels or implement additional controls to meet these standards. Although ambient air quality is not monitored at the national level, state governments are required to maintain monitoring systems in more polluted areas.

Federal regulations and economic instruments aimed at transport-related pollution focus on controlling automobile emissions and fuel quality. These regulations involve the use of state-of-the-art technology, emission standards for heavy vehicles, periodic inspection of older vehicles, and bans on leaded gasoline and certain fuel additives. Economic incentives in regulating emissions include reduced taxes on cars with three-way catalytic converters and on vehicles that use unleaded gasoline or that have diesel engines with lower particulate emissions.

Germany also has implemented a fairly elaborate system of smog control in which the states designate areas with high concentrations of air pollutants

---

[3]The term *immission* refers in this context to the concentration of a substance in an environmental medium.

that lead to smog incidents. At the federal level, three grades of smog intensity are defined: When the second level is exceeded, traffic restrictions are issued; when the third level is exceeded, industrial activity is halted. Smog areas are defined in both western and eastern Germany, and in recent years, smog levels in the west rarely have triggered a second-level warning. The new government has signaled that it will make summer smog restrictions tighter and enforce them more strictly.

Until recently, Germany did not use voluntary agreements for air pollution control, and economic incentives were used only in a limited fashion to reduce motor vehicle emissions. The Schroeder government, however, has indicated that it will reform the existing regulatory framework for the environment, particularly by increasing the use of voluntary agreements and economic instruments. These reforms have yet to be introduced.

Germany is a leader in the global movement to protect the environment. The country is party to many international agreements setting overall emission reduction goals and standards for transborder air pollution control as well as global measures. Germany also is a strong supporter of global efforts to prevent climate change and to protect the ozone layer. For example, Germany was the first country to have completed the CFC reductions called for under the Montreal Protocol.

Contemporary Dynamics

Like the United States and Japan, Germany has committed to reducing its greenhouse gas emissions under the FCCC and the Kyoto Protocol. Despite stringent and successful emission controls, however, growth in the number of motor vehicles and their increased use make it seem unlikely that the country will meet its air quality standards, particularly regarding CO_2 emissions. Germany anticipates a 45 percent growth in freight traffic up to 2010 and a 32–43 percent growth in passenger traffic. The eastern region of the country in particular is expected to have increasing transport-related emission problems as motor vehicle use rises in response to increasing levels of economic activity, increased affluence that leads to increase motor vehicle ownership and usage, the opening of an extensive new highway system, and the opening of borders to eastern and central European countries. Overall the demand for road-based transport is continuing unabated. Germany is the EU's largest emitter of greenhouse gases, and CO_2 is by far the most abundant emission. Unification significantly worsened the CO_2 balance in the country; in 1990, for example, 30 percent of German CO_2 emissions came from the five new states. In this context the government has placed further CO_2 emission reductions on the country's institutional agenda.

In the 1990s recognition of the continuing problems arising from transport activities prompted the center-right Kohl government to set additional quantitative targets aimed at reducing CO_2 emissions. Taking 1987 as the base year, the Kohl government planned to reduce CO_2 emissions by 25 percent by 2005 (this target was reconfirmed in 1992). The target was strengthened in 1995, with the base year reset to 1990, when CO_2 emissions were 5 percent lower than in 1987. This is an ambitious target that goes well beyond Germany's international commitments as well as those made by most other industrialized countries.

The ability to set such stringent targets emerged from an unusual agenda-setting experience. In 1987 the government set up a nonpartisan inquiry commission (the Enquete Commission) to study climate change. In 1990 this commission issued three reports that created the basis for a common definition of the problem, climate change, while recommending the adoption of strict emission reduction targets. Because the commission, rather than political parties, the Bundestag, interest groups, or ministries, reached this conclusion, it was possible to establish a broad national consensus around which to act. The commission's reports raised the public's awareness of climate change issues and set the institutional agenda for reform via a mobilization model.

To formulate policies necessary to achieve these lofty goals, an interministerial working group on CO_2 reduction was created. Thus far the use of voluntary agreements in this area is limited but not insignificant. For example, the German government entered into an agreement with automobile manufacturers calling for a 25 percent reduction in automobiles' average fuel consumption between 1990 and 2005. The government also relies heavily on economic instruments to incorporate the environmental cost of transport into fuel costs (including fuel taxes to discourage driving, subsidies to encourage public transport and for traffic management systems, road taxes and pricing, and fiscal measures to promote sales of fuel-efficient vehicles). Because Germany emphasizes informal consultations in the policy-making process, particularly with industry but also with environmental groups, these policy measures have not been strongly opposed by industry or the general public. The German population tends to be relatively more environmentally aware and environmentally demanding than the public in other industrialized countries and traditionally is less likely to oppose significant environmental reforms. These policies are associated with no unusual implementation concerns.

Despite public consensus on global warming problems, an effort to extend Germany's frequent use of economic instruments to a CO_2 tax was unsuccessful. Environmental interest groups, the Green Party, scientists, and the center-left Social Democratic Party favored developing such a tax, and in 1996 the Social Democratic Party and the Free Democratic Party together proposed a CO_2 tax in the Bundestag. The decision-making stage of this proposal was marked by a great deal of controversy. The proposal was immediately denounced by the Christian Democratic Union/Christian Social Union as unfeasible and expensive. Fearing a loss of international competitiveness, German industrial associations also opposed the proposal and instead pushed for a voluntary agreement. The government was not prepared to force the adoption of a tax despite it being a necessary means to reach the country's ambitious emission reduction target. Instead, industry's opposition ruled the day, and the government conceded to industry's calls for voluntary agreements.

Since 1992, little more has been achieved in policy reform regarding climate change. The costs of unification, growing budget deficits, and high and rising unemployment combined to reduce the importance of environmental issues to political leaders and the public. Until recently there was little discussion of measures to ensure that the targeted emission reductions will be achieved.

The Green Party, as the junior partner in the current governing coalition, is placing considerable pressure on the Social Democrats to rectify this situation. The Schroeder government has renewed Germany's commitment to achieving the Kohl government's ambitious target of reducing CO_2 emissions by 25 percent over 1990 levels by 2005. The government also has proposed a wide range of transport-related initiatives, including reforms designed to increase rail and water transport, reduce road transport, increase taxes on energy consumption (which would be accompanied by reduced taxes on labor income), and gradually introduce a tax on energy consumption (which went into effect in 1999).

Because the German public is relatively mobilized on environmental issues (as evidenced by the presence of the industrialized countries' oldest and most successful Green Party and the activities of a variety of environmental interest groups), the country has a substantial environmental policy reform record. Despite this commitment and public mobilization, the move to more stringent economic instruments to control CO_2 emissions was no more successful in Germany than in the other industrialized countries examined in this book. The failure to adopt an environmental tax to meet the country's stringent emission targets can be explained by both economic and political factors. Concerns about the competitive position of the German economy mean that policy choices must be justified to both the public and industry in terms of their cost neutrality. Thus arguments that environmental policies destroy jobs and reduce industrial competitiveness carry significant weight in policy debates. Measures seen as threatening to economic growth or the country's global competitiveness are destined to fail, especially given the corporatist arrangements that exist between government and industry. The pattern of close consultation in policy making between these players means that any measures perceived as harmful to industry are less likely to succeed.

France

Background: Policy Process and Policy History

Environmental policy in France has been managed by the Ministry of the Environment since 1971. This is a large bureaucratic organization with wide-ranging responsibilities, covering most areas of environmental protection and overseeing a large number of environmental agencies in the country. For example, the ministry oversees twenty-four regional directorates of industry, research, and environment (DRIREs), along with twenty-six regional departments of the environment. The DRIREs include among their responsibilities air quality management and local implementation of national policies. The ministry's financial resources were increased in the early 1990s to improve its ability to implement and enforce policies. The minister of the environment also leads an interministerial committee for environmental affairs that includes representatives from all government ministries and is charged with ensuring the integration of policies across ministries and reviewing the actions of ministries to ensure that they reflect environmental requirements. In general, the environmental policy process in France has involved central-level actors playing a key role in both policy making and implementation.

Since 1990, a more fully integrated approach to environmental pollution control and prevention has been pursued in France under the new National Environment Plan. This plan was especially targeted toward strengthening environmental policy implementation. Most environmental policies in France are adopted at the national level (although some regions also have their own administrative structures) and are then implemented at the lower levels of government, particularly at the department level through the local branches of different ministries. Many useful policy coordination mechanisms are at work in this system. In general, the environmental policy process in France is relatively well managed and effective.

Although France came later to the process of environmental protection than many of its European neighbors, its record on air quality management, which came into full force in the 1980s, is still viewed as being comprehensive, well coordinated, and effective. The government uses a variety of policy options for environmental protection, relying most heavily on direct regulations and economic instruments. The focus of these policies is on integrated pollution control. France has transposed most of the EU's environmental directives into national law, has made a serious attempt to implement these laws, and is a strong supporter of further EU action on the environment.

The majority of environmental policies directed toward air pollution in France are direct regulations. The French government first set air quality objectives with the 1961 Law on the Control of Atmospheric Pollution and Odors; these objectives were further defined in a 1977 law on classified facilities, which set standards for emissions from stationary sources based on best available technology. A national air quality monitoring system introduced in 1974 is run by associations throughout the country that operate with the approval of the Ministry of the Environment.

France also uses economic instruments to control industrial emissions. Charges on emissions from stationary sources were introduced in 1985 and extended in 1990 and 1995. Taxes on petroleum products, in the form of gasoline and diesel taxes, are high compared to other industrialized countries. French gasoline taxes were the highest in the OECD in 1995. France uses voluntary agreements with industry in a limited fashion, primarily to reduce CO_2 emissions and curtail energy use.

The French government supports and participates actively in international cooperative efforts on the environment. France is a signatory to all the major international agreements with regard to the major air pollutants and on more global issues such as ozone-depleting substances. France's record on meeting international environmental standards, both globally and within the EU, is among the best of the industrialized countries.

Contemporary Dynamics

France has ratified the FCCC and is a signatory to the Kyoto Protocol. The French government committed itself in 1994 to reducing the country's green-house gas emissions to 1990 levels by 2000. Although France is expected to meet its own 2000 CO_2 emission targets, its emission levels will be 9 percent higher than 1990 levels. With CO_2 emissions expected to continue to increase, the country must develop policies to meet the new targets introduced under the Kyoto Protocol. Despite recent improvements in fuel efficiency and motor vehicle emissions, the country's expanding transport sector places increasing pressure on air quality through the increased volume of emissions of many pollutants, especially CO_2.

Between 1970 and 1994, private vehicle traffic in France doubled, air transport increased by an average of 6 percent annually, and goods transport by road rose by 70 percent; between 1985 and 1995, freight traffic by road increased by 5 percent annually (OECD 1997: 159). In addition, vehicle ownership has risen and vehicles have increased in size, while their fuel efficiency has declined. As a result, in 1997, transport (especially road transport) in France was responsible for 33 percent of CO_2 emissions; of the 6 percent increase in net CO_2 emissions forecast for the country from 1990 to 2005, 80 percent will come from road transport. Although France's CO_2 emissions dropped by 27 percent from 1980 to 1994, they still account for 81 percent of the country's green-house gas emissions.

France has a less severe problem with CO_2 emissions than other industrialized countries. France has already reduced CO_2 emissions more per capita than any other EU country, and only Sweden has done better among the OECD countries. France has fewer energy-based and industrial sources of CO_2; for example, the country's use of nuclear power reduces the need for burning fossil fuel. Nonetheless, increasing transport-related emissions continue to make CO_2 levels a source of concern.

As in the other industrialized countries, these environmental issues arrived on France's systemic agenda as a result of external pressures, but they have yet to achieve important status on the institutional agenda. Because France previously reduced CO_2 emission levels substantially, the country tends to rest on its laurels. The primary French response to its international commitments has been a continuation of its previous policies, particularly with reference to reducing emissions from the transport sector.

Most French policies to control CO_2 emissions are economic instruments (including government subsidies for public transport and cleaner technology development, road taxes and pricing, and fiscal measures to promote sales of fuel-efficient vehicles). Recognizing that fuel consumption and CO_2 emissions are directly proportional, the French government effectively uses fuel taxes to control transport emissions—these taxes were the highest in the OECD countries in 1995 (at 81 percent of the pump price of gasoline). Regulatory policy in this area is limited to greater speed limit enforcement and vehicle inspections, and voluntary agreements have been signed with car manufacturers to limit CO_2 emissions by 2005. Government and industry also set up a working group on reducing these emissions and entered into a voluntary agreement for the development of alternatively powered vehicles.

Such policy reforms have been introduced and supported by governments of the left and right. Most of these policies were introduced by the mid-1990s and continue to be supported more recently by the Jospin government. Further reforms are not currently contemplated. The major political parties have tended to downplay environmental (and especially climate change) concerns. Although public opposition to existing transport-related policies is scant, climate change issues are not a large concern overall; thus little pressure exists for additional government action. The general feeling is that France makes a minor contribution to a global problem that it cannot do much about. Further, this attitude is not condemned by the environmental movement, which tends to focus its efforts on local rather than national initiatives. Although France has several green parties (one of which currently participates in the governing coalition), these parties and the environmental movement overall have tended to be divided and weak, with little influence on the policy process. For the most part, industry also is cooperative in the emission reduction process, especially concerning voluntary cooperation. As in the other industrialized countries, France's support for policies that rely more heavily on increasing taxes or instituting strict emission targets is far less strong. Taken together, these attitudes result in little political will to act on these issues.

France has no technical implementation concerns related to existing air quality policies—although to the extent that some of these policies involve real economic costs for users, they will be easier to implement in times of economic growth than in an economic downturn. Some complaints have been lodged about increasing consumers' costs through even higher taxes, but evidence indicates that the country's history of high fuel taxes gives the government more leeway in raising these rates, on the theory that they are already so high that people will not notice paying a few cents more.

Given that the continued increase in CO_2 emissions is expected to come primarily from the transport sector, policymakers will need to develop more restrictive policies in this sector and to better integrate environmental and transport policies. Policies currently under discussion include additional increases in fuel taxes and encouragement of an EU-wide CO_2 taxation scheme. France is also actively pressing the EU for harmonization in fuel taxation and prices, a proposal that has not made much headway.

The absence of further reforms to meet the more stringent targets the country faces under the Kyoto Protocol is the result of a lack of mobilization on these issues among the French public. In part, public indifference is the result of concerns about economic growth and competitiveness in the country, and neither the public nor the government has any interest in new policy measures that will increase the costs of transport and production. Further, substantial reductions in the past have significantly reduced the public's and the government's sense of urgency, putting little pressure on the government to act. Thus the absence of a substantial movement for reform, combined with concerns about international competitiveness and the belief that France has already made substantial progress, means that further reform has not occurred.

United Kingdom

Background: Policy Process and Policy History

Environmental policy in the United Kingdom traditionally was controlled at the central level through the Department of the Environment. Since 1990 the country's environmental policy making and implementation structure has undergone substantial restructuring. The 1990 Environmental Protection Act created a new system known as integrated pollution control (IPC). Under this system, Her Majesty's Inspectorate for Pollution is the enforcement agency responsible in England and Wales for regulating releases to air, water, and land from the most polluting industrial processes (in Scotland, regulation is the responsibility of the Scottish Environmental Protection Agency). Local authorities in the United Kingdom also play an important role in environmental protection, particularly for responding to problems not addressed by the IPC system. Control over environmental policies is one of the powers currently being devolved to the new parliaments in Northern Ireland, Scotland, and Wales.

IPC is designed to minimize the risk of environmental pollution through the use of pollution prevention measures at the source. Ultimately the system is intended to regulate all polluters that discharge more than one pollutant, although to date the system is directed at large polluters. IPC represents a significant change in environmental management policy, not only for the United Kingdom but also when compared to the environmental management approaches found in the other industrialized countries.

IPC involves two parallel pollution control systems. First, industrial processes considered potentially the most polluting must obtain a single authorization for all releases to air, land, and water. Obtaining such authorization requires an environmental impact assessment of all releases, a determination of the "best practical environmental option," and application of the principle of "best available techniques not entailing excessive cost" for pollution prevention and abatement.

The second pollution control system applies to more minor polluters. These facilities must obtain authorization from local authorities and apply the principle of best available techniques for air emissions only. Both central and local authorities are required by the 1990 act to track best available technologies and upgrade standards as appropriate, with authorizations renewed every four years. The act does not specifically indicate which industrial activities are subject to IPC, and thus far definition of such processes is difficult. As such, development of consistent environmental and economic assessment policies is an ongoing process.

IPC also represents a significant departure in environmental policy in the United Kingdom because of a much stricter enforcement mechanism. If a pollution producer fails to receive authorization, violates its authorization, or fails to comply with any legal requirements, unlimited fines may be imposed. In addition, regulatory authorities are strongly encouraged and more likely to initiate charges for violators. The number of pollution control inspectors also is increased.

The United Kingdom has a long history of environmental policy making that has emphasized pollution control rather than pollution prevention. Environmental policies in the United Kingdom involve the use of direct regulations, economic instruments, and international agreements. The United Kingdom has made an effort to adopt and implement all EC environmental directives and is a strong supporter of an even more integrated European environmental program.

In the past, and continuing under the new IPC structure, British environmental policy has stressed the use of direct regulation. Until recently, air quality, was controlled primarily under the provisions of the 1956 Clean Air Act (revised in 1968 and consolidated in 1993), which regulated emissions of particulates. Some air quality issues formerly covered under this act are now covered under IPC. In the area of air quality, the United Kingdom has resisted pressure to set quantitative targets for air pollution emission reductions or ambient air quality standards. When such targets were set, it was generally in response to requirements imposed by EC directives or international agreements. Under the provisions of the 1995 Environment Act, the secretary of state for the environment was charged with producing a national air quality strategy that involved targets and standards to serve as a general framework for air quality management efforts.

The 1997 National Air Quality Strategy set standards for eight common air pollutants, based primarily on their effects on human health but also with attention paid to their broader environmental effects (seven of these objectives were later incorporated into the 1997 Air Quality Regulation Act). This strategy requires local authorities (under a system known as local air pollution control created by the 1990 Environmental Protection Act) to monitor air quality in their localities and, where these standards are not likely to be met by 2005, to create air quality management areas and develop plans for meeting these goals in these areas. The Labour government completed a review of this strategy in 1998 and introduced new standards based on this review in early 2000.

The United Kingdom has a regular system for testing and inspecting motor vehicles for exhaust emissions and has introduced but not yet implemented a plan for roadside vehicle emission testing. Motor vehicle emissions are controlled under the 1972 and 1974 Road Traffic Acts. Since 1991, the United Kingdom has tested hydrocarbon and CO_2 emissions, and smoke emissions from light diesel vehicles have been tested since 1993. In addition, since 1992, all new vehicles must be fitted with catalytic converters. Regulatory policies also govern fuel quality, although the sulfur content of fuel is regulated only in London and leaded fuel has not been banned.

The British government has encouraged the use of unleaded fuel through tax differentials for leaded and unleaded gasoline since 1986. Although the use of economic instruments is otherwise limited, a number of additional uses are being considered as part of the IPC system, and government proposals in 1998 indicate an intention to provide further economic incentives for environmental protection.

Voluntary agreements are not used extensively in the United Kingdom. In part this reflects a pattern of close consultation between government and industry in environmental regulatory policy development. In some areas with some air quality problems, voluntary codes of conduct have been developed, but their use is not widespread.

The United Kingdom has a strong record on developing, ratifying, and fully implementing international environmental agreements. In a departure from its domestic environmental policies, the British government advocates creating and using quantitative targets to reach international environmental policy goals. The United Kingdom also supports European efforts to reduce transborder air pollution (a large portion of which the United Kingdom produces) and is a strong supporter of the major global agreements on ozone depletion, acid rain, and prevention of climate change. The British government advocates developing measures that allow for the effective implementation and enforcement of these agreements and supports future environmental cooperation among countries.

Contemporary Dynamics

Despite some improvements in air quality during the 1980s and 1990s, CO_2 emissions in the United Kingdom, particularly in urban areas, continue to increase as a result of the growth in motor vehicle use. In 1970 there were some 10 million passenger cars in the country; by 1994 there were well over 20 million, and the amount of traffic per year had nearly doubled (OECD 1994d: 94). From 1990 to 1996, total CO_2 emissions in the United Kingdom fell by 3 percent as result of switching from coal to natural gas in industry. However, transport is now the fastest growing source of CO_2 emissions in the United Kingdom. In 1996 the percentage of CO_2 emissions deriving from the transport sector was 20 percent, and road transport's share of CO_2 emissions are forecast to increase to 25 percent of emissions in 2000 (from 20 percent in 1990). In fact, transport is expected to account for all of the country's projected increases in CO_2 emissions between 1970 and 2020. In this context, the government has placed further CO_2 emission reductions on the country's institutional agenda.

Policy formulation with respect to transport and the environment continues the government's tradition of close consultation between regulatory agencies and industry. Because core policy networks in the United Kingdom remain strong, meaning that at best environmental groups are consulted only intermittently in the policy process, these closed policy communities have been successful at preventing stricter emission controls and defending producer interests. The new Labour government, through the creation of several discussion forums, has worked to encourage this consultative process. There is no green party movement in the United Kingdom, although a strong and well-organized lobby for the environment exists.

To meet its commitments under the FCCC, the United Kingdom's Conservative government issued its first climate change program in 1994. This program passed through a long consultative process with a wide range of affected interests before being proposed in the House of Commons. A carbon/energy tax was ardently resisted by the policy communities around ministries such as the Treasury, the Department of Trade and Industry, and the Department of Transport, which fought against the tax because it would influence industrial competitiveness. Consequently the use of such economic instruments was ruled out. To date, the United Kingdom has used a mix of regulatory instruments, such as traffic management, development of climate change program guidelines, mandatory transport plans for companies, and efforts to integrate transport and land use planning, and economic instruments, such as fuel taxes, tax exemptions or reductions to promote the use of certain fuels, government subsidies to encourage use of public transport, and fiscal advantages for public transport companies. Fuel taxes have increased annually in the United Kingdom since 1993 (with an average annual increase of 6.75 percent for unleaded gasoline, 7.75 percent for leaded, and 8.25 percent for diesel).

The new Labour government extended the United Kingdom's commitment to reducing CO_2 emissions to 20 percent of their 1990 levels by 2010 (higher than the Kyoto target), which will require dramatic policy changes. The Labour government initially favored annual increases in fuel taxes of at least 6 percent on average above inflation (1 percent higher than the previous government's commitment). In 1999, however, the government announced its decision to eliminate these annual increases (the so-called fuel tax escalator) in response to industrial pressures. The Labour government also entered into voluntary agreements with auto manufacturers to meet vehicle fuel-efficiency targets. The Greener Motoring Forum, a voluntary grouping of about 70 organizations that have an interest in transport issues, was established in 1994 to develop a common message about environmentally responsible motoring. Along these same lines, the government formed the Cleaner Vehicles Forum to bring together government, the motor and oil industries, and environmentalists to promote fuel efficiency and the development of less polluting new vehicles. The government also sponsors the Air Quality Forum, which brings together stakeholders and allows them to express their views on air quality management issues. Finally, a new superministry, the Department of the Environment, Transport, and the Regions, was created to improve policy integration and implementation.

In 1999 the government announced its intention to introduce a so-called climate change levy in April 2001 that will apply to business use of electricity, gas, and solid fuels. In an effort to ward off business opposition, the revenue from this tax will be recycled to businesses, primarily through reductions in employer national insurance contributions and will be used to support new plans to promote energy efficiency and renewable energy. The government has pointed out that it is not creating a new revenue source with the tax, and negotiations with affected interests are under way.

The increasing size and volume of transport in the United Kingdom means that much remains to be done to effectively reduce CO_2 emissions from this sector, especially in the face of the new binding targets set at Kyoto. To meet these new targets, the Labour government's New Deal for Transport (introduced in 1998) includes plans for increasing the tax differential on diesel and gasoline fuels, further focusing the tax system to deliver its environmental objectives and increasing public awareness of the need to reduce road transport. At the same time the U.K. Strategy for Sustainable Development makes a commitment to reducing transport's environmental impact. The government has also announced plans to improve the integration of transport, environmental, and energy policies to improve policy implementation. What remains to be seen is the manner and speed with which these commitments are translated into specific policy measures once the consultation process gets under way.

The nature of adopted policy reforms in the United Kingdom reflects the influence of those concerned about economic costs and international competitiveness. Despite its commitment to significant reductions in CO_2 emissions, the government has not been successful in pursuing the policies necessary to achieve these goals. The failure to adopt new environmental taxes and a recent decision to halt regular increases in gasoline taxation levels reflect the ability of industrial concerns to shape environmental policies. Industrial concerns have this ability because the policy formulation process is based on close consultative arrangements between industry and business that usually excludes advocates for more stringent environmental policies. At the decision-making stage, single-party government ensures that policy decisions made in this consultation process survive in the resulting legislation and that they are implemented effectively.

Italy

Background: Policy Process and Policy History

Government policies for environmental protection in Italy begin with the 1947 Italian constitution, which guarantees individuals' right to health and safeguards the natural, historic, and cultural heritage of the nation. Environmental legislation may be drafted by the Italian parliament, by the government, or by regional authorities. Protection of the environment also is pursued through decrees issued by the president of the republic, the president of the Council of Ministers, or by an individual minister with delegation from the parliament.

Environmental policies in Italy are drafted at the level of central government and implemented by lower levels of government, which can result in varying levels of implementation across regions. The 20 regions and 103 provinces have varying abilities to carry out these responsibilities owing to differences in size, resources, and administrative structures. The effectiveness of Italian environmental policies is generally viewed as being limited by the weaknesses of regional and provincial institutions and by a lack of coordination and linkage between central and regional levels, particularly in terms of defining responsibilities and providing adequate financial support for implementation costs. In addition, the Italian government's rigid regulatory framework provides local authorities with little to no discretion in the policy implementation process.

Italy established a national-level Ministry of the Environment in 1986 that coordinates and integrates environmental activities in the country and creates new policy instruments. This and other central-level environmental institutions are relatively short on human and financial resources. The ministry is charged with developing and administrating Italy's relatively new three-year environmental management programs, which lay out plans for allocating central revenues to the regions and provinces for environmental expenditures. These plans are the primary source of environmental money for subnational levels of government.

Italy faces real challenges regarding environmental policy coordination between central, regional, and other levels of government. National-level institutions lack both the resources and organizational strength to manage the policy process effectively. In addition to their own weaknesses, central government agencies thus far have had great difficulty in guaranteeing uniform implementation of regulations across regions, reflecting a high degree of subnational government autonomy. To improve this coordination, additional monetary resources, stronger enforcement mechanisms, and improved monitoring capabilities are needed at the central and regional levels. Such improvements will be possible only to the degree that the regional and local administrative units are strengthened (institutionally and financially) so that they can effectively fulfill their responsibilities.

The Italian government has been developing policies to improve air quality since the 1960s. Laws governing air quality are extremely complex and inconsistently implemented. Policies focus primarily on eliminating pollution rather than preventing it and include a combination of direct regulations, economic incentives, and voluntary and international agreements. Italian environmental laws reflect the content of nearly all EU environmental directives.

The main thrust of the Italian government's air quality management effort is through direct regulation. Italy's first comprehensive air quality legislation, the Clean Air Law, was adopted in 1966. Before this legislation, Italian air quality policies were piecemeal efforts that addressed specific, localized problems. Air pollution is now regulated under the 1988 Industrial Air Pollution Law, which allocates a wide range of responsibilities to the regions for both improving and monitoring air quality. Regions are charged with developing plans for protecting, conserving, and cleaning up their territories while complying with national air quality limits; setting emission limits based on best available technology within national guidelines; establishing air pollution monitoring; and reporting annually on air quality. Provinces are also required to monitor air emissions to meet national criteria.

Italy controls industrial emissions by issuing licensing permits for new and existing installations. Regional authorities issue permits to facilities that can demonstrate that emissions will fall within existing limits and that measures will be taken to prevent air pollution with current technology. In some regions, these responsibilities are passed on to the provinces. These requirements resulted in a large number of industrial plants requiring inspection and monitoring (estimated at between 300,000 and 600,000 premises) in an environment of limited resources and fragmented administration. Given these problems, a system of self-certification has been adopted.

The Italian government has introduced motor vehicle emission controls, including requiring all newly registered cars to be low-emission vehicles (equipped with three-way catalytic converters), in line with EU directives. Italy currently requires periodic emission inspections for all vehicles. The government also has proposed economic incentives to eliminate older vehicles and has adopted policies regarding fuel quality. Since 1978, taxes on all motor vehicle fuels have increased to such a degree that in 1994 Italy's fuel prices and taxes were the highest among the OECD countries. In 1992, fuel taxes were 66.3 percent of the full price for diesel, 75.8 percent for leaded gasoline, and 73.2 percent for unleaded gasoline (OECD 1994a: 75).

To control air pollution, Italy uses several mechanisms designed to control traffic in regions where severe pollution is a problem, particularly where air pollution has damaged historical buildings and artifacts. These measures typically include restricting access to the regions to public transport and low-emission vehicles or instituting odd-even plate access on alternate days.

Voluntary agreements among the government, trade unions, and auto manufacturers encourage the development of electric cars and the development of low-emission public transport. Agreements with oil industries also are used to improve fuel quality through lead and benzene content restrictions for gasoline and sulfur limits for diesel fuel.

Italy is an active participant in international cooperative efforts, both within the EU and on regional and global levels. The country has ratified most international air quality agreements and has integrated most EU air quality directives into national law. A lack of financial and personnel resources at the national, regional, and local levels, however, has resulted in an incomplete record with respect to the implementation and monitoring of these agreements. Italy has the dubious distinction of being the EU member state most frequently brought before the European Court of Justice for failing to comply adequately with EU environmental directives.

Contemporary Dynamics

Italy is also a party to the FCCC and has signed the Kyoto Protocol. A rise in CO_2 emission levels from the transport sector presents a challenge to Italian policymakers, particularly in the face of increasing passenger and freight traffic (an increase of 132 percent between 1970 and 1991, which is among the largest increases found in the industrialized countries). Emissions in the transport sector increased between 12 and 32 percent for various pollutants during the 1980s and continued to rise in the 1990s (OECD 1994a: 68). Although Italy CO_2 has one of the lowest levels of CO_2 emissions per capita among the OECD countries, the country's total emissions have increased since the 1980s. Like other industrialized countries, the gains achieved by existing emission policies are being offset by transport emissions, and stricter and more comprehensive policies are needed, particularly because current target levels of CO_2 are unlikely to be achieved at current rates of expansion in the transport sector. The government has placed further CO_2 emissions reductions on the country's institutional agenda.

Italy's official climate change strategy appears to be thin in content, especially regarding the transport sector. In 1994 the Ministry of the Environment formulated the National Program for Limiting CO_2 Emissions, which approaches CO_2 emission control largely through the use of economic instruments such as government subsidies for public transport, traffic management systems, alternatively powered vehicle development, and new technologies; fiscal measures to support sales of fuel-efficient vehicles; and vehicle fleet renewal. Italy has yet to use voluntary agreements to address CO_2 concerns, and specific regulations have been developed that relate only to speed limits outside of cities.

The decision-making stage of the 1994 program reflected the fact that industrial and energy producers were influential and able to protect their own interests. As a result, none of the program's measures placed limits on industrial or energy-related emissions. Since that time, climate change policy has appeared intermittently on the systemic agenda but with little real effect. The general political upheaval that Italy experienced in the first half of the 1990s hindered consistent environmental policy development, especially as the office of environment minister changed hands several times, and none of the office's occupants took environmental issues that seriously. Internal pressures have not played much of a role in environmental policy making in Italy. Although in the 1980s Italy had an active green party movement, by the 1990s the party had become fragmented and factionalized. Environmental issues have not been a high priority for mainstream partisan organizations. For example, recent attempts by the Ministry of the Environment to introduce environmentally conscious taxation and economic incentives in the Italian Financial Law did not succeed because partisan consensus about the problem is lacking. Although environmental interest groups have some ability to affect the policy process, they have not had a significant impact in this issue area of late, in particular because of a lack of citizen mobilization.

As in other areas of environmental policy, any air pollution policy measures face implementation difficulties in Italy because of a lack of coordination at the national, regional, and local levels and because of a lack of resources to monitor fully the process. Much remains for the Italian government to do when it comes to controlling CO_2 emissions. In particular, concrete measures concerning the transport sector are needed. For example, Italy has not gone as far as other industrialized countries with respect to vehicle inspections, exhaust emission controls, or the promotion of alternatives to road transport. In addition, Italy has yet to eliminate many of the country's transport-related tax deductions.

The lack of any substantial efforts to meet Italy's international commitments may be explained by economic, political, and institutional factors. Italian industrial and business interests have blocked the introduction of strong economic instruments for CO_2 emission controls on the grounds that such instruments will reduce the country's economic competitiveness and hinder economic growth. Given a general sense of economic uncertainty, the Italian government has been receptive to these claims. Politically, the Italian green parties are ineffective environmental policy advocates, the mainstream political parties are uninterested in the environment, and the environmental interest groups are not important actors. As a result, the government faces little political pressure to act. Institutionally, the political disarray in Italy for much of the 1990s resulted in environmental issues dropping off the systemic and institutional agendas.

Cross-national Trends

We are now able to consider the overall approach to air quality management in these six countries, as well as how effective their policies have been in improving air quality. As we review these broader cross-national trends, we observe a striking similarity with respect to policy choices and outcomes. These patterns of environmental policy reform may be attributed to the interaction of cultural, political, economic, and institutional factors.

Policy Choices

Direct regulations were by far the most common policy instrument used by the countries examined in this book to address air quality management. For the most part, air quality management policies involve varying degrees of emission controls and limits, usually by controlling pollution at its source through a national set of targeted emission levels. The exceptions to this pattern are Germany and Japan, where such measures also are accompanied by regulations that strongly encourage the development of new technologies and the use of best available technologies.

The use of economic incentives is not a common policy choice among the industrialized countries, although these countries have an increasing tendency to utilize an economic approach to pollution control. In countries where economic incentives are a part of air quality policy frameworks, they most commonly involve fuel taxes. Such incentives include direct taxes on gasoline sales, differential tax rates for leaded and unleaded gasoline, and reduced taxes on fuel-efficient vehicles or on vehicles that use unleaded gasoline. The Italian government traditionally has led the way with such policies—in 1994 it imposed the highest fuel taxes in the OECD—although by 1997 this leading position was occupied by France. Germany and the United Kingdom also have enacted fuel taxation policies. The United States is a clear outlier when it comes to fuel taxation. Policymakers in the United States exhibit little inclination to attempt to reduce fuel consumption by using taxes to increase fuel prices.

Several countries, including the United States, have experimented with other economic incentive policies, such as emission trading or deposit-refund systems, tax rebates for technology development, or fees for emissions, but the use of such policies is not widespread. This cross-national pattern of low usage has begun to change, however. Policymakers have been more likely to consider alternative policy mechanisms, such as product charges and tradable permit systems, because regulatory devices are viewed as having reached their effective limits and pressures are increasing to improve the cost-effectiveness of solutions to environmental problems. Even so, regulatory mechanisms are likely to remain the primary environmental policy instrument for most industrialized countries.

A pattern of cross-national variation also is observed with respect to the use of voluntary agreements. Such agreements are by far the most infrequently used air pollution policy instrument. Some countries do not use them at all. Even in countries that use such agreements to a limited degree, they are only a small part of the nation's overall air pollution policy framework. The extreme exception to this pattern is Japan, where some 40,000 voluntary agreements between government and industry have been signed and effectively implemented. Since the early 1990s, however, the use of such agreements appears to be on the rise in all countries.

Finally, all six countries are willing participants in transborder and international air quality management agreements. Most of these countries are leaders in the movement to address environmental issues on a global scale. All six countries have implemented the major international agreements on air pollution control, albeit with varying degrees of compliance and effectiveness. These international agreements play an important role in agenda setting in these countries.

Policy Outcomes

Several trends can be observed in the effects of air quality policy during the 1980s and 1990s. First, the policies implemented by these six countries have generally been effective in reducing air emission levels and improving ambient air quality. Second, although substantial gains have been made, some of this progress has been eroded by continuing hazardous emissions in some sectors, particularly from the transport sector. Third, cross-national differences in policy implementation and coordination have resulted in a pattern of differential policy outcomes.

How well have these countries done in reducing their levels of the most common air pollutants—that is, of SO_x, NO_x, and CO_2? As Table 11–1 indicates, their records are mixed, with a significant degree of cross-national variation. All six countries reduced their levels of air pollutants and improved ambient air quality during the 1980s and early 1990s. However, some countries have made far more progress in this effort than others.

Although several countries have reduced air emission levels significantly for some pollutants, emission levels for other pollutants have been reduced only marginally, or even increased, in some of these countries. Emission levels for most air pollutants remain above OECD averages, and the levels of many pollutants continue to rise. In the United States, this trend implies that air quality and economic growth continue to be strongly related and also reflects an

Table 11-1 Trends in Atmospheric Emissions

Country	Emissions of SO_x (thousands of metric tons)			Emissions of NO_x (thousands of metric tons)			CO_2 Emissions from Energy Use (millions of metric tons)		
	1980	1995	Percent Change	1980	1995	Percent Change	1980	1997	Percent Change
France	3,348	959	−71.4%	1,646	1,729	5.0%	485	363	−25.2%
Germany	5,321ᵃ	2,118	−60.2	2,709ᵃ	2,007	−25.9	981ᵃ	884	−9.9
Italy	3,757	1,322	−64.8	1,638	1,768	7.9	374	424	13.4
Japan	1,277	903ᵇ	−29.3	1,622	1,409ᵃ	−13.1	917	1,173	27.9
United Kingdom	4,894	2,351	−52.0	2,460	2,145	−12.8	593	555	−6.4
United States	23,501	17,408	−25.9	22,258	21,561	−3.1	4,785	5,470	14.3

SOURCE: *OECD Environmental Data, Compendium 1999* (Paris: Organisation for Economic Co-operation and Development, 1999).

ᵃ 1990 data.

ᵇ 1992 data.

energy-intensive consumption pattern. The best record on air quality management is found in Germany, where the major air pollutant emissions levels are the most strictly controlled and effectively reduced.

Although these six countries have made good progress since the 1970s in improving air quality, reducing emission levels, and removing health risks, they are all in danger of sacrificing these gains to increased emission levels, especially from the transport sector. Since 1980, industrialized countries have experienced a remarkable increase in the size of their motor vehicle stocks, an accompanying increase in motor vehicle usage, and an increase in the size of their transport infrastructures (Table 11–2).

Paradoxically, although individual motor vehicle emission levels have decreased in these countries, the tremendous increases in motor vehicle volume and usage have rapidly eroded these gains. In all six countries, the transport sector's relative contribution to air pollution, especially CO_2 emissions, has increased dramatically since 1980 (Table 11–3). The increased emission levels generated by these enlarged transport sectors might well eliminate the air quality gains of the past twenty years—and reduce these countries' chances of meeting their targets for CO_2 emission reductions.

The challenge for governments, as they seek to further reduce greenhouse gas emissions, is to continue to devise strategies for reducing motor vehicle use, both by private individuals and by business and industry. This goal may be achieved through policies that encourage the development of alternative forms of transportation (in particular, public mass transportation systems) and that provide better incentives to citizens to use these systems (for example, through increased use of economic policy instruments, such as higher taxes on vehicles and fuel). Other alternatives include increased emphasis on research and development on new technologies (for example, for the development of vehicles fueled by cleaner alternatives to gasoline) or the provision of infor-

Table 11-2 Trends in the Transport Sector

Country	Road Network Length (thousands of kilometers)			Total Number of Motor Vehicles (thousands)			Road Traffic Volume (billions of kilometers traveled)		
	1980	1997	Percent Change	1980	1997	Percent Change	1980	1997	Percent Change
France	793	893	12.6%	21,705	31,239	43.9%	296	472	59.5%
Germany	636ᵃ	656	3.1	38,532ᵃ	44,035	14.3	574ᵃ	619	7.8
Italy	297	308	3.7	19,379	33,889	74.9	227	474	108.8
Japan	1,113	1,153	3.6	37,067	69,210	86.7	389	756	94.3
United Kingdom	339	399	17.7	17,358	29,824	71.8	242	445	83.9
United States	6,212	6,315	1.7	155,796	210,224	34.9	2,442	4,090	67.5

SOURCE: *OECD Environmental Data, Compendium 1999* (Paris: Organisation for Economic Co-operation and Development, 1999).

ᵃ1991 data.

Table 11-3 CO$_2$ Emissions from Transport, 1980–1997

Country	CO$_2$ Emissions (millions of metric tons)		
	1980	1997	Percent Change
France	95.5	141.2	47.9%
Germany	138.8	188.9	36.1
Italy	76.1	118.1	55.2
Japan	160.7	267.0	66.1
United Kingdom	99.5	148.1	48.8
United States	1,257.5	1,658.4	31.9

SOURCE: *OECD Environmental Data, Compendium 1999* (Paris: Organisation for Economic Co-operation and Development, 1999).

mation and education to change public behavior, in particular with the goal of increasing public transport usage and stabilizing private vehicle use.

Countries with more coordinated environmental policy structures have had a greater degree of success in implementing and monitoring environmental control systems. For example, the German environmental bureaucracy involves a substantial degree of coordination between federal and state authorities. In addressing air pollution problems, this system has allowed for comprehensive management programs that are implemented uniformly across the country and are effective in achieving their objectives. Similarly, Japan has well-coordinated and integrated environmental policy making and implementation processes, which has resulted in generally more favorable policy outcomes in that country.

The complexity of the relationships between different levels of government in the United States is a complicating factor in establishing effective air pollution control, although controls are managed somewhat through stricter national-level enforcement of regulations. These differences were not related solely to the policy coordination difficulties often found between levels of government in federal systems. The United Kingdom, despite its unitary system of government, traditionally had an environmental policy process that was also hampered by coordination and implementation difficulties and that reduced policy effectiveness. Recently these shortcomings have been addressed through the creation of an integrated pollution control system. Thus, despite a general cross-national pattern of air pollution policy convergence, marked differences in management of the policy implementation process have produced variation in policy outcomes.

Understanding Policy Reform

The case studies indicate that the interaction of cultural, economic, political, and institutional variables is key to understanding environmental policy reform. In particular, these variables are important for understanding why none of the six countries adopted the more stringent economic measures (for example, some form of an environmental tax on CO_2 emissions) believed to be necessary to reach the ambitious CO_2 emission reduction targets of the Kyoto Protocol.

Citizens' expectations about their rights and freedom with respect to the environment were a strong influence in the reform process only in the United States. There, the fact that citizens are strongly attached to their right to own and operate a vehicle, as well as the culture of the open road, limits the possibility that the government will adopt tax measures that increase the cost of motor vehicle use. The other industrialized countries have, in fact, increased the costs of motor vehicle use in order to reduce CO_2 emission levels to a far greater degree than is observed in the United States. In particular, the other countries have higher gasoline taxes.

The difficulty the six countries experienced in introducing strict economic measures was partly related to a lack of citizen mobilization around climate change issues. Although several of these countries have active environmental movements, such movements tend not to be highly effective in mobilizing the general public around climate change issues, in part because of the long-term nature of the problem. Citizens tend to be more aroused about environmental issues whose effects they already observe. In countries where climate change has yet to arouse public concern, such as the United States, Italy, and France, governments faced greater difficulty in enacting reforms. The French government, for example, failed to even place such measures on the country's institutional agenda. Even in countries where the population was more involved, however, the political influence of those opposed to the introduction of more stringent measures was often sufficient to override popular opinion, as we saw in Germany.

Economic factors greatly influenced the six countries' policy response to emission reduction goals. The introduction of environmental taxes to achieve CO_2 emission reductions was opposed in all six countries for reasons of international economic competitiveness. Environmental taxes were ruled out because they were seen to reduce industrial profitability. Because these proposed reforms impose costs on private economic interests, such interests are highly motivated to prevent their adoption. Thus, in an environment in which high priority is given to economic growth and industrial competitiveness, environmental reforms that increase the costs to industry or consumers fail to be enacted. As a result, less effective voluntary agreements are introduced as alternatives to environmental taxes.

In all six countries a variety of institutional frameworks benefit the interests groups opposed to economic instruments. More specifically, this reform situation reflects the power of industrial interests. Whether through the operation of closed policy networks, corporatist arrangements, or intensive lobbying efforts, industrial lobbies were successful in all six countries in opposing the introduction of economic measures. Thus a close connection exists between industry and government in this policy area in a variety of institutional settings, and industry has the ability to influence both policy formulation and policy decision making.

SUGGESTED READINGS

Andersen, Mikael, and Duncan Liefferink, eds. 1997. *European Environmental Policy: The Pioneers.* Manchester: Manchester University Press.

Braded, John, Henk Folmer, and Thomas S. Ulen, eds. 1996. *Environmental Policy with Political and Economic Integration: The European Union and the United States.* Brookfield, Vt.: Edward Elgar.

Caldwell, Lynton, and Robert Bartlett. 1997. *Environmental Policy: Transnational Issues and National Trends.* Westport, Conn.: Quorum Books.

Collier, Ute, and Ragnar Lofstedt. 1997. *Cases in Climate Change Policy.* London: Earthscan Publications.

Hanf, Kenneth, and Alf-Inge Jansen, eds. 1998. *Governance and Environment in Western Europe: Politics, Policy and Administration.* New York: Longman.

O'Riordan, Tim, and Jill Jager. 1996. *Politics of Climate Change: A European Perspective.* New York: Routledge.

Portney, Paul, ed. 1990. *Public Policies for Environmental Protection.* Washington, D.C.: Resources for the Future.

Rosenbaum, Walter A. 1998. *Environmental Politics and Policy.* 4th ed. Washington, D.C.: CQ Press.

Scheberle, Denise. 1997. *Federalism and Environmental Policy: Trust and the Politics of Implementation.* Washington, D.C.: Georgetown University Press.

Vig, Norman J., and Michael E. Kraft, eds. 2000. *Environmental Policy: New Directions for the Twenty-first Century.* Washington, D.C.: CQ Press.

Weale, Albert. 1992. *The New Politics of Pollution.* Manchester: Manchester University Press.

Chapter 12 **Conclusion**

Diverse policy-making contexts shaped different reform dynamics in the six countries examined in this book. The differences in the countries' cultural norms, public opinion, economic conditions, political party systems, interest group politics, and governing institutions clearly are meaningful. Amid this diversity, however, two major trends stand out. First, many issues formerly considered to be domestic concerns are becoming increasingly internationalized. Second, in virtually all seven of the policy areas examined in this book, cost-control concerns are a more visible influence on policy making than they were in past decades.

Contemporary Trends

Given the diversity of policy concerns addressed in this book, some people might expect that no clear trends could be identified across seven policy areas in six countries. Even though all six countries are industrialized and wealthy, with relatively large economies compared to most of the world, they are quite different from one another in many respects. Some countries have centralized government systems (France, Japan, and the United Kingdom), and others are much more decentralized (Germany and the United States). Some countries have been world economic powers for centuries (France and the United Kingdom), whereas the economies of others took off only after World War II (Italy and Japan). In the 1980s and 1990s, some countries embarked on sweeping political reform (Italy and Japan). Other polities have been marked by visible partisan conflicts and voter swings (France and the United States). In the same time period, two countries (Germany and the United Kingdom) had remarkably durable governments with one party controlling the prime ministry for nearly two decades without interruption.

Through the case studies in the preceding chapters we have seen different situations in which cultural, economic, political, and institutional distinctions among these countries have shaped policy making. For example, we have seen multiple illustrations of how the Westminster system of government is best suited to the party government model of policy making. British chief executives faced the smallest number of defeats in the legislature. At the same time, however, we observed in the poll tax affair that the Westminster model makes it possible for governments to pursue measures that are visibly out of line with public opinion. When that occurs, the clear line of accountability can disrupt the government in charge.

Conversely we saw several situations in which coalition governments in France and Italy were supported by unstable voting majorities and public opinion trends. In many instances this volatility increased tensions or resulted in reversals of past policies—perhaps most visibly in the December 1995 general strike in France against the Juppe government's proposed spending cuts. Japanese governments, for the first time in decades, also faced some of these same pressures from unstable voting trends and weak ties among political parties in some of the governing coalitions.

Coalition government need not, however, be synonymous with policy volatility. If the coalition parties can agree on a platform and the voters demonstrate stable support for those parties, the prospects for more coherent policy making over time are considerable. We observed this situation in many policy areas in Germany during the enduring Kohl government of the 1980s and 1990s. Perhaps the most visible tension in the coalition of Christian Democrats and Free Democrats occurred in disputes over tax policy; on most other issues (including, eventually, asylum law reform) the two coalition partners were able to agree on how to proceed.

The United States case studies demonstrated why Charles Lindblom developed the incrementalist decision-making model through the study of U.S. policy making. The many decision points in the U.S. system, resulting from its mix of federalism and presidentialism, combine with undisciplined political parties to make major reforms more difficult to push through the system. In most policy areas in the 1990s, a series of incremental reforms were made to existing policies. The major exception to that trend is in social policy. After many years of criticism of existing policies, through public opinion, in the media, and within the Republican Party, President Clinton signed into law a series of major social policy changes in 1996. Major reform is not impossible in the U.S. institutional framework, but it tends to be time consuming.

The Increasing Internationalization of Public Policy

International agreements and international economic forces have in various ways worked to shape the policy agenda and to frame viable policy options in the policy formulation and decision-making stages. In several of these policy areas, industrialized countries' commitments to various external directives, accords, or binding agreements influenced their policy agendas. In immigration policy, for example, the European countries were faced with questions about what to do about population inflows that arose as a result of the elimination of border controls between European Union member states. For Italy, in particular, this meant substantial external pressures from other EU member states to strengthen the country's border controls, resulting in the adoption of many new policies. Contemporary environmental policy agendas reflected all six countries' participation in international accords to reduce greenhouse gas emissions. Further, the Maastricht budget deficit targets provided the impetus for deficit reduction in France, Germany, and Italy.

Internationalization had an effect on policy decisions in all six countries beyond the efforts these countries made to fulfill their obligations under international agreements. We also observed the effects of increasing international economic competition on policy reform decisions. In education, for example, the reform pressures that all six countries experienced in the 1980s and 1990s were a direct result of citizens' and industry's perceptions that educational systems had to be improved to increase these countries' international economic competitiveness. Similar arguments were used to oppose the use of costly economic instruments to reduce carbon dioxide emissions. Industrial interests in these six countries consistently and effectively argued that increased taxation or environmental charges would hurt these countries' global economic positions. Fiscal policies in these countries also were visibly influenced by global economic factors—specifically, by the requirements of European integration, by the increased interdependence among countries, or in some cases by both factors. These factors affected both fiscal policy agenda setting and the policy decision-making stage. The quest to reduce budget deficits that resulted from international financial market pressures and economic integration motivated these governments to increase revenues through tax policy reform.

Concern for Spending Restraint

Another major trend evident in these six countries was a desire to constrain the growth of overall public expenditures. Calls for fiscal restraint have been so common since the 1980s that they are now part of the normal state of affairs. The contemporary period marks the end of a long upswing in government spending. From the end of World War II through 1985, government expenditures as a percentage of gross domestic product (GDP) rose steadily in these and other industrialized countries. As Table 12–1 indicates, by 1985, spending met or approached 40 percent of the GDP in all but Japan and the United States.

In the late 1980s and 1990s, however, the pace of spending expansion slowed everywhere. In some countries (including the United States and the United Kingdom), government spending as a percentage of GDP declined from 1985 to 1995. In other countries, slight spending increases came not from new initiatives but rather from the maintenance of prior commitments in health care, pensions, and debt service, which grew faster than the GDP. In the second half of the 1990s, public spending declined in almost all industrialized countries. The only country that increased public spending between 1995 and 1999 was Japan. As we saw in Chapter 6, the Japanese government increased spending in an effort to escape the economy's deepest recession in decades.

Table 12-1 Government Spending as a Percentage of GDP, 1960–1999

Country	1960	1970	1975	1980	1985	1990	1995	1999
France	34.6%	38.9%	43.5%	46.2%	51.8%	49.6%	53.5%	52.2%
Germany	32.0	37.6	47.1	46.9	45.6	43.8	46.3	45.6
Italy	30.1	34.2	43.2	45.6	50.6	53.1	52.3	48.3
Japan	20.7	19.3	27.3	32.7	31.6	31.3	35.6	38.1
United Kingdom	32.6	39.3	46.9	44.6	45.2	41.8	44.4	39.3
United States	27.8	32.2	35.4	33.2	33.8	33.6	32.9	30.1
Average	*29.6*	*33.6*	*40.6*	*41.5*	*43.1*	*42.2*	*44.4*	*42.3*
Australia	22.1	25.5	32.4	34.1	37.3	33.5	35.5	32.3
Austria	32.1	39.2	46.1	48.5	50.1	48.5	52.6	50.7
Belgium	30.3	36.5	44.5	51.7	57.3	50.7	50.1	47.9
Canada	28.9	35.7	40.8	40.7	46.0	46.7	46.3	40.2
Finland	26.7	31.3	37.1	38.2	41.8	44.4	54.3	47.1
Greece	17.4	22.4	26.7	30.3	42.3	47.8	46.6	43.5
Ireland	28.0	39.6	47.2	N.A.	48.6	37.8	36.0	31.5
Netherlands	33.7	45.5	55.9	62.5	51.9	49.4	47.7	43.2
Norway	29.9	41.0	46.6	49.4	41.5	49.7	47.6	46.1
Portugal	17.0	21.6	30.2	N.A.	40.2	40.6	44.5	44.7
Spain	13.7	22.2	24.7	32.4	37.7	39.7	42.5	38.6
Sweden	31.1	43.7	49.0	65.7	60.3	56.2	62.4	55.9
Average	*25.9*	*33.7*	*40.1*	*45.4*	*46.3*	*45.4*	*47.2*	*43.5*
Average for all	*27.2%*	*33.7%*	*40.3%*	*43.9%*	*45.2%*	*44.3%*	*46.2%*	*43.1%*

SOURCE: For the years 1960–1980, data are from OECD (1982). For the years 1985–1999, data are from OECD (2000).

N.A. = not available.

Why are most industrialized countries so concerned with restraining expenditures? As noted earlier, part of this fiscal pressure comes from international currency and financial markets. The speed with which today's financial markets react to events makes countries risk averse in their fiscal policies. National governments would rather be seen as fiscally sound than risk a run against their currency or a loss of demand for government bonds.

Today's fiscal conservatism also stems from a growing realization that current government commitments in pension and health policy are headed for financial trouble because of demographic changes. Specifically, as the populations of these countries age, the ratio of workers paying into the system per pensioner is on the decline and will fall significantly in the early decades of the twenty-first century. To compensate for this decline, governments may decide to decrease the amount of benefits paid out, increase the tax rate, or both. This decision presents a major difficulty for governments because publicly managed pensions have come to be seen as guarantees provided to the citizenry.

This sense of entitlement derives from two sources. First, in all six countries pensions are funded on a social insurance basis: All citizens who have made certain contributions are eligible at retirement age for a pension—regardless of income. Second, today's workers have spent their lives paying into the system in anticipation of receiving a pension that provides for a certain standard of living.

The politics of pensions put governments in a real bind. Almost all voting-age citizens have a stake in the defense of current pension benefits because either they are already retirees or they have begun to pay into the pension system. However, governments fear that raising tax levels to maintain benefit levels will also generate political opposition. Governments face a true dilemma in which raising payroll taxes and reducing benefits are both bound to generate discontent. As a result, many governments have made only minor reforms thus far to their pension systems. Italy, where the pension system was running the largest deficit, is the only one of these countries that visibly reshaped its pension system in the 1990s.

In the absence of major pension reform, knowledge of the coming deficitary pressure has been used as a political argument in favor of fiscal restraint in other policy areas. We saw that argument emerge in regard to health care and social policy, in particular. Calls for fiscal responsibility in the 1990s drew on three major sources: a need to prepare for the retirement of the baby-boom generation, a need to improve governments' positions in international financial markets, and, in France, Germany, and Italy, a desire to meet the fiscal targets placed in the monetary unification effort.

Learning Lessons by Comparing Policies

We have offered in this book many examples that suggest the limitations of the extent to which countries may learn from one another. The cultural, economic, political, and institutional context of policy making as well as the decisions made by individual human beings can block the adoption of policies deemed desirable by some or perhaps even many policy analysts and sectors of society. For example, the United States's history as a country of immigrants colors the debate over restrictive immigration legislation. Italy's political, economic, and geographic divisions made it difficult to reduce the deficit in a series of governments pledged to do so. France has increased only slightly the use of direct taxes over the years because of a long suspicion that tax avoidance and tax evasion are widespread responses to such tax instruments. Japanese cultural norms slowed the adoption of long-term health care policies and have made implementation more difficult. The liberal tradition of individualism in the United Kingdom has led that country to adopt mainly means-tested social policies whereas most European countries chose a more universalistic approach. A variety of forces in Germany have supported expanding the adoption of user pays instruments in environmental protection; however, a host of economic problems (and tax hikes) associated with reunification blocked the enactment of such measures in the 1990s.

In short, the construction of public policies involves a variety of considerations that may constrain the usefulness of comparisons with other countries. Countries may face slightly different problems. They may confront similar problems but in different political, economic, or sociocultural contexts. In particular, the dynamics of the policy subsector in each country often plays a crucial role in determining the precise policy mix chosen.

Nevertheless, cross-national comparisons can and do help in the effort to meet citizens' needs via the design, passage, and implementation of public policies. We have seen many examples of a broad consensus in policy choice— a consensus built on an examination of national and cross-national experiences. Countries desiring to limit the flow of immigration have learned that restrictive immigration laws require enhanced enforcement measures for effective implementation. Countries with different political parties in charge have attempted to control their deficits in order to avoid the currency instability found in countries with higher deficits. Throughout the twentieth century, governments moved to an increasing use of direct taxes because such instruments permit a more nuanced use of tax expenditures as well as the pursuit of tax progressivity goals. Industrialized countries have learned that an effective set of public health initiatives is a crucial first step toward the achievement of better health outcomes. In the curative care sector, countries have learned that global budgeting for hospital care is the most effective cost-control measure available. Governments know that social insurance policies are useful for guaranteeing political (and financial) support for national pension systems. Compulsory public education at the primary and secondary levels is a response to the achievements of the first countries to adopt this policy. In environmental policy, countries are realizing that regulation is of limited effectiveness and are beginning to supplement regulation with the use of economic incentives.

In many situations, comparisons among countries can be useful. Even when comparisons do not lead to the virtually wholesale adoption of another country's policy, comparisons can often shift the national debate in a new, useful direction. We hope, therefore, that this book has helped readers to brainstorm more constructively about building solutions to public problems at home and abroad.

Glossary

absolute poverty A poverty measure that establishes a basic needs threshold beneath which citizens are said to be poor.

access to schooling The issue of who receives schooling.

actuarial fairness An approach to medical insurance that groups people according to their risk factors. Healthy individuals in low-risk occupations are grouped with similar individuals and pay lower insurance rates, whereas high-risk patients are forced to pay higher insurance rates in recognition of the greater likelihood that they will require care.

administrative evaluation One of the three major arenas of policy evaluation, in which the government itself evaluates public policies.

agenda setting The stage of the policy-making process at which problems come to the attention of policymakers.

asylum seekers Individuals who are already present in a country where refuge is sought or who are at the border requesting entry.

back door immigration Illegal entry into a country.

ballotage system A two-round variation of the single-member district plurality electoral system that requires a majority to win in the first round. If no candidate wins, the top vote-getters compete again under plurality rules.

basic needs An approach to social insurance programs in which the government sets benefit levels based on a certain standard below which no individual should fall.

behavioralism The school of thought in political science that focuses on the political behavior of individuals and groups throughout society.

bottom-up implementation A view of implementation that focuses on how informal customs and considerations, faced by those who implement policies, block the fulfillment of what policy decision makers originally intended.

capitation A system for reimbursing physicians based on how many patients they treat, not how many services they provide.

catch-all parties Coalitions of voters with weaker organizational structures, memberships drawn from disparate backgrounds, and programs based on less clearly defined goals or visions than are found in more traditional parties.

chronically poor Individuals who are of working age but who have a hard time escaping poverty.

command and control policies Environmental policies that involve direct regulation and monitoring by government.

consolidation A model of agenda setting in which the government places on the institutional agenda an issue already visible on the systemic agenda. The government does not need to mobilize support for maintaining the issue on the institutional agenda; instead it relies on existing public interest in the issue.

convergence thesis The theory that as countries industrialize, they develop similar policy concerns.

copayment A partial payment for medical services that patients are required to pay at the time that care is delivered.

corporatism A pattern of interest group activity in which fewer, larger groups participate actively in the policy-making process and government tries more often to include these major groups in systematic discussions of policy-making issues relevant to the policy network.

cost-benefit analysis Under the rational decision-making model, this type of analysis is used to identify all benefits (positive impacts) and costs (negative impacts) of a policy proposal and to select the option most likely to reach policymakers' goals at an acceptable cost.

countercyclical fiscal policies The practice of running deficits to escape recession and running surpluses in times of economic growth.

curriculum The course of study that educational institutions follow.

dealignment The weakening of voters' ties to existing political parties and a resulting shift in voter behavior.

debt service The interest and principal payments made on a country's national debt.

decision making The stage of the policy-making process at which the relevant public authority decides to create a new policy, to modify an existing policy, or to take no new action.

deficit The situation that occurs when governments spend more money than they take in.

depolarization The tendency for political parties to move toward the moderate center of the political spectrum.

direct government instruments Public policies that include direct regulations, the direct provision of services, the operation of state-owned enterprises, and the like.

direct regulations Environmental policies that involve the setting of restrictions and requirements by government.

direct taxes Tax instruments that are levied as a percentage of income earned by a person or a firm.

divided government A situation in which the executive and the legislature are controlled by different political parties.

economic incentives Environmental policy instruments that use market mechanisms, such as tax breaks, pollution charges, or deposit systems, to reduce pollution.

employer-mandate An approach to health care in which premiums are tied to wages.

entitlements Social insurance programs under which citizens cannot be denied benefits.

equality of opportunity The assumption that school systems can compensate for existing social and economic inequalities in a society. Universal access to schooling is believed to serve as a leveler, as opposed to less open educational systems that perpetuate existing social or economic divisions.

equality of provision The attempt to ensure that all students in an educational system are receiving the same type of education, particularly with respect to subject matter.

excise tax A tax charged on a particular good, such as tobacco or liquor.

external controls Illegal-immigration control measures designed to prevent foreigners from entering the country without permission, such as more effective policing of borders and airports.

family of nations A group of countries whose cultural similarities help to produce similar policy-making dynamics and in some cases comparable policy decisions.

family reunification Legal immigration that involves entry into a country by the spouses and children of legal residents and citizens.

federal political system A political system in which one or two meaningful levels of government exist above the local level; each level has its own constitutionally defined policy-making responsibilities.

fee-for-service A system for reimbursing physicians in which doctors are paid a fee for each service performed.

flat tax Income-neutral direct taxes that charge all citizens a uniform rate.

front door immigration Legal entry into a country, usually for family reunification or through employment-based immigration.

fusion of powers The constitutional division of authority in which the executive derives from and is responsible to the legislature.

garbage can decision-making A policy decision-making model that rejects the idea that governments systematically weigh policy alternatives. Decisions are instead the result of multiple factors interacting in the policy environment, or garbage can.

gatekeeper system A health care organization cost-cutting mechanism that requires patients to see a general practitioner to receive a referral before seeing a specialist.

globalization The idea that a country's national political, economic, and social life is increasingly affected by what occurs beyond the country's borders.

globalization of the environment The fact that the environment in one country is not distinct from the environment in another and that environmental problems do not respect national territorial boundaries.

government bonds Instruments created by governments to make up for a budget deficit. Investors purchase the bonds, and the government agrees to pay back the value of the bond plus interest over a certain period of time.

greenhouse gases Atmospheric gases that allow heat from the sun to enter the earth's atmosphere and then trap it, creating a greenhouse effect.

gridlock A situation that occurs when political, ideological, or other differences between the executive and the legislature make it more difficult for the government to develop policies.

guest worker programs Foreign labor recruitment programs in which foreign workers are given temporary work residence permits.

health maintenance organizations A form of health insurance in the United States in which premiums are used to hire a group of physicians who provide a comprehensive range of services to the plan's members.

humanitarian immigration Immigration of asylum seekers and refugees, who seek entry into a country as protection from political or other forms of persecution in their home countries.

illegal immigration The unauthorized entry of immigrants into a country, typically through clandestine means or visa overstaying.

income-neutral A tax system that has no impact on the distribution of income in a country.

incremental decision-making A descriptive model of decision making according to which political factors constrain decision makers from the pursuit of all possible alternatives; the result is that only marginal changes are made to existing policies.

indirect taxes Tax instruments that are not based on taxpayers' incomes. These instruments include sales taxes or the value-added tax.

individual equity An approach to social insurance programs in which citizens receive benefits in accordance with their level of contributions.

inside initiation A model of agenda setting in which interest groups attempt to influence the institutional agenda almost entirely in private. Where this model exists, no attempt is made to expand the visibility of the policy debate on the systemic agenda.

institutional agenda Issues that have attracted the attention of government officials and have become the focus of public policy making.

interest aggregation The process of taking a wide range of citizen viewpoints and demands and translating them into a more manageable and more specific number of policy alternatives.

interest groups Private organizations that set out to influence public policy in specific areas of concern to their members.

internal controls Illegal-immigration control measures that allow for the legal supervision of immigrants in order to guarantee that they leave when their visas expire and that they do not work without authorization.

iron triangle A political subsystem controlled by the relevant bureaucratic agencies, the relevant legislative subcommittees, and the major interest groups dedicated to a given policy area. Together these three groups exert influence in the policy area, and policy decisions in that area are closed to outside influence.

issue network A political subsystem in which a loose mix of government and non-government actors are actively involved in policy formulation. Membership in the network is flexible over time.

issue voting The tendency of voters to base their votes on the policy programs of competing parties on issues that matter to them, rather than on their strong sense of identification with a particular party.

judicial evaluation Policy evaluation conducted by the courts in response to a specific legal complaint against a public policy.

Kaldor criterion Standards for evaluating cost-benefit analyses, according to which policy decisions must provide more benefits than costs to society as a whole (even if some people suffer net losses). When applied, the preferred policy option is the one that provides the highest net benefits.

Keynesianism The school of thought in economics that argues for deficit spending as a government policy tool to help the economy grow out of tough times.

legal immigration Immigration for the purposes of family reunification or for employment sanctioned by government.

legislative judicial review The power of courts to declare legislation and executive actions unconstitutional and, thereby, to nullify laws.

liberal versus vocational education The debate over whether education should be aimed at reducing social and economic inequalities or at promoting global competitiveness. Proponents of liberal, or general, education advocate traditional training of students in the classics, reading, writing, and arithmetic in order to provide for the full development of the individual. Vocational, or technical, training supporters emphasize the development of useful skills that translate directly into specific occupational opportunities.

limits on technology acquisition A health care cost-control measure that places limits on the acquisition of medical technology by hospitals and private physicians.

mandatory national health insurance An approach to health care in which the government guarantees all citizens access to care, with multiple payers and multiple providers.

manifestly unfounded claims Asylum seekers' petitions for entry into a country that fail to demonstrate absolute proof of political persecution.

market economies Economic systems based on private ownership and the market, not the government, as the central economic coordinating mechanism.

market instruments Public policies that attempt to motivate certain behaviors within a largely free market.

market-maximized An approach to health care in which the government provides no guarantee of access through either public hospitals or mandatory health insurance.

mass party A well-organized political party that has a large number of active members drawn from a particular social cleavage and that is committed to pursuing a particular political ideology or a distinctive set of policy goals.

means-tested A method for determining eligibility for social assistance that is based on recipients' economic need.

median voter model The explanation of partisan trends that argues that political parties try to develop policies that will appeal to the widest range of voters, regardless of whether those policy positions contradict their traditional perspective on the issue at hand. This process results in the emergence of catch-all parties.

merit The belief that access to education should reflect the fact that individuals differ innately in their capabilities and are not equally capable of benefiting from an education. Those who emphasize merit oppose equal access to education for all.

mixed economies Economic systems that combine capitalist free-market principles, including private ownership, with some level of state ownership, some central economic planning, and a higher level of government regulation.

mixed instruments Public policies that rely on some combination of direct government intervention, market incentives, and voluntary persuasion.

mobilization A model of agenda setting in which the government is the group interested in setting the institutional agenda.

moderate pluralism A description of political systems in which political parties tend toward the center of the political spectrum.

multiparty system A political system in which multiple parties enter elections and achieve elected office. Parties represent a narrow range of interests and do very little interest aggregation.

national debt The sum total of the future financial obligations that the government owes to others.

national health service An approach to health care in which citizens are guaranteed access to most services through a system paid for and administered directly by the government.

new institutionalism An approach to the study of the policy-making process that focuses on institutional influences on policy making. This approach emphasizes formal rules and informal norms and patterns in governmental institutions, as well as the role of institutional considerations in framing nongovernmental organizations' participation in policy making.

non-refoulement principle The principle in international law that imposes legal and moral obligations on countries not to reject foreign asylum applicants if such rejection entails their being returned to a place where they are in danger of being persecuted.

optimizing adjustment A model of policy decision making in which decision makers do not consider widely divergent options but are willing to consider fairly significant changes from the status quo.

outside initiation An agenda-setting model in which organized interest groups attempt to raise the profile of an issue on the systemic agenda. By forming allegiances with other groups, raising citizen awareness, and lobbying the government these groups attempt to move their concerns onto the institutional agenda.

overloaded government A situation in which the sum total of the demands placed on government grows faster than both public spending and public revenues.

Pareto optimality The criterion that states that when evaluating the results of a cost-benefit analysis, policy decisions must make at least one person better off while making no one worse off.

parliamentary systems Governmental systems in which the chief executive is elected by the legislature and can be removed for any reason by the legislature as it sees fit.

partisanship thesis A theory of policy making that holds that parties are central to the policy process. In particular, political parties tied to the organized labor movement are argued to support an expansion in the scope of government activity in policy areas supported by labor unions, and the range of government activity is more likely to expand when such parties are in power.

party discipline The likelihood of legislators voting with their own party in the legislature.

party government A governing situation in which one party controls the executive branch and holds a majority in the legislative branch.

party system The number of parties that are viewed as having a serious chance of winning elections in a country, as well as the extent of competition between these parties.

pluralism A pattern of group activity in which many interest groups or other actors compete openly for the government's attention and in which political power is dispersed.

plurality In electoral systems, the requirement that the winning candidate must receive the most votes cast in an election.

pocketbook voting A pattern of voting behavior in which election results reflect the state of the national economy and, at times, individual economic fortunes. For example, if the country's economy is seen as reasonably strong, the incumbent party tends to do well with many voters—regardless of their traditional party ties or ideology.

point of service plan A hybrid form of managed care health insurance in the United States in which patients can choose to see a specialist who does not participate in the plan if they are willing to pay a higher copayment.

polarization In party systems, the degree of emotional or political distance between political parties.

polarized pluralism A description of political systems in which political parties tend to be more ideologically distant from one another. In such systems, parties tend to move away from the center of the political system toward the left and right poles.

policy evaluation The stage of the policy-making process at which judgments are made about the effects of public policies.

policy formulation The stage of the policy-making process at which proposed policy alternatives are weighed, the nature of the problem itself is debated, and policy proposals are developed.

policy implementation The stage of the policy-making process at which public policies are put into effect.

policy instruments The specific actions taken by government to put public policies into effect.

policy network All of the different actors who usually participate actively in a given policy area. A policy network is defined by the nature of the relationship between government and nongovernment participants.

policy outcomes The consequences of government activity, or what public policies produce.

policy outputs The government's actions to carry out and enforce its policies.

policy science A field of study focusing on what governments do rather than how institutions are organized.

political evaluation An arena of policy evaluation that takes place within existing policy networks, with interest groups providing feedback to government and influencing public opinion.

polluter pays principles Economic incentive policies in which individuals are charged for their environmentally harmful activities.

postentry controls Immigration policies that attempt to control immigrants', especially asylum seekers', activities and experiences once they are within a country's borders.

postindustrial A description of the changed employment structure of industrialized countries, with greater employment opportunities in the service sector than in manufacturing or agriculture.

postmaterialism A description of the changed attitudinal structure of industrialized countries, with citizens placing greater emphasis on freedom of expression, quality of life, greater political participation, the environment, or gender and sexual equality concerns than on physical or material well-being.

preentry controls External immigration-control mechanisms designed to prevent immigrants from making it across a country's borders.

preference system An immigration policy instrument that allocates a certain number of visas per year for particular categories of immigrants.

preferred provider organizations The gatekeeper system used in the United States, which not only requires patients to be referred to a specialist by a general practitioner but also usually limits patients to the selection of doctors who agree to the insurer's fee schedule.

presidential systems Governmental systems in which the chief executive is elected separately from the legislature to a fixed term and can be removed by the legislature only upon charges of dereliction of duty.

principal-agent model A model of bureaucratic activity in which the bureaucratic agents' control of information and expertise limits the authority of the principal political officials.

progressive A tax system in which the wealthy to pay a higher percentage of their income in taxes than the poor. Such a system redistributes income from the rich to the poor.

pronatalist family policies Social policies that reward parents for having additional children and that encourage increasing family size.

proportional representation The allocation of legislative seats in an electoral district roughly according to the proportion of the vote that a party's slate received.

public assistance A social policy benefit model in which eligibility for benefits is means tested.

public goods Services generally deemed necessary for a basic quality of life that are unlikely to be provided by the marketplace because it is not in any individual's self-interest to produce them.

public policies Intentional courses of action designed by government bodies and officials to accomplish specific goals or objectives.

public versus private schooling An education debate involving the question of permitting religious schools to exist and, where they exist, of the appropriate allocation of public funds.

pull factors A country's characteristics that make it attractive to immigrants.

push factors A country's characteristics that affect individuals' decisions to emigrate, including overpopulation, poverty, unemployment, natural disaster, or war.

rational decision-making A prescriptive model of decision making that emphasizes the even-handed consideration of all alternatives and the consequences of those alternatives.

realignment The process whereby individuals form attachments to new political parties corresponding to new forms of social identification.

referendum An election in which voters choose among specific policy options, typically involving a yes-no vote on one issue.

refugees Individuals found outside their home country (typically in refugee camps) who are seeking entry into another country for protection from persecution.

regressive A tax system that forces the poor to pay a higher percentage of their income in taxes than the rich. Such a system redistributes income from the poor to the wealthy.

regularization programs Immigration programs that provide legal amnesty (and usually naturalized citizenship) for illegal immigrants who satisfy certain conditions such as entry into the country before a certain date, good health, regular employment, or a valid passport.

relative poverty A poverty measure that creates a relative standard to assess comparable levels of poverty across a society or across countries.

risk-pooling An approach to medical insurance that groups people based on the principle that everyone is at risk of needing care due to chronic illness or accidents. This risk is pooled across a large number of currently healthy and unhealthy individuals to provide maximal coverage at lowest cost.

satisficing decision-making A descriptive model of decision making in which the bounded rationality of decision makers limits their ability to give full consideration to all alternatives and their consequences.

separation of mandate In presidential systems, the fact that the chief executive derives strength from his or her direct election independently from the legislature. The executive has a personal mandate to govern, whereas the legislature also has its own independent electoral mandate.

separation of powers The constitutional division of authority among the executive, legislative, and judicial branches of government.

side door immigration Entry to a country through temporary immigration programs.

single-member district plurality The allocation of legislative seats based on the division of the country into a relatively large number of legislative districts; each district is assigned one seat in the legislature. Once an election is held and the results are tallied, the candidate who receives the most votes is the elected representative from that district.

single-payer An approach to health care that guarantees all citizens access via a single program in which almost all funds come from the government but care is provided privately.

situationally poor Individuals who for one reason or another (unemployment, illness, or old age) cannot support themselves.

social cleavages Social criteria by which people are grouped in a society.

social dumping The movement of low-skill individuals from countries that provide fewer social benefits to countries with more generous social benefits systems. Employers move to countries that provide fewer social benefits because of the lighter tax burdens associated with lower levels of benefits.

social insurance A model for determining access to social policy benefits in which all citizens in a given circumstance are eligible for assistance regardless of their degree of economic need.

social insurance programs Government programs that provide for health care, old age benefits, unemployment, and the like.

social market economy An economic system in which the government combines support for the private sector and the free market (with nearly all enterprises under private control). A high level of government intervention is designed to create a framework for economic growth.

subsidies A social policy instrument that involves the government spending money to make services available to the needy at abnormally low prices.

supply-side school The school of economists who believe that decreasing taxes and increasing government spending will stimulate investment and economic growth.

surplus The situation that occurs when governments take in more money than they spend.

swing voters Voters who demonstrate no strong loyalty to any political party from one election to another but instead base their voting choices on candidates' personalities, perceptions of candidates' competence and leadership abilities, more specific policy promises of one party or another, and the like.

systemic agenda The set of citizens' concerns and issues that may be placed on a country's institutional agenda.

tax avoidance The practice of managing money in such a way as to minimize the tax liability.

tax brackets In tax systems, the increments used to determine taxation rates for specific levels of income.

tax credits A feature of some tax systems in which the cost of a particular activity is counted as a credit toward the taxes owed.

tax deductions A feature of some tax systems in which the government allows citizens to reduce their amount of taxable income by taking into account charitable contributions and the like.

tax evasion The illegal refusal to pay taxes owed under the law.

tax expenditures Public policies in which the government reduces citizens' tax obligations when they spend their money for certain purposes, such as through lower sales taxes on food or tax deductions for home ownership.

tax protest Citizens' opposition to taxes that is generated by perceived injustice.

tax revolt Citizens' opposition to taxes that results from a perception that taxation is unjust in its execution and unfair in principle.

top-down implementation A view of implementation that focuses on how policy design at the leadership level frames how policies will be implemented.

traditionalism Political science analyses that focus on formal government institutions and that make normative judgments about preferred institutional forms.

transfers Government economic assistance provided to citizens via direct cash payments to individuals or in-kind benefits.

two-party system A political system in which two major political parties present broad policy alternatives to the electorate in an effort to appeal to the broadest possible segment of the electorate.

unitary political system A political system in which only one meaningful level of government exists above the local level. In such systems, only the central government has constitutionally derived policy-making authority (for all stages of the policy-making process).

user pays principles Economic incentive policies that involve additional costs for consumers of environmentally hazardous products.

volatility A tendency for patterns of partisan support to shift dramatically from election to election as both the issues of the day and parties' and the electorate's positions change.

voluntary agreements Nonbinding agreements between government and producers to reduce pollution levels.

voluntary instruments Public policies in which speeches by public officials and publicly authorized commercials encourage people to adopt certain behaviors.

vouchers Coupons, representing tax dollars, that parents use to pay tuition at the school of their choice, public or private.

welfare states States that provide extensive social insurance benefits to their citizens.

Westminster model A model of government in which a parliamentary system is combined with a plurality electoral system.

References

Abel-Smith, Brian. 1994. *The Reform of Health Care Systems: A Review of Seventeen OECD Countries.* Paris: Organisation for Economic Co-operation and Development.

Ambler, John. 1987. "Constraints on Policy Innovation in Education: Thatcher's Britain and Mitterrand's France." *Comparative Politics* 20:85–105.

Anderson, Odin. 1972. *Health Care: Can There Be Equity?* New York: Wiley.

Atkinson, Anthony, Lee Rainwater, and Timothy Smeeding. 1995. *Income Distribution in OECD Countries.* Paris: Organisation for Economic Co-operation and Development.

Baker, Maureen. 1995. *Canadian Family Policies: Cross-National Comparisons.* Toronto: University of Toronto Press.

Baldwin-Edwards, Martin, and Martin Schain. 1994. "The Politics of Immigration: Introduction." In *The Politics of Immigration in Western Europe,* edited by Martin Baldwin-Edwards and Martin Schain. London: Frank Cass.

Betz, Hans-George. 1991. *Post-modern Politics in Germany: The Politics of Resentment.* London: Macmillan.

Betz, Hans-George. 1994. *Radical Right-wing Populism in Western Europe.* Basingstoke, U.K.: Macmillan.

Blendon, Robert, et al. 1990. "Satisfaction with Health Systems in Ten Nations." *Health Affairs* 9: 185–192.

Boyd, William. 1996. "The Politics of Choice and Market-Oriented School Reform in Britain and the United States." In *The Reconstruction of Education,* edited by Judith Chapman, William Boyd, Rolf Lander, and David Reynolds. London: Cassell.

Boyd, William, and Charles Kerchner. 1987. "Introduction." In *The Politics of Excellence and Choice in Education,* edited by William Boyd and Charles Kerchner. Philadelphia: Falmer Press.

Brochman, Grete, and Tomas Hammar, eds. 1999. *Mechanisms of Immigration Control: A Comparative Analysis of European Regulation Policies.* Oxford: Berg Publishers.

Cameron, David. 1978. "The Expansion of the Public Economy: A Comparative Analysis." *American Political Science Review* 72:1243–1261.

Castles, Francis, ed. 1982a. *The Impact of Parties: Politics and Policies in Democratic Capitalist States.* London: Sage.

Castles, Francis. 1982b. "The Impact of Parties on Public Expenditure." In *The Impact of Parties: Politics and Policies in Democratic Capitalist States,* edited by Francis Castles. London: Sage.

Castles, Francis, ed. 1993. *Families of Nations: Patterns of Public Policy in Western Democracies.* Aldershot, U.K.: Dartmouth Publishing.

Castles, Francis, and Deborah Mitchell. 1993. "Worlds of Welfare and Families of Nations." In *Families of Nations: Patterns of Public Policy in Western Democracies,* edited by Francis Castles. Aldershot, U.K.: Dartmouth Publishing.

Castles, Francis, and Rudolf Wildenmann, eds. 1986. *The Future of Party Government.* Vol. 1: *Visions and Realities of Party Government.* New York: DeGruyter.

Center for Educational Research and Innovation. 1998. *Education at a Glance: OECD Indicators, 1998.* Paris: Organisation for Economic Co-operation and Development.

Chubb, John, and Terry Moe. 1990. *Politics, Markets and America's Schools.* Washington, D.C.: Brookings Institution Press.

Cibulka, James. 1996. "The Evolution of Education Reform in Great Britain and the United States: Implementation Convergence of Two Macro-policy Approaches." In *The Reconstruction of Education,* edited by Judith Chapman, William Boyd, Rolf Lander, and David Reynolds. London: Cassell.

Cigler, Allan J., and Burdett A. Loomis, eds. 1998. *Interest Group Politics,* 5th ed. Washington, D.C.: CQ Press.

Cobb, Roger, Jennie-Keith Ross, and Marc Howard Ross. 1976. "Agenda Building as a Comparative Political Process." *American Political Science Review* 70:126–138.

Cohen, Wesley, and Daniel Levinthal. 1990. "Absorptive Capacity: A New Perspective on Learning and Innovation." *Administrative Science Quarterly* 35:128–152.

Collier, Ute, and Ragnar Lofstedt. 1997. "Comparative Analysis and Conclusions ." In *Cases in Climate Change Policy,* edited by Ute Collier and Ragnar E. Lofstedt. London: Earthscan Publications.

Confalonieri, Maria, and Kenneth Newton. 1995. "Taxing and Spending: Tax Revolt or Tax Protest?" In *The Scope of Government,* edited by Ole Borre and Elinor Scarbrough. Oxford: Oxford University Press.

Conradt, David. 1996. *The Germany Polity.* New York: Longman.

Coombs, Philip. 1985. *The World Crisis in Education: The View from the Eighties.* New York: Oxford University Press.

Cornelius, Wayne, Philip Martin, and James Hollifield. 1994. "Introduction: The Ambivalent Quest for Immigration Control." In *Controlling Immigration: A Global Perspective,* edited by Wayne Cornelius, Philip Martin, and James Hollifield. Stanford: Stanford University Press.

Cowart, A. T. 1978. "The Economic Policies of European Governments, Part II: Fiscal Policy." *British Journal of Political Science* 8:425–439.

Crepaz, Markus. 1995. "Explaining National Variations of Air Pollution Levels: Political Institutions and Their Impact on Environmental Policy-making." *Environmental Politics* 4:391–414.

Duclaud-Williams, Roger. 1988. "Policy Implementation in the French Public Bureaucracy: The Case of Education." *West European Politics* 11:81–101.

Eckstein, Harry. 1960. *Pressure Group Politics: The Case of the British Medical Association.* London: Allen and Unwin.

Eliason, Leslie. 1996. "Educational Decentralization as a Policy Strategy in an Era of Fiscal Stress." In *The Reconstruction of Education,* edited by Judith Chapman, William Boyd, Rolf Lander, and David Reynolds. London: Cassell.

Elmore, Richard. 1997. "The Politics of Education Reform." *Issues in Science and Technology* 14:41–50.

Enloe, Cynthia. 1975. *The Politics of Pollution in Comparative Perspective: Ecology and Power in Four Nations.* New York: David McKay.

Esping-Andersen, Gøsta. 1990. *The Three Worlds of Welfare Capitalism.* Princeton: Princeton University Press.

Flora, Peter, and Jens Alber. 1981. "Modernization, Democratization and the Development of Welfare States in Western Europe." In *The Development of Welfare States in Europe and America,* edited by Peter Flora and Arnold Heidenheimer. New Brunswick, N.J.: Transaction.

Fowler, Frances, William Boyd, and David Plank. 1993. "International School Reform: Political Considerations." In *Reforming Education: The Emerging Systemic Approach,* edited by Stephen Jacobson and Robert Berne. Thousand Oaks, Calif.: Corwin Press.

Freeman, Gary. 1995. "Modes of Immigration Politics in Liberal Democratic Societies." *International Migration Review* 29:881–903.

Freeman, Gary. 1998. "The Decline of Sovereignty? Politics and Immigration Restriction in Liberal States." In *Challenge to the Nation-state,* edited by Christian Joppke. Oxford: Oxford University Press.

George, Vic. 1996. "The Demand for Welfare." In *European Welfare Policy: Squaring the Welfare Circle,* edited by Vic George and Peter Taylor-Gooby. London: Macmillan.

George, Vic, and S. Miller, eds. 1994. *Social Policy Towards 2000: Squaring the Welfare Circle.* London: Routledge.

Gimpel, James, and James Edwards. 1998. *The Congressional Politics of Immigration Control.* Boston: Allyn and Bacon.

Ginsburg, M., et al. 1990. "National and World System Explanations of Education Reform." *Comparative Education Review* 34:474–499.

Glaser, William. 1978. *Health Insurance Bargaining: Foreign Lessons for Americans.* New York: Gardener.

Gould, Arthur. 1993. *Capitalist Welfare Systems: A Comparison of Japan, Britain, and Sweden.* London: Longman.

Greider, William. 1981. "The Education of David Stockman." *Atlantic Monthly,* December, pp. 27–54.

Grilli, V., D. Masciandaro, and G. Tabellini. 1991. "Political and Monetary Institutions and Public Financial Policies in the Industrial Countries." *Economic Policy* 10:341–392.

Grindle, Merilee, and John Thomas. 1991. *Public Choices and Policy Change: The Political Economy of Reform in Developing Countries.* Baltimore: Johns Hopkins University Press.

Hadenius, Axel. 1985. "Citizens Strike a Balance: Discontent with Taxes, Content with Spending." *Journal of Public Policy* 5:349–363.

Hagemann, R., B. Jones, and R. Montador. 1988. "Tax Reform in OECD Countries: Motives, Constraints, and Practice." *OECD Economic Studies* 10:185–226.

Hahm, Sung Deuk, Mark Kamlet, and David Mowery. 1996. "The Political Economy of Deficit Spending in Nine Industrialized Parliamentary Democracies." *Comparative Political Studies* 29:52–77.

Hall, Peter. 1986. *Governing the Economy: The Politics of State Intervention in Britain and France.* New York: Oxford University Press.

Hall, Peter. 1990. "Policy Paradigms, Experts, and the State: The Case of Economic Policy-making in Britain." In *Social Scientists, Policy, and the State,* edited by Stephen Brooks and Alain Gagnon. New York: Praeger.

Hanf, Kenneth, and Alf-Inge Jansen. 1998. "Environmental Policy: The Outcome of Strategic Action and Institutional Characteristics." In *Governance and Environ-*

ment in Western Europe: Politics, Policy and Administration, edited by Kenneth Hanf and Alf-Inge Jansen. New York: Longman.

Hansen, John Mark. 1998. "Individuals, Institutions, and Public Preferences over Public Finance." *American Political Science Review* 92:513–532.

Haycraft, John. 1987. *Italian Labyrinth.* London: Penguin.

Heclo, Hugh. 1978. "Issue Networks and the Executive Establishment." In *The New American Political System,* edited by Anthony King. Washington, D.C.: American Enterprise Institute.

Heisler, Martin. 1986. "Transnational Migration as a Small Window on the Diminished Autonomy of the State." *The Annals* 485:153–166.

Hicks, Alexander, and Duane Swank. 1992. "Politics, Institutions, and Welfare Spending in Industrialized Democracies, 1960–1982." *American Political Science Review* 86:658–674.

Hofferth, S. L., and D. A. Phillips. 1991. "Child Care Policy Research." *Journal of Social Issues* 9:1–13.

Hollifield, James. 1992. *Immigrants, Markets and States.* Cambridge: Cambridge University Press.

Huseby, Beate. 1995. "Attitudes Toward the Size of Government." In *The Scope of Government,* edited by Ole Borre and Elinor Scarbrough. Oxford: Oxford University Press.

Iannacone, Lawrence. 1988. "From Equity to Excellence." In *The Politics of Excellence and Choice in Education,* edited by William Boyd and Charles Kerchner. Philadelphia: Falmer Press.

Immergut, Ellen. 1992. *Health Politics: Interests and Institutions in Western Europe.* Cambridge: Cambridge University Press.

IMF. 1995. *Government Finance Statistics Yearbook 1995.* Washington, D.C.: International Monetary Fund.

Jacobs, Lawrence. 1993. *The Health of Nations: Public Opinion and the Making of American and British Health Policy.* Ithaca: Cornell University Press.

Jacobson, David. 1996. *Rights Across Borders.* Baltimore: Johns Hopkins University Press.

Jager, Jill, and Tim O'Riordan. 1996. "The History of Climate Change Science and Politics." In *Politics of Climate Change: A European Perspective,* edited by Tim O'Riordan and Jill Jager. New York: Routledge.

Jansen, Alf-Inge, Oddgeir Osland, and Kenneth Hanf. 1998. "Environmental Challenges and Institutional Changes." In *Governance and Environment in Western Europe: Politics, Policy and Administration,* edited by Kenneth Hanf and Alf-Inge Jansen. New York: Longman.

Jenson, Jane. 1989. "Paradigms and Political Discourse: Protective Legislation in France and the United States Before 1914." *Canadian Journal of Political Science* 22:235–258.

Joppke, Christian. 1998. "Immigration Challenges the Nation-state." In *Challenge to the Nation-state,* edited by Christian Joppke. Oxford: Oxford University Press.

Joppke, Christian. 1999. *Immigration and the Nation-state.* Oxford: Oxford University Press.

Kawashima, Yasuko. 1997. "A Comparative Analysis of the Decision-making Processes of Developed Countries toward CO_2 Emissions Reduction Targets." *International Environmental Affairs* 9:95–126.

Kindleberger, Charles. 1967. *Europe's Postwar Growth: The Role of the Labor Supply.* Cambridge: Harvard University Press.

King, Anthony. 1973. "Ideas, Institutions and the Policies of Governments: A Comparative Analysis—Part III." *British Journal of Political Science* 3:409–423.

King, Anthony. 1975. "Overload: Problems of Governing in the 1970s." *Political Studies* 23:284–296.

Klein, Rudolf. 1995. *The New Politics of the National Health Service,* 3d ed. New York: Longman.

Kogan, Maurice. 1971. *The Politics of Education.* New York: Penguin.

Lasswell, Harold. 1951. "The Policy Orientation." In *The Policy Sciences: Recent Developments in Scope and Method,* edited by Daniel Lerner and Harold Lasswell. Stanford: Stanford University Press.

Lauglo, Jon. 1996. "Forms of Decentralization and Their Implication for Education." In *The Reconstruction of Education,* edited by Judith Chapman, William Boyd, Rolf Lander, and David Reynolds. London: Cassell.

Layard, Richard, and Stephen Glaister, eds. 1994. *Cost-Benefit Analysis.* Cambridge: Cambridge University Press.

Layton-Henry, Zig. 1992. *The Politics of Immigration Control.* Oxford: Blackwell.

Lindblom, Charles. 1959. "The Science of Muddling Through." *Public Administration Review* 39:79–88.

Lindblom, Charles. 1968. *The Policy-making Process.* Englewood Cliffs, N.J.: Prentice-Hall.

Linder, Stephen, and B. Guy Peters. 1989. "Instruments of Government: Perceptions and Contexts." *Journal of Public Policy* 9:35–58.

Lundqvist, Lennart. 1974. *Environmental Policies in Canada, Sweden and the United States: A Comparative Overview.* Beverly Hills, Calif.: Sage.

Lundqvist, Lennart. 1980. *The Hare and the Tortoise: Clean Air Policies in the United States and Sweden.* Ann Arbor: University of Michigan Press.

March, James, and Johan Olsen. 1976. "Organization Choice Under Ambiguity." In *Ambiguity and Choice in Organizations,* edited by James March and Johan Olsen. Bergen, Norway: Universitetsforlaget.

March, James, and Johan Olsen. 1984. "The New Institutionalism: Organizational Factors in Political Life." *American Political Science Review* 78:734–749.

Marmor, Theodore. 1997. "Global Health Policy Reform: Misleading Mythology or Learning Opportunity." In *Health Policy Reform, National Variations and Globalization,* edited by Christa Altenstetter and James Björkman. New York: St. Martin's Press (for the International Political Science Association).

Marmor, Theodore, and David Thomas. 1972. "Doctors, Politics and Pay Disputes: 'Pressure Group Politics' Revisited." *British Journal of Political Science* 2:421–442.

Marshall, Catherine, Douglas Mitchell, and Frederick Wirt. 1989. *Culture and Education Policy in the American States.* New York: Falmer Press.

May, Peter. 1991. "Reconsidering Policy Design: Policies and Publics." *Journal of Public Policy* 11:187–206.

McLean, Martin. 1988. "The Conservative Education Policy in Comparative Perspective." *British Journal of Educational Studies* 36:200–217.

McLean, Martin. 1995. *Educational Traditions Compared.* London: David Fulton Publishers.

Messere, Ken, ed. 1998. *The Tax System in Industrialized Countries.* Oxford: Oxford University Press.

Messina, Anthony. 1989. *Race and Party Competition in Europe.* Oxford: Clarendon Press.

Messina, Anthony. 1990. "Political Impediments to the Resumption of Labour Migration in Western Europe." *West European Politics* 3:31–46.

Messina, Anthony. 1995. "Immigration as a Political Dilemma in Britain: Implications for Western Europe." *Policy Studies Journal* 23:686–699.

Money, Jeannette. 1999. *Fences and Neighbors: The Political Geography of Immigration Control.* Ithaca: Cornell University Press.

Morone, James. 1995. "Nativism, Hollow Corporations, and Managed Competition: Why the Clinton Health Care Reform Failed." *Journal of Health Politics, Policy and Law* 20:391–398.

Morrissey, Oliver, and Sven Steinmo. 1987. "The Influence of Party Competition on Post-war UK Tax Rates." *Politics and Policy* 15:195–206.

Norton, Philip, ed. 1999. *Parliaments and Pressure Groups in Western Europe.* London: Frank Cass.

OECD. 1982. *OECD Economic Outlook: Historical Statistics 1960–1980.* Paris: Organisation for Economic Co-operation and Development.

OECD. 1994a. *Environmental Performance Reviews: Italy.* Paris: Organisation for Economic Co-operation and Development.

OECD. 1994b. *Environmental Performance Reviews: Japan.* Paris: Organisation for Economic Co-operation and Development.

OECD. 1994d. *Environmental Performance Reviews: United Kingdom.* Paris: Organznisation for Economic Co-operation and Development.

OECD. 1994c. *New Orientations for Social Policy.* Paris: Organisation for Economic Co-operation and Development.

OECD. 1997. *Environmental Performance Reviews: France.* Paris: Organisation for Economic Co-operation and Development.

OECD. 2000. *OECD Economic Outlook,* No. 67. Paris: Organisation for Economic Co-operation and Development.

O'Riordan, Tim, and Andrew Jordan. 1996. "Social Institutions and Climate Change." In *Politics of Climate Change: A European Perspective,* edited by Tim O'Riordan and Jill Jager. New York: Routledge.

Ozawa, Martha. 1991. "Child Welfare Programs in Japan." *Social Service Review* 65:2.

Passow, A. Harry. 1990. "Whither (or Wither?) School Reform." In *Education Reform: Making Sense of It All,* edited by Samuel B. Bacharach. New York: Allyn and Bacon.

Patel, Kant, and Mark Rushefsky. 1999. *Politics, Power and Policy Making: The Case of Health Care Reform in the 1990s,* 2d ed. New York: M.E. Sharpe.

Pempel, T. J., ed. 1990. *Uncommon Democracies: The One-party Dominant Regimes.* Ithaca: Cornell University Press.

Pempel, T. J. 1992. "Bureaucracy in Japan." *PS: Political Science and Politics* 25:19–24.

Perlmutter, Ted. 1996. "Bringing Parties Back In: Comments on 'Modes of Immigration Politics in Liberal Democratic Societies.'" *International Migration Review* 30:375–389.

Peters, B. Guy. 1991. *The Politics of Taxation: A Comparative Perspective.* Cambridge: Basil Blackwell.

Peters, B. Guy. 1995. *The Politics of Bureaucracy*, 4th ed. New York: Longman.

Pressman, Jeffrey, and Aaron Wildavsky. 1973. *Implementation: How Great Expectations in Washington are Dashed in Oakland*. Berkeley: University of California Press.

Raffel, Marshall. 1997. "Dominant Issues: Convergence, Decentralization, Competition, Health Services." In *Health Care and Reform in Industrialized Countries*, edited by Marshall Raffel. University Park: Pennsylvania State University Press.

Ravitch, Diane. 1995. *National Standards in American Education*. Washington, D.C.: Brookings Institution Press.

Rich, Paul. 1990. *Race and Empire in British Politics*. Cambridge: Cambridge University Press.

Roemer, Milton. 1977. *Comparative National Policies on Health Care*. New York: Marcel Dekker.

Roller, Edeltraud. 1995. "The Welfare State: The Equality Dimension." In *The Scope of Government*, edited by Ole Borre and Elinor Scarbrough. Oxford: Oxford University Press.

Rose, Richard, and Terrance Karran. 1986. *Taxation by Political Inertia*. London: Macmillan.

Roubini, Nouriel, and Jeffrey Sachs. 1989. "Political and Economic Determinants of Budget Deficits in the Industrial Democracies." *European Economic Review* 33:903–938.

Rust, Val, and Kenneth Blakemore. 1990. "Educational Reform in England and the United States." *Comparative Education Review* 17:160–179.

Sassen, Saskia. 1998. "The De Facto Transnationalizing of Immigration Policy." In *Challenge to the Nation-state*, edited by Christian Joppke. Oxford: Oxford University Press.

Sassen, Saskia. 1999. *Guests and Aliens*. New York: The New Press.

Schain, Martin. 1987. "The National Front in France and the Construction of Political Legitimacy." *West European Politics* 10:229–252.

Schain, Martin. 1988. "Immigration and Changes in the French Party System." *European Journal of Political Research* 16:597–621.

Scharpf, Fritz. 1997. *Games Real Actors Play: Actor-Centered Institutionalism in Policy Research*. Boulder: Westview.

Schlesinger, Mark, and Taeku Lee. 1994. "Is Health Care Different? Popular Support of Federal Health and Social Policies." In *The Politics of Health Care Reform*, edited by James Morone and Gary Belkin. Durham: Duke University Press.

Schmidt, Manfred. 1982. "The Role of Parties in Shaping Macroeconomic Policy." In *The Impact of Parties: Politics and Policies in Democratic Capitalist States*, edited by Francis Castles. London: Sage.

Schnapper, Dominique. 1994. "The Debate on Immigration and the Crisis of National Identity." In *The Politics of Immigration in Western Europe*, edited by Martin Baldwin-Edwards and Martin Schain. London: Frank Cass.

Scruggs, Lyle. 1999. "Institutions and Environmental Performance in Seventeen Western Democracies." *British Journal of Political Science* 29:1–32.

Sears, David, and Jack Citrin. 1985. *Tax Revolt: Something for Nothing in California*. Cambridge: Harvard University Press.

Shapiro, Martin, and Alec Stone. 1994. "The New Constitutional Politics of Europe." *Comparative Political Studies* 26:397–420.

Simon, Herbert. 1957. *Models of Man: Social and Rational.* New York: Wiley.

Sinfield, A. 1984. "The Wider Impact of Unemployment." In *High Unemployment,* edited by OECD. Paris: Organisation for Economic Co-operation and Development.

Smith, Martin. 1994. "Policy Networks and State Autonomy." In *The Political Influence of Ideas: Policy Communities and the Social Sciences,* edited by Stephen Brooks and Alain Gagnon. New York: Praeger.

Soysal, Yasemin. 1994. *The Limits of Citizenship.* Chicago: University of Chicago Press.

Spring, Joel. 1988. *Conflict of Interests: The Politics of American Education.* New York: Longman.

Starr, Paul. 1982. *The Social Transformation of American Medicine.* New York: Basic Books.

Steinmo, Sven. 1993. *Taxation and Democracy: Swedish, British, and American Approaches to Financing the Modern State.* New Haven: Yale University Press.

Stone, Deborah. 1980. *The Limits of Professional Power.* Chicago: University of Chicago Press.

Tuohy, Carolyn. 1999. *Accidental Logics: The Dynamics of Change in the Health Care Arena in the United States, Britain, and Canada.* New York: Oxford University Press.

van Waarden, Frans. 1992. "Dimensions and Types of Policy Networks," *European Journal of Political Research* 21:29–52.

Vernon, Raymond. 1993. "Behind the Scenes: How Policymaking in the European Community, Japan and the United States Affects Global Negotiations." *Environment* 35:12–29.

Vogel, David. 1986. *National Styles of Regulation: Environmental Policy in Great Britain and the United States.* Ithaca: Cornell University Press.

Weale, Albert. 1992. *The New Politics of Pollution.* Manchester, U.K.: Manchester University Press.

Weaver, R. Kent, and Bert Rockman. 1993a. "Assessing the Effects of Institutions." In *Do Institutions Matter? Government Capabilities in the United States and Abroad,* edited by R. Kent Weaver and Bert Rockman. Washington, D.C.: Brookings Institution Press.

Weaver, R. Kent, and Bert Rockman. 1993b. "When and How Do Institutions Matter?" In *Do Institutions Matter? Government Capabilities in the United States and Abroad,* edited by R. Kent Weaver and Bert Rockman. Washington, D.C.: Brookings Institution Press.

Welch, Susan. 1985. "The 'More for Less' Paradox: Public Attitudes on Taxing and Spending." *Public Opinion Quarterly* 49:310–316.

White, Joseph. 1995. *Competing Solutions: American Health Care Proposals and International Experience.* Washington, D.C.: Brookings Institution Press.

Wildavsky, Aaron. 1975. *Budgeting: A Comparative Theory of Budgeting Processes.* Boston: Little, Brown.

Wilensky, Harold. 1975. *The Welfare State and Equality.* Berkeley: University of California Press.

Wilson, James. 1989. *Bureaucracy: What Government Agencies Do and Why They Do It.* New York: Basic Books.

Wirt, Frederick, and Grant Hartman. 1986. *Education, Recession and the World Village: A Comparative Political Economy of Education.* Philadelphia: Falmer Press.

Wray, Harry. 1999. *Japanese and American Education: Attitudes and Practices.* Westport, Conn.: Bergin and Garvey.

Yergin, Daniel, and Joseph Stanislaw. 1998. *The Commanding Heights: The Battle Between Government and the Marketplace That Is Remaking the Modern World.* New York: Simon and Schuster.

Index